JEWS AMONG MUSLIMS

Jews among Muslims

Communities in the Precolonial Middle East

Edited by

Shlomo Deshen
Professor of Anthropology
Tel-Aviv University

and

Walter P. Zenner
Professor of Anthropology
University of Albany, New York

NEW YORK UNIVERSITY PRESS
Washington Square, New York

Selection, editorial matter and Chapter 1 © Shlomo Deshen
and Walter P. Zenner 1996
Chapters 2–19 © Macmillan Press Ltd

All rights reserved

First published in the U.S.A. in 1996 by
NEW YORK UNIVERSITY PRESS
Washington Square
New York, N.Y. 10003

Library of Congress Cataloging-in-Publication Data
available from the Library of Congress

ISBN 0–8147–9675–3 (hardcover)
ISBN 0–8147–9676–1 (paperback)

Contents

Preface vii

Notes on the Contributors viii

Acknowledgements ix

Part I Introduction 1

1. Jews Among Muslims in Precolonial Times: An Introductory Survey 3
   Walter P. Zenner and Shlomo Deshen

2. Traditional Jewish Society and Modern Society 25
   Jacob Katz

3. Jewish Acculturation in Premodern Societies 35
   Stephen Sharot

4. Islam and the Jews: Myth, Counter-Myth, History 50
   Mark Cohen

5. Sephardic Rabbinic Responses to Modernity: Some Central Characteristics 64
   Zvi Zohar

Part II Morocco 81

6. Patronage and Protection: The Status of Jews in Precolonial Morocco 83
   Allan R. Meyers

7. Community Life in Nineteenth-Century Moroccan Jewry 98
   Shlomo Deshen

8. Jewish Existence in a Berber Environment 109
   Moshe Shokeid

9. Saddiq and Marabout in Morocco 121
   Norman Stillman

Part III Tunisia and Tripolitania 131

10. Southern Tunisian Jewry in the Early Twentieth Century 133
    Shlomo Deshen

| 11 | Communal Organization of the Jews of Tripolitania during the Late Ottoman Period
Harvey E. Goldberg | 144 |

Part IV Syria and Iraq — 159

12	Syrian Jews and their Non-Jewish Neighbors in Late Ottoman Times *Walter P. Zenner*	161
13	Jews in Late Ottoman Syria: Community, Family and Religion *Walter P. Zenner*	173
14	Baghdad Jewry in Late Ottoman Times: The Emergence of Social Classes and of Secularization *Shlomo Deshen*	187
15	The Religious World of Jewish Women in Kurdistan *Susan Starr Sered*	197

Part V Yemen — 215

| 16 | The Social Structure of Jewish Education in Yemen
Shlomo D. Goitein | 217 |
| 17 | The Authority of the Community of San'ā in Yemenite Jewry
Yosef Tobi | 232 |

Part VI Iran — 245

| 18 | Dhimmi Status and Jewish Roles in Iranian Society
Laurence D. Loeb | 247 |
| 19 | Prestige and Piety in the Iranian Synagogue
Laurence D. Loeb | 261 |

| *Recommended Readings* | 271 |
| *Index* | 280 |

Preface

This work stems from many decades of effort and affection which we, as social anthropologists, have invested in research on Jews from Muslim lands for over thirty years. We have been engaged in uncovering the present-day life of Middle Eastern Jews in Israel, the United States, in other countries in Europe and the Americas, as well as North Africa. Together with our interest in the present, we both have a lively interest in the social history of these people.

In 1982, we published a volume of selections which tried to reconstruct the lives in Jews in traditional Middle Eastern societies, as well as syntheses by anthropologists and historians. *Jewish Societies in the Middle East: Community, Culture and Authority* was well received at the time.

But, since 1982, much has been published on the Jews of North Africa and Southwest Asia, both by professional historians and anthropologists. Anthropological thinking has become more critical of earlier theoretical approaches. The perspectives of scholars have been affected by political changes in the relationship of Israel and her Arab neighbors. We decided to respond to these developments by editing a new volume.

The present book incorporates several of the articles which appeared in Jewish Societies in the Middle East, These have been edited and abridged and we have added new articles, both general synthetic pieces and historical ethnographies which present new perspectives.

Several colleagues, most notably Norman Stillman, Kevin Avruch, and Jane Gerber, encouraged us to publish this work. We also would like to thank Niko Pfund and Jennifer Hammer of New York University Press and Tim Farmiloe and Gráinne Twomey for their assistance in publication. Keith Povey has helped us greatly in copy-editing and indexing. This work would have been impossible without the work of our colleagues who allowed us to republish their articles. The patience, support, criticism and assistance of our wives, Hilda Deshen and Linda Zenner, have been invaluable throughout the years in keeping us on track.

We want to dedicate the work to the memory of the many Jewish communities of North Africa and Southwest Asia which have been deserted, destroyed and transplanted in the course of the twentieth century.

SHLOMO DESHEN
WALTER P. ZENNER

Notes on the Contributors

Mark Cohen is Professor of History at Princeton University.

Shlomo Deshen is Professor of Anthropology at Tel-Aviv University.

Shlomo D. Goitein was associated with the Institute of Advanced Studies at Princeton at the time of his death in 1985.

Harvey E. Goldberg is Professor of Social Anthropology at the Hebrew University in Jerusalem.

Jacob Katz is Professor Emeritus of Social History at the Hebrew University in Jerusalem.

Laurence D. Loeb is Associate Professor of Anthropology at the University of Utah in Salt Lake City.

Allan R. Meyers is Assistant Professor of Anthropology in the School of Public Health at Boston University.

Susan Starr Sered is Associate Professor of Anthropology at Bar-Ilan University.

Stephen Sharot is Professor of Sociology at Ben-Gurion University in Beersheba.

Moshe Shokeid is Professor of Anthropology at Tel-Aviv University.

Norman Stillman holds the Schusterman/Josey Chair in Judaic History at the University of Oklahoma.

Yosef Tobi is Associate Professor of History and Comparative Literature at Haifa University.

Walter P. Zenner is Professor of Anthropology and Jewish Studies at the University of Albany (State University of New York).

Zvi Zohar is Senior Scholar at the Shalom Hartman Institute in Jerusalem.

Acknowledgements

The editors and publishers are grateful to the following for permission to reproduce copyright material: Harvey Goldberg and the Jerusalem Center for Public Affairs for H. Goldberg, 'Communal Organization of the Jewish of Tripolitania during the Late Ottoman Period', *Jewish Political Studies Review*, 5, 3 & 4, Autumn 1993; Norman Stillman and Magnes Press for 'Saddiq and Marabout', in *Sephardim and Oriental Jewish Heritage*, 1982; Mark Cohen for 'Islam and the Jews', *Jerusalem Quarterly*, 38, 1986; Laurence D. Loeb for 'Dhimmi Status and Jewish Roles in Iranian Society', *Ethnic Groups*, 1, 1976, and 'Prestige and Piety in the Iranian Synagogue', *Anthropological Quarterly*, 51, 1978; Yosef Tubi for 'The Authority of the Community of Sun'ā in Yemenite Jewry', in *Jewish Societies in the Middle East*, ed. S. Deshen and W.P. Zenner (University Press of America, 1982); Allen R. Meyers for 'Patronage and Protection: The Status of Jews in Precolonial Morocco', in *Jewish Societies in the Middle East*, ed. S. Deshen and W.P. Zenner (University Press of America, 1982).

Every effort has been made to contact all the copyright-holders, but if any have been inadvertently omitted the publishers will be pleased to make the necessary arrangement at the earliest opportunity.

Part I
Introduction

1 Jews among Muslims in Precolonial Times: An Introductory Survey
Walter P. Zenner and Shlomo Deshen

An American Jewish soldier was in China during the Second World War. He walked into a building one Saturday. Lo and behold, he saw a small group of Chinese men, chanting in Hebrew and reading from a scroll. To his amazement, he realized that they were Jews. After the service, he went up to the cantor and told him, that he too was a Jew. The cantor looked at him in astonishment and finally asked in broken English, 'Funny, you no look Jewish'.

While not necessarily true of China in the 1940s, this anecdote could, with minor variations, be applied to the experiences of American Jewish tourists in Morocco or Central Asia or elsewhere in the non-Western world. While the physiognomy of the congregants and their pronunciation of Hebrew may be unfamiliar, the fact that one is in a synagogue, worshipping with essentially the same text, is obvious. Clearly, traditional Jewry is a coat of many colors. Jewish life and society were different in Morocco from what they were in Iraq, in Germany from Tripolitania.

Presently, in America, however, and indeed elsewhere, this is not generally realized. All too often, one encounters persons, who, while concerned with matters of Jewry and Jewish culture, conceive of this subject in an ethnocentric European-oriented framework. The prevailing conception is one in which the European *shtetl* community is naturally assumed as a prototype and model of traditional Jewry on the eve of nineteenth century modernization and later destruction. In this view, traditional Jewry equals the *shtetl* society. Jewish communities which differ from this model are deemed to require justification or improvement, but they are not perceived for what they are, simply traditional manifestations of Jewry. Moreover, the image of the Eastern European *shtetl*, as popularized in modern literature, art, and theater is not well-grounded in sober historically informed knowledge.

Scholarly research into the Jewish communities which stretched from Morocco to India has been increasing, although large lacunae in our knowledge still exist. In this volume, we bring together some of the most insightful studies of these communities. In this way, we aim to contribute toward greater understanding in the area of comparative Jewish ethnology. We have chosen selections on the following bases: (*a*) they contain descriptions of significant social institutions, such as the economy, religion and education, or deal with important relationships such as between Jews and Gentiles or inter-class connections; (*b*) they are descriptive, with an orientation to a broad picture of the society and are not merely a collection of disjointed data of a purely folkloristic or ethnographic nature; (*c*) they deal with the penultimate 'premodern' period; (*d*) they are grounded in historically well-informed research.

When we first prepared a collection of papers along these lines over a decade ago, our choices were fairly limited. The history of Jews under Islam was limited mainly to the period from the seventh to thirteenth centuries of the Christian era, with spasmodic attention given to Jews in the Ottoman Empire in the sixteenth and seventeenth centuries and the Damascus affair of 1840. New interest in the Jews of the Middle East developed as a result of the mass immigration to Israel. One immediate result of this immigration was practical sociological research. Several of the contributors to this volume, including the editors, began their careers by doing studies relating to the acculturation of Middle Eastern immigrants to Israeli society. This has been followed in the past decade by doctoral dissertations, books, monographs, and conferences dealing with the Jews under Islam. In fact, important contributions are now being made by individuals whose origins lie in Middle Eastern lands, such as Yosef Tobi, represented in our volume. At a more profound level, the new interest in non-Western Jewry is probably rooted in the Holocaust background of contemporary Judaic studies. There may operate a feeling that after the uprooting of European Jewry, a wide-ranging exploration of sources of Jewish vitality is called for, and those traditional Jewries that survived physically intact to the present arouse a special interest.

Eight of the authors whose selections we chose are social scientists, particularly social anthropologists. In most cases, they initially undertook the investigation of the recent past of their communities in order to interpret better the present situations of Jews from those communities. Most of the investigators studied the communities first in Israel (Goitein, Goldberg, Deshen, Sered, Shokeid, Zenner), while some (Meyers, Loeb) did field work in the country of origin. In some cases, the anthropologists used a variety of materials, in addition to participant-observation, including historical documents, secondary sources, supplemented by oral testimonies and the use of the present situation as a clue to the past.

Not all those using this eclectic approach are anthropologists, however.

The late Shlomo Goitein was trained in the philological approaches of German orientalism, but in his researches on both the Yemenite Jews and the 'Geniza People' (the communities represented in documents of the Cairo Geniza), he used a similar approach. A close reading of Goitein's *A Mediterranean Society* (in which he presents an historic ethnography of Jewish society mainly in Tunisia and Egypt between the tenth and thirteenth centuries) will reveal that he used his experiences among Yemenites and other Middle Eastern Jews in Israel, as well as drawing parallels with American Jewry. The remainder of our authors are generally historians, although several of these have been informed by anthropological work, most notably Norman Stillman. One interest which most of the authors, whether anthropologists or historians, whose work is represented here, share is an interest in using particular details and events for generalizations. This leads us to discussion on higher levels of abstraction than ordinarily engaged in by historians. The two disciplines also share a concern with the problems inherent in historical reconstruction and interpretation.

Our work is part of a general effort which has borne fruit. Prior to the 1980s, a number of authors had written syntheses of the histories and ethnographies of Middle Eastern communities. Notable among these were Chouraqui (1968), Patai (1971), Hirschberg (1974), Hayim J. Cohen (1973) and Stillman (1979, see also 1991), as well as the many Middle Eastern entries in the *Encyclopaedia Judaica*. But we differ from these in our social anthropological perspective.

Locating the societies of which we speak in time and space is often problematic. Sources may come from more than one community, and localities may differ from each other. Sources may also refer to more than one period. In dealing with sources, one must translate the language of the document into the language of the social scientist. A document, such as a legal inquiry and response, has problems of its own; it often deals with legal cases which are unique and unusual, yet the social scientist may be tempted to see it as more typical than it is.

Use of other materials such as folktales, proverbs, oral testimonies, moralistic literature, and travellers' accounts have similar difficulties. Historical reconstruction based on oral reports is methodologically debatable, among both historians and anthropologists. Some have argued that such reports express mainly the current attitudes of the informants and contemporary conditions; they do not reliably reflect past situations as they refer to them. Others, however, view oral reports as valuable sources of information when controlled and used critically through parallel data of other types, primarily written sources and participation-observation. Anthropologists infer aspects of the culture of the past from the present. For instance, the way in which Jews in Shiraz in the 1960s, described below by Laurence Loeb, competed for honor in their synagogues can be seen as a retention from their lives over the past century. When Loeb draws such inferences, it is done with the full knowledge that the present context differs from the situation of a hundred years ago, and that the inference must be tested with more direct documentation.

Some of the theoretical concerns of social anthropology thus inform the selection of the materials that constitute the bulk of this volume, as do the generalizations we tentatively attempt to draw in this introduction. We operate with two sets of concepts, one sociological and one ethnographic. On the sociological plane, we aim to illuminate spheres of social activity in the political sphere, economy, religion, the family and kin, and schooling. We are interested in relating our work to general conceptualizations of cultural development, such as those of Jacob Katz and Stephen Sharot (chs 2 and 3 below).

We define the subject of this volume as 'traditional Jewish communities,' and one of our first selections is Jacob Katz's essay, in which he differentiates 'traditional' from 'modern' society in the context of Jewry. This requires explanation. In the 1950s and 1960s, many applied social scientists in the United States and Israel were concerned with how to help 'traditional peoples' acquire the means to become modern, to acquire the blessings which modernization would supposedly bring. This sanguine view of modernity and its opposite, tradition, have long been attacked from various directions. The notion of 'traditional society' has been criticized as simplistic, and 'modernity' has come to be seen as an ideological notion implying the effort of dominant groups to control others, sometimes in near-totalitarian fashion (e.g. Rabinow, 1989).

While recognizing the validity of some of the criticisms of 'modernity' and 'tradition', we still find value in certain limited, specific formulations. Thus following Katz, we use the distinction between 'tradition' and 'modernity' as ideal types only, in the Weberian tradition. While we may speak of 'traditional times', we recognize that aspects of 'tradition' persist to this day, and that the transition is a matter of degree. In addition, many of the studies which are included here and which we cite were done in societies which had begun to experience modernization. The fact that the so-called 'post-modernists' invest time in developing a model of modernity suggests that, despite their critique of typologies in the social sciences in general, they, too, see that such types have heuristic value. In sum therefore, the generalizations which we make about traditional Jewish societies in the Middle East should be seen as hypotheses to be tested and refined, not as established facts.

The term, 'Middle Eastern Jews' is roughly coincident with Jews living in areas where Muslims dominate. Most of the Jewish communities under consideration are found in Northern Africa and Southwestern Asia. While we recognize that there are a variety of social patterns in Islamic societies (and that these societies like all others, must adapt to social, economic, and ecological conditions which may override various particular religious prescriptions), we assume that religious prescriptions play a major role in relations between Jews and Gentiles. While all Muslim societies tend to favor the dominant religion, the way in which such privilege is carried out may vary. On the one hand there may be a policy which allows for Jewish officials, and for open display of wealth by members of the minority, and on the other hand there may be severe restriction on minority people. The issue will concern us further below.

CULTURE AREAS OF JEWS AMONG MUSLIMS

The concept of 'culture area', though not unproblematic, is useful in delineating the variety of Jewish societies under Islamic rule. We paint the culture areas in broad strokes, stressing the ethnic and linguistic mix, the political map of the premodern period, and certain characteristics of the Jewish population. One area is Morocco, which shares with the other Maghreb countries an ethnic mix of Arabic- and Berber-speaking peoples. Morocco has maintained a distinct existence as an independent kingdom for centuries, while the other North African countries fell under the Ottoman Empire. Spain, Portugal, France, and the Italian states played important roles in the Maghreb. Most Jews there spoke Maghrebine Arabic; there were also important enclaves of Spanish and Italian Jews in the area. As will be noted in the chapters by Shokeid, Deshen, Stillman, and Goldberg, Morocco, as against the eastern countries of the region, developed different patterns of communal leadership and religion.

In Egypt, Syria, and Iraq, Jewish and Christian minorities coexisted with Muslims, divided among themselves into numerous sects, including Sunnis, Shi'is, Druzes, and Alawis. The area attracted numerous sojourners and immigrants, of various religions, from other parts of Southwest Asia, North Africa and Europe. Partly by reason of being part of the Ottoman Empire, the diversity of religious groups in the region created a pattern of interaction different from that of North Africa.

Turkish and Balkan Jewry constitutes yet another distinctive cultural enclave, marked by the dominance of Jews speaking Ladino (or Judezmo), a language stemming from Spanish and written for a long time in Hebrew characters. The area included the western parts of Anatolia and most of the Balkan countries, where Jews lived in a highly polyglot environment. Even though the Muslim Ottoman Empire controlled most of this area for centuries, many regions had Orthodox Christian majorities. Even more than in the Fertile Crescent, Jews were caught in struggles between Christians and Muslims, especially after the establishment of independent Balkan states in the nineteenth century. Like Jews of the Maghreb and Syria and Egypt, Turkish and Balkan Jewry had close commercial and cultural ties with Jews in Italy, especially the community of Leghorn (Livorno). Yemen in the southern part of the Arabian peninsula, the Northern Tier (Kurdistan and Azerbaijan), and 'Persia', comprising the Jewries of Iran, Afghanistan, Uzbekistan, and Tajikistan constitute still other culture areas. Numbering seven in all, these comprise the bulk of Jews in the Middle East, though smaller groupings not contained within them can be considered separate culture-areas or enclaves (e.g. the Jews of Georgia, the Egyptian Karaites).

The differences between the culture areas can be illustrated by considering the Jews of the Northern Tier in comparison with those of Yemen. The Northern Tier was a most heterogeneous environment, comprising ancient sects, besides Jews. The languages spoken in the area include the Indo-European Kurdish languages (which is why much of this area is called Kurdistan), as well as Aramaic, used by Jews and many Christians, Turkish (or Azeri), Arabic, Persian, and Armenian. From accounts of Kurdistani Jews, we hear of considerable and often friendly social interaction between Jews and Gentiles (Noy, 1974). The communities were small and people wandered far to make a living. The Jews in the region maintained a cultural communal life that was relatively open. Internal Jewish communal institutions in the Northern Tier were few and often weakly developed, and Jews of this region were not known for their learning. Synagogues were mainly active on Sabbaths and festivals, not during the week. Altogether religious institutions were not very vigorous (Feitelson, 1959; Shai, 1982). It is possible that the easy interaction of Jews with their neighbors in Kurdistan can help explain this weakness, as Jews were not driven to develop their institutions defensively.

Yemenite Jewry stands in sharp contrast to that of the Northern Tier. Yemen has been a much more closed society than the former. In parts of Yemen stratification was rigid, and has been described as a virtual caste system. Principles of social and religious exclusiveness operated in relations between Jews and their Muslim neighbors. There were also unique oppressive laws, such as the forcible conversion of orphaned Jewish children to Islam (Goitein, 1955b: 77–81). The development of many symbols of Jewish distinctiveness was stimulated by the challenges of the political environment (see the chapters by Goitein and Tobi). While communal institutions in Yemen were also not highly developed, the family there took on additional roles. Goitein indicates how education was embedded in the family, and how Jewish fathers took care to ensure that their sons were learned in the tradition. Hence Yemenite Jewry has often been described as passionately, virtually uniformly, attached to Jewish tradition.

But in the period between World War I and their exodus around 1950, the Jews of the Northern Tier were caught in conflicts between various governments and rebellious ethnic groups. Fighting between Turks, Armenians, and Assyrians in Urmia (Iranian Azerbaijan), in which Jews were killed, and the murder of a Jewish family in Urfa (Turkey) which led to the departure of Jews from that city, are two examples (Joseph, 1961; Zenner, 1989/90). Loeb's description of the Southeastern Yemenite Jewish community of Habban (1980) shows a group which faced severe pressures from the physical environment rather than from neighbors, who were not particularly intolerant. This comparison of culture areas demonstrates that the concept is useful for formulating hypotheses, but the conclusions must be subjected to testing, refinement, and/or rejection.

We proceed to summarize the main features of the major social activities of Jews in the Middle East, beginning with the pervasive area of religion.

JEWISH TRADITION, LITERACY AND RELIGION

While we are primarily concerned with what distinguishes Jews under Islam from other Jewries, it is important to keep in mind that before modern times, Jews everywhere adapted their religion, within broad parameters of faithfulness to *halakha* (the Talmudic code), to meet the vicissitudes of material and political conditions. Traditional Jews deemed their own version of Judaism as legitimate and authentic, and disavowed the fact of innovation. This denial made it possible for gradual change to occur painlessly, while, at the same time, preventing radical breaks with the past. Zvi Zohar (ch. 5) shows how even in the late nineteenth century Sephardic rabbis dealt with change in this fashion. Jews in traditional times maintained a basic unity that crossed the boundaries of Gentile polities and cultures. The channels of communication between traditional Jewish societies, remained open as late as the period of the European Enlightenment, when modern national political boundaries began to block communication.

Until the late eighteenth century the basic uniformity of Judaism as a socio-religious phenomenon, was characterized by a precarious balance between this- and other-worldliness. On the side of spiritual life, there was also a valuation, albeit qualified and delimited, of achievement in material matters and in secular scholarship. In Europe, by the late nineteenth century, as a result of new Jewish religious movements in Eastern Europe, this had changed, and the balance among committed traditional Jews tilted in favor of spirituality and other-worldliness. On the other hand, powerful new forces for secularization led to the emergence of a vast stratum of Jews who loosened their Jewish commitments.

The Middle East was spared such developments for over a century. Traditional Torah-learning remained a requisite practice for self-respect in many communities, and honor and esteem awaited ranking scholars. Only in the late nineteenth century were the effects of European modernization beginning to be felt in Jewry under Islam, especially in the Balkans, Iraq, and Algeria. While the events in themselves were not entirely different in Europe and in the Middle East, there was a time lag in their occurrence. In many Muslim countries traditional Judaism remained viable well into the present century, in some regions until the time of mass emigration in the 1940s and 1950s. But in this book we are mainly concerned with the traditional past, and only those European parallels which apply to traditional times are pertinent.

In those times, considerable differences developed between the branches of Judaism in Christian and in Muslim countries. Despite a reluctance to acculturate to their non-Jewish neighbors, these differences mirrored differences between Christianity and Islam, as Sharot (this volume, ch. 3) points out. One such difference was that Christianity began its development as a minority religion. This led, especially in the west, to the transformation of the Church as a power-center separate from the state, while under Islam no distinction was made between religion and the state. As Sharot points out, this difference had ramifications for Jewish communities under each religion. Similarly there were parallel differences between the intellectual styles of Christianity and Islam on the one hand, and European and Middle Eastern Jewries on the other, which are less well understood. Unlike either Judaism or Islam, Christianity was marked by the application of a sophisticated casuistry to theological questions. Except for a short-lived phase of similar concern with doctrine during the Middle Ages, theology was not as developed in either Islam or Judaism. On the other hand, both Judaism and Islam developed sophisticated bodies of legal interpretation.

Here again, we find interesting differences between Jews in Europe and the Middle East. Northern European Jews, in particular, developed a casuistic argumentative legal style, which has become part of the intellectual style of East European Jews, even those who are secularized (Ben-Sasson, 1959: 22–3; 171, 191; Zborowski and Herzog, 1953: 88–104). While the intellectual style of Middle Eastern Jews has been little studied, it is clearly more straightforward. Goitein's study of Yemeni education (ch. 16) gives some insights, and also the more recent sophisticated work of Boyarin (1989). More work on other communities needs to be done, comparable to Eickelman's study of Muslim academies in Morocco (1978).

Another important dichotomy between European and Middle Eastern Jewries lies in the area of popular religion and mysticism. While in Europe powerful moves to rid Judaism of magic and mysticism appeared beginning in the eighteenth century, such a division did not occur in the Middle East. Among many Middle Eastern Jews, the *hakham* or rabbi remained legal authority, scholar, and pastoral leader. While non-believers and scorners appeared in modernizing communities from Algiers to Baghdad, many continued to make pilgrimages to reputed tombs of ancients (such as the tombs of Esther and Mordecai in Iran) and to those of recent dignitaries in Morocco (see Stillman, this volume, ch. 9). Some rabbis in Israel and elsewhere continue to write talismans to protect against frights and diseases.

The various religions of the Middle East are embedded in literate traditions, but must appeal to many people who are barely literate. Among Middle Eastern Jews in recent times, much of the tradition was transmitted orally, while European Jewry was more dependent on written texts. In the hagiographies of saintly rabbis, one may note that in Morocco the saint is sometimes praised as not having to refer to books even for complex problems of ritual or law. In parallel Tunisian stories, the rabbis are praised as not resolving even simple problems without recourse to scholarly books. Most, but not all, Middle Eastern communities tended towards the Moroccan model. While ideally Jewish boys throughout the region went to school, in some areas as in Kurdistan generally, and among lower classes in Syria and North Africa, the degree of literacy was low. In other areas and social classes a high level of Hebrew literacy and even rabbinic scholarship was achieved.

The Hebrew and Aramaic word in the holy books had a sanctity all its own, whether or not the reader understood the meaning of the word, and thus literacy was sometimes ritualized (Deshen, 1975). The talisman with its permutation of the Divine Name is an example of this. Further examples are the recitation of prayers by the illiterate, the reading and study of the Zohar, a mystical text, largely incomprehensible to the uninitiated

(Stahl, 1979), as well as the adoration of the Torah scroll as a sacred artifact. Another common denominator of all traditional Jewish communities is the illiteracy of most women. While girls and women in their child-rearing years did not go to the synagogue frequently, women did resort to *hakhamim* for spiritual needs, such as advice, amulets to guard against disease, the evil eye, and barrenness. Older women were more likely to go to synagogue, or on pilgrimage to various shrines. Such participation in the reverence of saints' tombs may be a reaction to the subordinate status of women and lower-class men, as argued by Mernissi (1977). And Susan Sered (ch. 15) argues that women's religiosity had a different character from that of the men.

The synagogue was the major arena for public life. Besides their religious functions, synagogues filled important roles, such as encouraging leadership and social control. This has been shown in studies of Moroccan synagogues in Israel and Morocco (Shokeid, 1985; Deshen, 1989), Israeli Tunisian synagogues (Deshen, 1970), and Persian ones (Loeb, ch. 19), and even contemporary American synagogues (Heilman, 1976). These studies focus on the intersection of the sacred and the secular. Politicking, gossip, competition for status, and expression of ethnicity, are among the activities uncovered. Loeb observes 'status juggling' in Shirazi synagogues, which he attributes to traditional Persian etiquette and the generally low status of the Jews in Iran.

The modes of expressing religious sentiments differ from area to area in terms of language, pronunciation, music, and other emphases. Loeb (1976) has attempted to compare the way in which different senses are stimulated by synagogue ritual among Persian and Yemeni Jews, including sight, hearing, tactility, and olfaction. After some Syrian Sabbath synagogue services in both the United States and Israel, people will sprinkle rosewater on the worshipper's hands. This will give the worshipper a different sensory association with the Sabbath than would be true if this were not done. While such subtleties are ill-understood, they show the persistent cultural distance between the Jews of different parts of the Middle East, and between the Jews of the Middle East and Europe generally.

THE ECONOMIC BASIS

Jews everywhere lived as minority groups within larger societies, and tended to specialize in particular crafts or lines of trade. There is a tendency for small powerless groups to be drawn into niches in the economy which are not attractive to the elite or to the masses (Zenner, 1991). Such positions often require unusually hard work or involve unpleasant tasks (such as the work of tanners and dyers who acquire odors in the course of their work), or activities which are looked down upon for religious reasons (such as work with precious metals under Islam). While most social systems dictate a connection between social status and occupation, in the Middle East there are particular features as to the economic roles and statuses ascribed to Jews.

Goitein (1971) contrasted the fixed, caste-like character of Yemen in the nineteenth century to the competitiveness and openness of medieval Egypt. Morocco in recent centuries has been described as individualistic (Rosen, 1984), but even there Jews tended to concentrate in a limited set of occupations. While early Jewry was agricultural, the transformation to landless craftsmen and traders seems to have been completed by the end of the first millennium (Goitein, 1955b). In a few places even in our times, such as in Iraqi Kurdistan and parts of Yemen, one still found Jews who cultivated at least part of the time (Feitelson, 1959; Goitein, 1955a).

Most Middle Eastern Jews in traditional times were engaged either in the crafts or in commerce. The trades included textiles, metals, upholstery, and food preparation, and many lived in tribal areas. Others were itinerant craftsmen or peddlers who left their families in town, and traveled for extended periods among isolated tribes or in the villages. These men were 'strangers' in Simmel's sense. They had regular relations with the tribesmen whom they served, and occupied positions in the rural social structure that were reserved for those not of the tribe. These positions, based on fixed relations with particular Gentiles, afforded Jews protection from harm in societies that lacked universalistic forms of law and order. In many parts of the Middle East, Jewish traders maintained variants of patron–client relationships with local potentates, which assured them basic security. These relationships were of a particular nature, and required the Jew to offer his wares or services to the patron, in return for the latter's extended protection (see this volume, Deshen, ch. 7; Meyers, ch. 6). But there were differences of nuance in various parts of the Middle East. In southern Morocco, for instance, Shokeid (ch. 8) describes a system that was relatively closed. The patron–client tie was formalized by a sacrificial act, and there are signs that such relationships were often hereditary. In Kurdistan, the patron–client relationship was even more stifling and sometimes amounted to virtual serfdom (Ben-Ya'akob, 1961). In Yemen the system was less constricted and Jews could establish ties with several local dignitaries, which presumably gave them greater freedom.

Another facet of the Jews' position was that they were outside the hurly-burly of political conflict, including feuds. This role of institutionalized stranger was one which was common to smiths, traders, and shamans in many Old World societies (Simmel, 1908; Zenner, 1991: 1–45; Rosen, 1984; Chouraqui, 1968: 131–3; Goldberg, 1981). The paradox of the stranger role is that one may be a native of a place and still be a stranger to one's neighbors, by virtue of caste and/or religion. Traders are often strangers, because of the contradiction between the reciprocity expected of kin and the hard-headedness required in business. It is thus not surprising that Jerban Muslims from Southern Tunisia were grocers in northern cities, but local, non-migrant Jews were the merchants on the island of Jerba (Stone, 1974; Deshen, ch. 10). While many of the rural traders dealt with a wide variety of merchandise, others were highly specialized, such as a lowland Yemeni weavers' village (Goitein, 1955a), the itinerant silversmiths of Habban (South Yemen) (Loeb, 1980), or the Hara Sghira community in Jerba, where the Jews engaged in processing wool (Deshen, this volume, ch. 10).

In large cities, the economic activities of Jews were more diversified, though they still tended to concentrate in certain branches of the economy. In Istanbul around 1900, for instance, there were Jewish wholesale and retail traders, porters, fishermen, boatmen, goldsmiths, and moneychangers. In this city in the early stages of modernization, there were also several Jewish banks, factories making novelty items, ready-made wear, and a glassworks. The community included rich, middle-income, and poor people (Broyde and Gottheil, 1903). As traders and artisans, the Jews were subject to the vagaries of international commerce. The decline of the caravan trade across the deserts, and severe competition from European industry, had an adverse effect on many Middle Eastern Jews. Still, Jewish entrepreneurs, such as those in Istanbul, were among the first industrial manufacturers in the area (Quataert, 1994: 134). Jewish merchants were often involved in sending Middle Eastern commodities, like Egyptian cotton and Syrian silk, to Europe and importing European fabrics. Jewish peddlers distributed the European woolen and cotton cloth in rural areas such as in Anatolia, Syria, and Kurdistan.

THE POLITICAL SYSTEM: THE ROLE OF THE STATE AND INTERETHNIC RELATIONS

In the study of encapsulated, caste-like groups, much of life is determined by the domination of wielders of power outside the group. This can be seen with regard to Jews among Muslims. Jews and Christians living in the Muslim world had a special status, that of *dhimmis*, tolerated 'protected' minorities. They were permitted to practice their religions and earn their livelihood, as long as they deferred to Muslim authority and kept a low profile. What the last meant varied from period to period. Among the restrictions which recur was the prohibition to build new, non-Muslim houses of worship, repair them, or to be officials with authority over Muslims. There were humiliating regulations, such as obliging Jews to wear a distinctive garb, prohibition on riding horses or crossing the path of Muslims. In Shi'ite Iran in the nineteenth century, Jews were barred from the streets on rainy days (Loeb, this volume, ch. 18). Though there were places and times when these regulations were not fully enforced, the special position of *dhimmi* was a reality (Goitein, 1955b: 62–88). Jews were often useful to their Muslim neighbors, because of their occupational specialties, and some of these and their ramifications are indicated in local proverbs.

One type of proverb takes the form, 'Eat at A's but sleep at B's'. A Lebanese Christian formulation runs, 'Eat at a Druze's (home), but sleep at a Christian's (house)'. Frayha (1953: Nos. 1174, 1175) interprets this in terms of the hospitality of the Druzes coupled with the mutual hostility of Druze and Christian in Lebanon, which made Christians fear for their lives in Druze homes. In Iraq, a Jewish formulation was 'Eat in a Muslim's (home), but sleep in a Christian (house)'. Here the similarity of Jewish and Muslim dietary laws dictated eating. On the other hand, if a Jew would die at night, the Muslim might bury the circumcised Jew in a Muslim cemetery, hence the preference for Christian lodgings. While the Iraqi formulation implies interreligious tension, it is not suffused with hostility. Jews and non-Jews had a variety of relationships including sharing magic and personal counseling. Wise men of all religions were consulted when needed, and visits were made to shrines of saints of all groups. In times of drought and plague, all religions prayed and held processions to alleviate the divine decree (Goldberg, 1981; Feitelson, 1959; Zenner, this volume, ch. 12). Similarly, if the client of a local potentate was attacked, this was an affront to that individual, who might retaliate. The shielding of Jewish clients sometimes continued right into the period of the Arab–Israeli struggle. In Tedif-al-Yahud, a village near Aleppo, the local headman protected the synagogue at the Jewish shrine of the biblical Ezra, when it was threatened in 1947 (Zenner, this volume, ch. 12). Goldberg (1990) and Rosen (1984) describe similar situations elsewhere.

In urban centers of government individual Jews who had the most contact with high officials were the latter's clients, and those individuals were usually wealthy, and powerful within the Jewish community. There were numerous incidents when individual Jews briefly became retainers of the powerful, to fall from grace with rapidity, sometimes provoking anti-Jewish riots in their wake (see Romanelli, 1989; also Deshen, ch. 7, where the effect of these conditions on the autonomy of the Jewish community is indicated). The power of Jewish retainers was sometimes exaggerated, as in a sarcastic medieval poem from Egypt:

> Today the Jews have reached the summit of their hopes and have become aristocrats. Power and riches have they, and from among them are councillors and princes chosen. Egyptians, I advise you, become Jews, for the very sky has become Jewish! (Fischel, 1969: 88)

The favored Jews have become, to that writer, symbols of illegitimate *dhimmi* influence, and they are convenient scapegoats (Zenner, 1990).

A balanced view of the treatment of *dhimmis* in Islamic societies must take into account the formal status with its implied inequality, the interpersonal ties in everyday life, and the ambiguities of the patron–client relationship, and there were considerable differences. In North Yemen a law mandated that orphaned Jewish children be converted, whereas in South Yemen this was unknown (Loeb, 1980). Elsewhere, the murder of Jews was attributed, as often as not, to general insecurity and brigandage in the countryside, rather than to acts of Jew-hatred (Chouraqui, 1968: 54–5; Braver, 1945/6; also Deshen, this volume, ch. 7). The presence of Christians, and of other minorities not part of the Islamic majority (such as Shi'ites, Alawis, and Druzes), added additional contours to the shape of Muslim–Jewish relations. Through the nineteenth century and until the rise of Arab and Jewish nationalism, Jews and Christians were often competitors for both the favors of Muslim patrons and of the representatives of European powers. In this context, Jews appeared as less of a threat to Islam than did the Christians (Zenner, this volume, ch. 12). The Druze, who were seen either as heretics or as non-Muslims, were not a protected group, though they did receive *de facto* recognition. Therefore Druzes preferred to have *dhimmi* neighbors, rather than Sunnis who might look askance at them. Consequently many Christians lived among Druzes, and most village Jews in south Syria, Lebanon, and northern Palestine lived near Druzes.

The interpretation of interethnic relations in the Middle East is often caught up in polemic. Since the nineteenth century they have been used either to embroider a myth of a 'Golden Age' of Islamic tolerance (as opposed to Christian bigotry), or to embellish a counter-myth of Muslim fanaticism (as opposed to Christian love and Western liberalism). In the nineteenth century, the first was utilized by Western liberals as evidence of the benefits of religious tolerance and liberal reform. In our times also, both the myth and the counter-myth have political uses in the Arab–Israeli conflict as indicated by Mark Cohen (ch. 4). But there is no straightforward characterization of the Islamic treatment of minorities that is true for all times and places.

THE POLITICAL SYSTEM: INTERNAL COMMUNITY ORGANIZATION

The internal organization of Jewish communities is the product of both external forces and of Jewish tradition. Those who adhere to traditional Judaism seek to reproduce a certain blueprint wherever they live. The synagogue, the school for teaching Torah, the rabbinic court, provision of charity for the poor, regulation of kosher meat, maintenance of the ritual bath and the cemetery, all these are among the institutions, roles, and activities of this blueprint. The precolonial Jewish community had considerable judicial autonomy, and this went well beyond the areas of marriage, divorce, and inheritance recognized under Ottoman law. The legal writings of Jewish sages shows how far-reaching this jurisdiction was. All business law and some aspects of housing, as well as marital law and ritual, were considered by the rabbinic courts. Jewish authorities were able to impose fines, ostracism, and mete out corporal punishment, indirectly through the organs of the ruler. While Jews could turn to Islamic courts, as they sometimes did, the web of Jewish family and economic ties and socio-religious sanctions made this difficult. Muslim courts were sometimes seen as corrupt and required payment of bribes (Zenner, this volume, chs 12 and 13).

An autonomous Jewish community had to have its own system of finances. The sources for funds included indirect and direct taxes, such as a tax on kosher meat, gifts in exchange for synagogue honors (see below Loeb, ch. 19), and voluntary contributions. The communities often worked in an informal manner. Goitein termed the system of medieval Egyptian communities 'a medieval religious democracy', as they lacked the formal framework of modern representative government, in which procedures are explicitly written out. Rather, informal mechanisms developed by which the people made their will known, such as protests during synagogue services. The small size of most communities, even in large cities, made this possible, as most people knew each other and were mutually involved.

While Goitein's use of the term 'democracy' is an exaggeration, his usage underlines the need to scrutinize the data to identify ways in which different segments of the people participated in public affairs. Public opinion might control and limit the power of local potentates, leading us to look beyond formal procedures and the specificity of roles. Several principles operated in the selection of community leaders, such as lineage, personal attributes including wealth, integrity, and governmental connections. There was considerable variation in community leadership in the region. Goitein (1953) summarized the situation in Yemen: community leaders had both secular and sacred authority. While the hereditary principle was followed, an individual had to be qualified in his own right. There were no formal elections; representatives of extended families made the selection. But Muslim authorities intervened when the community was divided by factionalism. In San'aa, the capital, Jewish leaders had considerable influence over Jews in the rest of the country (see also Tobi below, ch. 17).

Community organization was often related to the size of the Jewish population. Most Yemeni Jews did not live in prestigious San'ā, but were dispersed in small communities, often consisting of no more than one or two extended families. Thus the elder of the family was the community leader. Yemeni community organization, familistic, often ascriptive, yet achievement oriented, is only one of several types which we encounter, in the fascinating variety that constitutes Middle Eastern internal Jewish politics. In Morocco, we encounter established aristocratic lineages, which provide religious and secular leadership, within the context of larger communities that were heterogeneous in terms of family composition (Shokeid, this volume, ch. 8). In Southern Tunisia, there is another political system: communities governed by relatively formal ordinances that prevail over the power of local families (Deshen, this volume, ch. 10).

The leaders of local Jewish communities had ties to local ruling elites and to the outer world. Small communities often turned to prestigious rabbinical courts of larger communities for authoritative decisions, as well as for material support and intervention with Gentile authorities in case of need. The Tuscan port of Leghorn was a center for Hebrew scholarship during the eighteenth and nineteenth centuries, and many volumes of rabbinic literature, by rabbis throughout the Mediterranean, were published there. Also, many leaders of Jewish communities from Morocco to Syria had familial ties with Italian Jewry. Though the Jewish communities of Palestine were not centers of trade, they had a special place in this communications network. Pilgrims went back and forth between their homes and the four 'holy cities' (Jerusalem, Safed, Tiberias, and Hebron), even during periods of unrest. Emissaries were sent by these communities to obtain financial support, and they provided adjudication and learned advice to otherwise isolated communities. A striking example of this is the case of the Central Asian community of Bukhara, which underwent thorough reform and revitalization as a result of the activity of one such emissary at the end of the eighteenth century (Moshavi, 1974: 329–31). Through their communications network, and the patronage of wealthy and powerful Jews in market-towns and large international cities, the Jews in small isolated communities, from the Atlas mountains of Morocco to Central Asia, remained connected to Jews throughout the world.

THE FAMILY AND GENDER ROLES

Zealous concern with male control of women's sexuality and behavior marks Islamic societies in comparison with other societies. This includes veiling, gender segregation, and the honor and shame code. One aspect of gender segregation is the opening of space to enable men to circulate in public, while secluding and protecting women's domestic activities. Houses are designed so that strange men cannot see the women of the house (Abu-Lughod, 1987). The honor–shame code ties the honor of the family and its males to the chastity of its women, and to the assertiveness and generosity of its men. Women are expected to defer to males, and of course to enter marriage as virgins. These practices were particularly rigorous among upper-class urban Muslims. Lower down on the scale this was less so. In that context minority women, both Jewish and Christian, were less likely to be fully secluded and veiled. But both minorities held attitudes similar to those of Muslims, as shown by Rahel Wasserfall (1990). Susan Sered (below, ch. 15) shows how segregated Jewish Kurdish women were from men, and how different their experiences were from those of men in every sphere of life.

The emphasis on male superiority is manifold: male heirs are desired, while female offspring are not. While male circumcisions after birth were elaborately celebrated, the births of girls generally were not celebrated (though there were slight exceptions, see Deshen, 1970: 140–7). In many places, virginity of the bride was examined by female relatives of bride and groom, if not publicly displayed. In general, Middle Eastern Jews conformed to a common regional family-type, patriarchal, recognizing the authority of senior males over others. Inheritance passed from fathers and sons, even more than among Muslims, since Jewish women generally did not inherit property from their fathers, while Muslim women did. The preferred residence pattern was the household based on elder parents, their married male children, and their dependents. Marriage of all first cousins, and also between uncles and nieces was permitted and sometimes encouraged (Goldschmidt et al., 1960), while Muslims permit first cousin marriage but forbid uncle–niece marriage. Rules of preferred marriage and residence however, are not coterminous with actual decisions. As Harvey Goldberg (1967) has pointed out in relation to the Middle East generally, non-kin factors lead to varying rates of cousin marriage in different communities. The same is true about choices concerning place of residence.

The minority status of Jews affected gender relations. It was often difficult for an unarmed minority to defend effectively the chastity of its women, when the person who harassed a Jewish woman was a powerful member of the majority group. In Kurdistan, stories about the seduction and rape of Jewish women by Muslims are common (Zenner, 1972a,b; Shai, 1982; Feitelson, 1959). There are occasional reports of Jewish women who were entertainers or prostitutes (Cohen, 1973: 158–9; Loeb, 1977). Since Jews were considered non-combatants in conflicts among Muslims, they were in a position comparable to that of women. Sometimes, therefore, Muslims emphasized the shame of Jews by prohibiting Jewish women from fully covering their faces, exposing them and their menfolk as low-class people, thus degrading the minority.

MODERNIZATION

When 'traditional times' began and ended are complex socio-historical questions which we do not tackle here (but see Deshen, 1989, ch. 1). Suffice it to say that the point of beginning lies somewhere in the Middle Ages, when normative rabbinical tradition crystallized and came to predominate, after its victory over the Karaite alternative formulation of Judaism. In any case, the question of the beginning of traditional times is not of immediate concern to us, because we concentrate on the period beginning with the late eighteenth and the nineteenth centuries, as indicated earlier. The end point is, in our case, more pertinent. One can view the end of traditional times in terms of increasing interdependence with the West: when European powers penetrated the Muslim world, traditional times ended. Yet contact with Europe is age-old, and the degree of modern commercial and colonial penetration was uneven. Pending detailed research on the subject, we conceive of the end of traditional times in the Jewish Middle East as linked to the transformation of traditional educational institutions. Education has functioned as a catalyzing factor for change in many areas of society. During the nineteenth century, schooling became linked to increasing political and economic dependency of Middle Eastern Jewries on European powers and European Jewries. Major Jewish communities throughout the region became involved with Protestant missions and the French Alliance Israélite Universelle organization. The latter sought to defend Jews from persecution, besides providing education, that would make the Jews 'productive' and self-supporting, as understood by emancipated Western Jewish bourgeoise.

Later, other Jewish organizations, German, British, American, and Israeli, made similar efforts. The results achieved by each were ambiguous, as they furthered alienation of Middle Eastern Jews from both their non-Jewish neighbors and from their own traditions, while preparing them for work in the Westernized sectors of the local economies (Netzer, 1989; Rodrigue, 1990). The same pattern was repeated among other Middle Eastern minorities, and was a factor contributing to their insecurity in the era of nationalism (Joseph, 1961; Naby, 1977; Sanjian, 1965). Outside intervention, while giving the communities material, political, and cultural support in the short run, weakened them in some ways, and disrupted the old *modus vivendi* between them and the ruling Muslims.

Following this approach one might see the beginning of significant modernization and Europeanization with the establishment of modern Jewish schools. But such periodization cannot be precise, because in some communities Jewish children had already begun earlier to attend Christian mission schools. In any case, by the late nineteenth century, Jews in much of the Middle East had long worked for European agents, and were thus involved in the world market. But the opening of Alliance schools, which occurred in numerous communities, in Edirne (Turkey) in 1867, Aleppo (1869), Istanbul (1875), Fez (1883), and Teheran in 1898, and numerous other places, was a mainline phenomenon. More and more young Jews now saw themselves through a European mirror, and the communities turned an important historical corner.

In the chapters of this volume, we are concerned with Jews in Islamic lands on the eve of this transition. Indeed, our understanding of these societies remains imperfect, but the generalizations, conclusions, models and hypotheses formulated by scholars working in the field are promising. We have progressed to a stage where significant questions are being raised.

References

Abu-Lughod, Janet L. (1987) 'The Islamic City: Historic Myth, Islamic essence, and Contemporary Relevance,' *International Journal of Middle Eastern Studies* 19: 155–176.

Ben-Sasson, Haim H. (1959) *Hagut VeHanhagah* (Hebrew) (Jerusalem: Bialik Institute).
Ben-Ya'akob, Abraham (1961) *The Jewish Communities of Kurdistan* (Hebrew) (Jerusalem: Ben Zvi Institute).
Boyarin, Daniel (1989) *Sephardic Speculations: A Study in Methods of Talmudic Interpretation* (Hebrew) (Jerusalem: Ben-Zvi Institute).
Braver, Abraham J. (1945–6) 'The Jews of Damascus after the Blood Libel of 1840,' *Zion* 10: 83–108 (Hebrew).
Broyde, I. and Gottheil, R. 'Constantinople,' *Jewish Encyclopedia* IV (1903): 241–2.
Chouraqui, André (1968) *Between East and West: a History of the Jews in North Africa* (Philadelphia: Jewish Publication Society).
Cohen, Hayim J. (1973) *The Jews of the Middle East: 1860–1972* (Jerusalem: Israel Universities Press).
Deshen, Shlomo (1970) *Immigrant Voters in Israel: Parties and Congregations in a Local Election Campaign* (Manchester: Manchester University Press).
—— (1975) 'Ritualization of Literacy: The Works of Tunisian Scholars in Israel,' *American Ethnologist* 2: 251–9.
—— (1989) *The Mellah Society: Jewish Community Life in Sherifian Morocco* (Chicago: University of Chicago Press).
Deshen, Shlomo and Shokeid, Moshe (1974) *The Predicament of Homecoming: Cultural and Social Life of North African Immigrants in Israel* (Ithaca, NY: Cornell University Press).
Eickelman, Dale (1978) 'The Art of Memory: Islamic Education and Its Social Reproduction,' *Comparative Studies in Society and History* 20: 485–516.
Feitelson, Dina (1959) 'Aspects of the Social Life of Kurdish Jews,' *Jewish Journal of Sociology* I: 201–16.
Fischel, Walter (1969) *Jews in the Economic and Political Life of Medieval Islam* (New York: Ktav) (Reprint with new material; original edition, London, 1937).
Frayha, Anis (1953) *Modern Lebanese Proverbs* (Beirut: American University of Beirut).
Goitein, Shlomo D. (1953) 'On the Communal Life of Jews in Yemen,' in *Mordecai M. Kaplan Jubilee Volume* (New York: Jewish Theological Seminary, Hebrew Section) 43–61.
—— (1955a) 'Portrait of a Yemenite Weavers Village,' *Jewish Social Studies* 16: 3–26.
—— (1955b) *Jews and Arabs* (New York: Schocken Books).
—— (1969–94) *A Mediterranean Society*, 5 vols (Berkeley: University of California Press).
Goldberg, Harvey (1967) 'Father's Brother's Daughter Marriage among Tripolitanian Jews in Israel,' *Southwestern Journal of Anthropology* 23: 176–91.
—— (1981) *Mordecai's Story* (Philadelphia: Institute for the Study of Human Issue).
—— (1990) *Jewish Life in Muslim Tripoli: Rivals and Relatives* (Chicago: University of Chicago Press).
Goldschmidt, E.A., Ronen, A. and Ronen, I. (1960) 'Changing Marriage Systems in Jewish Communities in Israel,' *Annals of Human Genetics* 24: 191–204.
Heilman, Samuel (1976) *Synagogue Life* (Chicago: University of Chicago Press).
Hirschberg, Hayim Z. (1974) *A History of the Jews in North Africa* (Leiden: Brill).

Joseph, John (1961) *The Nestorians and Their Muslim Neighbors* (Princeton: Princeton University Press).
Loeb, Laurence D. (1976) 'Sense Stimulation and Ritual Response: A Classification of the Religious Symbolic Behavior of Persian and Yemenite Jews,' in A. Bharati (ed.), *The Realm of the Extra-Human* (The Hague: Mouton) 167–77.
—— (1977) *Outcaste: Jewish Life in Southern Iran* (London: Gordon and Breach).
—— (1980) 'Jewish Life in Habban: A Tentative Reconstruction,' in F. Talmage (ed.), *Studies in Jewish Folklore* (Cambridge Mass.: Association for Jewish Studies) 201–19.
Mernissi, Fatima (1977) 'Women, Saints, and Sanctuaries,' *Signs* 3: 101–12.
Moshavi, Barukh (1974) *Customs and Folklore among Nineteenth Century Bukharian Jews in Central Asia* (PhD Dissertation, Yeshiva University, 1974) (Ann Arbor: University Microfilms International).
Naby, Eden (1977) 'The Assyrians of Iran: Reunification of a "Millet,"' *International Journal of Middle Eastern Studies* 8: 237–49.
Netzer, Amnon (1989) 'Jewish Education in Iran,' in H.S. Himmelfarb and S. Della Pergola (eds), *Studies in Judaism: Jewish Education Worldwide* (Lanham Md.: University Press of America) 447–61.
Noy, Dov (1974) *Jewish–Gentile Relationships as Reflected in the Folktales of the Jews of Kurdistan*. Paper delivered at the International Conference on Jewish Communities in Muslim Lands (Jerusalem: Institute of Asian and African studies and the Ben Zvi Institute).
Patai, Raphael (1971) *The Tents of Jacob* (Englewood Cliffs, NJ: Prentice-Hall).
Quataert, Donald (ed.) (1994) *Manufacturing in the Ottoman Empire and Turkey, 1500–1950* (Albany, NY: State University of New York Press).
Rabinow, Paul (1989) *French Modern: Norms and Forms of the Social Environment* (Cambridge Mass.: MIT Press).
Rodrigue, Aron (1990) *French Jews, Turkish Jews: The Politics of Jewish Schooling in Turkey, 1860–1925* (Bloomington: Indiana University Press).
Romanelli, Samuel (1989) *Travail in an Arab Land*. Translated by Y. and N. Stillman (Tuscaloosa: University of Alabama Press).
Rosen, Lawrence (1984) *Bargaining for Reality: The Construction of Social Relations in a Muslim Community* (Chicago: University of Chicago Press).
Sanjian, Avedis (1965) *Armenian Communities in Syria Under Ottoman Dominion* (Cambridge, Mass.: Harvard University Press).
Shai, Donna (1982) 'Family Conflict and Cooperation in Folksongs of Kurdish Jews.' S. Deshen and W.P. Zenner (eds), in *Jewish Societies in the Middle East: Community, Culture and Authority* (Washington DC: University Press of America) 273–84.
Shokeid, Moshe (1985) *The Dual Heritage: Immigrants from the Atlas Mountains in an Israeli Village* (Manchester: Manchester University Press, 1971; augmented edition, Transaction Books, 1985).
Simmel, Georg (1908) 'Der Fremde,' in *Soziologie* (Leipzig: Duncker & Humbolt).
Stahl, Abraham (1979) 'Ritualist Reading among Oriental Jews,' *Anthropological Quarterly* 52: 115–20.
Stillman, Norman (1979) *The Jews of Arab Lands: A History and Sourcebook* (Philadelphia: Jewish Publication Society).
—— (1991) *The Jews of Arab Lands in Modern Times: A History and Sourcebook* (Philadelphia: Jewish Publication Society).

Stone, Russell (1974) 'Religious Ethic and the Spirit of Capitalism in Tunisia,' *International Journal of Middle Eastern Studies* 5: 260–73.

Wasserfall, Rahel (1990) 'Bargaining for Gender Identity: Love, Sex, and Money in an Israeli Moshav,' *Ethnology* 29: 327–40.

Zborowski, Mark and Herzog, Elizabeth (1953) *Life is With People* (New York: International Universities Press).

Zenner, Walter P. (1972a) 'Some Aspects of Ethnic Stereotype Content in the Galilee: A Trial Formulation,' *Middle Eastern Studies* 8: 405–16.

—— (1972b) 'Aqiili Agha: The Strongman in the Ethnic Relations of the Galilee,' *Comparative Studies in Society and History* 14: 169–88.

—— (1989–90) 'Chicago's Sephardim: A Historical Exploration,' *American Jewish History* 79: 221–41.

—— (1990) 'Jewish Retainers as Power Brokers,' *Jewish Quarterly Review* 81: 127–49.

—— (1991) *Minorities in the Middle* (Albany, NY: State University of New York Press).

2 Traditional Jewish Society and Modern Society
Jacob Katz

To the observer of the contemporary scene it sometimes appears as if great social and cultural differences separate such Jewries as those of Yemen and Hungary, and those of Morocco and Poland. The aim of this chapter is to give the reader a historical and sociological perspective on this matter. Jacob Katz, Professor Emeritus of Social History at the Hebrew University of Jerusalem, and one of the leading Judaics scholars of our time, traces the general characteristics of Jewish traditionalism in various spheres of social life, particularly in the area of education. These characteristics are generally common to all premodern Jews. They vary only in matters of relative detail from one premodern type of Jewish community to the next. As against this, the great differences between Jewish communities, that strike one's attention in modern times, stem from processes of modernization which operated in different ways in various Jewish communities. Katz formulated this thesis in the 1950s, in terms customary among sociologists, for the benefit of Israeli educators. The paper was influential, at that time, in helping to counteract prejudices among officials who were not familiar with the cultures of the new immigrants. Despite the passing of time, Katz's thesis is still fresh, for prejudices of all kinds are still very much alive. Moreover, cultural and sub-ethnic consciousness among Middle Eastern Jews, in Israel and also in the West, is on the rise. This sometimes causes differences to be emphasized to an extent beyond acceptable historical and sociological proportions. The chapter serves to develop a balanced position on a crucial issue of Jewish diversity.

A great deal has been said about the cultural differences between various ethnic groups in Israel, and doubtless such differences do exist. The issue I would like to raise is whether these differences ought to be considered as elements that separate specific ethnic groups or rather ought to be considered as all-encompassing differences between two types of society,

Source: Abbreviated translation of 'Traditional and Modern Societies', *Megamot* X (1960): 304–11. By permission of Henrietta Szold Institute: The National Institute for Research in the Behavioral Sciences, Jerusalem. © Copyright 1960.

the traditional type and the modern type. Professor Goitein has compared the Jewish–Yemenite educational system with the educational system of the Talmudic period. Goitein was able to interpret Talmudic sources by virtue of the comparison with what he actually saw at work in Yemenite Jewish society. Alternatively, he was also able to understand much of what he found in Yemenite society on the basis of the comparison with the original sources of traditional Jewry. Goitein concluded that the differences between the variety of traditional Jewish societies are minor and should be seen in the context of a fundamental principle that is common to all of them. In all traditional societies, man's aspiration lies in seeking religious justification for his existence. This stands in contrast to modern man whose main aspirations lie in other fields, those of financial success, standard of living, and so forth.

I do not discuss this distinction here, but merely state that I shall proceed on the assumption that traditional society is an all-encompassing type, within which there is a variety of historical manifestations. I shall use the sociological concept 'traditional society' to designate societies that, although not primitive, are not societies of the type in which we live today. The key-term for comprehension of the concept 'traditional society' is 'tradition'. Rather than founding their existence and aspirations on values and on knowledge yet to be discovered and developed, people in traditional societies assume that all the practical and theoretical knowledge that they require has been inherited by them from their forefathers, and that it is man's duty to act in accordance with the ancient customs. Furthermore, there is the added assumption that there is no essential difference between the various spheres of human activity, in the sense that all activities require justification in terms of religion. This assumption of people in traditional societies does not, however, imply that traditional society undergoes no changes. There can in fact be no society that does not change. Karl Mannheim long ago suggested that we attempt to imagine a society in which no children are ever born. Though such a society would appear like any other, it would, in actual fact, be lacking one of the most important elements of social dynamics, the coming and going of generations. All societies in actuality are based on generational turnover, and this perforce entails social change. Historical sources, in particular those that deal with the history of education, indicate that even in traditional societies people complained that times were changing and that the younger generation was not faithful to customs of the fathers. It appears that a certain amount of friction between generations is inevitable everywhere and at all times. This friction is a consequence of differences that distinguish each generation from its predecessor.

We know that traditional societies underwent changes in such matters as technology and fashions of dress. We also know that there was development on a spiritual level. Thus there was a time in Yemen when the Zohar was unknown. Only later did the Zohar penetrate the lives of the Jews of Yemen, and eventually became a guiding religious source, directing thought, emotion, religious experience and outlook. This is also pertinent to halakhic literature. The acceptance of the Shulhan Arukh by Yemenite Jews was a definite change in the community. How can these facts be resolved with the claim of traditional society that it bases its present on the past? Evidently in using the term 'traditional society', we do not wish to suggest that this is a society without change, but rather, that it is a society that does not wish or aspire to change. Indeed people in traditional society attempt to resolve changes in the light of tradition and tend to declare what is novel to be old. This state of affairs stands in contrast to that in modern society wherein the old is declared to be new, in order to facilitate its acceptance. Traditional society, though in fact undergoing changes, makes itself out to be static, while modern society on the other hand, aspires toward change. It is difficult for modern man to attribute value to anything just by virtue of its being inherited from the past. The fact that our forefathers acted in a particular way does not provide modern man with the confidence that this indeed is the correct manner. Man in modern society feels compelled to justify his behavior on another level altogether, on a rational, scientific or pseudo-scientific base, that does not rest on the acceptance of values of the past.

At this juncture lies the real distinction between traditional and non-traditional society. Traditional society seeks justification for its way of life from within the realm of tradition, and it tends to blur distinctions between the different spheres of activity, and to adopt a single measure of legitimization *vis-à-vis* one and all. In modern society, on the other hand, the state of the heritage of the past varies from sphere to sphere. As regards technology, for instance, tradition is not held to be valid at all. On the other hand, to the extent that modern society does admit to religious values, it does not deny that these are to be derived from the traditional sources. Aside from the source of individual emotions, religion even in modern society is supported by institutions which cannot possibly be renewed every generation or even periodically every year. As regards other spheres of life we find that compromises are made. Thus for instance, in the sphere of education, while efforts are made to train students to understand their present and to be prepared for the future, some subjects of study are based on traditional principles, and religious education is not the only such subject. The study of language and literature, for instance, is based on what has been absorbed from the past, and there is no attempt to make daily innovations. Also in the area of education of behavior and good manners, the past controls the present to a considerable extent. Similarly, in the study of national history the past determines ongoing life. The opposite, however, is the case in the study of the natural sciences, where there is barely any study of their history, but rather an attempt to teach the latest scientific accomplishments (to the extent that these can be conveyed to the young generation).

These essential distinctions between areas of life in modern society do not hold for traditional society. At this point we come to the central issue. In traditional society, at least theoretically, there is no distinction between different spheres of activity. When we say that traditional Jewish society is religious, we mean that the religious world-view penetrates into areas which we would not regard as associated with religion. Certain customs concerning dress, language, and manners are accepted only by virtue of their being in accordance with tradition, while the tradition itself is validated on the basis of religious beliefs. There were, however, always differences of opinion as to the degree of the validity of tradition, and it is possible to distinguish between two attitudes. On the one hand there is traditionalism based on direct acceptance of the tradition conveyed through social channels. Every traditional Jewish community, whether located in Yemen, Iraq, or in Ashkenazic Europe, accepted the rabbinic Jewish tradition, that had been passed down through the generations by means of a written compilation. On the other hand, each Jewish culture area had its own specific local traditions, which were conveyed through the generations by unmediated personal contact, rather than through the impersonal and formal literature. Here the child meets the tradition, not by studying books in which it receives its theoretical formulation, but by the very fact of his being born and brought up within traditional society. The sense of value attributed to the tradition is not founded on theoretical justifications provided by men of ideas; rather, the person is absorbed into traditional society by the very fact of his education. The conceptual world is molded by the unmediated impressions created on the child which convey a satisfying and safe world. Thus, the link between the child of the society and the tradition is created.

The fundamental education in traditional society is based on the study and absorption of formal knowledge from books and written sources, but the essence of the power of the tradition is created through the unmediated contact with the surroundings. This straightforward attitude toward the personal and local tradition sometimes acquired theoretical justification; there were those who claimed that the legitimization of customs lay in the very fact of their practice throughout the generations. There was, however, another outlook according to which only those customs that can be justified by reference to the traditional literature, are binding. Both attitudes towards custom regarded themselves, and rightly so, as traditional, but the one referred to traditional written sources for legitimization, while the other was satisfied with the very fact of practice of the customs for their legitimization. It now seems to me that the Jewish communities of the Middle East are particularly associated to the latter type, where justification for tradition lies in its very existence and practice and in the personal link of the individual to his society.

As I stated earlier, all spheres of life in traditional society, such as family life, practices of government and law-maintenance, the educational system and religious activities, are governed by a similar world-view. Let us begin with the family. The Jewish family has an ancient tradition. In the same way that Goitein succeeded in carrying out a comparison between the Yemenite education system and that of the period of the Talmud, it should not be difficult to compare the traditional Jewish family (of which there are still remnants), and the Jewish family during the period of the Talmud, even though the differences are considerable. The Jewish family in seventeenth-century Poland is similar to the Yemenite family of both the past and, to a certain extent, of the present day. In both, religion-based tradition legitimizes internal family relations, including the relationship between husband and wife and relations between the generations. The father, who regards himself as having the right to determine the fate of his children in their studies, in their choice of profession and of marriage-partner, is supported by the firm belief that tradition legitimizes his actions. The same holds for the control of the wife by the husband; although sources in *halakha* and homiletics suggest an idealized image of harmony and consideration in this area (and indeed something of that has remained in every Jewish home), much of the behavior within the family does not coincide with the ideal. Again, the justification for actual behavior lies in the stamp of custom through the generations.

Let us turn next to the area of education. In traditional Jewish societies education has one major function: to convey traditional values from generation to generation. Here the great difference between traditional and modern societies can be seen best. Education in modern society aspires to provide the child with knowledge that will stand him in good stead from a practical point of view, and to develop his inner capabilities, so that he will be able to come to a happy combination between his personal needs and the benefit that he can contribute to society. Traditional society knows no such aims, and educators in Israel are faced with problems that arise when immigrants who are accustomed to a traditional educational system are confronted with the demands of a modern educational system.

In traditional society, institutional education is responsible for providing the child with knowledge of Judaism. All other matters, such as preparation for earning a living and training in the practical aspects of daily life, are given over to other agencies. The *heder* of Ashkenazi Jewry, which has its equivalents in all other traditional Jewish societies, was never an institution that provided technical or practical training of any kind. The struggle that did take place within traditional society, particularly in the Ashkenazi communities, as to the provision of practical knowledge to the younger generation, did not focus on the question as to whether these studies be permitted or not, but rather as to which educational institutions, public or semi-public, were to be charged with them. It was admitted that a man must train himself for a craft, trade or some occupation that would provide him with a living, and children were permitted, at the correct time, to be apprenticed to a craftsman, particularly if the community's economy was based on crafts. Similarly, there was no opposition in traditional Jewish society to the study of useful subjects, such as languages, mathematics and other subjects of general knowledge, and there were always small groups that engaged in these.

When traditional society was viable, total and all-encompassing, at least parts of the communities were compelled to engage in matters that deviated from the fostering of the tradition in its restricted sense, such as certain occupations or diplomatic activities. There was no opposition to this, but the problem remained as to which community agencies would bear the responsibility for preparing people for these positions. The traditional institutions saw themselves as responsible for the teaching of religious and cultural values, and they refused to take on themselves the teaching of secular matters. A similar situation exists to this day in the major traditional institutions in Israel, *talmudei torah* and *yeshivot*. Many of these schools, though not opposed to practical studies and to general knowledge, do not wish to become involved in their teaching and prefer to rely on other bodies for these functions. If *yeshivot* do engage in the teaching of these matters it is with great reluctance. The great achievement to which we are witness in today's religious educational establishments, albeit in the non-extremist institutions, is the attempt to combine the two. The problem, however, has not been entirely solved: one still has the feeling that one corner of the school belongs to the traditional world, while other corners emanate an entirely different atmosphere. At certain hours of the day the child finds himself in the traditional *heder*, not very different from what it must have looked a few hundred years ago, and at other moments, in a modern school. For someone who is only familiar with the traditional image of these institutions, this is evidence of revolutionary measures, and it appears as if the sacred and the profane have gotten mixed up with each other, and as if the inner unity of the sacred institutions has collapsed.

These remarks are also pertinent to the family sphere. A person who has been brought up within the framework of traditional society, and accepts the almost unrestricted authority of the father, will find it difficult to become accustomed to the sharing of this authority with other agencies and persons such as the mother and elder siblings of the younger generation. This divided authority implies that the principles on which he has based his existence hitherto are now being fundamentally undermined. This is also true for other areas of activity, such as the sphere of socializing and unmediated contact between people. Traditional society is never ascetic up to the point of denying social pleasures. Social enjoyments exist everywhere, and there are institutions that provide opportunities for people to meet each other for no other reason than to enjoy each other's company. Jewish traditional society is no exception to this, although there have been attempts to impose restrictions on social amusements. The Gaon of Vilna (in the late eighteenth century) advised his wife to pray at home rather than at synagogue in order to avoid idle chatter. He was ready for her to forego the religious satisfaction attached to public prayer in order to avoid contact with the profane. But the attitude of the Gaon of Vilna was unusual; on the whole traditional society does offer scope for social enjoyment as long as this takes place under the auspices of the existing social institutions, whose legitimization is rooted in tradition. Thus, for instance, it was permitted to engage in leisure activities in the study-house, in addition to the activities for which it was created. Also, traditional wedding festivities were sometimes extended over more than the seven days of customary feasting, and included festivities before the actual wedding ceremony, and sometimes even before and after betrothal. In other words, enjoyment for its own sake was forbidden; it had to be given justification from within the accepted traditional framework. The usage of the concept *seudat mitzva*, that is a festive meal of religious significance, was greatly extended over time. In the early halakhic sources the concept was very restricted, and festive meals that would today be classified as *seudot mitzva* were originally not considered as such. Over time the concept grew less restricted and the legal authorities exerted themselves to classify more and more social occasions under this heading. One gets the impression that they wished to be generous in permitting social gatherings, and thus to give these occasions a religious seal, in accordance with tradition.

This phenomenon, whereby people in traditional society were able to satisfy their needs for friendship and socializing in accordance with traditional requirements, gave society much resilience and adaptability. Although there were always moralists who disapproved of recently-legitimized social gatherings and festivities, it was nevertheless possible to live in traditional society without the perception of enjoyment as misconduct. It was considered wrong only if a man invited his friend to a festive gathering for no explicit reason. This close link between the sphere of social life and religious beliefs is just one illustration of the unity of different spheres of activity within traditional society. But what happens when such a society shakes itself free of tradition? Then sociability and enjoyment for their own sake become acceptable. Both young and old discover that they have the right to go out and enjoy themselves for no reason other than their own pleasure. We are witness to such a process when young people, brought up in a traditional society, find themselves in modern society and discover the facilities available for enjoyment. But more important, these young people also discover that modern society sees no harm in the fact that a man, at the end of his working day, goes out and looks for relaxation in an activity for which there is no explicit religious or moral justification. This, in my opinion, is one of the outstanding examples of the gradual separation of institutions that were originally combined, which occurs in the transition from life under traditional conditions to modern conditions.

Further examples may be drawn from the fields of government and economics. The term 'government' refers to arrangements determined by the ruling authorities, which are obeyed by those further down the social hierarchy. We do not need to explain the secret of government, why it is that those below obey those above; this is one of the basic sociological facts. Government is an institution for which every society provides its own particular form of legitimization. In a society founded on a secular–rational basis the tendency is to justify the organs of government by referring to necessity, namely that society cannot exist without some form of law-maintenance. In fact education towards good citizenship in modern societies seeks to ensure the identification of the younger generation with the authorities that direct the society. Traditional societies, on the other hand, work on a quite different basis. Those societies are usually much smaller than modern mass societies; therefore contact between the ruler and the ruled is more personal, direct and unmediated. The governor is often personally known to the public and, most crucially, his position in accordance with religious tradition, is believed to be blessed from above.

Government in modern society is founded on the rational concept of the decentralization of power (such as the principle that the executive body is answerable to the legislative body, and both of these are answerable to the judiciary). The principles governing decentralization are so abstract that they cannot be deduced from simple observation of the workings of the government. Someone who has no notion of the functional significance of a Parliament, and who is witness to groups of people arguing vehemently, sometimes aggressively, is likely to be repelled by the apparent lack of meaning. On the other hand, such a person observing the president at a ceremony will become aware of the existence of the governing body, by virtue of the concrete manifestation, and he will be more likely to identify with it. Now traditional society combines the two elements: the governor is both the institution and its symbolic representative. Modern government, on the other hand, is based on the separation of its symbolic and functional aspects. This is one reason why newcomers from traditional society have not easily adjusted to modern political functions. Though such people may identify with the symbolic aspects of government, their initial understanding of the inner workings of politics are limited.

Let us address ourselves to the economic issue. Economics is surely a rational matter: man works in order to earn a living and provide for his family. Here, seemingly, tradition cannot have much say. But in fact this is not the case. Modern economic activity assumes that man is rational, and rationality in the sphere of economics implies optimal material success by the easiest means feasible. People in traditional society also aspire to material success, though not necessarily by the easiest means possible. Economic activity in traditional society is carried out in accordance with custom. Thus for instance, where it was accepted that a particular skill be passed down through the generations, the individual was not given the opportunity to choose his profession according to his own will. This contrasts with modern life, where the trend is to direct the individual to that profession which will be best for the individual and for the community. But that is unfamiliar to people who were raised in traditional society.

Before concluding let me add a more general comment. Traditional Jewish society in the diaspora was characterized by the fact that it was never a whole society. Jewish society took on the form of a sect or of a caste, not in the full sense of the term as used by sociologists, but certainly in the sense of a group that fulfilled roles within strict limitations, some of them self-imposed and some of them imposed from the outside. In traditional society man was not able to achieve much for his children, and the future, though secure, promised very little variety. His steps were guided by tradition; he could not and did not have to make far-reaching decisions. Now one of the great consequences of the establishment of the State of Israel is the fact that Jewish society has become whole, and is able to offer its citizens a wide choice of professions, thus accommodating the needs of both individual and society. However, people who are unfamiliar with the modern outlook, and who are accustomed to have their existence largely defined by their circumstances, find this a situation in which they lose control over their world. They often do not comprehend the potential benefits inherent in the new situation. Integration into the new society requires that people from the traditional world cut themselves off from much that has guided their way in the past. Otherwise, that which is a potential advantage in modern society remains a disadvantage for them.

Let us summarize. A society is classified as traditional, not because it has no future or no present. Society can only continue to exist by virtue of the past that molds its present, and each generation adds its particular contribution to the heritage of the past. Traditional society is thus compelled to adjust to changes that occur in its midst. In traditional society, however, it is the traditional frame of reference that provides justification for changes. In modern society the situation is radically different, and little value is attributed to tradition. Though there are still hesitant attempts to establish links with the tradition, on the whole it is assumed that the activity of people in various areas of life is to be based on the inner rationale of each particular activity. Thus, economic activity proceeds according to its own rules, and similarly in matters of government, education, family and leisure time. For those who come from traditional societies all this raises profound existential problems and inevitable clashes between the two worlds. These clashes are particularly evident in Israel, where the situation I have outlined is not the consequence of a historical process, but of the sudden transition through migration from one type of society to another.

3 Jewish Acculturation in Premodern Societies
Stephen Sharot

Stephen Sharot, Professor of Sociology at Ben-Gurion University in Beersheba, stresses differences between traditional Jewries, in contrast to Katz's emphasis on their uniformity. Sharot compares four major Jewish culture-areas: China, India, the Islamic Middle East, and Christian Europe. The comparison deals with the degree of socio-cultural openness, as opposed to closure, which these Jewries exhibited towards their respective Gentile environments. The Jews in India and China were the most open to Gentile influence, while those in premodern Europe were the least open, and Jews under Islam stood between these two poles. The differences are explained by characteristics of the host-societies. We have omitted the European material from this edited version of the study.

An obvious place to begin a comparison of levels of acculturation among Jewish communities is the Middle East; in contrast with Europe and the Far East, the Jews had not transplanted their culture to an alien environment, but were, from the outset, a part of the indigenous culture. The expansion of the Arab empire facilitated the dispersion of Jews over the Middle East, but in many areas Jews were established before the advent of Islam. In its formative stages, Islam incorporated many religious, legal, and moral conceptions from the Jews, and even after the boundaries between Islam and Judaism were drawn, Jews and Muslims continued to share many beliefs and practices.

Levels of Jewish acculturation to Islamic societies have varied over different areas and periods. Although following the Islamic conquests, significant numbers of Jews were totally assimilated, often by conversion, into the 'host' population, the rate of assimilation was rarely high enough to reduce the overall numbers. In contrast to the Christians and Zoroastrians, who were unable to adjust to their newly acquired minority status, the number of Jews increased in the centuries after the Islamic conquests. The

---

Source: Abbreviation of Stephen Sharot, *Judaism: A Sociology* (Newton Abbot: David & Charles, 1976) 5–36; 190–2. © Copyright 1976 by Stephen Sharot. Reprinted by permission of Stephen Sharot and David & Charles.

Jews remained a distinct socio-cultural group under Islam, but they shared far more of the culture of their non-Jewish neighbors than the Jews in Europe. The influence of Judaism on early Islam had been considerable, but, after its crystallization, Islam in turn had an influence on Middle Eastern Judaism. As in most cases, the subordinate minority acculturated to the dominant majority, rather than the other way round.

In general, there was little that outwardly distinguished Jew and Muslim: they spoke the same language and wore the same clothes, despite occasional regulations seeking to differentiate Muslim and Jewish dress. It has often been said that the Middle Eastern Jews were 'Arab in all but religion', but this oversimplifies and distorts the true situation. Religion pervaded Middle Eastern culture and a distinction between 'religious' and 'secular' areas of culture is often difficult to make. For example, adoption of the dominant language was bound to have implications for the minority's religion. By about CE 1000 the majority of Middle Eastern Jews had, like the rest of the population, adopted Arabic, and this involved the adoption of Arabic ways of thinking and Arabic religious concepts. The Jews used Arabic for translating and teaching the Bible, as well as discussing Jewish law and ritual. Although the Muslim's emphasis on the study of the Arabic language also influenced the Jews to study Hebrew, the use of Arabic for both secular and religious purposes contrasts with the development of language barriers between Jews and Christians in Europe.

Furthermore, if we take the term 'religion' to mean not just the 'orthodox' doctrines of Judaism and Islam but all the supernatural beliefs and practices found among the Middle Eastern population, then there was considerable overlap between the religion of Muslim and Jew. Much of the 'popular' religion shared by Muslim and Jew was preIslamic. One central cult, especially important in North Africa, which had many preIslamic elements but which was brought into the framework of both Islam and Judaism in the Middle East, was that of pilgrimage to the tombs of saints. Both Muslims and Jews sought the intercession and protection of the saints, offering them candles and oil lamps and performing rituals by their tombs. Family pilgrimages were made when important family events occurred and collective pilgrimages were made on the anniversary of the death of the saint. In addition to certain saints worshipped by both Muslims and Jews, the two religious groups shared many magical practices and beliefs associated with witchcraft, sorcery, divination, ecstatic prophecy, demons, the evil eye, the magical significance of numbers, and the protective power of amulets. In many cases, the 'popular' cults appear to have attained a greater place in the total religious system of Middle Eastern Jews than the distinctive beliefs and practices of Judaism. The trend from local religious diversity to Talmudic uniformity, which had occurred under the Roman and Persian empires and which was at first strengthened under Islam, was reversed in the later Middle Ages when local religious customs again assumed importance...

In addition to sharing much of the 'popular' religion of their neighbors, Jews were also influenced by more 'orthodox' Islamic practices. The short, intense features of Muslim prayer impressed Middle Eastern Jews, and their services displayed far more decorum than European Jewish services. Like the Muslims, the Jews practiced polygamy, and the religious position of Jewish women deteriorated in Islamic environments. In the highlands of Yemen, where Islamic women did not attend the mosque, Jewish women did not attend the synagogue and were completely cut off from the religious life of the men.

Although most Middle Eastern Jewish communities shared much of their culture with their Muslim neighbors, their distinctiveness as religious minorities varied greatly, even among those who had little or no contact with other Jewish communities. For example, the Yemenite Jews had no contact with Jewish communities outside Yemen, but their religio-culture remained very distinct from that of their non-Jewish neighbors; they had evolved certain unique religious practices, but, like the Jews of Europe, prayer in the synagogue and study of the Talmud were central. They provide a sharp contrast with other isolated communities which were highly acculturated, such as the Mountain Jews of the Caucasus (Tats), the Jews in Kurdistan, and many communities in the interior of North Africa...

The Jewish communities under Islam varied greatly in their levels of acculturation to the culture of the majority, but, on a continuum of religious acculturation, most of the Middle Eastern communities may be placed mid-way between the highly acculturated Jewish communities of the Far East (India and China) and the very strong sub-cultural distinctiveness of the pre-nineteenth century European Jewish communities. In the early Middle Ages, Jews migrated from the Middle Eastern centers and transplanted their religio-culture to 'alien' environments: the majority migrated to Europe and a much smaller number migrated farther east. The contrast between the development of Judaism in East and West is striking: in the West the Jews not only retained but reinforced their religio-cultural distinctiveness, while in the East the Jews adopted much of the local culture and religion into their own system.

The Jews of China provide one of the few documented Jewish communities which were entirely absorbed, culturally and socially, by a 'host' society. There were probably a number of small Jewish communities in both inland and coastal Chinese towns by CE1200, and a number of communities, some quite large, are known to have existed in coastal towns between the fourteenth and seventeenth centuries, but the community in

Kaifeng was the only one to survive into the nineteenth century. By the end of the nineteenth century, the Jews of Kaifeng too had almost entirely disappeared through assimilation, but there is historical evidence of their substantial acculturation long before this.

There is no doubt that the first Jewish settlers in Kaifeng were Talmudic Jews; in 1850 they still had all the prayer books and scrolls required for daily and Sabbath services and for all the festivals and fasts. It appears, however, that Chinese influences entered the Jews' beliefs and practices at an early stage, and Western visitors in the seventeenth and eighteenth centuries found a highly acculturated community whose religion combined certain distinctively Jewish beliefs and practices with beliefs and practices from the environmental Confucian, Buddhist, and Taoist religions. The Jewish temple was still flourishing, and the Jews still practiced a number of traditional Jewish commandments such as abstinence from pork, but the attenuation of their Judaism was observed in their poor Hebrew and ignorance of many Jewish rites and festivals. The influence of the non-Jewish religious environment was clearly visible in the architecture of their temple, the use of non-Jewish ritual objects, the observance of Chinese seasonal festivals, ancestor worship, and absorption of Chinese rituals into the rites of passage, and the use of inscriptions written on stone tablets for the transmission of religious beliefs. The inscriptions on both the stone tablets and temple archways were written in Chinese, used Chinese terms for God, contained quotations from Confucian writing, and proclaimed that the principles of Confucianism and the religion of the Chinese Jews were the same.

Unlike the Chinese Jews, the Jews in India increased in number, but during their period of comparative isolation from other Jewish communities, their Judaism lost much of its distinctiveness; they adopted many Hindu customs, and they were assimilated into the caste system. In the sixteenth and seventeenth centuries, European Jews migrated to India and established an orthodox form of Judaism among the Cochin Jews. The Jews from Europe probably intermarried with the wealthiest families of the established Jewish community, but they came to form a White Jewish caste and completely distinguished themselves from the indigenous Black Jews. A third caste, composed of slave and servant converts of the White Jews, also emerged.

Little is known of the religion of the Cochin Jews before their contacts with Western Jews, but it is evident from the thirteenth century tombstones that even then they had an imperfect knowledge of Hebrew and the Bible. There is more information of the preWesternized Judaism of the Bene Israel who, unlike the Cochin Jews, did not come into sustained contact with early European Jewish immigrants to India. A more distinctive

Judaism was introduced to the Bene Israel in the nineteenth century by Cochin Jews, Jewish immigrants from the Middle East, and, somewhat paradoxically, by Christian missionaries who translated the Bible into Marathi and taught Hebrew. But before the recent period of contact with non-Bene Israel Jews, the Judaism of the Bene Israel took highly acculturated forms. The Bene Israel observed the Sabbath, some of the holy days, some dietary regulations, and circumcision, but knowledge of Hebrew had been lost, and they had adopted a number of religious beliefs and practices from their Hindu neighbors, especially from the higher castes – they objected to the remarriage of widows and they believed that the eating of beef was prohibited by the Jewish religion.

The Bene Israel held a comparatively low-caste position; in the villages of Konkan their traditional caste occupation was oil pressing, and in Bombay, where they concentrated in the nineteenth century, they became a caste of clerks. In addition, the Bene Israel were divided into two sub-castes: the *Gora* or 'White' Bene Israel, who claimed they were pure descendants of the first Jewish settlers in India, and the lower caste *Kala* or 'Black' Bene Israel.

Although most Jewish communities under Islam retained a greater religio-cultural distinctiveness than the Jews of China and India, it is the Ashkenazi Jewish communities of medieval and early modern Europe that provide the strongest contrast with the Jewish communities of the East. The Ashkenazi came to put an enormous emphasis on the strict interpretation of religious law and the observance of religious ritual; a 'wall' was built around the Torah to lessen the possibility of ritualistic mistakes. In the twelfth and thirteenth centuries, the *Hasidei Ashkenaz* ('pious men of Germany') established more rigid precepts against contact with Christian symbols and imposed upon themselves an even stricter ritualism than that required by the Talmud. The cultural distinctiveness of the Jews was not limited to religious beliefs and practices, but came to encompass such spheres as everyday language and clothes. Yiddish developed as the distinctive everyday language of the Jews, and in eastern Europe, from the seventeenth to the early twentieth centuries, Jewish appearance and clothes visibly set them apart from non-Jews: the men grew long beards and sidelocks and wore long black caftans and large hats. That special clothes came to signify the orthodox Jew illustrates the encompassing importance of Judaism to Jewish society in Europe...

Jewish society in the medieval and early modern period was a traditional one in the sense that change was only accepted if it could be legitimized by values and practices handed down from the past. Legitimacy had to be found in the codes of religious law, and this gave enormous significance to religious scholarship. Men were regarded as superior to women since they were the main 'carriers' of the religion, bearing the major part of the 'yoke of the Law.' Women had only to learn enough to read their prayers and perform their special ritual activities, but it was the duty of every man to study, and a large proportion did devote part of the day or a certain day of the week to the study of the law. It was common for the wife of a scholar to manage both the home and a business while her husband devoted his time to study of the sacred texts . . .

The three major status attributes in the traditional Jewish community were learning, wealth, and lineage (the scholarship and wealth of ancestors and relatives). Since wealth was not always sufficient to achieve status in the community, many prominent merchants and bankers sought to obtain rabbinic standing. If a man could not achieve high scholarly status, the next best thing was to support his son-in-law while he studied. Marriage and dowries were arranged according to the bridegroom's religious scholarship . . .

Jews and Christians held many magical beliefs in common, but even in this sphere there were important differences between them. The invocation of demons and the distinction between white and black magic were of minor significance for the Jews, compared with their importance in the Christian religio-culture. Another difference was that magic did not have an anti-establishment function among the Jews; the more scholarly Jews emphasized the need for both adherence to the legalistic rabbinical system and for knowledge of the mystical cabbalistic writings. Talmudical scholars were often the greatest miracle workers. Thus, although there was some cultural overlap in magic between Christians and Jews, this was of limited significance, and in general the religio-cultural distinctiveness of the Ashkenazi Jews remained very marked in most parts of Europe up to the end of the eighteenth century.

In comparison with the Ashkenazi, the Sephardi Jews of the Iberian peninsula adopted a greater part of the dominant culture. Judaism was less encompassing in the socio-cultural system of the Sephardim, and from the thirteenth century onwards references to non-observance of the religious law by the Jews in Spain are common. The Ashkenazi observed a greater number of rituals, interpreted the religious law in a stricter fashion, and took greater heed of their rabbis.

ENVIRONMENTAL CULTURE AND SOCIAL STRUCTURE

Any explanation of the different levels of acculturation among Jewish communities must take into consideration demographic distribution. The

Jewish population in each single community was not, however, a significant independent variable: urban concentration did not guarantee, and rural distribution did not necessarily weaken, continuing socio-cultural distinctiveness. A few of the Chinese urban communities were fairly large at one time, but they disappeared, while Jewish communities in rural areas in India, the Middle East, and Europe increased in number. The largest urban communities were found in the Near Eastern and Mediterranean areas where many Jewish communities occupied entire quarters of the towns. In Europe most communities were not large; the number of Jewish families in a few commercial centers reached the hundreds, but European Jewry was widely distributed in many towns and villages, especially in eastern Europe.

Far more significant than the number in each community was contact with other communities, and here the greater density and communication of Jews within Europe must be considered. In the High Middle Ages, western and central Europe contained most of the European Jews, but there was a movement east in the latter part of the medieval period, and, in the early modern period, the vast majority of European Jews lived in eastern Europe. In the premodern societies, mobility between communities was low, but the Jews were more mobile than most, and, although often infrequent and irregular, the network of contacts and ties between the European communities supported the knowledge of, and identification with, a 'people' which stretched far beyond the immediate community. This was not the case for the Jews of the East and some parts of the Middle East, many of whom knew little or nothing of a Jewish people outside their own immediate community.

Although the most acculturated communities are to be found among those isolated for long periods from the centers of Jewish settlement, there are also examples of isolated communities which retained a very high level of religio-cultural distinctiveness, and the history of Western Jewry since the eighteenth century has shown that large numbers, extensive communication, and a sense of identity with a far-ranging 'people' do not prevent substantial acculturation. It is clear that small numbers and lack of contact with other communities only made a community particularly susceptible to an absorbent environment. An explanation of variations in the level of Jewish religious acculturation requires, therefore, an analysis of those aspects of the religio-culture and social structure of the 'host' societies which would affect the cultural and social barriers between minority and majority.

In the cultural environments of the premodern societies under discussion, religion was central and played a very important part in the dominant groups' orientations to religious minorities. The major religions in China were both syncretistic and culturally pluralistic; they combined and reconciled diverse beliefs and practices, and little or no attempt was made to demand the exclusive allegiance of believers. In accommodating non-Jewish practices into their religion, the Chinese Jews were following the general Chinese practice of observing sacraments from a number of religious traditions – Buddhist, Taoist, etc. – side by side.

Confucianism, the official Chinese state doctrine, was neither a state religion nor a church in the Western sense; the literati espoused a doctrinal orthodoxy and emphasized the necessity of performing certain rites, but there was little or no attempt to coerce others. The Chinese political elite permitted and encouraged religious syncretism if it was politically efficacious, and it tolerated diverse religions, as long as they were not hostile to the state. Max Weber (1964: 213–4) wrote, 'the most important and absolute limit to practical tolerance for the Confucian state consisted in the fundamental importance of the ancestor cult and this-worldly piety for the docility of the patrimonial subject.' There was little or no formal constraint on Chinese Jews to conform to non-Jewish beliefs and practices, as long as they recognized the ancestral cult and religious status of the Chinese emperor. In addition, neither religious nor nationalist notions predisposed the dominant group to separate the Jews from other Chinese. The concept of nationalism or of a nation did not arise in China since the empire was regarded as the universe, composed of concentric circles, becoming increasingly barbarous the farther they lay from the Chinese core. Like the Muslims, with whom they were sometimes categorized, the Chinese Jews lived within the universe and were not, therefore, subject to any differential legal, political, economic or social treatment.

The important elements of the Chinese social structure, the extended family, clan, and political rule by a centralized bureaucracy, did not dispose the Jews to enter a peculiar structural niche in the society. The original Jewish settlers in Kaifeng were probably specialists in manufacturing, dyeing, or pattern printing of cotton fabrics, but economic diversity among native Kaifeng Jews is illustrated by a 1512 inscription which mentions degree-holders, civil and military officials, farmers, artisans, traders, and shopkeepers. In the fifteenth, sixteenth, and seventeenth centuries, a number of Jews attained high political and military posts, and others were successful as physicians and scholars.

The majority of Kaifeng Jews were members of the small Chinese merchant-artisan class which occupied a social position between the mass peasant base and the literati. But from the beginning of the fourteenth century, Kaifeng Jews entered the scholar-official class in increasing numbers, and some held important positions. In contrast to the free towns in Europe, Chinese towns were seats of the mandarinate, and the ambition of most merchant families in the towns was to break into the scholar-official class. The literati was not a completely closed class, and in the large, wealthy, imperial city of Kaifeng, Jews, as much as others, could take advantage of the limited opportunities for mobility. Song Nai Rhee has argued that the civil service system transformed Jewish intellectuals into Confucian literati, a transformation which affected their total philosophical and religious perspective. Some members of the Jewish community, who were more conscious of their religious distinctiveness, disapproved of the Confucianization of the Jewish intellectuals, but as members of the Chinese elite, the Jewish scholar-officials were bound to have an important influence on the whole community. In addition, participation in the civil service contributed towards intermarriage and assimilation; the Jewish literati had to leave Kaifeng since, like all other civil servants, they were prohibited from holding official positions in the place of their birth. It may be hypothesized, therefore, that the substantial acculturation and assimilation of the Chinese Jews was related both to the Chinese cultural orientations (religious syncretism and pluralism) and to the Chinese social structure which permitted the socio-economic integration of the Jews in Chinese society.

Like the Chinese religions, the general dispositions of Indian Hinduism towards minority religions were syncretistic and culturally pluralistic. The dominant Hindus tolerated other religions which did not threaten the caste system and the supremacy of the Brahmins. But although they were pluralistic in the sense that they did not actively attempt to enforce a Hindu monopoly, the assimilative character of the caste system and the syncretism of the Hindu religion resulted in a virtual monopoly of Hinduism over much of India. Although the Bene Israel had only acquired the status of a low caste, it had presumably been to their advantage to accept voluntarily certain Hindu rituals and the caste system; it was difficult for an alien and therefore impure group, which was not economically self-sufficient, to exist outside the Hindu community. Once the Jews had adopted the caste system and some principal practices of Hinduism, their own distinctive beliefs and rituals were tolerated within the Hindu community itself.

Although the general orientations of Hinduism strongly disposed the Jews to substantial acculturation, the Indian social structure did not strongly dispose them to substantial assimilation. Anthropologist Srinivas has described Indian society as subject to two opposed types of solidarity: the solidarity of village and the solidarity of caste. Indian villages were largely autonomous units; there were no large-scale interregional religious institutions in India, and the authority of the secular rulers rarely extended to the internal affairs of the village. For many centuries the Bene Israel resided in the villages of Konkan, and it is clear that their close association with non-Bene Israel occasionally resulted in intermarriage. However, the solidarity of caste reinforced the social boundaries of the Bene Israel and enabled them to increase in number. As in China, the Indian Jews were not singled out for differential treatment as Jews, but unlike in China, the very integration of the Jews into the Hindu religio-social system contributed to their social preservation.

In contrast to the syncretistic religions of the East, Islam developed out of a monotheistic tradition and inherited from it strong dispositions to doctrinism. Islam was flexible in incorporating folk beliefs and practices of the nominal Muslim population, but its syncretism was slight in comparison with the inclusive tendencies of the Eastern religions, and the dominant Islamic groups were consistent in their rejection of distinctive Judaic beliefs and practices. Again, in contrast with Eastern religions, which were generally content to coexist peacefully with other religions, Islam has often been markedly monopolistic; it has sought, often with success, to establish itself as the only religion in a particular area by converting or eliminating non-Islamic religious groups. Islamic monopolism was, however, mainly directed towards pagans or non-monotheists, and the Islamic disposition toward the Jews was, in general, more pluralistic than monopolistic. Mohammed established the general principle that adherents of non-Islamic monotheistic faiths should be allowed to live under Muslim rule. Although in its early warrior phase this principle was not consistently upheld, Arab religious pluralism became firmly established once the Arabs had conquered vast territories containing large non-Islamic populations.

The broad pluralist disposition of the dominant Arabs towards other monotheists was formulated in a number of treaties which provided for the protection of the persons, property, and religious observances of minorities in return for payment to the Islamic rulers. During the High Middle Ages this pluralism was interrupted by two outbreaks of monopolism, limited in time and scope: one in Egypt from 1012 to 1019 under the Khalif al-Hakim and the other under the Almohad conquerors of North Africa and Spain in the 1140s. In both cases, Christians, as well as Jews, were given the choice of conversion to Islam or death. Such occurrences were, however, very rare in the Arab world. The general condition of non-military castes in the fourteenth and fifteenth centuries revived under the Ottoman Turks in the sixteenth and seventeenth centuries, and then deteriorated again. But over long periods and up to recent times, the Jews under Islam enjoyed a comparatively secure existence, free from persecution.

Within the framework of general religious pluralism, the Jews were subject to a certain amount of differential treatment, although, again, this varied considerably between periods and provinces. Some of this differential treatment was motivated by a desire to secure the monopoly of Islam over its nominal adherents and to protect Islam from 'deviant' religions. In order to demonstrate the superiority of Islam over other religions, numerous restrictions on non-Muslims were introduced concerning such matters as modes of dress, size of buildings, and interfaith contacts. These restrictions, which applied to Jews as well as other religious minorities, were seldom enforced, and in fact, discrimination was very intermittent. Nontolerant and segregationist policies were more likely to be found where the Muslim population adhered to a sectarian form of Islam. In the Yemen, under the rule of the Sh'ites, conditions were particularly oppressive; Jews were regarded as ritually unclean, they were subject to many restrictions, and in the seventeenth century they were forced out of the towns to live in special areas on the outskirts. As the only non-Muslim religious minority in the Yemen, the Jews were without rights, and they were forced to seek Muslim patrons who would provide them with protection in exchange for payment.

Many Jewish communities under Islam were subject to heavy fiscal discrimination, but with a few exceptions, such as the Yemen, other forms of discrimination were slight or non-existent. The Jews had undergone a transformation from an agricultural people to one of merchants and artisans in the seventh and eighth centuries, but since there were few restrictions in the economic sphere, they undertook a great variety of occupations and did not become economically differentiated from urban Muslims. The Middle Eastern Jews shared both in the prosperous mercantile period from the ninth to the thirteenth centuries and in the decline thereafter.

In most cases, the residential separation of the Jews was voluntary: there were no legally segregated quarters, but predominantly homogeneous religious quarters were customary in Muslim towns, and there was no degradation associated with living in one. The Jews also had their own semi-autonomous community organization to which Islamic rulers delegated substantial political authority, and which was entrusted with the task of collecting taxes. But despite fairly distinct living quarters and community organization, close and intimate association with Muslims was not uncommon...

Like Islam, Christianity was an insular religion with only limited dispositions to syncretism. The Christian Church was flexible in incorporating pagan folk beliefs and practices which did not present articulate religious alternatives or challenges, but it was consistent in establishing clear boundaries with alternative religious systems, such as Judaism. The Christian Church differed from Islam, however, in so far as it was far less disposed to take a pluralistic stance towards other monotheistic faiths.

The fact that the Jews were the only deviant religious group whose existence was tolerated by the central organs of the Church is important to an understanding of the situation of the Jews in medieval Europe. Muslims were not tolerated except on a temporary basis in Spanish and Italian areas, and Christian heretics were bloodily suppressed. The Jews were the sole recognized representatives of religious dissent, the only group to fall outside the otherwise complete religious monopoly of the Church. The ecclesiastical doctrine, formulated by the Church fathers and the early popes, stated that the Jews should be tolerated in a submissive state until the end of days, at which time their conversion would herald the second coming of Christ. The Church taught that the exile and submissive state of the Jews was a God-inflicted penalty for the Jewish repudiation of Christ, and could thus be regarded as evidence for the truth of Christianity. This doctrine did not mean that the Church should not attempt to convert Jews, but conversion by force was in general officially prohibited.

The policy of limited pluralism with regard to the Jews was held relatively consistently by the Papacy and the higher ranks of the Church throughout the medieval period. With a few exceptions, the central offices of the Church counselled tolerance and restraint during intolerant periods, and they passed decrees whose purpose was to protect Jews and safeguard their property. The Church had little executive power outside the pontifical states and feudal lordships of individual bishops, but the principles of the Church toward the Jews were very influential in determining the policies of secular rulers, who generally found that the existence of a Jewish community was congruent with their economic and fiscal interests. The official Church policy of limited tolerance was, however, little appreciated or known by the Christian masses and the lower levels of the Church hierarchy. Local and regional clerics, particularly parish priests and wandering monks, were often supporters or leaders of anti-Jewish outbreaks. During periods of unrest, such as the times of the Crusades and the Black Death, neither the church nor most secular authorities were able or willing to prevent massacres of whole Jewish communities. Thus, although European Jews were often protected by sovereign powers, outbreaks of persecution were far more frequent under Christianity than under Islam . . .

CONCLUSIONS

It is now possible to make a number of statements accounting for the gross differences in levels of Jewish acculturation in the societies discussed. It should be emphasized, however, that with regard to a number of the 'isolated' communities, our conclusions will have to be very tentative. The historical data is often sparse and, in some cases, almost non-existent. It is not possible to trace the religio-cultural developments of the Chinese, Indian, and many Middle Eastern communities over the centuries since much of our information derives from Europeans who visited and described the communities after they were 'discovered'. In many cases, we can only compare a number of static pictures of communities at the end of their periods of isolation, and from these attempt to reconstruct their histories. However, what independent historical evidence we do have suggests that, where the distinctiveness of Judaism became highly attenuated, the process occurred over a long period and cannot be explained in terms of the characteristics and orientations of the first generation of Jewish settlers. If the original Jewish settlers had been predisposed to cultural and social absorption by the 'host' society, the community would not have survived centuries of isolation from other Jewish communities, even in a highly attenuated form.

The size of the Jewish community and the distance from the major centers of Jewish settlement are important variables but should not be overemphasized. Comparatively small numbers, and lack of contact with other Jewish communities, could only make a community particularly malleable to its cultural and social environments. One important cultural dimension was the strength of the boundaries of the dominant religion of the majority. Jewish acculturation was much greater in those societies where the dominant religion was syncretic, than in those societies where the dominant religion was insular. Although the differences between Judaism and the environmental religious systems were initially much greater in China and India than in the Middle East and Europe, the syncretism of the Eastern religions contributed to the much greater loss of Jewish religio-cultural distinctiveness in the East.

Another important dimension was the strength of the dominant group's disposition to demand allegiance to its religion within its defined territory. As might be expected, syncretic religions were more disposed to monopolism. The greater the tendency of the dominant group to coerce the Jews into accepting the majority religion, the more the Jews emphasized their religio-cultural distinctiveness. The greater the tendency of the dominant group to accept the existence of Judaism, the more likely the Jews would acculturate to the majority or core culture.

Both religio-cultural and social structural dimensions influenced the extent to which the Jews were separated socially from non-Jews. Where Jews were separated, they were less likely to adopt the non-Jewish religio-culture. Where Jews were not so separated and social contacts with non-Jews were more frequent and intimate, acculturation was far more likely. The extent to which the Jews were separated within a society was often related to the dominant group's disposition to monopolism or pluralism. A total monopolistic policy, if successful, would have resulted in the disappearance of the Jews, but successful monopolism was very rare. Even when Jews were forced to convert to Christianity, they often remained unassimilated, and this drove the dominant group to segregate them still further.

Although attempts at a total monopolism by means of massacres, forced conversions, and expulsions were not uncommon in Christian Europe, periods of pluralism were generally longer. Variations in social separation have, therefore, to be considered within the framework of pluralism, although it is obvious that Jews were more likely to be separated from non-Jews in those societies whose pluralist stance was of a comparatively limited form. In some cases, segregation of the Jews was motivated by the dominant group's desire to impose or retain its religious monopoly over the non-Jewish population. In medieval Europe, however, the Jews were segregated by more encompassing barriers long after Judaism had ceased to be a threat to Christian monopolism.

Some spheres of separation of Jews from non-Jews were little related, at least in any direct way, to the religious motives and orientations of the dominant group. Differences in the social structures of 'host' societies were also relevant. The feudal structure of European societies made for the separation of Jews in the economic, social, and political spheres. Jews were less segregated in Middle Eastern societies, but the convergence of religion and state under Islam involved the political separation of religious minorities. In China and India, Jews were not politically separated and corporate Jewish polities did not develop. The Indian caste system did make for some social separation of Jews, but, in contrast to the Middle East and Europe, the Jews were separated within the dominant religious system and not outside it. The social separation of Jews as a caste in India implied a substantial Jewish acculturation, while in the Middle East and Europe, the greater the social separation of Jews from non-Jews, the greater the tendency of Jews to retain or reinforce their religio-cultural distinctiveness.

References

Leslie, D.D. (1972) *The Survival of the Chinese Jews: The Jewish Community of Kaifeng* (Leiden: Brill).

Rhee, S.N. (1973) 'Jewish Assimilation: The Case of the Chinese Jews,' *Comparative Studies in Society and History* 15: 115–26.
Srinivas, M.N. (1952) *Religion and Society among the Coorgs of South India* (Oxford: Oxford University Press).
Strizower, S. (1971) *The Children of Israel: The Bene Israel of Bombay* (Oxford: Blackwell).
Weber, Max (1964) *The Religion of China* (New York: Free Press).

4 Islam and the Jews: Myth, Counter-Myth, History
Mark Cohen

In this chapter we begin to narrow focus onto Muslim lands. Mark Cohen, Professor of History at Princeton University, presents a comparative overview of the conditions of Jews under medieval Islam and under Christianity. In particular Cohen discusses the contrasting political, economic and religious settings, and argues that these led to more favorable situations for Jews under Islam than under Christianity. Cohen participates in this paper in a discussion that has long engaged scholars of many disciplines, as well as other social commentators, for contemporary political as well as scholarly reasons.

> You know, my brethren, that on account of our sins God has cast us into the midst of this people, the nation of Ishmael, who persecute us severely, and who devise ways to harm us and to debase us ... No nation has ever done more harm to Israel. None has been able to reduce us as they have.

Thus wrote Maimonides to the persecuted Jews of Yemen late in the twelfth century. In recent years the issue addressed by him has aroused new and impassioned interest – indeed, a highly politicized debate, in books, articles, and public forums, on the question: How did the Jews fare under Islamic rule in the Middle Ages? Were they treated better than their brethren in Europe, or was their situation perhaps similar to, if not, as Maimonides suggests, worse than, that of the persecuted Jews of Christendom? Two radically divergent answers to this question have been offered. One is the well-known thesis – or rather, *myth* – of the Jewish Islamic interfaith utopia, a 'golden age' of toleration, of political achievement, and of remarkably integrated cultural efflorescence. This myth was invented by nineteenth-century European Jewish intellectuals frustrated by the tortuously slow progress of their own integration into gentile society in the age of emancipation; it went hand-in-hand with the so-called 'lachrymose conception' of European Jewish history, according to which Jewish life in medieval Christian Europe was one long chain of suffering.

Source: Paper in *Jerusalem Quarterly*, 38 (1986): 125–37; also in M.R. Cohen, *Under Crescent and Cross*, Princeton University Press, 1994.

Originally promulgated by Jewish writers, the myth of Judeo–Islamic harmony (contrasted with Judeo–Christian conflict) has in our own time been appropriated by Arabs and by Western sympathizers with the Arab struggle against Israel, who attempt, through the use of history, to explain and in fact justify modern Arab anti-Zionism and anti-Semitism. They argue, explicitly or implicitly, that the current disharmony between Jews and Arabs is not to be attributed to any long-standing Arab or Islamic anti-Semitism. Rather, as Jewish historians themselves have claimed, Jews and Arabs lived in peace and friendship for centuries; therefore, the source of modern Arab antipathy towards Israel is the Jews themselves, who destroyed the old harmony when they began to threaten Muslim-Arab rights to the land of Palestine.

An early example of this adoption of the Jewish myth of the interfaith utopia can be found in George Antonius' book, *The Arab Awakening*.[1] Among more recent publications are Ibrahim Amin Ghali's *Le monde arabe et les juifs*,[2] and, in Arabic, Qāsim 'Abduh Qāsim's *al-yahūd fī Misr mundh al-fath al-islāmi hattā al-ghazw al-'uthmāni* (*The Jews of Egypt from the Islamic Conquest to the Ottoman Invasion*),[3] as well as the paper given by Said Abdel Fattah Ashour at the Fourth Conference of the Academy of Islamic Research at al-Azhar University in Cairo in September, 1968. (Entitled 'al-yahūd fī 'l-'usūr al-wustā: dirāsa muqārina bayn al-sharq wa-'l-gharb', it was published both in the Arabic original[4] and in the official English translation of the conference proceedings[5] under the title, 'Jews in the Middle Ages: Comparative Study of East and West').

Dismayed by contemporary Arab exploitation of the myth of the interfaith utopia in the service of the cause against Israel, some Jewish writers have, lamentably, invented a 'counter-myth' to take its place. Echoing and often citing Maimonides' dark view of Islamic treatment of the Jews, these writers indict Islam as congenitally and relentlessly persecutory. And, by transposing the theory of Jewish suffering from Christendom to Islam, they have created what we may call the 'neo-lachrymose' conception of the Jewish past.[6]

One well known promulgator of this revisionist trend suffered personal humiliation when she was expelled along with other Jews from Egypt in 1956. Writing under the pseudonym Bat Ye'or, 'Daughter of the Nile', she has published several pamphlets and books sounding the theme of congenital and unremitting Arab-Islamic persecution of the non-Muslim religions. Her French book on the subject has just appeared in an expanded English version called *The Dhimmi: Jews and Christians Under Islam*[7] and it constitutes a classic example of this revisionist trend. Another is journalist Joan Peters' *From Time Immemorial: The Origins of the Arab–*

Jewish Conflict over Palestine.[8] This work has gained considerable notoriety for its provocative assault upon the historical argument defending Arab claims to the land of Palestine. In her introductory chapters Peters presents a litany of instances of anti-Jewish persecution in the premodern Islamic world, arguing overtly against Arab rhetoric espousing the myth of the interfaith utopia as well as against the view, shared by many Jewish and non-Jewish writers alike, 'that the Jews were, during certain periods in the Arab lands, "better off" than they were in Christian lands of Europe.'

While the myth of the interfaith utopia was certainly in need of correction, the counter-myth, with its implicit transvaluation of the older conception of the relative status of the Jews of the West and the East, does not represent a fairer reading of the past. A more balanced approach, such as that taken by Bernard Lewis in his recent book, *The Jews of Islam*,[9] or by Norman Stillman in the historical introduction to his source book, *The Jews of Arab Lands*,[10] is badly needed. That is because, as any careful and systematic reading of the historical sources shows, despite the theological intolerance that Islam shared with Christendom, the Jews of Islam experienced far greater security and far more integration with the majority society than their brethren in Europe. During the first six centuries of Islam, the period embracing the so-called 'Golden Age' that has been the focus of attention by proponents of both the old myth and the new counter-myth, the incidence of violent persecution, with great loss of life, was comparatively low. The discriminatory restrictions of the so-called Pact of 'Umar, most of them adopted from Byzantine-Christian anti-Jewish legislation, were more often than not observed in the breach. Such irrational conceptions as the association of the Jews with the Devil, a well-known feature of the medieval Christian attitude towards the Jew, had little place even in the popular Arab imagination. Blood libels – in Europe a by-product of the popular perception of the diabolical Jew – were absent during these centuries. Expulsions did not occur. And we hear practically nothing during this period about prosecution of Jewish converts to Islam for alleged unfaithfulness to the new religion.

If theology did not dispose Muslims to treat Jews better than they were treated in Christendom, what accounts for the relatively more favorable position of the Jews of the medieval Islamic world? The answer, as might be expected, is complex and nuanced, involving economic, political and social factors that interacted in history in ways that elude simple description. Moreover, the contrast is starker for Northern than for Southern Europe, where the persistence of pre-Christian Roman traditions and the older settlement of Jews, bordering on indigenous habitation, seem to have fostered a more tolerant and economically and socially more integrated environment. What we shall have to say, therefore, in what follows takes northern Christendom as its point of comparison so that the contrast will be sharpened with more meaningful distinctions brought to bear on the discussion.

As is well known, Jews came to Europe during the early Middle Ages principally as international merchants. Christian rulers, particularly the Carolingian kings, encouraged Jewish traders to settle in their realms by offering them favorable conditions of residency and commercial mobility. The Jews, indeed, fulfilled an important function in this predominantly rural and agricultural setting. However, their economic role was simultaneously a cause of social resentment. As merchants, Jews found themselves practitioners of a marginal and despised profession. Continuing a prejudice characteristic of Roman society, early medieval Christendom held the trader in relatively low repute. Always on the move and lacking firm roots in any given locale, the merchant appeared quintessentially alien. This attitude was reinforced by Christian doctrines about the 'just price' that placed commerce at the bottom end of the scale of religiously acceptable occupations. From the very outset, therefore, the identification – however exaggerated – of Jews with a despised occupation accentuated their own alien religious status within Christian society.

This situation degenerated when, with the revival of urban life in eleventh-century Europe, Christians began to enter commerce on a large scale. Formerly the despised, alien merchant in a backward rural environment, the Jewish merchant now became a resented commercial competitor. As commercial guilds developed, Jews were excluded from membership on account of their inability to take the required Christian oath of initiation. The result, well known to all, is that Jews who were involved in commerce gradually transferred their energies to usury. And other Jews who for various reasons were pressured out of productive occupations also found their only means of livelihood in making loans to Christians. Jewish banking complemented European economic expansion during the High Middle Ages, and, because Jewish profits from moneylending steadily filled and refilled royal treasuries in the form of tax revenues, secular rulers sanctioned and gave legal support to this enterprise.

If kings and emperors tolerated the Jews on account of their economic benefit to the royal treasury, in Christian society at large moneylending bred anti-Jewish contempt. Jewish usurers were universally hated. Hatred emanated both from the common folk, who were the Jews' main pawn-broking customers, and from elements of the new Christian bourgeoisie, who resented the royal support for Jewish usury. Dependence upon the Jewish moneylender created an improper inversion of the well-defined hierarchical relationship between Christianity and Judaism and intensified the degree of discomfort with the alien Jewish presence. These anti-Jewish sentiments were further reinforced by the Catholic church's vigorous campaign against the evil of usury beginning in the twelfth century. Although only sporadically successful in gaining the support of secular rulers, it had a devastating effect on Jewish economic well-being wherever it fell upon receptive ears. In short, economic factors, intertwined with religious conceptions, played an ongoing role in molding the negative attitude towards the Jews in Europe of the Middle Ages and in creating the rigid boundaries that separated Jews and Christians from one another.

In Islam, by contrast, religious conceptions and economic realities combined to produce a different state of affairs. Unlike Christianity, Islam, influenced by the mercantile background of Muhammad's native city Mecca, was born with a positive attitude towards commerce. The example of Muhammad's own life, as well as statements in the Qur'ān and in other Islamic holy literature, lent strong support to the mercantile life. And, since many of the jurists in the early Islamic period were themselves merchants, Islamic law was shaped to meet the needs of a mercantile economy. On purely religious grounds, therefore, there was no basis in Islam for the kind of prejudicial attitude towards the Jewish merchant that existed from the outset in Christendom.

In addition to this fundamental distinction in economic 'theory', economic realities during the early Islamic centuries prevented the development of the competitive atmosphere that heightened anti-Jewish sentiment in the West during the period of urban-commercial expansion. The Islamic conquest, with its political unification of the entire Mediterranean and all of southwest Asia, set in motion an enormous commercial revolution and created unlimited economic opportunities. As a result, whereas in Europe the new Christian merchants of the high Middle Ages viewed the old Jewish merchants as competitors to be displaced, in Islam Muslim merchants of the early centuries following the conquest saw the Jews as equal participants in a burgeoning imperial economy. Interdenominational cooperation was common, and commercial guilds excluding all but coconfessors of the dominant faith did not yet exist. Moreover, the Jews enjoyed extensive economic diversification. This made the Jews more 'like' their non-Jewish neighbors and reduced the level of hostility, which in Europe resulted in part from their economic marginality. Of equal importance, the Jews of Islam during this period (and later on, for that matter) were never restricted to moneylending, as were their coreligionists in Northern Europe by about the twelfth century. Jews and Muslims borrowed and lent from and to one another, and the sticky issue of usurious lending to gentiles that caused so much consternation and insecurity for Jews in medieval Europe, leading rabbis to inveigh against the practice, had virtually no counterpart either within or without the Jewish community of medieval Islam.

While economically the Jews of Islam experienced much more freedom and integration into gentile society than their brethren in Europe, legally their situation appears comparable, if not worse. Proponents of the counter-myth regularly point to the humiliating disabilities imposed upon the Jews (and Christians) in the Pact of 'Umar and kindred Islamic sources. These stipulations include prohibitions against building or repairing houses of worship, against holding public religious ceremonies, against bearing arms or riding anything but the least honorable mounts, against holding public office, as well as a poll tax (*jizya*) levied in humiliating fashion. It is often noted, too, that the infamous 'Jewish badge' introduced in Europe for the first time in the thirteenth century existed centuries earlier in the Pact of 'Umar stipulations requiring distinctive dress. The twin themes of segregation and humiliation that run through the Islamic sources seem to rival if not exceed the legal restrictions and pariah status imposed upon the Jews in the Christian West.

Historically, however, theory and practice diverged. Even some proponents of the counter-myth concede that by and large the restrictions of the Pact of 'Umar were very unevenly and sporadically enforced during the centuries under discussion here. The large number of synagogues that were built to accommodate the new Jewish communities of the expanding Islamic world, and the frequent reference in our sources to the reimposition of the Pact of 'Umar restrictions, testify to the relative ease with which Jews and Christians evaded the heavy hand of the law.

Moreover, in assessing the legal position of the Jews of Islam it is important to reassert that the basic terminology defining their legal status, the *dhimma*, conveys the idea of 'protection', which the Pact of 'Umar explicitly guarantees the Jews and Christians (*dhimmīs*) in return for their recognition of the superiority of Islam. The latest publication espousing the counter-myth of 'thirteen centuries of sufferings and humiliations' under Islam – Bat Ye'or's abovementioned book – creates a grossly misleading impression by characterizing every bleak aspect of the Judeo-Islamic experience as 'the *dhimmī* condition.'

Equally important, any comparative analysis of the position of the Jews under medieval Islam and Christianity must take into account a fundamental political difference between the two societies. Medieval Christendom had two competing authority structures, the state and the church, which were plagued by endless conflict. Popes and secular rulers battled with words and sometimes with armies for supreme authority over the Christian masses, and each side vied for hegemony over the Jews as well. Kings and emperors claimed the prerogative to protect the Jews, whom some began to call 'serfs of the royal chamber'. Relegated to a special legal status, Jews became subjects to all the advantages and disadvantages of unmediated dependence upon the secular ruler. When central authority was strong, Jews could generally count on royal or baronial protection. But this protection was accompanied by rapacious taxation that sorely threatened Jewish financial security. When central power was weak, or when the ruler was far away, popular hostility towards the Jews often spilled over, unchecked, into physical violence.

The Roman church, for its part, strove to achieve the universalist ideal of a Christendom ruled by direct apostolic successors to Peter. Beginning in the thirteenth century, it asserted the theological doctrine of the 'perpetual servitude' of the Jews. The church insisted that secular rulers eliminate state-supported Jewish usury and segregate Jews from their Christian neighbors. The tribulations which afflicted the Jews as a result of the church's partial, and in the case of Jewish moneylending occasionally greater-than-expected success in enforcing its will in these matters – like the very fact of the Jews' tenuous direct dependence upon the protection of the kings and emperors of Europe – may be credited to their unenviable position as pawns in the battle between church and state in the Middle Ages.

The somewhat less precarious position of the Jews in the medieval Islamic world has much to do with the fundamentally different organization of political authority in Islam. Unlike Christendom, classical Islam, being an ecclesiastical polity, knows no formal division between church and state. The caliph embodies secular and religious leadership in one and the same person. Consequently, medieval Islam did not experience a church–state struggle, nor its untoward side-effects on the Jewish minority. To be sure, Islamic rulers were not immune to the conservative sentiments of clerics who favored strict enforcement of the Pact of 'Umar and even the revocation of its protective guarantees when *dhimmīs* violated its ordinances. Many instances of anti-Jewish and anti-Christian oppression can be traced directly to the intolerant voices of these *ulamā*. Nonetheless, this was relatively rare during the first six centuries of Islam, when religious scholars had somewhat less influence in public affairs than they did later on. Moreover, as A.L. Udovitch has pointed out in an important essay,[11] in Islamic law the status of the Jews is nowhere treated as a separate issue. Rather, stipulations are incorporated subject by subject into the conventional categories of the classical Islamic law codes. This stands in sharp contrast to the isolation of Jewry law provisions in the law of medieval Christian states and is a reflection of the greater degree of integration of the Jew in medieval Muslim society. Also, by way of contrast, the Jews of Islam never became direct, legal dependents of the ruler; nor did the Pact of 'Umar link toleration of Jews to their economic utility, as was the case in Europe. These differences surely help explain why the expulsions of the Jews in the West were not duplicated in the medieval Islamic world.

Not only were there differences in the legal policies of Christendom and Islam towards the Jews. The Jews held a disparate status within the social structure of the two societies as well. As noted above, the mercantile activities of the Jews accentuated their image in Christian Europe as a marginal group. Nonetheless, they experienced a considerable degree of security and prosperity, especially in the Carolingian kingdom. This was largely a consequence of the pluralistic structure of early medieval European civilization, which was still imperfectly Christianized and in which the Barbarian legal principle of the personality of law was still strong. In this heterogeneous environment, the Jews could be tolerated despite their own religious non-conformity and cultural and legal distinctiveness. By the eleventh century, however, the last remaining pagans of Western Europe had been converted to Christianity, leaving the Jews as the only non-Christian entity in society. The concomitant spread of the notion of a universalistic Catholicism, mediated to the masses by the monastic orders, also dealt a blow to the tolerance that was associated with the earlier, more pluralistic age. By this time, these and other transformations in Western Christendom, including the growing economic competition, set the stage for the anti-Jewish violence of the age of the Crusades.

The position of the Jew in medieval Near Eastern society stands in sharp contrast. The Jews were, first of all, indigenous inhabitants of the area, not, as in Western Christendom, immigrant aliens. In addition, pluralism and religious heterogeneity were more deeply and more permanently ingrained in Islamic than in European Christian society. A multiplicity of ethnic Muslim groups – Arabs, Turks, Berbers, and Iranians – populated the social landscape along with the Jews. As religious dissenters, moreover, Jews were not unique. They shared their *dhimmî* status with other non-Muslim groups, principally the Christians and Zoroastrians. As a result, Muslim religious discrimination was directed at the *dhimmî* class as a whole, rather than at the Jews in particular. And while it is true that the Qur'ān and later Arabic literature occasionally distinguish between the two subordinate monotheistic religions, evincing a certain slight preference for the Christians, it is also accurate to say that contempt for nonbelievers in Islam was usually more or less evenly distributed across the *dhimmî* class. Moreover, when the restrictive clauses of the Pact of 'Umar were, on occasion, rigorously enforced, they were usually directed in the first instance at the far more numerous Christians. For all these reasons, therefore, the negative psychological impact of second-class status was substantially blunted for the Jews. To be sure, as in Christian Europe, the Jews were always and everywhere viewed by Muslims as social and religious inferiors. In practice, however, the Jews of Islam were less rigidly set off from the majority society than were the Jews of Christendom.

The permeability of boundaries between Jews and Muslims was fostered by yet another distinguishing characteristic of Islamic society – it was far less corporate than its European counterpart. In Islam there did not exist to the same extent the more or less rigidly defined identity (reinforced by royal concessions of legal autonomy) that Western corporate organization formally assigned to such groups as the nobility, merchant guilds, the clergy, municipalities, and, of course, the Jews. Rather, social agglutinates relied on informal ties of loyalty and group identity that by their very nature allowed for flexibility and an overlapping of roles and tended to mitigate the marginality to which official Islamic theology assigned the Jews. Though deprived of the right to bear arms, and hence excluded from one of the most powerful groups in Muslim society, namely, the army, Jews participated in most of its other major social categories: the merchant class, the crafts, the government bureaucracy, and even the agricultural sector. Moreover, the absence of rigid corporate social organization in Islam meant that collective guilt for alleged crimes against the host society and its religion, so commonly assigned in Christendom to the Jewish corporate entity, did not become an operative motif in the Islamic–Jewish relationship. These realities were reinforced by the persistence in Islam of the principles of the personality of law long after it was replaced in Christendom by territorial and municipal legal codes that relegated the Jews to the position of a grudgingly tolerated, separate and alien non-Christian corporate group.

Economic, political, and social factors acted in Islam as a counterweight to the fundamental theological hostility towards the religion of Judaism – branded as an inferior version of monotheism – and towards the Jews – stigmatized, along with the Christians, as contemptible infidels. However, even the theological position of Islam *vis-à-vis* the Jews differed significantly from that of Christianity. In Christendom, theological opposition to Judaism and the Jews was firmly rooted in the historical situation attending the rise of the new religion; it formed an organic and essential ingredient in Christian thought. Born directly out of Judaism, promulgated originally by professing Jews, and lacking an independent ethnic base,

Christianity, from its inception, found itself locked in a bitter struggle to incorporate and then differentiate itself from its Jewish parent. Desperately needing to win converts from among the 'gentiles' in order to insure its existence, the early church bitterly resented Jewish proselytizing among the Roman pagans, not to speak of Jewish resistance to the Christian mission. Moreover, until the fourth century the Roman government suspected the Christian community of messianic subversion and relentlessly persecuted the neophytes while continuing its ancient policy of recognizing the legitimacy of Judaism and protecting the Jews. In an effort to win its own recognition from pagan Rome and to justify its own sense of superiority, the nascent church developed an elaborate anti-Jewish theological doctrine. This doctrine stated that since the Jews had rejected Christ, God had rejected the Jews and had chosen the Christians in their stead as the new Israel.

When Christianity became the official religion of the Roman Empire, following the conversion of Emperor Constantine at the beginning of the fourth century, the theology of divine rejection was systematically employed to whittle away at the protective provisions of Roman Jewry law. At the same time, the spiritual Fathers of the Church, led by St Augustine, developed a theological rationale for the continued presence of the Jews in Christian society. This was the well-known doctrine of 'witness', according to which God had preserved the Jews as living testimony, by virtue of their abject state, to the victory of Christianity. And, with their conversion to Christianity at the time of the Second Coming, they would bear witness to the truth of Jesus' Messianic essence. This official church doctrine provided a rationale for protecting the Jews and served to temper the theological animosity that informed the earliest phase of the Judeo–Christian relationship.

In the Middle Ages, the heightened piety of the age of the Crusades brought a new, popular brand of Christian anti-Jewishness to the fore. Its most ominous manifestation was the wholesale massacre of the Jews of the Rhineland in the Crusader pogroms of 1096. Popular mentality, partly to justify the violence, and fed by uneducated local clergy, embellished the official Catholic theology of rejection by fixating on the Jew as the ally of the devil, bent on destroying Christendom. The vulgar anti-Jewish theology of the High and Later Middle Ages, with its frequent blood libels and pogroms, was paralleled by a somewhat more civilized, though no less threatening, assault on the religion of Judaism, manifested in disputations designed to persuade Jews to convert to Christianity.

From statements in the Qur'ān, the Prophetic traditions (the *hadīth*), and other portions of its religious and secular literature, Islam appears similar to Christianity in its theological opposition to the Jews and Judaism. Moreover, while in Christendom, massacres of the Jews began relatively late in the history of the relationship of the two faiths, in Islam the very first encounter between Islam and Judaism produced a violent anti-Jewish pogrom. The Prophet Muhammad, having experienced ridicule and opposition from the Jews of Medina, lashed out violently by expelling some and massacring an entire Jewish tribe. However, that brutal anti-Jewish episode in the early Judeo–Islamic relationship turned out to have been – relatively speaking – an isolated one. This can be explained comparatively by the particular historical circumstances in which Islam originated and spread.

Unlike Christianity, Islam did not need to establish its identity at the expense of its Jewish parent. Islam was established on a solid ethnic foundation, the tribes of the Arabian Peninsula, who were swiftly won over to the new religion. Conquering within decades the rest of the Near Eastern and the North African world, Islam achieved virtually overnight what it had taken Christianity nearly three centuries to accomplish. There was even less reason, therefore, to continue the aggressive struggle against Judaism, let alone devise a theology of divine rejection.

In addition, because Muhammad was not a Messiah, Islam, unlike Christianity, never conceived of itself as being a messianic fulfillment of Judaism. Rather, Islam saw itself as a restoration and purification of Abrahamic monotheism, which had become eroded in earlier divinely inspired religions, in Christianity more than in Judaism. The Jewish rejection of Muhammad, therefore, never entailed the same theological challenge to Islam that was implicit in the Jewish rejection of Jesus. Hence, Islam did not invest anywhere near the same polemical energies expended by Christendom to refute Judaism and to convert the Jews.

Characteristically, the Muslim attitude towards Jewish Scripture differed from that of its Christian counterpart. Christianity needed the Jewish Bible – the Old Testament, in its parlance – as witness to the incarnation and mission of Christ described in the New Testament. Islam viewed its Scripture differently, as a replacement of the divinely revealed, yet humanly distorted, Scriptures of both Judaism and Christianity. Muhammad, having personally rediscovered pure, Abrahamic monotheism through a new divine revelation, did not need the Jewish Bible for the justification of Islam. And indeed, the various attempts by medieval Muslim writers to find annunciations of the mission of Muhammad in biblical verses pale in significance when compared to the massive Christological exegesis of Jewish Scripture. Rabbinic exegesis of the Bible – so repugnant to Christian theologians – bothered Muslim clerics only insofar as it distorted pristine Abrahamic monotheism. Thus the Islamic polemic against the rabbis was much less virulent and had far less serious repercussions. The Talmud was burned in Paris, not in Cairo or Baghdad.

More secure than their brethren in the Christian West, the Jews of Islam took a correspondingly more conciliatory view of their masters. In Europe, the Jews nurtured a pronounced hatred for Christians, whom they considered to be idolaters subject to the anti-pagan discriminatory provisions of the ancient Mishnah. Moreover, when faced with the choice between death and conversion, the Jews of Northern Europe usually chose martyrdom rather than 'the polluting waters of the baptismal font', as they called it in Hebrew. The Jews of Islam had a markedly different attitude towards the religion of their masters. Staunch Muslim opposition to polytheism convinced Jewish thinkers like Maimonides of Islam's unimpeachable monotheism. This essentially 'tolerant' Jewish view of Islam echoed Islam's own respect for the Jewish 'people of the Book' and doubtless constituted a factor – alongside the extensive interface in the economic and social spheres that tended to blur the boundaries between Jew and Muslim – disposing Jews faced with persecution at the hands of Islam to convert rather than suffer martyrdom.

Equally revealing of the contrast are the divergent Jewish perceptions of their own disabilities and suffering. The Jews of Christendom – hated, oppressed, and frequently physically attacked – poured out their grief in a long string of lachrymose dirges and chronicles that they incorporated into their liturgy. The commemoration of their suffering was branded on the collective Jewish consciousness and was the basis for the so-called 'lachrymose' interpretation of Jewish history in modern Jewish historiography. The Jews of Islam, at least in the period under discussion, largely refrained from such exercise of literary woe. The event that evoked Jewish responses most closely approximating the European writings was the terrible persecution, massacre, and forced conversion of Jews and Christians in mid-twelfth-century Spain and North Africa under the Almohades. These include the mournful phrases at the end of the chronicle of rabbinic history by the twelfth-century Spanish Jewish philosopher, Abraham ibn Daud, the doleful Hebrew poem of Abraham ibn Ezra on the destruction of Jewish communities in North Africa, and the litany of cruel suffering by Judah ben Joseph ibn 'Aqnin. (Very like the Northern European dirges in tone, this last passage, found in ibn 'Aqnin's philosophical treatise, 'Therapy of the Soul', has been reproduced for the first time in an English translation in the anthology section of Bat Ye'or's *The Dhimmí*.) These texts bear eloquent witness to the trauma experienced by Jews during those difficult times. It is, indeed, against the background of this unprecedented persecution that Maimonides, himself a refugee from Almohade terror, wrote the lines quoted at the beginning of this essay.

Similarly, as Bernard Septimus has shown,[12] it was apparently the Almohade persecution that gave rise to a new Jewish saying (a purposeful distortion of an ancient Midrashic utterance): 'Better (to live) under Edom [i.e., Christendom] than under Ishmael [i.e. Islam].' This claim that Christendom provided a more secure home for the Jews than Islam, first made by refugees from Almohade persecution who had found a haven across the border in the Christian kingdoms of Northern Spain, has unknowingly been revived in our own day in the writings of proponents of what I have called here, alternatively, the 'counter-myth' of unrelenting Islamic persecution of the Jews, or the 'neo-lachrymose' interpretation of Jewish history.

Contemporaries of the Almohade persecution, like Maimonides, perceived that an era of relative security and cultural integration was drawing to a close. Indeed, the later Islamic Middle Ages, from the late twelfth or early thirteenth century on, saw – as even the architects of the myth of the interfaith utopia acknowledged – a steady decline in Jewish fortunes. There were many causes for this reversal, and the process, with its remissions, especially under Ottoman rule in the sixteenth century – a period often called the second 'Golden Age' of Jewish life under Islam – is well described in the books by Bernard Lewis and Norman Stillman mentioned above. The extent to which one can speak of a deterioration in the situation of the Jews in later medieval Islam, similar to the position of the Jews in medieval Christendom; the degree to which one can apply the adjective 'lachrymose' to the life and history of the Jews of Islam in recent centuries; and the extent to which modern Arab anti-Semitism – modeled in the first instance largely upon Christian stereotypes imported from the West and now nurtured by indigenous Islamic theological hostility – has become an unmovable impediment to peaceful rapprochement between Israel and her Arab neighbors, are all matters for further reflection.

Notes

1 New York: Capricorn Books, 1965, especially 391–2, 410 (originally published 1946).
2 Paris: Editions Cujas, 1972.
3 Beirut: al-Madrasa al-'Arabiyya li 'l-Dirāsāt wa-'l-Nashr, 1980.

4   Cairo: Matba'at al-Madani, n.d., II, 349–61.
5   Cairo: General Organization for Government Printing Office, 1970, 497–505.
6   Some examples: Saul S. Friedlander, 'The Myth of Arab Toleration,' *Midstream* 16, no. 1 (January, 1970) 56–9; Maurice M. Roumani in collaboration with Deborah Goldman and Helene Korn, 'The Persecution of Jews in Arab Lands,' in *The Case of the Jews from Arab Countries: A Neglected Issue*, vol. 1 (Jerusalem: World Organization of Jews from Arab Countries, 1975) 41–57; Martin Gilbert, *The Jews of Arab Lands: Their History in Maps* (London: Furnival Press, 1975); Rose Lewis, 'Muslim Grandeur and the Spanish Jews,' *Midstream* 23, no. 2 (February, 1977) 26–37; idem, 'Maimonides and the Muslims,' *ibid.* 25, no. 9 (November, 1979) 16–22; Eliezer Whartman, 'Islam vs. the Jews, Zionism and Israel,' *Newsview* (July 5, 1983) 12–17.
7   Rutherford, New Jersey: Fairleigh Dickinson University Press, 1985.
8   New York: Harper and Row, 1984. The quotation at the end of this paragraph is from page 75.
9   Princeton: Princeton University Press, 1984.
10 Philadelphia: Jewish Publication Society of America, 1979. The present writer reviewed this book in the *Association for Jewish Studies Newsletter*, no. 28 (March, 1981) 13–14.
11 'The Jews and Islam in the High Middle Ages: A Case of the Muslim View of Difference,' in *Gli ebrei nell'alto medioevo* (Spoleto, 1980), II, 682–3. This paper presents a balanced and well reasoned analysis of the subject. Some of the responses to the paper at the symposium at which it was given, which were published in the volume, betray what we have called here the counter-myth of the 'neo-lachrymose' trend.
12 'Better under Edom than under Ishmael: The History of a Saying' (in Hebrew), *Zion* 47 (1982) 103–11, with an English summary.

5 Sephardic Rabbinic Responses to Modernity: Some Central Characteristics
Zvi Zohar

One of the major issues of the cultural anthropology of Jewry is to define the details of difference, in social structure and culture, in various Jewish societies. The main categories of societies conceptualized in comparative studies in Jewish societies have mostly been, as in this introductory part of the volume, embarrassingly broad – the dichotomy of Sephardic as against Ashkenazic societies. Also in this introductory section, the chapters so far have mainly explored the major sociological components of differences between clusters of Jewish societies. The contribution of Zvi Zohar, Senior Scholar at the Shalom Hartman Institute in Jerusalem, now thrusts this exploration into the heart of Jewish culture, the legal doings of rabbis. On the base of extensive study of the writings of nineteenth and twentieth century Sephardic sages, he outlines a portrait of the style and content of their religio-legal rulings, which contrast markedly with those of comparable Ashkenazic rabbis. The material on which Zohar bases his conclusions pertains, as he indicates in the title, to the 'response to modernity.' Study of the rulings of Sephardic sages of an earlier period, who did not contend with modernity, might have led to a picture not that much different from their Ashkenazic peers. That in fact is the general thesis of this introductory section. But the volume is not devoted exclusively to traditional times, and many of the contributions treat transition to conditions of colonialism, migration and secularism. While Zohar's work contributes only indirectly to the issue of diversity in traditional Jewish societies, this study illuminates the issue in the context of Westernization.

In this article I seek to characterize the response of Sephardic rabbis to the challenges of modernity. My thesis is that their response is different, in significant and interesting ways, from that of their Ashkenazic-European peers. I suggest that these differences can be understood as stemming from two, synergetic factors: (i) major differences between the experience of modernization in European and in Islamic lands; and (ii) the cultural heritage of the Sephardic rabbinic elite. The article fleshes out the thesis by discussing concrete cases of Sephardic response to change, which together present major aspects of the 'ideal-type' of a Sephardic-Oriental rabbinic ethos. I begin with a brief background survey of the responses of European Jewry to modernity.

THE COALESCENCE OF ORTHODOXY IN EUROPE

In the eighteenth and nineteenth centuries, European Jewry underwent processes of enlightenment and secularization, accompanied by internal social and ideological tensions. Many rabbis felt that these changes threatened the existence of traditional Judaism and, to counter this, they formulated a counter-strategy which became known as 'Orthodoxy'. As historian Nathaniel Katzburg writes:

> Orthodoxy, as a well-defined and separate phenomenon within Jewry, crystallized in response to the challenge of the changes which occurred in Jewish society in Europe in the first half of the 19th century: Reform, the Haskalah [enlightenment], and trends towards secularization.[1]

Orthodox leaders declared that they were simply preserving and continuing the ways of life and the beliefs of premodern Judaism. However, this contention is at variance with socio-historical reality, writes historian Jacob Katz:

> The claim of the Orthodox to be no more than the guardians of the pure Judaism of old is a fiction. In fact, Orthodoxy was a method of confronting deviant trends, and of responding to the very same stimuli which produced these trends, albeit with a conscious effort to deny such extrinsic motivations.[2]

Orthodoxy's goal, then, was to oppose the radical moves of Jewish modernists, which were seen to endanger the future of Jewish life. Orthodoxy's strategy, as formulated by its leaders, was to totally deny the legitimacy of all modernist innovations, by stating that *halakha* (Jewish religious 'law') was an eternal, fixed corpus of normative directives. This view of *halakha* was encapsulated in the Orthodox slogan 'Torah prohibits the New'.[3] This strategy deeply affected European *halakha* in modern times. One result is described by Menahem Elon:

> Leading respondents have increasingly declared – and with regard to many important matters – that they fear the responsibility and will seek

therefore to refrain from rendering a clear and decisive judgment... This
reluctance to make rulings [termed *yirat horaah*], began to spread in the
19th century, and has become a serious source of concern in the 20th.[4]

The connection between Orthodox strategy and the phenomenon described
by Elon is that the assertion 'Torah prohibits the New' undermines the
validity not only of 'dangerous' innovations but also of *any* new halakhic
ruling. *Yirat horaah* is an understandable concomitant of Orthodox thought.
In sum: Orthodoxy was, first and foremost, a rejection of Reform and
enlightenment; but the internal logic of its rejectionist strategy severely
impaired the ability of Orthodox rabbis to respond to other aspects of
modernity in a creative halakhic manner.[5]

Is the Orthodox mode of response to modernity somehow inherent to
halakhic Judaism? Fortunately, this is not a 'what-if' question, a counter-
factual of the type so disparaged by historians. Students of modern Jewish
religion and culture have a readily accessible test-case available – the
experience of Sephardic-Oriental Jewry's encounter with modernity.

SEPHARDIC-ORIENTAL JEWS IN MODERN TIMES

Under the caption 'Sephardic-Oriental' I include those Jews who lived,
over the past few centuries, in the Islamic countries of the Middle East and
North Africa.[6] The Jews of these lands were heterogeneous, including
diverse communities and sub-groupings.[7] One thing all Sephardic-Oriental
Jews have in common, however, is a communal self-identity according to
which their religio-cultural world bears the stamp of influences exerted by
Sephardic exiles since the fifteenth and sixteenth centuries.[8]

The Jews of the Middle East and North Africa were exposed to the
influences of modern Europe from the fourth decade of the nineteenth
century. In 1830, France conquered Algeria; in 1831, Egypt conquered
Palestine and Syria, and soon thereafter extended legal equality to non-
Muslim inhabitants; in 1839 the Ottoman Empire followed suit with a
declaration on civil rights. In addition to increasing general European
influence in the Middle East and North Africa, Jews of these lands were
directly influenced by another factor – West European Jewry. The latter
mobilized to assist their 'downtrodden' Oriental brethren and established
international organizations dedicated to that task. In addition to political
lobbying aimed at efficating European diplomatic intervention for the protection of Oriental Jews, the organizations (and private philanthropists) also
sought to enlighten those Jews by providing modern, western education.

Since the mid-nineteenth century, generations of young Jews and Jewesses in Islamic lands received a Francophone and basically secular (though not anti-religious) education, in Alliance Israélite Universelle and similar schools. Many others studied in schools established by European-Christian organizations.

The activities of gentile and Jewish Europeans were augmented by local government policy: legal and politico-structural reforms were initiated during the nineteenth century by both Ottoman and Egyptian governments, seeking to modernize their states so as to withstand external pressures. New technologies – in communications, transport, industry, agriculture, urban development – reached the area, and had far-reaching effects, especially in the urban centers. Thus, on the eve of World War I, Mediterranean Jews were significantly affected by modernity, in direct proportion to their economic status, education and urban location.[9] The inter-war years saw the extension of modernization to large sectors of the Jewish middle class, and by the late 1940s a large proportion of Sephardic-Oriental Jews in their countries of birth were quite modernized. Nevertheless, the typical response of the Sephardic rabbinic elite to these developments was very different from that of their European peers. Sephardic rabbis, therefore, cannot be characterized as Orthodox in the correct sense of that term.

CONTEXTUAL DIFFERENCES

Modernization in Islamic lands was very different from that of Europe.[10] I underline one variable of modernization – the lack, in Islamic lands, of anti-clericalism as found in Europe. Also, Islamic religious leaders did not respond to modernity by the formation of radically different forms of Islamic religious life.[11] Rather, even those Muslims who criticized the current socio-political and cultural situation of their society chose to characterize the sought-for changes as compatible with the spirit and norms of Islam.[12] In this respect, Jews of Islamic lands were similar to their Muslim compatriots: attacking rabbis as backward and criticizing halakhic Judaism as obscurantist were not done in the Sephardic-Oriental milieu. Movements which advocated abandonment of rabbinic Judaism in favor of some brave, new definition of Jewish identity did not develop there.[13] Even those sectors of the Jewish community whose lifestyle reflected religion in only the most minimal way, including those who advocated modern political ideologies, did not insult the community's rabbis or traditions.[14]

In the absence of Jewish ideological attacks upon Judaism or against rabbinic authority per-se, there was no external impetus for Sephardic-

Oriental rabbis to formulate a policy stating that 'Torah prohibits the New', or to refrain from reaching novel halakhic decisions, if warranted by specific socio-historical developments. However, lack of such external factors is not enough; considerations internal to Sephardic halakhic discourse might conceivably lead rabbis to reject halakhic change. Let us see then, how Sephardic halakhic writers regarded change in *halakha*.

HALAKHA AS A DYNAMIC RELIGIOUS PHENOMENON – AS SEEN BY SEPHARDIC RABBIS

Examining writings of Sephardic rabbis of the nineteenth and twentieth centuries, we find that the prevailing attitude was that there were no immanent features in *halakha* requiring rabbis to refrain from formulating new halakhic rulings, in new circumstances. Rather, they held that the greatness and eternal vitality of *halakha* lie in its capacity to express Judaism's values in a variety of forms, as appropriate to changing circumstances. The following three examples illustrate this:

1. In nineteenth-century Europe, some voices were heard calling for the revision of Maimonides' Principles of Jewish Faith. Inter alia, it was suggested that the article affirming belief in the eternality of Torah be rephrased, so as to provide Jews with the capability of accommodating Judaism to modern conditions. Rabbi Eliyahu Hazan[15] responded that Torah as we have it requires no change at all, in order to enable response to contemporary historical developments. The reason, he wrote, is:

> Since the Holy Torah was given to physical human beings, who are always subject to changes stemming from differences in history and time, in rulers and decrees, in nature and climate, in states and realms – therefore, all Torah's words were given in marvelous, wise ambiguity; thus, they can receive any true interpretation at any time. . . . Indeed, the Torah of Truth, inscribed by God's finger, engraved upon the Tablets – will not change nor be renewed, for ever and ever.[16]

The words of the Holy Torah are thus eternal; yet the eternality of Torah is manifest specifically in its inexhaustible capacity to yield multiple meanings, each appropriate to a different human reality.

2. In the introduction to a volume of his responsa, Rabbi Ben-Zion Meir Hai Uzziel[17] rejects the central premise of Orthodoxy, and stresses that *halakha* must respond to modern developments:

> In every generation, conditions of life, changes in values, and technical and scientific discoveries – create new questions and problems that require solution. We may not avert our eyes from these issues and say 'Torah prohibits the New,' i.e. anything not expressly mentioned by earlier sages is ipso facto forbidden. A-fortiori, we may not simply declare such matters permissible. Nor, may we let them remain vague and unclear, each person acting with regard to them as he wishes. Rather, it is our duty to search halakhic sources, and to derive, from what they explicate, responses to currently moot issues ... In all my responsa, I never inclined towards leniency or strictness according to my personal opinions; rather, my intention and striving were always to search and discover the truth. To the extent that my understanding enabled me, I walked in the light of earlier halakhic masters, whose waters we drink and whose light enlightens us; With this holy light, which issues from the source of the hidden, concealed Light, I illuminated my eyes....[18]

In this paragraph, Rabbi Uzziel rejects the path of Orthodoxy, of Reform, and of those 'afraid to decide' described by Elon, above. He states that *halakha* can and should develop through hermeneutics and analogy, applied by halakhists deeply motivated to discover the truth. His sentences are replete with what may be termed mystical rationalism, which bring to mind Maimonides' introduction to the *Guide of the Perplexed*.[19] Clearly, Uzziel sees *halakha* as a far from finite set of normative dicta. He requires halakhists to discover anew how Jews should relate to developments in human life, values and science – following the light contained in earlier rabbinic writings.

3. A third illustration is to be found in the thought of Rabbi Hayyim David HaLevi, currently chief rabbi of Tel-Aviv.[20] In response to criticism directed against him by an Orthodox rabbi, HaLevi rejects that rabbi's assertion that commitment to Judaism entails refraint from halakhic creativity. Since all legislation known to humans requires nearly constant revision due to 'changes in the conditions of life', how is it, asks HaLevi, that the laws of our Holy Torah, revealed to us thousands of years ago, can still function and guide us, today? He responds:

> This is possible only because permission was given to Israel's sages in each generation to renew *halakha* as appropriate to the changes of times and events. Only by virtue of this was the continuous existence of Torah in Israel possible, enabling Jews to follow the way of Torah.... There is nothing so flexible as the flexibility of Torah ... it is only by virtue of that flexibility that the people of Israel, through

the many novel and useful rulings innovated by Israel's sages over the generations, could follow the path of Torah and its commandments for thousands of years.[21]

Perennial renewal is a sine qua non of authentic *halakha*. The basic orientation of Sephardic rabbis, reflected in these quotations, is different from that of Ashkenazic orthodox rabbis in that the former advocate a dynamic *halakha*, while the latter identify commitment to Torah as requiring adherence to the pre-modern halakhic status quo.

Focusing on the notion of dynamic *halakha*, we have not yet clarified anything about its substantive contents and values. One type of dynamic response to modernity could conceivably lead in the direction of entrenchment and strictness; indeed, that is how Sammet characterizes certain aspects of Orthodox halakha: 'To the extent that any new decisions were rendered, they were in one direction only – increasing strictness.'[22] I proceed then to present salient characteristics of Sephardic-Oriental halakha, illustrated by citations from the works of Sephardic rabbis of the last 150 years.

SUPPORT FOR THE INTEGRATION OF SECULAR STUDIES INTO THE JEWISH CURRICULUM

In pre-modern times, almost all Jewish boys received several years of elementary schooling. However, the traditional curriculum was concerned only with the mastery of reading and language skills necessary for participation in synagogue life. A major issue in modern Jewish history was the reform of the elementary-school curriculum so as to include secular subjects. By and large, Sephardic rabbis favored such an integrated program. Thus Rabbi Joseph Hayyim[23] was asked about a change planned for the Baghdad Jewish school, in which context children would receive lessons in arithmetic, Arabic and commercial correspondence – in addition to the traditional program of Torah studies. Rabbi Hayyim supported the inclusion of these subjects in the curriculum, but ruled that they should not be taught inside the actual prayer hall (where classes in Torah subjects were held), but in other premises. He added:

> ... like they do in schools. For in our times, in each city there is a school, for the teaching of writing and languages. But, they construct or rent a building for these studies, and do not conduct them in the synagogues or in the yeshivoth.[24]

Rabbi Hayyim thus clearly advocates that Baghdadi Jews follow the modern model of schools as a community institution, physically differentiated from the sites of prayer and Torah-study. He sees no problem with regard to the curriculum change per se. There is a gap between his position and the one typical of European Orthodoxy. Note, for instance, the 1891 decision of the heads of the Russian yeshiva of Volozhin to close down the institution, rather than to agree to the inclusion of secular topics in the curriculum as required by Russian authorities; and the anathema declared by Jerusalem's Ashkenazic rabbis in 1853 against anyone who sent his children to a newly-founded modern school.[25] Interestingly, Rabbi Hayyim presents his position as 'stringent', relative to the ruling of another leading Sephardic rabbi, Israel Moshe Hazan.[26] Rabbi Hazan supported the conduct of an integrated program of Torah and secular studies inside the synagogue itself. Furthermore, he wrote that if gentile parents insisted on sending their children to such a Jewish study-program, it was permissible to accept them.[27]

POSITIVE REGARD FOR MODERN SCIENCE AND TECHNOLOGY

Sephardic rabbis expressed positive regard for modern science and technology. Thus, Rabbi Raphael Aharon Ben-Shim'on[28] writes:

> New inventions of many types have proliferated in our times, for human technological ingenuity has increased as a result of knowledge gained by research into the basic elements of creation – fire, air, water and earth. New inventions – not even imagined by our forefathers – blossom forth daily . . .[29]

Rabbi Ben-Shim'on is aware of the dependency of technological progress upon scientific research. He regards such research not as antithetical to religion, but rather as an involvement in the understanding of Creation, i.e., as a quasi-religious enterprise. (His endorsement of such activity, however, has not yet led him to give up traditional terminology – as may be seen in his (pre-modern) listing of the 'elements'.) This citation is from a responsum in which Ben-Shim'on discusses whether one may light matches and electrical lights on holidays.[30]

A fascinating discussion of electrical lighting is provided by Rabbi Joseph Mesas.[31] Writing in 1935, he permits use of electric bulbs to light Hanukkah candelabra, instead of the traditional oil-wick candles. He explains:

> I hold it to be clear and simple that, if electrical lighting had been extant in Temple times, most certainly it would have been employed in the Temple candelabrum. For it is inconceivable that we should illuminate

our private homes with that great, wonderful electric light, which is verily after a heavenly model – and yet illuminate God's holy palace with olive-oil, which even the poorest of the poor despise in our time. It is therefore obvious that we shall illuminate the future Temple, may it be built speedily in our days, with electrical lights. Amen.[32]

The implications of this statement are rich. First, while electrical light is 'after a heavenly model', it was unknown in antiquity, and discovered only recently. Thus modern science uncovers sublime aspects of creation, hitherto hidden from humankind. Second, there is an understandable ratio between God's 'home' (the Temple) and the homes of ordinary folk. The Temple must impress the pilgrims who make their way to it from all corners of the earth. It must be (at least) the equal of the most outstanding architectural feats of humanity. A situation in which human dwellings are more advanced in any way than is God's Temple is patently untenable. It follows that advances in science and technology must find their expression in the design of the Temple and its equipment.[33]

A third implication flows from the above. Extensive passages in the Torah and in rabbinic sources discuss the structure of the Temple candelabrum, the preparation of pure olive-oil for use therein, and the manner in which to clean the wicks and light new ones. All these passages, it now transpires, are technologically contingent. Their underlying significance is, that the Temple should be illuminated by the best and most impressive light available to humankind. Thus, true commitment to Torah entails that the halakhic details of Temple illumination be re-determined from time to time, in accordance with technological progress. What a contrast with the notion that 'Torah prohibits the New'!

A SENSE OF SOLIDARITY WITH CONTEMPORARY NON-JEWISH SOCIETY AND STATE

Modern times saw innovations in political thought, which led many countries to adopt policies recognizing Jews as equals. Many Sephardic-Oriental rabbis expressed positive regard for these changes. In some cases, emancipation was also judged to have halakhic consequences, Here is an example from nineteenth century Ottoman Baghdad:

Rabbi 'Abdallah Somekh[34] was asked, whether it was permissible to hire a gentile who would extinguish the synagogue's gas-lighting after Friday evening services.[35] The congregation posing the question added that Rabbi Jacob Poppers[36] had permitted employing such a worker. That sage had reasoned, that failure to extinguish synagogue lighting might enable a fire to break out in the synagogue; the fire might spread to surrounding homes of gentiles, who would then accuse the Jews of arson. If such a situation were to develop, wrote Poppers, the Jews would have to personally engage in fire-fighting and might be physically attacked by angry gentiles. To forestall such developments, it was better that the Jews hire a gentile to extinguish the synagogue lights. Rabbi Somekh answered, that with all due respect to Poppers, it would be wrong to rely on his ruling, for times had changed:

> In our times, thank God, Jewish life in exile has been sweetened, especially in the cities of Europe, and also in Turkey. And they will not cast libel upon us, if a fire happens to break out, and no-one will raise his voice to say, that Jews started the fire in order to harm Gentiles; for all have become almost as one people. In addition, when a fire breaks out, Jews are not required to personally extinguish it, for in such a case the firemen come quickly, with all their equipment, and it is them whose task it is to put out fires. Therefore, all the reasons offered by Rabbi Poppers are irrelevant in our times.[37]

Somekh relies on two distinct developments. First, the new spirit of brotherhood between Gentiles and Jews lessens the probability of physical attack. Secondly, developments in modern society – the delegation of fire-fighting to professionals – remove from urban residents (in our case, from Jews) the responsibility for extinguishing fires, whenever they occur. Thus, Jews need not face the problematics of extinguishing fires on the Sabbath.[38] Both developments are favorable, in Somekh's eyes; yet their halakhic implications are towards greater stringency, since what was permitted in the past (employment of a 'Shabbes Goy' to extinguish synagogue lights) is now to be forbidden.[39]

ACKNOWLEDGEMENT OF A COMMON RATIONALITY WHICH ENCOMPASSES THE REALM OF HALAKHA

In the eyes of many Sephardic scholars, the rationality characteristic of Judaic – including halakhic – culture is essentially the same as the rationality characteristic of the intellectual elite of enlightened, non-Jewish society. Early twentieth-century Egypt offers an illustration. Contemporary Egyptian law empowered the courts of each ethnic-religious community ('millet') to deal with matters of marriage and divorce concerning the members of their community.[40] As part of the official Egyptian court system, 'millet' courts allowed lawyers accredited to that system to represent clients whose case came before the court. Thus, a Coptic lawyer could represent a Jewish client in a divorce hearing held in a rabbinic court. Naturally, that lawyer needed to know the substantive content of Jewish divorce law, in order to represent his client. Similarly, the heads of the Ministry of Justice wanted to know the law that Jewish judges followed in their judgments, since state agencies were expected to recognize and enforce them. However, Jewish law was effectively inaccessible to anyone not steeped in rabbinic texts.

In response to the widespread demand for knowledge of Jewish law in the realm of 'personal status', Rabbi Mas'ud Hai Ben-Shim'on,[41] head of Cairo's rabbinic court, composed a major two-volume work, *Kitab al-Ahkam ash-Shar'iyyah fi-l-Akhwal ash-Shakhsiyyah li-l-Israiliyyin*.[42] In this work he presented in modern literary Arabic a survey of the halakhic norms that courts of the Jewish millet followed. The enterprise reflects an acknowledgment of the substantive accessibility of *halakha* to a non-Jew. This implicit recognition of a joint universe of discourse is explicated in an epistle of commendation and support, sent to the author by Rabbi Abraham Abikhezir of Alexandria,[43] who writes:

> Your opus, work of a wise man and a thinker, is sui generis. No gold can equal its value, nor any silver pay its worth. You devoted days and nights, and banished sleep from your eyes, in order to retrieve pearls from the depth of the sea of Talmud and Poskim. And from them you fashioned a necklace, inlaid with precious onyx and jasper, to adorn the members of your nation and to publicly sanctify the Name of Heaven ... And, so that it not be as a sealed book for a person who does not understand our pure and holy tongue, you toiled – and succeeded – to edit it in the language spoken here in Egypt, the harmonious and pleasant Arabic tongue. In doing so, you followed in the footsteps of our intellectual giants of old, Sa'adiah Gaon and Maimonides, of blessed memory. Thereby, you fulfilled a keenly-felt lack. The people treading in darkness, who have never seen the light of Torah, will now see a great light, and happily rejoice. The lawmakers and the lawyers, of all peoples and tongues, will taste of this honeycomb and say, 'Hurrah! we have become warmed and enlightened by just laws and regulations!' They will thank and praise your name, for you will be to them a father and a teacher of justice. And they will sanctify the God of Jacob, and give adoration to the Laws of Israel, saying: 'What great people has laws so just, as the laws of Torah which Moses set before the people of Israel?!'[44]

In other words, making *halakha* accessible to a non-Jewish public, in their own language, will not only be of assistance to them, but will also sanctify God's Name – a very high value in Torah's scale. The epistle explicates that such sanctification will occur as a result of the positive appreciation that Egyptian legalists will express for the content of Jewish marriage and divorce laws. Such a positive evaluation is meaningful only if one assumes that Jews and Gentiles share a world of rational discourse, which enables mutual evaluation and critique.[45] Further, the author's esteem for the Arabic language is noteworthy. Indeed, Rabbi Mas'ud Hai goes further in this respect than did medieval sages. They wrote in Arabic, but employed Hebrew letters, while he employs original Arabic typeface.[46] The use of modern literary Arabic, and the concern for the esteem of Egyptian gentile lawyers, provide another illustration of Sephardic rabbis' sense of solidarity with contemporary non-Jewish society.

HALAKHIC AFFIRMATION OF CERTAIN VALUES CENTRAL TO EUROPEAN MODERNITY

Major Sephardic sages identified with certain values crucial to modern European political thought. One such value is the notion that basic legal and political rights follow from man's creation 'in God's image'.

After Palestine was occupied by Great Britain in 1917/18, Jews resident in the country engaged in internal deliberations for electing an assembly that would represent them *vis-à-vis* the new authorities. One controversial issue was that of women's suffrage. Not surprisingly, the Old Yishuv rejected this innovation (supported in this matter, surprisingly, by Rabbi Isaac HaCohen Kook, whose Zionist credentials were impeccable). Those who rejected women's suffrage based themselves on Jewish precedent: in premodern Jewish communities women never had political rights. One Rabbi Dr. Ritter asserted, that women had not been accorded status in the Biblical definition of the Israelite polity: they were not regarded as 'Qahal' or as 'Edah, were neither counted in the census nor included in Israel's genealogical lists.[47] Rabbi Ben-Zion Meir Hai Uzziel responded:

> Let us grant that they are neither Qahal, nor Edah . . . nor anything. But are they not creatures, created in the Divine image and endowed with intelligence? And are they not connected to matters within the competence of the proposed assembly or of the committee it shall designate, whose directives they shall be required to obey . . . ?[48]

The fact that women were 'created in the Divine Image and endowed with intelligence', and that they would be expected to obey the elected leadership, entails an halakhic decision by Rabbi Uzziel according to which, Torah sees women as possessing an inalienable right to vote. The conception of man as having been created in the Divine Image is Biblical; yet the derivation of political rights from this conception is definitely modern – as is the notion that the duty of obedience to political authority is linked to one's right to vote. Rabbi Uzziel affirms the halakhic validity not only of the Biblical notion of man's Divine Image, but also the modern political implications derived (by non-Jews!) from that notion.[49]

Another value of modern political thought lies in the assertion that international reality should be more than a meeting of vectors of force. One people should not subjugate another. Rather, every people has a right to sovereignty, irrespective of that people's military power. Rabbi Haim David HaLevi writes, that this ethos of international relations is the vision of Isaiah, which, he claims, began to be accepted after World War I, when the victorious Allies recognized the right of peoples to self-determination. It further progressed after World War II but was constrained by the cold war. However, the break-up of the Soviet Union has re-enabled progress towards actualization of this ethos.

> Before our very eyes, the vision of our holy prophet 'wolf shall dwell with sheep, and leopard lie beside lamb' is in the process of realization. Thousands of years passed until the world understood the great values of peace and equality between nations, envisioned by Israel's prophets of old, and sincerely strives [sic!] to concretize those values in praxis . . . This encourages belief in the more distant, eschatological vision, 'They shall beat their swords into plowshares, and their spears into pruninghooks'. . . . Before our eyes, and in our very own days, we behold the victory of the messianic vision of Israel's spirit.[50]

Just as Rabbi Uzziel halakhically affirmed the contemporary political-legal implications derived by non-Jews from the Biblical concept of man's Divine Image, so too does Haim David HaLevi affirm the Judaic value and significance of twentieth century progress in the ethos of international relations – as a modern expression of a major Biblical prophetic vision.[51]

CONCLUSION

While noting that a direct sense of threat affecting Ashkenazic rabbis was not felt by their Sephardic-Oriental peers, I argued that lack of external threat was not a sufficient condition for openness to halakhic change, for an internal halakhic ethos rejecting change might exist in the Sephardic tradition. Upon examination, however, it transpired that the cultural heritage of the Sephardic rabbinic elite incorporated a view of *halakha* as an inherently dynamic religious phenomenon. This view of *halakha* enabled Sephardic-Oriental rabbis acting in the context of modernity to hold what they believed to be an authentic Jewish outlook. This consisted of many elements: Support for the integration of secular studies into the Jewish curriculum; Positive regard for modern science and technology; A sense of solidarity with contemporary non-Jewish society and state; Acknowledgement of a common, Jewish–Gentile rationality which encompasses (inter alia) the realm of *halakha*; halakhic affirmation of certain values central to European modernity. These elements can be seen as components of an 'ideal-type' of a Sephardic-Oriental rabbinic ethos in modern times. Clearly, there is more than one authentic modern continuation of pre-modern halakhic Judaism.

Notes

1   N. Katzburg, 'Orthodoxy,' in *Encyclopaedia Judaica* 12: 1486–7.
2   J. Katz, 'Orthodoxy in Historical Perspective,' in *Studies in Contemporary Jewry* 2 (1986) 3–17; the citation is from 4–5.
3   This slogan was coined by the founder and leader of the Orthodox movement, Rabbi Moses Sofer (1762–1839) also known (after an acronym) as Hatam Sofer. A classic article on Rabbi Sofer is Jacob Katz's *Outline of a Biography of Hatam Sofer*, first published in 1968 and re-published in Katz's *Halakha ve-Kabbalah* (Jerusalem 1984) 353–86. A brief presentation of Rabbi Sofer's life and views may be found in Moshe Sammet's article in Encyclopedia Judaica 15: 77–79. Sammet wrote a dissertation entitled 'Halakha ve-Reforma' ('Halakha and Reform'), Jerusalem, Hebrew University, 1969. A concise overview of his findings may be found in his 'Teguvat ha-Halakha 'al ha-Modernizatzia' ('The Response of Halakha to Modernization') in *De'ot* 36 (1969), 26–30.
4   M. Elon, *Jewish Law – History, Sources, Principles*, Jewish Publication Society, Philadelphia, 1994, vol. 3, 1493–4.
5   For a fuller analysis of this matter, see my 'Halakha u-Modernizatzia' ('Halakha and Modernization'), Jerusalem, Shalom Hartman Institute, 1982.
6   Specifically, the Jews of Turkey, Iraq, Syria-Lebanon, Palestine, Egypt, Libya, Tunisia, Algeria and Morocco. Probably, the Jews of the Balkans can be included, and also those of Yemen.
7   For example, the Jews of Tunis included two distinct ethnic groups – Grana

and Touansa; the Jews of the island of Jerba, in southern Tunisia, are a third socio-cultural group, in that same country.

8   The depth of this Sephardic identity was not contingent upon actual influx of Iberian exiles into the community. A fine example is provided by Rabbi Joseph Hayyim (d. 1909), the greatest rabbinic leader of Iraqi Jewry in modern times. Very few Jewish exiles from Spain reached Iraq; yet Rabbi Hayyim writes that Iraqi Jews must follow the rulings of the Sephardic halakhic code, *Shulkhan 'Arukh*, 'for we the Sephardim are bound to follow the decisions of [the Sephardic] Rabbi Caro' (*Ben Ish Hai*, first year, *parashat Devarim*).

9   That is to say, a wealthy, Alliance-educated Jew living in a newly-built quarter of Cairo was quite modernized, while a lower-class, traditionally-educated Jew living in a Kurdish village was little touched by modernization.

10 For a concise presentation, see my article 'The Halakhic Teachings of Modern Egyptian Rabbis,' *Pe'amim* 16 (1983), 65–88 (Hebrew).

11 The so-called 'Islamic reform' movement, which was an important factor in Middle Eastern Islam in the early twentieth century under the leadership of Afghani and 'Abduh, was much less radical than European-Christian reform.

12 *Inter alia*, this was the path adopted by most Arab communists.

13 A very unusual exception to this rule was Rabbi Raphael Katzin's attempt to establish a 'reform' congregation in Aleppo c.1862, described by Yaron Harel in *Hebrew Union College Annual* 63 (1992), XIX–XXXV (Hebrew).

14 That is not to say that rabbinical leaders were never openly criticized. Thus, many Cairene Jews in the early 1920s severely criticized the behavior of the incumbent Chief Rabbi as high-handed. In the late 1940s, Baghdadi Jews participated in a mass demonstration against Chief Rabbi Khaduri, whom they regarded as cowardly *vis-à-vis* the anti-Semitic regime. But, importantly, these critiques were ad hominem.

15 Eliyahu Hazan was born c. 1847 in Izmir and grew up in Jerusalem. He served as rabbi of Tripoli and then of Alexandria, until his death in 1908. His published works include four volumes of responsa and a volume on the traditions of Alexandrian Jewry.

16 Eliyahu Hazan, *Zikhron Yerushalayim*, Livorno, 1874, 57.

17 Rabbi Uzziel (1880–1953) was born in Jerusalem, served as Sephardic rabbi of Tel-Aviv (1912–1939) and until his death as Sephardic Chief Rabbi of Israel. He composed seven volumes of responsa, two volumes on *halakha* concerning orphans and widows and legal guardianship, and many works of theology and homilies.

18 Introduction to the first volume of his *Mishpetei Uzziel*, Tel-Aviv 1935, IX–X.

19 The greatest rationalistic philosophical work of medieval Judaism.

20 Born in Jerusalem in 1924, HaLevi served as rabbi of Rishon-LeZiyyon, and since 1973 as Chief Rabbi of Tel-Aviv. HaLevi has written hundreds of articles on a wide range of Jewish topics, and published 25 volumes.

21 Hayyim David HaLevi, "Al gemishuta shel ha-halakha (On the flexibility of Halakha)', in *Shana be-Shana* 1989, pp. 183–6.

22 Sammet, see above note 3.

23 See above, note 8.

24	Joseph Hayyim, responsa *Rav Pe'alim*, part 2, *Orah-Hayyim*, responsum 22.
25	On the Volozhin incident see *EJ* 16: 217. On the opposition to the school, see *EJ* 9: 300.
26	Israel Moshe Hazan (born in 1808) grew up in Jerusalem and became a member of its rabbinic court. Around 1842 he went on a fund-raising mission to Europe and was offered the post of chief rabbi of Rome. Later he became rabbi of Corfu and of Alexandria. Hazan composed works of responsa, published from manuscript a collection of Geonic responsa, *Iyyei HaYam*, to which he added an interesting commentary, and published other works, in which he propounded a fascinating approach to Jewish religious thought and life. See Joseph Faur's biography, *Rabbi Israel Moshe Hazan, ha-Ish u-Mishnato*, Jerusalem, 1977.
27	Israel Moshe Hazan, *Sh'erit ha-Nahalah*, Alexandria, 1862, 13–16.
28	1848–1928. Born in Rabat, Morocco, he grew up in Jerusalem and served as chief rabbi of Cairo from 1891 to 1921. He wrote volumes of halakhic works.
29	*UmiTsur Devash*, Jerusalem, 1912, responsum 9.
30	Holidays are days of rest, according to Torah. What activities are not consonant with 'rest' is a matter to which post-Biblical Jewish sources deliberate. As matches and electrical lighting are recent inventions, the question of their use during holidays had not been dealt with.
31	Meknes, 1892–Haifa, 1975. Educated in Meknes, Rabbi Mesas served as rabbi of Tlemcen, Algeria in 1924–1940, as a rabbinical judge in Meknes (1940–1964) and chief rabbi of Haifa until his death. His published opus includes many volumes of responsa and other works of traditional Judaica.
32	J. Mesas, *Ner Mitzvah*, Fez, 1939, 15.
33	Rabbi Mesas' understanding on this matter would seem to be a reasonable conclusion from Maimonides' understanding of the principles guiding the planning of the Temple and its precincts. See *Guide of the Perplexed* III: 45.
34	Baghdad, 1813–1889. Rabbi Somekh, one of the two great sages produced by Iraqi Jewry in modern times, was the founder of Baghdad's 'Beit Zilkha' Talmudical academy which produced nearly all rabbis of modern Iraq.
35	The lighting and extinguishing of fire on Sabbath is forbidden by *halakha*. Moreover, the sages of antiquity decreed that Jews may not utilize gentiles to circumvent the original rule and to perform forbidden actions for the sake of Jews. Yet this latter decree was leniently interpreted by medieval halakhists, thus creating the institution known in Europe as 'Shabbes Goy', i.e. a Gentile employed by Jews to assist them on Sabbath.
36	Rabbi of Frankfurt 1718–1740.
37	A. Somekh, *Zivhei Tzedek ha-Hadashot*, Jerusalem, 1981, responsum 134.
38	Although formally unconnected, both developments stem from the internal 'logic' of modern, civil society: on the one hand, the move towards a political–territorial group identity, non-dependent on religious affiliation; and on the other, the assumption by local and national government of an ever-widening range of societal responsibilities, fulfilled via bureaucratic agencies.
39	See also my Hebrew article 'New Horizons: A Major 19th Century Baghdadi Rabbi's Heightened Awareness of Socio-Cultural Variety and Change,' *Pe'amim* 36 (1988), 89–107.

40 This applied only to nationals of Egypt. If even one party to a legal dispute was a foreign national, the complex 'Capitulations' agreements usually resulted in the case being tried before a consular or a 'mixed' court.
41 Jerusalem, 1869–Cairo, 1925.
42 *The Book of Religious Laws of the Jews in Matters of Personal Status*, Cairo, 2 vols, 1912–1919.
43 Born in Morocco in 1866 and raised in Jerusalem. In 1892 he became assistant to Alexandria's chief rabbi, and later head of the rabbinical court.
44 Rabbi Abikhezir's letter was published in the introduction to *Kitab alAhkam*, 28–9.
45 The assumption does not originate with Rabbi Abikhezir. Indeed, the expectation that all human beings would acknowledge the values of justice expressed in the laws of Torah is itself biblical (*Deuteronomy* IV: 5–8). What Rabbi Abikhezir's words teach us is the extent to which the sense of a joint world of discourse was vital in modern times, and the extent to which Sephardic rabbis valued activity aimed at deepening Torah's accessibility to non-Jews.
46 In medieval and modern times, most Jews who wrote Arabic employed Hebrew letters; compare Yiddish, which, similarly, is basically a German dialect, written in Hebrew characters. I am grateful to Professor Deshen for reminding me to stress the significance of the fact that Rabbi Mas'ud uses Arabic letters.
47 'Qahal' and 'Edah' are Biblical terms, usually translated as 'community' or 'congregation'. Rabbi Dr. Bernhard Loebel Ritter, Chief Rabbi of Rotterdam in the years 1885–1928, was a determined opponent of Zionism.
48 *Mishpetei Uzziel, Hoshen Mishpat*, responsum 6; reprinted in *Piskei Uzziel bi-Shelot ha-Zeman*, Jerusalem 1978, responsum 44.
49 I analyzed Rabbi Uzziel's position in my article, 'Un grand decisionnaire sepharade defend les droits de la femme,' *Pardes* 2 (1985), pp. 128–148. A detailed comparison between his views and those of Rabbi Abraham Isaac HaCohen Kook may be found in my forthcoming article, 'Traditional Flexibility and Modern Strictness: A Comparative Analysis of the Halakhic Positions of Rabbi Kook and Rabbi Uzziel on Women's Suffrage,' in Harvey Goldberg (ed.), *Sephardi and Middle Eastern Jewier: History and Culture in the Modern Period*, in press, Indiana University Press.
50 Rabbi H.D. HaLevi, 'Athalta di-Geulat 'Olam be-Tav-Shin-Nun,' *HaTsofe*, 19 Jan. 1990.
51 Aspects of the theology of Rabbi HaLevi are discussed in my article, 'Sephardic Hakhamim, Modernity, and the Theology of Haim David HaLevi,' in Kevin Avruch and Walter Zenner (eds), *Critical Essays on Israeli Society, Religion, and Politics (Books on Israel* IV) (Albany, NY: State University of New York Press, forthcoming).

Part II
Morocco

6 Patronage and Protection: The Status of Jews in Precolonial Morocco
Allan R. Meyers

> *Basing himself on Arab and European historical sources, Allan Meyers, who teaches in the School of Public Health at Boston University, explores the issue raised in the previous chapter, the position of Jews under Muslim rule, focusing on pre-colonial Morocco. In that context, Meyers argues, different relationships obtained in different parts of the country. The crucial factors were the degree of power which local potentates and the central government wielded respectively. Communal protection obtained where the government was strong, and individual patrol–client relationships were forged where local strongmen ruled.*

INTRODUCTION

The history of Jewish–Muslim relations in Morocco begins with the Islamic conquest of North Africa, in the seventh and eighth centuries, and continues to the present time. However, until very recently, Moroccan Jewish studies have fallen into the interstices between two traditions of scholarly research. On the one hand, there have been studies of Moroccan history and ethnography, in which Jews appear as important, though secondary participants. On the other, there have been studies of Moroccan Jewish history and social life with some reference to the broader historical, social, cultural, and political context within which this history has taken place.[1] Each of these scholarly traditions has produced studies of lasting and even monumental importance, but neither has been able to adequately set Moroccan Jewish communities in their Moroccan milieux.

Within the past ten to 15 years, the mutual isolation of these two traditions has begun to break down, as sociologists and anthropologists who

---

Source: 'Patronage and Protection: The Status of Jews in Pre-colonial Morocco,' in S. Deshen and W.P. Zenner (eds), *Jewish Societies in the Middle East* (Washington DC: University Press of America, 1982) 85–104.

have studied Moroccan Jews in Israel have tried to reconstruct Jewish life in Morocco, mainly to determine the influence of the Moroccan past upon the immigrants' adaptation to life in Israel (Willner and Kohls, 1962; Shokeid, 1971), and as North Africanist historians and ethnographers have begun to study Moroccan Jews in the context of Moroccan Islam. In this latter regard, the most interesting development has been an exchange involving Lawrence Rosen, an anthropologist, who has written about Jewish–Muslim relations in Morocco (Rosen, 1968; 1972; cf., 1979; Stillman, 1973), and Norman Stillman, an Orientalist and historian, who has responded with a short and highly critical note (Stillman, 1976).

Both Stillman's and Rosen's papers represent only preliminary efforts, and their respective conclusions may be modified by more intensive research. However, since they are both highly qualified North Africanists, each in his respective discipline, and since they disagree so sharply in their conclusions, it is instructive to examine their controversy in greater depth.

THE CONTROVERSY

Rosen's papers deal mainly with the town of Sefrou, southeast of Fez, where he did ethnographic fieldwork between 1967 and 1968; he was in Sefrou during the Six-Day War of 1967, when there were rumors and threats of reprisals by Muslims against Jews. Using both direct observation and retrospective data, Rosen studies Muslim–Jewish relations, in normal times and in times of stress. He concluded that under normal circumstances, Jews and Muslims lived together in peace, if not harmony; indeed, he contends that many Jews were able to manipulate their relationships with their Muslim neighbors to considerable economic advantage. In times of danger, on the other hand, each Jewish family had a Muslim guarantor to whom it would turn; this person was supposed to protect them from injury and to avenge them if they were harmed.

To Rosen, dyadic relationships – i.e. relationships between two individuals – were of the essence of Sefriwi politics. In reference to Muslim–Jewish relations, a Muslim was the dominant superordinate member of each dyad, the patron; the subordinate member, the client, was a Jew:

> ... in most of central Morocco ... Jews were able to occupy an intermediate role between (Arabs and Berbers)[2] ... Largely unwilling to risk any of their independence in transactions with Arabs and frequently at odds with the urban-centered and Arab-dominated government of the sultan, Berbers preferred to have economic relations with local Jewish merchants and craftsmen. The relationship was, characteristically, a very

personal one involving a formal bond of protection granted a specific Jew by a specific Berber, a protection which was jealously guarded lest an unpunished act by a third party against a Jewish protégé be taken as a sign of weakness or unreliability on the part of a Berber protector. The Berber – or for that matter the Arab – usually developed a long-term and purely economic relationship with the Jew and one which . . . was generally characterized by that kind of friendship that so often attends a clearly symbiotic relationship. (Rosen, 1972: 444–5; cf., Geertz, 1979: 166)

Stillman criticizes Rosen for several reasons. First, he suggests that Rosen has treated Muslim–Jewish relations in Sefrou as though they were timeless: i.e. without justification, he has 'projected' the situation prevailing in the 1960s 'back in time', ignoring considerable historical change. Secondly, he suggests that Rosen has made a serious error by generalizing the experience of Sefrou to all of Morocco, because 'Sefrou was a notable exception to the rule even prior to the coming of the French' (Stillman, 1976: 13). Thirdly, Stillman states that Rosen's ideal portrayal of Muslim–Jewish relations has overlooked some of the most important and least attractive realities. Finally, by implication, he denies the importance which Rosen attaches to Muslim–Jewish dyads. Instead of the pre-eminent role of partners in dyads, Stillman stresses the Jews' status as *dhimmîs*, members of a subordinate *community*, *vis-à-vis* a superordinate *group*. Dyadic relationships might have had 'a localized, mitigating effect', but the essential character of Muslim–Jewish relations depended upon the *dhimma*, a relationship not of individuals, but of corporate groups (Stillman, 1976: 14).

In summary, there are fundamental differences between Rosen's and Stillman's interpretations of Jewish–Muslim relations in Morocco, not only in terms of data, but also in terms of the interpretation of data and the political uses to which these data are put. In fact, there is compelling ethnographic and historical evidence that both kinds of relationships existed simultaneously in Morocco, perhaps in the same locales. There was no single paradigm of Muslim–Jewish relations, but rather variations around a common theme. Moreover, and more importantly, the controversy which surrounds the interpretation of data, basically a political controversy, obscures a very important problem in historical and ethnographic research.

HISTORICAL AND ETHNOGRAPHIC BACKGROUND

Jews have lived in Morocco for centuries – perhaps, millennia (Hirschberg, 1974: 22) – and they have lived in as great a range of social, political and ecological circumstances as Jews in any other part of the Islamic world, the *dâr al-Islâm*. Like Jews in medieval Egypt, Iran, and Yemen, Moroccan Jews lived in imperial cities, smaller trading and administrative centers, mountain villages, and oasis towns. There is no complete continuous roster of the Jewish communities of Morocco, but there are episodic accounts which confirm the broad distribution of Moroccan Jews. For example, at the turn of the fifteenth and sixteenth centuries, following the Christian *reconquista* of the Iberian Peninsula, there were at least fifty *millâhs* (Jewish communities) in Morocco in all ecological zones (Epaullard, 1956; Mauny, 1967/1961: 459–62). In the 'modern' period – i.e. since the establishment of the present 'Alawî Dynasty in ca. 1664 – there is evidence for the continuous existence of a hundred or more (Zafrani, 1972; Foucauld, 1888: 395–403). These, too, have been widely distributed throughout the country, along the major trade axes, ranging in size from a few isolated individuals to twenty thousand people and more.

Moroccan Jews' subsistence and economic activities varied according to the ecologic zones in which they lived. For much of modern Moroccan history, Jews have controlled much of Morocco's international trade, especially with England, the Low Countries, and France. They have also participated extensively in related fields of government service, as customs agents, interpreters, and European consuls to the sultans' courts. In the cities and administrative and trading centers, Jews were concentrated in lesser forms of commerce, including trading, peddling, money-changing and money-lending, and a certain proportion served their own communities as rabbis, teachers, and scribes. Throughout Morocco, Jews were artisans and craftsmen; they sold and worked precious metals, they were tinkers, embroiderers, shoemakers, and tinsmiths, and in certain parts of the mountains and desert, they were expert gunsmiths, making weapons for both imperial soldiers and dissident tribes. In rural areas, Jews were sometimes farmers and shepherds, and finally, in urban areas, there was a large underclass of carters, day-laborers, bath keepers, butchers and prostitutes, who lived marginal existences, always on the verge of destitution, vulnerable to any sudden economic change. In summary, occupational inventories of Moroccan Jews (e.g. Flamand, 1959–1960: 29–37) show that they engaged in a broad range of economic activities, excluded only from military service and Muslim religious activities. Correspondingly, their economic states ranged from the broad mass, who were of very humble means, to a small minority, most of whom were engaged in international commerce, who appear to have had untold wealth.

Stillman has properly stressed the historical changes in Jews' status across nine or ten centuries of Moroccan history (Stillman, 1976: 13–14), but he fails to appreciate that there were also ethnographic and economic differences among Jews in Morocco and that these differences also affected the Jews' status in different parts of Morocco at the same historical epoch.

DHIMMA AND THE STATUS OF JEWS IN MOROCCO

At all times and in all places, Jewish–Muslim relations were governed by a single principle, the classical Islamic idea of *dhimma* (Goitein, 1955: 62–87). Put simply, this principle dictated that Jews were subject people who were obliged to pay a tax or tribute to the Muslim sovereign. In return, the sovereign was supposed to guarantee their physical and fiscal security, a measure of religious liberty, and political autonomy in matters of personal status (for example, education, marriage and divorce, and inheritance). However, this principle allowed for wide latitude in its application, depending upon the nature of sovereign authority, Jews' and Muslims' respective subsistence patterns, and the nature of Jewish communal life. In fact, there were several different expressions of *dhimma* in precolonial Morocco, depending upon the circumstances under which Jews and their Muslim protectors lived.

In the imperial cities, Muslim–Jewish relations most closely approximated the ideal of *dhimma*. Jews lived in their own quarter, the *millâh*, which was often separated by walls from the Muslim quarters, and they were often obliged to follow certain sumptuary laws. At various times, for example, these laws forbade them to ride horses or to wear visible jewelry or required them to go barefoot outside the *millâh* or to dress only in black.[3] Jews were enjoined from physically assaulting Muslims, even if they themselves were first assaulted, and they were expected to bear insults without complaint. In a representative passage, William Lempriere, a British surgeon from Gibraltar, described the *millâh* of Marrakech in 1789:

> The Jews who are at this place pretty numerous, have a separate town to themselves, walled in, and under the charge of the Alcaide, appointed by the emperor. It has two large gates, which are regularly shut every evening about nine o'clock, after which time no person whatever is permitted to enter or go out of the Jewry, till they are opened again the following morning. The Jews have a market of their own, and, as at Tarudant, when they enter the Moorish town, castle, or place, they are always compelled to be barefooted. (Lempriere, 1804: 197)

The Jewish community was also obliged to pay an annual tribute, called *jizîya* or *gharâma*, to the sultan or to his local delegate, usually either a *khalîfa* (regent) who was one of the sultan's brothers or sons, or a *qa'id*, a military governor (Michaux-Bellaire, 1904). In some cases, the payment was in cash or precious metal. In other cases, Jews paid their tribute in kind. In still other cases, the sultans exempted a community from paying its annual tribute in return for an economic service. Lempriere describes one such case:

> The Jews in general are obliged to pay to the emperor a certain annual sum, in proportion to their number, which is a considerable income, independent of his arbitrary exactions. Those of Morocco (Marrakech) were exempted by Sidi Mahomet from this tax, and in its rooms he compelled them to take goods of him, of which they were to dispose in the best manner they could, and pay him five times their value; by which means they were far greater sufferers than if they paid the annual tax. (Lempriere, 1804: 198)

In all cases, the tribute was based upon the community's size and the financial means of its residents and represented an explicit *quid pro quo*.

In return for the payment of *jizîya* or *gharâma*, the sultans and their officers allowed the Jews a number of prerogatives: for instance, they were allowed to collect their own taxes, including taxes to support Jewish officials and institutions, and they had watchmen and bailiffs at their disposal to enforce their decrees. But above all, the sultans guaranteed the Jews' security and the security of their property throughout their domains. In fact, when a royal chronicler wanted to characterize the reign of a powerful seventeenth-century sultan, he wrote '[in those days] the land was so secure that a woman or a Jew could walk from Oujda to the Wâd Nûn [in the Moroccan Sahara], without harm!' (al-Nâsiri, 1906–1907: 132).

However, not all sultans were so powerful, nor was the land always so secure. In general, these studies have represented traditional Moroccan politics as a tension between two polar tendencies: *makhzan*, central government by the sultan, and *sîba*, opposition to centralized authority, embodied in the resistance of towns, tribes, and charismatic holy men (*marabouts*).[4] In territorial terms, the *bilâd al-makhzan* was the territory which the sultan controlled at any given time, and the *bilâd al-sîba* was the residual category of all regions which were beyond imperial control. The *bilâd al-sîba* included many kinds of government – for example, local dynasties, strongmen, and tribal councils – and there was frequent significant political change. The *bilâd al-makhzan* was territorially discontinuous – for example, two neighboring cities might be under imperial control, while the territory between them was not – and the boundaries were subject to frequent change. Consequently, there were always limitations upon the effective powers of the imperial government. These limitations, in turn, placed corresponding limitations upon the effectiveness of the sultans' guarantees.

The restrictions upon the sultans' powers had a significant impact upon dhimma protection because many Jews lived in the *bilâd al-sîba* and many others had regularly to travel through dissident regions in pursuit of their livelihoods. The greatest number of Jews almost certainly lived in the major cities, especially the main administrative centers and the commercial ports, which were subject to fairly consistent government authority. But the greatest number of communities was inland, in the mountains and oases, far from imperial control.

People who lived or travelled in these regions had protection needs which were different from those of their urban counterparts. This is not to suggest that the sultans' *dhimma* was worthless in the *bilâd al-sîba*. In fact, the sultans often had considerable spiritual authority among dissident peoples, even when their temporal powers were limited, and this respect may have served, in an indirect way, to protect the sultans' protégés. However, people also required more predictable assurances, which only local people with their own bases of independent authority were able to provide.

Often, under these circumstances, Jews and Muslims lived together in the dissident regions in much the same kind of arrangement as in the *bilâd al-makhzan*, a kind of microcosmic *dhimma*: the Jewish community, through its leaders, paid tribute to the local powers in return for their personal security and partial political autonomy. Although there are only a few data describing such relationships, they seem to have prevailed in many of the smaller Berber 'kingdoms' of the Middle Atlas, the Anti-Atlas, and Sûs. Walter Harris, a British journalist and traveller with broad experience in Morocco, describes one such situation, in the Dadès Valley of southeastern Morocco, in 1894:

> Close to the village was a 'Mellah,' or 'Ghetto,' of Jews, living by themselves in a separate quarter, which also was undefended, from the fact that they do not in any way participate in the wars. The Jews exist at Dads, as elsewhere among the Berbers, under the system of *debeha*, or sacrifice, so called from the fact that a sheep or an ox is supposed originally to have been offered to the Berbers in order to obtain protection. The families of Jews here too live in a feudal state, each being dependent upon some Shleh family for immunity from ill-treatment and

robbery: in return for this they pay a small yearly tribute to their protector. (Harris, 1895: 173–4)

In other cases, however, Jews derived protection from dyadic relationships similar to the ones which Rosen described in Sefrou. In these cases, individual Jews paid annual tributes in cash or kind to individual Muslim patrons who, in return, guaranteed to protect persons and their property and who foreswore to avenge them if they came to any harm. There are many examples of this kind of agreement from all parts of Morocco; in a recent publication, David Hart has described one such situation among the Aith Waryaghar of the Moroccan *Rif*:

> ... in 1953–1955; there were some five Jewish families (all elementary or nuclear in character) located in northern Waryagharland, and two more at the Monday market of the Aith Hadhifa.
>
> Every male Jew was either a silversmith or goldsmith or a packsaddle maker; the usual pattern was that there was one of each resident at or near each market, and that he and his family were under the protection of a powerful *amghar* or *qaid*. The keynote of Jewish behavior was that of safety in humility; conversely, for a powerful man to have 'his own' Jew was considered a sign of prestige. Because the Jews stood entirely outside of the political system, and because their occupational services were much in demand, many informants said that to kill or even molest a Jew was an infinitely worse offense than to kill a fellow tribesman, for the Jew's protector would show absolutely no mercy to the killer. (Hart, 1976: 279–80)

Not all Jewish clients had such powerful patrons, though, obviously, it was important for them to associate themselves with as rich or powerful men as they possibly could: for example, merchants, political strongmen, or holy men (*marabout*).

It is not clear how clients chose their patrons – nor *vice versa* – but it appears that a number of factors intervened. First, many protection arrangements were hereditary, in which case, neither party had much control over the agreement, although, presumably, even hereditary arrangements might lapse if dues were not paid (Harris, 1895: 173; Foucauld, 1888: 400). Secondly, there was an economic consideration: more powerful protectors probably cost more, so that only some people could afford the tributary dues that they might demand. At the same time, not all people needed the same amount of protection, and it may have been that those Jews with particularly high risk occupations – itinerant tinkers and traders, for instance – needed the greatest amount of protection and were therefore willing to pay more.

There were also supplementary forms of protection of which these people could avail themselves; for example, many Moroccan tribes collected a form of tribute called *zattâta*, a kind of highway toll which ensured a traveller's safety within the tribal territory but for only a limited period of time, usually time enough to cross the territory. *Zattâta* was assessed upon every foreigner, but it was customarily higher for Jews. *Zattâta* was especially relevant to Jews who travelled extensively in dissident territory and was another means by which they could protect themselves against multiple contingencies (Westermarck, 1926, I: 518–69; Brunot and Bousquet, 1946: 353–70; Geertz, 1979: 137–8).

What advantages accrued to Jews who participated in patron–client dyads? The most obvious return was physical security – security for their lives and livelihoods – since the Muslim patrons were, in principal, obliged to protect 'their' Jews. In this respect, they differed but little from their urban counterparts. The other advantages are less clear; for example, there is no evidence that Jews who were in patron–client relationships were assured any communal political autonomy; indeed, on the basis of what is known about the political organization of rural Jewish communities, this was probably not even a relevant concern. Many individuals were highly mobile, and most communities were quite small: too small to maintain synagogues, schools, religious societies, or even cemeteries of their own (e.g., Flamand, 1959–60). This is not to suggest that rural Jews had no such facilities or that they made no use of them; only that these arrangements, such as they were, were not explicitly sanctioned by anything like a *dhimma*. Instead, the pacts of protection were more limited and specific relationships, not only because they involved fewer people, but also because they had more limited ramifications in the Jewish partners' lives.

SANCTIONS

Under normal circumstances, Jews in Morocco had little need for protection. By all accounts, they lived with their Muslim neighbors in peace, if not tranquility, and went about their activities unharmed. However, it was in times of stress that the protection pacts were important, and it was at just such times that the guarantees most often failed. Protectors sometimes punished those who harmed their proteges; for example, Captain John Braithwaite reported that on December 5, 1727:

> Five *Moors* were crucified for robbing and murdering a *Jew*. This was one of the principal *Jews* of Mequinez (Méknès), and great Industry and

Interest was made by the *Jews* to discover his Murderers. (Braithwaite, 1729: 200)

However, there is ample evidence that throughout Moroccan history, imperial troops plundered Jews who had faithfully paid their taxes, tribal marauders robbed Jews who had paid *zattâta*, and Muslims injured or killed protected Jews with impunity.

These violations may reflect individual or social pathology; for example, both European and Moroccan sources portray Mûlay al-Yazîd (fl. 1790–2), the sultan who directed terrible pogroms against the Jews of northern Morocco (cf. Stillman, 1978: 133–42), as a lunatic and renegade (Lourido Diaz, 1978: 323–33). But what is more important, they also reflect a fundamental contradiction in the entire protection complex: there were only relatively frail and inconsistent sanctions to underwrite the guarantees. Jews, themselves, were powerless to physically sanction recalcitrant protectors or patrons – whence their need for protection – and there is no evidence that higher authorities – tribal chiefs, sultans, or imperial officers – ever did so.

This did not mean that sanctions were non-existent. Such sanctions as existed were social and moral, rather than material, but this is not to say that they were without force. For example, terrific shame befell patrons who mistreated their Jewish clients or who allowed others to do so with impunity. In the former case, they appeared to be bullies; in the latter, weaklings, neither of which was an attractive image before neighbors and kin (Foucauld, 1888: 400). There might also have been ritual sanctions, particularly if the protectors were holy men or if the protection agreement were sealed by an oath (*âr*). In these cases, offenders risked supernatural sanctions, which might be applied to themselves, their families, or their tribespeople without prior warning and at any time (Westermarck, 1926, I: 518–64). Finally, the Jews were not totally without practical power; in extreme cases, they could withdraw their services from consistently recalcitrant patrons or protectors and in that way seriously affect their material well-being. Jews were often the only traders, money-lenders, or metalsmiths available. The withdrawal of services would have complicated and perhaps even significantly disrupted local economic life.

There is no evidence of Jewish 'boycotts' of towns or tribes or regions of Morocco. This may simply reflect the absence of data or the fact that people were compelled to make a living, even at the risk of their lives. Alternatively, it may also mean that there were relatively few egregious violations of protection agreements, for any number of reasons, and that protection agreements did, in fact, provide the kinds of protection which they were supposed to provide.

DISCUSSION

In principal, the Jews of Morocco were *dhimmis*, like their counterparts in other Muslim lands; they were physically and politically vulnerable unless they had Muslim protectors to guarantee their wellbeing. But in practice, the protection arrangements between Jews and Muslims in Morocco took different forms. In the *bilâd al-makhzan*, the Jews' status conformed closely to that of traditional *dhimmis*: Jewish communities, corporate entities, were the sultan's protégés. In the *bilâd al-sîba*, under different social, political, and economic circumstances, the status of Jews was more variable: communal protectorship existed, but more often, Jews formed patron–client pairs, similar to those which Rosen has described. However, neither Rosen nor Stillman has characterized the situation in all of its complexity, because no single model of behavior can adequately describe the relationship between Muslims and Jews in precolonial Morocco. There were certain general rules of conduct which applied universally in Morocco – for example, Jews always deferred to Muslims – but the essence of Jewish–Muslim relations has been variability: the accommodation of behavior to the prevailing circumstances.

This kind of variability is not unfamiliar to anthropologists, who learned long ago that formal prescriptions for human behavior, whether written or customary, must be treated more as approximate guidelines than as inviolable or inflexible rules. It is essential to understand the formal theoretical statements – in this case, the classical rules of *dhimma*, as they may have been modified in Morocco. But these alone are not sufficient; it is also necessary to study the practical applications of these principles, because there are often compromises, violations, and exceptions to the rules.

At the present time, there is no explanation for the distribution of protection regimes, why some Jews formed patron–client dyads and others belonged to protected groups. There are several possible explanations. For example, demography and subsistence patterns played major parts. Where there were small highly mobile Jewish populations, as in the Moroccan Rîf, it would have been difficult to maintain any communal life. Hence, dyadic relationships prevailed. The protectors' relationship with the *Makhzan* is another factor which may have been significant: i.e. by a process of diffusion, those tribes which were more loyal to the *Makhzan* or in more sustained contact with Islamic orthodoxy may have been more inclined to practice *dhimma*.

Finally, there may have been a social structural explanation for the variation. In fact, a French explorer, Charles de Foucauld, put forward such an explanation about ninety years ago! He suggested that tribes with 'despotic' governments inclined toward communal protection, while 'egalitarian' tribes were characterized by patron–client dyads:

> Among the tribes which have a democratic style of political organization, for example, the Beràber, each Jew has his own patron. Among those which are governed by a chief with absolute powers, such as the Mezgita or Tazarwalt, the Jews belong to the sheik and have no other *sîd* (lord or master) than he. In those regions where there are sheiks with limited powers, as at Tazenakht, among the Zenaga, the Jew owes him an annual tribute and cannot move to another place without redeeming himself from him; nevertheless, he also belongs to a particular master who has common rights over him. (Foucauld, 1888: 400)

Unfortunately, no one has tested Foucauld's hypothesis, but there are several ethnographic settings in Morocco where controlled comparative studies could take place: the southern face of the High Atlas Mountains is one example, the Central High Atlas another. In both of these regions Jews lived among tribal people some of whom were governed by councils and others by despots. And in both cases, Jewish–Muslim relations continued, with little outside interference, until well after World War II. Through a careful combination of both historical records and ethnographic fieldwork, in Morocco, France, and Israel, it should be possible to reconstruct not only the nature of Jewish life, but also the Muslim context in which it took place. Without such a detailed analysis, it is possible only to speculate about many aspects of Jewish–Muslim relations in tribal Morocco and also about many aspects of rural Jewish communal life. What is certain is that there were several possible kinds of protection and that they were not necessarily mutually exclusive; any individual may have been a party to two or more arrangements or even different kinds of arrangements at any time.

Finally, since Stillman has accused 'American anthropologists' of presenting an idealized – even idyllic – view of Jewish life in Morocco (Stillman, 1976: 13), it is necessary to comment upon the protégés' perception of the protectors' guarantees. Quite clearly, it is impossible to know whether Jews were happy with their status or whether the level of violations was high or acceptably low. Moreover, from an academic perspective, it is both irrelevant and misleading to ask. The data are highly ambiguous. On the one hand, the combination of personal and communal protection was remarkably resilient, because it maintained a viable Jewish community in Morocco for at least six centuries. On the other hand, it was clearly defective because Moroccan Jews, since at least the seventeenth century, sought the protection of Western European colonial powers in preference to that of sultans, *marabouts*, and tribal despots.

Such data as these are easily amenable to polemical purposes (Stillman, 1977a); indeed, they have been used polemically, to different and contradictory ends. It is inevitable – perhaps even desirable – that this should be the case. However, they also have an enduring interest for social scientists and comparative historians who are interested in functional and processual analysis. They provide insights into ethnic relationships in Islamic states, the processes by which they changed, and the relationship between the broader political environment and the protection regimes.

Acknowledgement

An earlier version of this paper was presented to a panel on 'Anthropological Perspectives on Jewish–Gentile Relations' at the annual meeting of the Association for Jewish Studies, Boston, 1977. I am grateful to Walter Zenner, convener of the panel, for his encouragement in the preparation and revision of this paper, and to Shlomo Deshen, Jerry Weiner, Magali Morsy, and David Hart for criticism and advice.

Notes

1   Each of these traditions relies upon very different source material. The tradition of Moroccan history uses Moroccan primary sources, mainly imperial chronicles, published accounts of European diplomats and travellers, and European diplomatic archives. The best bibliographic guide, restricted to a single period, is Lourido Diaz, 1967. Studies of Moroccan Jewish history are based mainly upon Jewish sources, mainly Rabbinic chronicles and decisions; the most comprehensive bibliography is Attal, 1973: 143–227. In more recent years, both traditions have relied heavily upon ethnographic field work and French and Spanish administrative accounts.
2   There is considerable controversy about the distinction between Arabs and Berbers in North Africa. Simply stated, Berbers are bilingual, speaking both Arabic and Berber, a distinct language of which there are three main dialects in Morocco. They inhabit the mountain regions and some parts of the desert, they claim to be descended from the autochthonous pre-Islamic

population of Morocco, and, historically, they were often associated with resistance to the power of the sultanate. Arabs, on the other hand, speak only Arabic, predominate among the urban population, and claim to be descended from Arab tribes who arrived in Morocco beginning in the Seventeenth century. A more comprehensive discussion and a more detailed description of the controversy appears in Gellner, 1969: 1–34 and Gellner and Micaud, 1972: 11–24.

3   While some of these requirements were clearly humiliating and disabling, others, such as residential segregation, may have come about at the request of Jewish authorities or may, at least, have served their purposes (Corcos, 1972; Zafrani, 1972: 141–7).

4   The intensity of the controversy which surrounds the concepts of *makhzan* and *sîba* in Morocco resembles that of the Arab–Berber debate (note 1). For a comprehensive and critical discussion, see Waterbury, 1970: 15–60.

References

Attal, Robert (1973) *Les Juifs d'Afrique du Nord: Bibliographie* (Jerusalem: Yad Ben Zvi).

Braithwaite, John (1729) *The History of the Revolutions in the Empire of Morocco* (London: Darby and Browne).

Brunot, Louis and Bousquet, G.-H. (1946) 'Contributions à l'étude des pactes de protection et d'alliance chez les Berbères au Maroc central,' *Hespéris* 33: 353–7.

Corcos, David (1972) 'Les Juifs au Maroc et leurs mellahs,' in *Zakhor le-Abraham/ Mélanges Abraham Elmaleh* (Jerusalem) 14–78.

Epaulard, A. (ed. and trans.) (1956) *Description de l'Afrique d'après Jean-Leon l'Africain*, 2 vols (Paris: Maisonneuve).

Flamand, Pierre (1959–60) *Diaspora en terre d'Islam*, 2 vols (Casablanca, I.H.E.M.).

Foucauld, Charles de (1988) *Reconnaissance au Marce, 1883–1884* (Paris).

Geertz, Clifford (1979) 'Suq: The Bazaar Economy in Sefrou,' in C. Geertz, L. Rosen and H. Geertz (eds), *Meaning and Order in Moroccan Society: Three Essays in Cultural Analysis* (Cambridge: Cambridge University Press) 123–314.

Gellner, Ernest (1969) *Saints of the Atlas* (Chicago: University of Chicago Press).

Gellner, Ernest and Micaud, Charles (eds) (1972) *Arabs and Berbers* (London: Duckworth).

Goitein, S.D. (1955) *Jews and Arabs: Their Contacts through the Ages* (New York: Schocken).

Harris, Walter B. (1895) *Tafilet* (London: Blackwood).

Hart, David (1976) *The Aith Waryaghar of the Moroccan Rif: An Ethnography and History* (Tucson: University of Arizona Press).

Hirschberg, H.Z. (1974) *A History of the Jews in North Africa* (Leiden: Brill).

Lempriere, William (1804) *A tour from Gibraltar to Tangier . . . and Thence Over Mount Atlas to Morocco* (London: Higham).

Lourido Díaz, Ramón (1967) *Ensayo historiográfico sobre el sultanato de Sidi Muhammad b. Abd Allah (1757–1790)* Serie Monográfica, I (Granada: Cuadernos de Historia del Islam).

Lourido Díaz, Ramón (1978) *Marruecos en la Segunda Mitad del Siglo XVIII* (Madrid: Instituto Hispano-Arabe de Cultura).
Mauny, Raymond (1967/1961) *Tableau géographique de l'Ouest Africain au Moyen Age*, 3 vols (Amsterdam: Swets & Zeitlange).
Michaux-Bellaire, Robert (1904) 'Les impôts marocains,' *Archives Marocaines*, 1.
Al-Nâsiri al-Salawî, Ahmed ibn Khalid (1906-7) *Kitâb al-Istiqsa*, trans. by E. Fumey, *Archives Marocaines*, 9-10.
Rosen, Lawrence (1967) 'A Moroccan Jewish Community During the Middle Eastern Crisis,' *American Scholar*, 37: 345-451.
Rosen, Lawrence (1972) 'Muslim-Jewish Relations in a Moroccan City,' *International Journal of Middle Eastern Studies*, 3: 435-449.
Rosen, Lawrence (1979) 'Social Identity and Points of Attachment: approaches to Social Organization,' in Geertz, Rosen and Geertz (eds), *Meaning and Order in Moroccan Society: Three Essays in Cultural Analysis* (Cambridge: Cambridge University Press) 19-122.
Rosen, Lawrence (1984) *Bargaining for Reality: The Construction of Social Relations in a Muslim Community* (Chicago: University of Chicago Press).
Shokeid, Moshe (1971) *The Dual Heritage: Immigrants from the Atlas Mountains in an Israeli Village* (Manchester: Manchester University Press).
Stillman, Norman (1973) 'The Sefrou Remnant,' *Jewish Social Studies* 35: 255-63.
Stillman, Norman (1976) 'The Moroccan Jewish Experience – A Revisionist View,' *Association for Jewish Studies Newsletter* 18: 13-14; also in *Jerusalem Quarterly* 9 (1978): 111-23.
Stillman, Norman (1977a) 'In His Cousin's House: The Jew in the Traditional Arab World,' *Middle East Review*, Winter 1976/1977: 37-40.
Stillman, Norman (1977b) 'Muslims and Jews in Morocco,' *Jerusalem Quarterly* 5: 74-83.
Stillman, Norman (1978) 'Two Accounts of the Persecution of the Jews of Tetouan in 1790,' *Michael* 5: 130-42.
Waterbury, John (1970) *Commander of the Faithful* (London: Weidenfeld & Nicolson).
Westermarck, Edward (1926) *Ritual and Belief in Morocco*, 2 vols (London: Macmillan).
Willner, Dorothy, and Kohls, Margot (1962) 'Jews in the High Atlas Mountains of Morocco: A Partial Reconstruction,' *Jewish Journal of Sociology* 4: 207-41.
Zafrani, Haim (1972) *Les Juifs du Maroc: vie sociale, économique, et religieuse* (Paris: Geuthner) t. I.

7 Community Life in Nineteenth-Century Moroccan Jewry
Shlomo Deshen

In this, and the chapter that follows, the debate on the Jewish condition in Morocco is further explored, and Moroccan Jewish communities are studied in two specific settings, the urban and the tribal. In the present chapter, drawing upon pertinent material from the writings of predominantly city-based Moroccan rabbis, Deshen summarizes some of the conclusions of his book on urban Moroccan Jewry, The Mellah Society. *The reader may find full notations there.*

This paper introduces into the study of the nature of Jewish life in Morocco, graphically descriptive material from an important source, the Hebrew legal correspondence of Moroccan rabbis of the eighteenth to nineteenth century, the 'responsa' literature. In the first section of the paper I address myself to the structure of Moroccan Muslim–Jewish relations in general, and in the second section I focus on the ramifications of these conditions in the urban Jewish community in particular.

THE STRUCTURE OF MUSLIM–JEWISH RELATIONS

The major urban *mellahs*, Jewish quarters, were located within the *blad el-makhzen*, the domain under the immediate and personal authority of the sultan. The latter's rule was based on relationships that were sustained by the descent from the Prophet and his being a 'Prince of the Faithful'. During most of the Sherifian period, Morocco had no state bureaucracy, not even a substantial imperial army. Frequently the sultan's armed forces did not amount to much more than a glorified bodyguard, and for strategic military purposes, the monarch depended upon the armed forces of loyal tribal potentates. Typically, the sultan maintained several capital cities,

---

Source: Abbreviated version of a chapter in W.M. Brinner and S.D. Ricks (eds) (1986), *Studies in Islamic and Judaic Traditions II* (Atlanta, GA: Scholars Press) 143–55.

and rotated his residence between them so as to maintain a periodic personal, *baraka*-laden presence, in the various parts of his domain.

Since the sultan lacked overpowering material coercive force, an important expression of his authority lay in the extent of the peace and order that prevailed in the cities of the *blad el-makhzen*. The security of urban Jews, the weakest and most exposed of the sultan's subject, was an important manifestation of his power. Attacking Jews of the cities close to the sultan was an affront to the sovereign. During unruly periods when the sultan's power was weak, the monarchs were particularly sensitive to the political implications of harassment of the Jews. In order to limit the exposure of Jews to insurgents and thereby expose their own impotence, the sultans enclosed Jewish communities within the confines of *mellah* walls. This confinement was viewed by Jews as 'a sudden and bitter exile', and it was probably partially motivated by the desire to isolate and ostracize the Jews. Confinement in the *mellahs* also aimed at the physical protection of the Jews, albeit for political and not altruistic reasons. But it lacked the predominant discriminatory motives, religious and social in nature, that motivated European rulers in their times to restrict Jews to ghettos. Characteristically a large number of the major Moroccan *mellahs*, particularly in Rabat, Marrakesh, Salé, Tetuan and Demnat, were imposed on Jews during the nineteenth century, at a time when the sultan's power was beleaguered by the advances of imperialism and the subsequent extortion of capitulation agreements. During the late seventeenth century and parts of the eighteenth century, when the sultan's power was at its height, one hears little of confining Jews within *mellah* walls.

However, even during quiet periods the sultan's protection was not sufficient to free the Jews from harassment. The reason for this is rooted in the nature of the Jewish economy. A study of nineteenth-century lists of Jewish occupations reveals that over half of the male urban Jews earned their living by travelling for extended periods in tribal areas away from the cities. The tribesmen of those regions, both Arabs and Berbers, though not necessarily denying the sovereignty of the sultan, usually behaved independently, being bound only by the rule of local potentates. The economic activities of lone travellers, particularly of unarmed and despised Jews, were possible only if formal and stable arrangements had been effected with the tribal chieftains. Thus it is seen that Jewish economic activities were dependent on the sultan's protection within the cities, and on tribal protection in other areas. The two kinds of protective ties complemented each other. The sultan's protection tended to be communal in nature. It encompassed an entire *mellah* community, providing security for urban Jews, including the women and children whose menfolk were absent. Tribal protection, on the other hand, tended to be individual in nature. It was extended to the individual Jew who required protection in a particular, idiosyncratically defined area. Because of individual economic connections with certain tribesmen, each Jew, or each small group of two or three trading partners, required a unique network of patrons that provided security along each particular route. Since tribesmen often controlled only short stretches of an individual's route, the latter (individually or on behalf of a small number of partners) perforce had to make arrangements with numerous potentates.

The rabbinical sources are replete with incidents concerning Jewish peddlers and craftsmen who lost their lives to robbers while travelling. However, the most common fear of travellers seems to have been not loss of life but rather loss of property. This fear is well demonstrated in the general statement of a nineteenth-century Tafilalt sage:

> We see that when [highwaymen] set out to rob, their intention is to take goods and to capture Jews, and hold them till they get redeemed.

Jews extricated themselves from such situations by activating ties with patrons. Such ties were often ramified beyond monetary payments. Frequently they included handicraft and business services that continued for a lifetime, sometimes even passing from one generation to the next. In this manner, patron–client relations were sometimes enhanced by family tradition, as well as feelings of loyalty and trust. Molesting a Jewish client clearly infringed upon the sphere of influence of the Muslim patron of that client. Although we do not know definitely to what extent the mechanisms of patron–client relationships afforded security, it appears that individual ties were more effective than the communal ones. This contention is supported by the fact that in the responsa there are numerous reports of urban Jews being attacked violently with loss of life, whereas from remote Tafilalt we have the relatively mild statement recorded above which conveys a less insecure situation. There are also theoretical considerations that would lead us to expect that the sultan's protection, the only protection available to sedentary Jews, would be far from fully effective. First, city Jews, although protected by the sultan, were natural targets for insurgents. Second, the cities were witnesses to the learned activities of Islamic scholars, the *ulamā*, whose very existence reminded the sultan of his religious duties as 'Prince of the Faithful', and these duties had clear negative implications *vis-à-vis* the Jewish position.

The patron–client relationship between a Muslim potentate and his individual Jew had many faces. It was both harsh-authoritative, and affective-friendly. On the latter plane, we find mutual visiting during family celebrations and even participation in a whole range of ritual activities.

These included visiting saintly graves hallowed by both Jews and Muslims, and prayers of Jews and Muslims during times of drought. One of these ritual activities, the Mimuna Jewish folk festival, has been carefully studied by Harvey Goldberg. Muslims fulfilled an important role in this festival by providing the first leavened food after the Passover festival, when Jews refrain from such food. The Jewish Mimuna festival thus functionally required the participation of Muslims. Some of the cases recorded in the rabbinical responsa reflect loyalty and devotion between individuals that cut across the religio-ethnic divide. We learn of the practice of eighteenth-century Meknes Jews who, when threatened by insurgents, gave their valuables for safekeeping to Muslim acquaintances. A nineteenth-century Sefrou source reports a case about two Jews, who were clients of different Muslim patrons, and owed money to each other. The source relates that the creditor did not pursue his case, because he was apprehensive lest the dispute lead to violence between the Muslim patrons, and he feared that his patron's life might be endangered. An eighteenth-century Meknes source reports an incident in which a local Muslim potentate visited a Jewish home together with a Jewish visitor. During the course of the visit the Jewish visitor asks the Muslim to arrange for him a match with the host's daughter. The note of intimacy is striking, extending even to the sensitive area of marital affairs.

THE SOCIAL CONTOURS OF *MELLAH* AUTONOMY

The personal dyadic ties between patrons and clients had important ramifications in the structure of the Jewish community. They cut across internal ties within the Jewish community, thus obstructing communal loyalty. The overall effect of the dyadic ties was to impede the development of communal institutions and of Jewish autonomy in general. The community often had individual members who were independent of community authority and institutions, and this was a potent social factor. In a moment of candor, an eighteenth-century Fez sage notes that judicial activities were hampered by powerful individuals of the community:

> The Judge must sometimes ignore things ... for who can prosecute the powerful, and what court can judge and convict them? ... And I have experienced such situations myself ...

The *nagid*, the community representative, who fulfilled important tasks in taxation matters and in mediating payment of extortion monies demanded by the authorities, was frequently appointed by the authorities and not by the community. This was especially so in the royal cities, such as eighteenth-century Meknes. The *nagid* was chosen from the most prosperous of the community's businessmen and artisans, and as such he must have had business affairs with Muslim potentates. His private business dealings, one must assume, had some effect on the public activities of the *nagid* within the Jewish community, and it is plausible that the public and private interests of the *nagid* sometimes conflicted. We read of *negidim* whose public and private affairs were so intertwined, that when they sought reimbursement from the community for public expenses they claimed to have incurred, they had difficulty in separating public from private expenditures. Altogether, community autonomy was not extensive enough to permit the role of the *nagid* to develop systematically into one of a civil servant of the community in the bureaucratic sense. Further, the absence of clear distinctions between the *nagid*'s public and private affairs obviated the role of the *nagid* from being fully independent of external social forces.

The synagogue was another important, perhaps the paramount, *mellah* institution. Synagogues were not usually operated by the community but rather by powerful individuals. In fact, most synagogues were owned by individuals. Even those synagogues that were community property were operated independently by individual sages, whose position was hereditary. The monetary income of the synagogues was not publicly controlled by the congregations; the income served primarily to support the particular sage who ran the synagogue. The sages considered themselves responsible for maintaining the facilities and providing services, and they personally provided the necessary funds. The position of an owner of a synagogue *vis-à-vis* the congregation was, as tersely phrased in one of our sources, 'as one who invites people to his home'. Synagogues provided a public service through private initiative, in a manner reminiscent of education and health services in many premodern societies. From the perspective of *mellah* sociology, the organization of synagogues was similar to the structure of the role of the *nagid*. In both cases community organs were not dominated by the community *per se*. Both the *nagid* and the synagogue were prone to influence by social forces outside of the community, in particular powerful Muslim patrons and their Jewish clients, who were powerful within the confines of the community. Thus we learn of a man in nineteenth-century Salé who was condemned for homosexuality, and forbidden by the Jewish court to participate in synagogue services (a form of partial excommunication). Thereupon the offender was invited by a powerful individual who owned a synagogue to worship there. The man received public honors in that synagogue and, with these, respectability.

The permeability of *mellah* community organs to outside forces had important ramifications in the relationships between the Jewish community leadership and the Muslim authorities. Jewish community leaders at all times sought to maintain asymmetric relationships with the local Gentile authorities, that is, the Jewish community endeavored to limit the sphere of influence of the Gentile authorities in community affairs. In the context of that policy the Jewish authorities prohibited individual Jews from having direct recourse to the Gentile authorities. Particularly in matters of litigation between members of the community, the Jewish authorities insisted on the exclusive jurisdiction of Jewish courts of law. Individual recourse to Gentile courts of law was regarded as a heinous sin. However, Jewish communities as corporate bodies did routinely have recourse to Gentile authorities, in cases of litigation between themselves and powerful Jewish individuals. In such instances, the Jewish authorities needed the legal and political backing of the Gentile authorities. Also, since Jewish authorities usually lacked executive power, such as a penal system, Gentile assistance was required to execute the law as adjudicated by Jewish courts. The asymmetry of the relationship lay in the fact that the Jewish authorities prohibited individuals from involving Gentile authorities in internal Jewish affairs, but retained for themselves as corporate bodies the prerogative of turning to the Gentile authorities and to their courts of law. This asymmetric relationship, and the efforts to maintain it under diaspora conditions, was one of the basic problems of Jewish autonomy: the asymmetry was never consistent and hence Jewish communal autonomy was not impervious to interference, both by Gentiles from the outside, and by members of the community from the inside.

In Sherifian Morocco, in particular, the asymmetric relationship *vis-à-vis* the Muslim authorities was far from perfect. We find numerous instances of turning to the Gentile authorities and to their courts of law, and also of Gentile authorities intervening with the Jewish authorities in favor of particular Jewish clients. Community leaders were suspicious and could not be sure that their deliberations remained private. They feared that internal matters would be leaked to the Muslim patrons of individual community leaders. In an eighteenth-century Sefrou source the following is said about the secrecy of communal deliberations *vis-à-vis* Muslim potentates:

> No one can say a thing against their will, or do anything about it, because they are so fearsome ... Everything is overheard and the wall has ears.

There are many accounts of individuals who evaded communal taxation by soliciting the protection of their Muslim patrons. Thus according to an eighteenth-century Fez source:

Many people get assistance from the lords of the land and procure for themselves official documents. Some people free themselves from all taxes; others arrange to pay a little just as they feel.

We also hear of legal cases in which Muslim potentates intervene in the Jewish court on behalf of their clients, and of litigants who evade the Jewish court in preference to a Muslim court, where their patron wields influence. We read about a Jewish court that could not operate, because a litigant failed to present himself before it 'because he is a Jew of the enemies'. The individual in question was a client of a Muslim patron who was then in armed conflict with the potentate of the area in which the court was located. In this case, the prevalence of patron–client relations between individual Muslims and Jews altogether obviated the operation of the Jewish court.

Muslim influence penetrated the community in yet another manner: through people whose business affairs were limited or nonexistent and who had no influential Muslim patrons. These people, often destitute and reduced to begging, nevertheless had a potent resource that enabled them to pressure the Jewish authorities: the threat of defecting from the community and converting to Islam. Such threats were voiced with particular frequency in connection with taxation problems and debts. Individuals unable to cope with exorbitant requests of Muslim potentates, as mediated by the *nagid* and Jewish community authorities, sought to escape their lot by converting. In times of unusual material pressure, the Fez chronicles recount, numerous people relieved themselves of the disadvantages of belonging to the humiliated and highly-taxed *dhimmī* strata, by converting to Islam. However, not all these conversions were permanent; some lived as crypto-Jews, and we also learn of converts who considered returning to Judaism.

The prevalent attitude towards conversion is manifested in an eighteenth-century Meknes court case. It is concerned with the father of a bride who broke a betrothal agreement, and the issue was whether he should pay a fine to the father of the groom. The defendant argued that he had discovered that the groom was tainted because he was 'an informer', that is, one who discloses private financial matters of members of the Jewish community to powerful Muslims. The court accepted the argument of the defendant, dismissed the case, and added the following striking gloss to the judgment:

Although some time ago the brother of the groom converted to Islam, and the father of the bride was aware of that at the time of betrothal and accepted it, it does not follow that he was also ready to accept this additional foul blemish. For in these times conversions are common, and people do not refrain from intermarrying with partners who have converted relatives. But this [being an informant] is a great blemish – the ears tingle upon hearing it!

It appears that the feeling towards conversion was less severe than towards the radically asocial act of 'informing'.

The reasons that drove Jews away from their community in times of despair were mainly material. Yet it is plausible that this relative readiness to convert was also linked with the view of Islam in Jewish eyes, and of Judaism in Muslim eyes. Stillman summarizes this latter attitude:

> There is no obsession with the Jews comparable to that found in medieval European literature. Most of the Moroccan stereotypes of Jews may be negative, but they are also peripheral. They are perceived primarily as *dhimmîs*, humbled, but protected subjects. As long as the Jew conforms to this role, he arouses little interest.

In contrast to the complex theological obsession of Christianity with Judaism, Islam is concerned mainly with its superior status. Indeed, it is obsessed with the belief that 'Islam is superior', but that is all. Moreover, the Muslim obsession with superiority does not relate to Judaism exclusively; it encompasses *dhimmî* religion in general. Judaism in Islam is far less prominent than in Christianity. The Muslim view of Judaism is paralleled by the Jewish view of Islam. Among the Jews in Sherifian Morocco, Islam was not regarded as a rival religion with theological content worthy of serious religious debate, nor do we have evidence that it was regarded as defiling, impure, or demonic. These two conceptions of the majority religion – its being a theological rival or a widely feared entity – were entertained at various times by European Jews about Christianity. Islamic religion, on the other hand, seems altogether to have aroused little interest among the Jews of Sherifian times, and whatever evidence of such interest that we do have indicates rather an attitude of aloof disdain. The Jews regarded Islam as largely vacuous, and believed that its substantive content had been drawn from Judaism. When the host religion is perceived in such terms it is plausible that it does not constitute a formidable opponent or, alternatively, a monster to be battled against or to be avoided at all costs. Theologically, Islam was certainly not the abomination to traditional Judaism that many other religions were. Thus, in times of stress, some people might be driven to Islam, and could rationalize their move by the argument that conversion was not apostasy to a serious rival, certainly not to an idolatrous creed. Sociologically, the effect of this attitude was yet again to make *mellah* society permeable to external social forces.

The weakness of the corporate element in *mellah* social structure was countervailed by the vitality of religious practice and of kinship relations. In the religious sphere, *mellah* society in Sherifian times was vibrant. The sages of the period produced numerous works of biblical exegesis, religious law, legal responsa, and religious poetry. Only part of this corpus has reached us, and less has been published. Yet even that amounts to dozens of large tomes. This creativity was the work of scholars, many of whom were members of a small number of families that produced learned men for many generations. But devotion to the religio-cultural heritage was not limited to the circles of these families. The noble sages operated family synagogues to which people flocked, thus accepting them as rabbis and community leaders. After their death, people often venerated the memory of sages, paralleling the common practice of North African folk religion. The *mellah* by and large stamped people with devotion to their religion and culture.

In the area of kinship, the family had patrilineal features that elicited loyalty and bound people together materially. Even in this area, however, there is evidence that family cohesion was not unshakable. In a Sefrou community regulation there is a remarkable revelation concerning the nature of social forces that are conceived of as inimical to domestic cohesion. The regulation concerns the practice of mutual visiting of elders whose offspring are linked by marriage ties. Specifically, the father of the groom, accompanied by adult male relatives and friends, used to visit the home of the father of the bride on festival days, absenting themselves from their own homes and neglecting domestic ritual duties in relation to their wives and children. In the regulation the rabbis condemn the custom in a characteristically Middle Eastern idiom. Instead of properly feasting and lording at home, the rabbis complain, the elders 'go and submit themselves to others'. The rabbis thus conceive domestic neglect as linked with social ties between individuals. These ties, in the view of the times, imply inequality, the acceptance of hospitality entailing admission of at least situational and temporary inferiority. The situation is part of the whole complex of patron–client relations, which, when fully developed, also includes elements of political and economic inequality.

We have presented data extracted from rabbinical sources that permit us to construct a general framework of the Jewish condition in the cities of Sherifian Morocco. After summarizing the general structure of political relationships of the period and the nature of the Jewish economy, we focused on the features of Jewish communal autonomy. We proceeded to the Jewish attitude toward Islam and conversion. Some of these features are not unique to Moroccan Jewry, and figure in other times and other places of the Jewish Diaspora. Thus, the Jewish attitude towards Islam that I have described, and the asymmetric political relationship between Jewish community leaders and the Gentile authorities and with their own rank-and-file, are widespread. But these features are not universal in the Jewish Diaspora and they vary in matters of intensity and detail. I contend that although the disparate details of social structure that I have described are not unique to Moroccan Jewry, the entire complex configuration of features is uniquely Jewish-Moroccan and, further, that it can readily be comprehended when viewed against the background setting of Sherifian times. The evidence we have indicates that Moroccan Jewish society was to a degree permeable to the influence of the Muslim majority. It was fractured by ties that linked individual Jews to Muslims, and these ties had ramifications in internal relationships within *mellah* society. The *mellah* situation as a whole was uniquely Moroccan, although some of its specific features were common to other parts of the traditional Jewish Diaspora.

There are indications that the situation I have described developed and became marked over time. A set of three distinct data demonstrate that, prior to the eighteenth century, local Moroccan elements were less potent than thereafter. First, there is the issue of public as against private dominance and ownership of synagogues. During the eighteenth and nineteenth century we encounter increasing tolerance on the part of communal leaders towards individuals who open their own synagogues. The phenomenon of private synagogues was frowned upon by sages of the past, prior to the nineteenth century, who based themselves on medieval Sephardic tradition. In the later period, however, we encounter a prominent sage who, while offering lip service and obeisance to the ancients, ruled directly against the medieval precedent. We encounter another sage, who states that, in the course of his long career as a judge, he changed his mind and came to adopt a milder position concerning private synagogues.

Second, there is a specific point in the management of private synagogues. In cases where the owner is personally unsuited for a position of religious leadership, the ancient practice was for him to engage a rabbi. The latter would receive all the income that came from the synagogue congregants, and out of that sum pay rent to the owner of the synagogue. In the nineteenth century, however, this changed. The owner would now receive all the income, and out of that he paid the rabbi a salary for his services. The change benefited the lay owner and contradicted ancient practice based on the Sephardic tradition. The change was, however, in line with the indigenous practice of Marrakesh and Southern Morocco, where Sephardic tradition had never fully taken root. In the course of the nineteenth century indigenous Moroccan tradition overcame the Sephardic tradition and became accepted in central Morocco by rabbis who were actually heirs of the Sephardic tradition, in addition to the south of the country where the indigenous had never been supplanted. The social implication of this legal mutation is that the power of the individual as such is heightened, at the expense of formal limitations governing statuses and roles.

Third, there is a shift in inheritance law. In traditional practice, upon a man's death his property was divided equally between the widow and her sons, and upon the widow's death her property was divided among the sons. In the nineteenth century the practice was changed, and the property was fully divided among the sons, upon a man's death, to the detriment of the widow. Again, the social implication of the new practice was to enhance the position of the individual. Whereas in the past some family property was held jointly through the widow, in the nineteenth century the role of the family, as a corporate property-holding group, declined.

The research of social anthropologists and historians on Morocco in the past 15 years has uncovered important features of the social networks and of the cultural assumptions within which Moroccans operate. The study of Moroccan Jews demonstrates that social relationships of the kind extant among the Muslim majority are also operative among the Jewish minority. The data derived from rabbinic responsa support Meyers' thesis that, at least in certain regions of Morocco and in particular spheres of activity, patron–client relationships were potent, profoundly affecting the situation of individuals. To this I would now add that these relationships also affected communal and individual interactions in the community. The boundaries of Jewish society, while theoretically clearly defined, were in fact permeable: Jews sometimes moved between the majority and minority societies. Also the autonomy of the community was not rigidly bounded in practice; intervention from the outside sometimes penetrated the intimacy of domestic and religious affairs. Finally, these individualistic features of Moroccan society seem to have gained greater emphasis over time, and to have become more accepted among Jews towards the end of the precolonial period.

8 Jewish Existence in a Berber Environment
Moshe Shokeid

The previous chapters were based on literary sources and on observations of Jewish life in Morocco. This chapter by Moshe Shokeid, Professor of Anthropology at Tel Aviv University, uses oral accounts given by Atlas Mountain Jews, about years after they immigrated to Israel. In contrast to the previous chapter, this chapter focuses on the communities of the tribal hinterland. Shokeid draws from the testimonies of people who had experience as merchants, peddlers, and itinerant craftsmen among the Berbers, and who interacted with their patrons and other neighbors. The data is used in conjunction with written sources to elaborate the picture of the Moroccan Jewish condition.

During the 1970s historians, sociologists and anthropologists assessed diversely the Jewish situation in Morocco. Polar answers were given to the question whether Jews were a persecuted minority forced to comply rigidly with the more humiliating and severe *dhimmi* regulations, or whether their relationships with the surrounding Muslim society were relatively congenial, particularly when compared with European Jewry. The Moroccan debate cannot be isolated from an assessment of the general scene of Jewish life in Muslim lands, which was permeated with the ambiguity engendered by the *dhimmi* status. That official charter of rights and obligations, applied to Jews and Christians alike, has given rise to contrasting and inconsistent descriptions and interpretations of tolerance versus oppression in Islamic society. Chouraqui was one of the first to emphasize the relatively harmonious elements in Jewish–Muslim relations in Morocco (1958: 54–5), and the controversy gained momentum when Rosen formulated his hypothesis for the sociological *raison d'être* of these harmonious relationships.

This approach to the Jewish situation in Morocco has been challenged by Stillman as idealizing the Jewish position and distorting the general

---

Source: Abbreviation of a paper in 'Actes du Colloque International de l'Institut d'Histoire des Pays d'Outre Mer,' Abbaye de Senanque, Octobre 1978, 62–91. © Copyright 1980 by Editions du Centre National de la Recherche Scientifique. Reprinted by permission of the Centre National de la Recherche Scientifique.

Moroccan scene through the application of a hypothesis pertinent mainly to the Sefrou case. Stillman reinforced his argument with historical and folkloric sources which depict the humble and vulnerable legal and social position of Moroccan Jews. Pointing to the pariah status of Moroccan Jews, Stillman contends that they were excluded from many trades and consequently forced into occupations forbidden to Muslims, such as gold- and silversmithing and the particularly despised occupation of moneylending. Stillman also cites records, and brings evidence as to the persecution of Jews. Against the background of these contradictory opinions, Meyers propounds that there has never been a single paradigm of Muslim–Jewish relations in Morocco. During different periods, as well as in different parts of the country, various patterns predominated, exhibiting different types of co-existence. According to this view, both Rosen and Stillman present only a partial perspective of a situation that is far more complex. An inquiry into the ambiguity of patterns and the general ambivalence in Muslim–Jewish relationships we find in Goldberg's analysis of the Mimuna ceremony, and this ambivalence of relationships forms the theme of many Jewish Moroccan folktales, in which contacts with non-Jews are tense and contentious.

My own investigation into the particular situation of Atlas Mountains Jews revealed that most of the writers who explored Jewish life under Berber rule in recent generations comment on the Jews' relative safety, emphasizing the cordial relationships with their neighbors. Some of these writers refer to symbiotic relationships between Jews and Berbers. Flamand concentrates on the economic dimension of this symbiosis; Willner, on the other hand, comments in general: 'The Jews of Ait Ardar lived in virtual symbiosis with their Berber neighbors, and enjoyed excellent relations with them and a high subsistence level' (1969: 263). These descriptions seem surprising considering the unstable political situation and the more difficult environmental circumstances of Berber tribal areas. The skeptic may query whether the mere fact that Jews continued to survive under Berber rule did not give rise to these idealized descriptions.

Whatever our conclusions on the Jewish situation in the Atlas Mountains and elsewhere, an important factor to be considered, both in past and possibly future debates, is that most of the studies and assessments on Jewish–Muslim relationships have been carried out after the majority of Moroccan Jewry immigrated to Israel or elsewhere. This factor inevitably circumscribed investigation, not only in studies of communities which do not have many written records (particularly communities from southern Morocco), but in other communities as well. Moreover, the collective and individual Jewish experience of the twentieth century, particularly the

Holocaust, Israeli statehood and, in its wake, mass immigration from Middle Eastern and North African countries might have colored, in various ways, the views both of Moroccan-born Jews and of those who informed about, or analyzed, the situation of Jews in Morocco.

The arguments of the above scientists and our specific reservations evince a problem rarely treated directly by the various disciplines, namely the interpretative dimension in the presentation and analysis of data. The issue was tackled in anthropology by Geertz (1973: 3–32) who exemplified his argument with observations he recorded in Morocco. The *dramatis personae* in his case were a Jewish trader from the highlands of central Morocco, his patron – a Berber sheikh – robbers from a neighboring Berber tribe who had attacked the trader and his guests, and a French colonial officer. The latter, anxious to enforce French law and order, messed up settlement of the dispute according to Berber custom, which would have granted the Jewish trader considerable indemnification in sheep by the attacker's tribe.

Discussing the quality of interpretation embedded in the presentation and analysis of observed or recorded behavior, Geertz claimed:

> What it means is that descriptions of Berber, Jewish or French culture must be cast in terms of the constructions we imagine Berbers, Jews or Frenchmen to place upon what they live through, the formulae they use to define what happens to them ... They must be cast in terms of the interpretations to which persons of a particular denomination subject their experience, because that is what they profess to be descriptions of. (1973: 15)

In analyzing my own data, I was constantly aware of the limitations in the study of the Jewish Moroccan situation. Through the experiences of a community from the Atlas Mountains transplanted to an Israeli village, which I called Romema,[1] I tentatively suggest some interpretations for the position of Jews in these parts of Morocco. My observations in Romema were carried out over a period of 18 months – from October 1965 to March 1967, and for three months during the summer of 1976. The people of Romema migrated to Israel in 1956 from a village, which I named Amran, located in the district of Ait Bou Oulli,[2] about 50 kilometers southeast of Demnate. I refrain from discussing the patterns of social and cultural life of Atlas Mountains Jews and possible cultural symbiotic elements with the surrounding Berber society.[3] Rather I concentrate on the basic material circumstances of their lives – residence, occupation, and safety. The present anthropological study will, I hope, further contribute to the descriptive and analytical spectrum of Jewish life in Morocco, through its assessment of the Jewish situation in some parts of the Atlas Mountains.

THE CIRCUMSTANCES OF JEWISH LIFE IN AMRAN

When I began to summarize my data on the relationships of the people of Amran with their neighbors (Shokeid, 1971/1985: 18–23), I realized that these could not be defined in clear-cut terms. The immigrants' spontaneous stories and discussions as well as their answers to my direct questions were sometimes reminiscent of the pathetic descriptions of the position of Atlas Mountains Jews by nineteenth and early twentieth-century travelers and geographers (e.g. Thomson, 1889; Slouschz, 1927; Montagne, 1930). In many of these accounts, the Jew is highly dependent on his Berber patron who protects him for his own interest. At times the patron himself might ransack his Jewish protégé's property. Aside from this harsh presentation, there are scores of stories on how the Jews ingeniously contrived to safeguard their wealth and to ensure their personal wellbeing. Often the storyteller, during his narrative, asked God's forgiveness for having duped the Muslims. Others are tales of mutual dependence, based on genuine mutual respect, which stress fairplay and personal friendship between the Jewish trader or craftsman and his Muslim client, partner, or patron.

Amran, an all-Jewish village which prior to immigration had a population of three hundred and fifty inhabitants, was divided into seven family groups. This familial division greatly overlapped the occupational division in the community. At the top of the economic and social ladder were the traders whose ancestor, according to family tradition, had been a merchant from Demnate, who, upon the invitation of a local sheikh, had settled in Amran. His sons and grandchildren, like him, were in trade; they contracted farming partnerships with their neighbors for whom they put up capital, and they owned flocks of sheep grazed by Muslims with whom they shared the lambs. However, much of the trade consisted of nuts and the import of sugar, oil, as well as of other items. The senior members of the family of traders had in recent generations headed the community, and acted on its behalf in dealing with the local sheikhs (in Israel their neighbors have accused them of collaborating with the Muslims).[4]

The other families followed various crafts – cobbling, carpentry, and smithing. The poor and unskilled worked at odd jobs for the wealthier and skilled members of the community. Some of the craftsmen worked at home – particularly those who made embroidered shoes – others plied their craft in nearby or distant Berber settlements. All male members of the community came into direct contact with the Muslim population on an economic basis. There were almost no Jewish communal functions which exclusively provided a livelihood. Also the religious leaders were at times engaged in some kind of economic transaction or occupation. Trade and plying their crafts took the Jews over wide stretches of territories, crossing tribal borders, or, as they put it: 'We travelled through different *memshalot* (governments)'. A former smith concluded his description of travels in search of work in Morocco with the sweeping statement, 'For us craftsmen there were no borders.'

Their houses and the land the Jews usually rented from the Berbers. However, some of the merchants owned property.[5] As far as the people of Romema could remember, they had not paid regular taxes before the advent of the French administration. The wealthy, however, made costly gifts to their influential neighbors on the occasion of family celebrations or on holidays. They also bribed their sheikh to intercede on their behalf in disputes with their Muslim partners or debtors. Prior to French rule in the region, the local Berber sheikh was elected yearly by a council of the tribal grouping of Ait Mezalt.[6]

Aside from their local sheikh and the landlords, Amran merchants and craftsmen were not necessarily permanently bound in business or by patronage to particular Berbers. Though they had sometimes developed special relationships with particular Berber families over a few generations, these ties could be cut off and new ones established without formality. However, their strongest ties were with those Berbers from whom they rented houses and land.[7] Their landlords would intervene in disputes with other Muslim families. The Jews, on the other hand, held aloof from any strife in which their patrons' patronymic or tribal groupings were engaged. They would stay at home and wait for the tension to cool off. The trader or craftsman might have moved to another close or distant community upon the invitation of an employer or client to live on his estate. This mobility prompted by the search for livelihood may explain the changing size of Jewish communities in the Atlas Mountains, from less than ten inhabitants to three hundred or more (see Flamand's census, 1959: 329–33).

The landlords and patrons were often intimately acquainted with their Jewish protégés' personal and communal affairs. Thus, for example, the Romemites recall that in settling arguments or disputes between family groups in Amran, particularly between merchants and craftsmen, Berber neighbors were often witnesses or arbitrators. The itinerant craftsman might have remained with his Berber employer for days, or even weeks. His employer saw to his personal needs. Only on the Sabbath might the journeying craftsman have stayed at a nearby Jewish community or visited the synagogue. The Muslims also might come to visit, stay, and partake of food and drink at their Jewish partners' or acquaintances' homes.[8] Friendship was at times expressed in gestures of physical contact, as in the story of the craftsman whose employer kissed his brow, begging him to stay with him overnight.

During the generation preceding immigration to Israel, two Jews from Amran converted to Islam, both of whom had been itinerant craftsmen. The wife and children of one of them immigrated to Israel. The horrified brethren of the erstwhile Jews explained that the Berber employers of the latter had practiced 'witchcraft' on them, while serving them tea. According to the Romemites' stories, however, it would seem that it was poverty and despair, at a particular hard time that drove the two to abandon their religion, family, and community. Altogether, conversion of individuals to Islam was a problem many communities in Morocco had to contend with.

The wealthier merchants on their major business trips to Demnate often became the target of robbers; for protection they took with them on these journeys some robust members of the community. Prior to the establishment of French rule, local sheikhs ransacked on a number of occasions the property of the family of traders in Amran. According to their account, the last time the family was plundered the women were driven out of the house and the men tied up, but none was hurt. However, since the documents of all financial transactions had been well hidden, the family could renew its business, and it continued to thrive. At other times, the merchant could count on his Muslim friends. When the last head of the community was caught by French custom officials with a load of unauthorized fabric, a commodity rationed at that time, he stopped on his way to the police station at one of his Muslim acquaintances' home, and managed to leave with him part of his merchandise, loading sacks of straw instead. The eldest son of the head of the community, in his frequent references to Amran, has vividly drawn the multi-faceted aspects of Jewish life in Morocco, as may be seen in the following succinct comment, phrased in a style often used in Romema in public debates and at ceremonies. This manner of speech interweaves metaphors with a somewhat archaic poetic language.[9] 'The Jew even if very rich was stripped of honor in front of the Arab, and had to bow down to his will. But the Jew was always better dressed, better fed, and his house better furnished and stocked!'

On the relative safety of Jewish life in the Atlas Mountains, as perceived by the Romemites, we can learn from the following discussion. One evening, in Romema, while leaving the synagogue after the service, a settler spoke of the Negev Beduin who were criss-crossing the borders of Jordan, Egypt and Israel, smuggling drugs into the country as well as all kinds of heavily taxable commodities. One of the listeners suggested that those who were caught should be 'slaughtered'. Upon which the son of the last head of the community, mentioned above, retorted with astonishment: 'But why? The Arabs didn't slaughter us when we were living among them!' Yet on other occasions, people spoke appreciatively of their changed circumstances in Israel: 'It is better to live in Israel because it is safe. In Morocco, you could be rich, but the Arab could come any time and rob you of your wealth. Here you are not afraid of anyone; you can shout at, and even throw out, the Jewish Agency people, if you want to!'[10]

The ambiguity in the position of Jews in Morocco, as well as the various modes of relating to their past existence among the Berbers, cropped up also in references by both former merchants and craftsmen to their manner of dress (though their tone and purpose of mentioning that point differed). The Jewish garb was usually white, but the merchants at times wore fancy and colorful clothes similar to the attire of Muslims. The craftsmen in recounting this added, not without a measure of satisfaction, that the proud merchants were the first to be molested not only by the highwaymen, but also by their Muslim patrons and neighbors.

THE INTERMEDIARY ROLE OF ATLAS MOUNTAIN JEWS

Today, when we try to assess what the Jewish situation had been in Muslim countries, we often compare it with the present situation in Israel or in Western countries. This is done also by the immigrants themselves, as evidenced by some of the earlier quotations, or in the following comment by a former shrewd merchant who was wont to speak of his methods of fooling his ignorant Muslim clients, and who, in Israel, had become a prosperous farmer:

> When we came to Israel we thought we would be given a small hut to live in and only bread to eat. I never dreamt we would have electricity and that I would own a refrigerator, a washing machine, and a tractor! There are Jews who return to the country of origin. Not me! I shall not go back to Morocco, even if I get thousands in cash! I shall not return to be cursed again by Arabs!

This former merchant has thus filtered his perspective of life in Morocco, *inter alia*, through his comprehension of personal achievements in Israel. These greatly surpassed his expectations, which at the time of immigration had been motivated by Messianic beliefs (Shokeid, 1971/1985: 32–3).

This brings us back to our introductory note on the interpretative factor embedded in the informants' apprehension of their past and present situation. But, as demonstrated earlier, the Romemites' recollections were not geared into a definitive formula of positive or negative interpretations of their social position and of their relationships with their neighbors in Morocco. Consistency in interpretation is, it seems, more typical of outsiders, including scholars, or to ideologically motivated 'natives.' As mentioned, in the Romemites' view of life in Morocco the Berbers at times played a prominent role in relationships of Jews among themselves (Shokeid, 1971: 26).

No doubt the Jews of Amran did not leave a 'paradise' behind them, a notion which may be inferred from those who refer to symbiotic relationships between Jews and Berbers. They were a low-class minority; an inferior status, which, however, did not deprive them in all spheres of life. The Berbers were highly dependent on their many and varied services, which were not confined only to those occupations prohibited to Muslims. The Jews were also not the lowest status group in the Atlas Mountains; lower, for example, were the blacks, the descendants of former slaves, who traditionally were servants or followed such crafts as pottery. Within this framework of economic relationships and interdependence, the prosperous Jew could own land and prove his economic achievements and the special social relationships he had established with influential Berbers through fancy 'non-Jewish' dress.

To obtain a broader perspective of Jewish life in the Islamic world we may compare the Atlas Mountains situation with the position of Jews as observed in Iran in the 1960s.[11] Iranian Jews were confined, well into the twentieth century, to the most despised occupations and forced to show humiliating signs of identity, and they were considered of low moral standing. Bodily contact with a Jew was still in some places polluting to his Muslim neighbor. A Jew's property, life, and honor were never secure. He learned to hide his material possessions, to look destitute and humble. Loeb (this volume, chapter 18) argues that the Iranian Jews' occupations as peddler, moneylender, entertainer, vendor of liquor and prostitution, which lead to interaction with diverse social groups, might have placed him in a position of communicator or disseminator of ideas. As an outcast however – humiliated and polluting – he, in fact, served to insulate the various segments of the population from one another, and thus performed an important service for the Persian elite.

The potential role of the Jew as mediator between various groups in society has been suggested as explaining the position of Jews in two polar extremes of Muslim environments: Rosen (1972) who analyzed the intermediary role of the Jew between Arabs and Berbers, and Loeb (this volume, chapter 18) who interpreted the Jew's communicatory potentiality as transformed into an insulating function. Though the approach of the intermediary role of the Jew cannot alone explain the complex Jewish situation, as manifest in Morocco or in Iran, it is a key variable in elucidating the Jewish situation in many places throughout the history of the Diaspora. In our case, the Jew cast in an intermediary role clarifies some aspects of Jewish existence in the Atlas Mountains.

In some parts of Morocco the Jew might have played an intermediary role between the two distinct ethnic categories of non-Jewish society, the Arabs and the Berbers. In the Atlas Mountains, the role of Jews was, *inter alia*, intermediary between different Berber tribal groupings – a hypothesis which calls for further research. The Atlas Mountains Jews were living in what is known as *bled es-siba*, or 'land of dissidence' and 'disorder.' The central administration of the Sultan was not effective in these parts of Morocco and even the advent of French rule had little influence. Only at a late stage of French occupation – since the second quarter of this century – were changes imposed. The surrounding Berber society was segmentary, organized agnatically, and in continuous inter- or intra-tribal conflict (see Gellner, 1972; Hart, 1972, 1976; Burke, 1976). Basic to the political tribal system were the *ingurramen* (marabouts), members of holy lineages, who did not belong to the tribal groupings, mediated in disputes, and applied tribal customs (such as the election of chiefs by rotation). They were endowed with *baraka* (divine grace), pacific, and their person was safe (Gellner, 1969, 1972).

The mosaic of Berber society, aside from these holy outsiders, comprised another network of communities of pacific and secure outsiders – the Jews – who rendered vital economic services, yet were powerless due to their lower status, which was manifest in their humble behavior. Therefore services rendered by Jews or trading with them was not socially committing, which would not have been the case had the interaction been with a Berber from another patronymic group, and that might have been degrading for one party. Lack of commitment was especially significant in partnerships with Jews, who put up the capital in farming and herding enterprises; but also in day-to-day trading with the Jewish merchant who extended credit to his clients. This vital interaction with the Berbers placed the Jewish merchants and traders in Ait Bou Oulli, in an advantageous position evidenced, *inter alia*, by their superior station in the Jewish community.

Hart's study of Jews shortly before immigration to Israel, and his recording of comments made by Berbers after the mass departure of Jews, succinctly encapsulate some features of Jewish existence observed by the other side:

> The keynote of Jewish behavior was that of safety in humility; conversely, for a powerful man to have 'his own' Jew was considered a sign of prestige. Because the Jews stood entirely outside the political system, and because their occupational services were much in demand, many informants said that to kill or even to molest a Jew was an infinitely worse offense than to kill a fellow tribesman. (Hart, 1976: 280)

Although these two sets of records, my own from Israel and Hart's from Morocco, do not originate with the same group of Jews and their Berber neighbors, they reflect complementary interpretations of some elements of Jewish existence in Morocco. As it appears from the Romemites' experience, the Jewish craftsman, peddler and merchant could live in his community or travel with little risk involved, and he was welcomed, though he did not enjoy an honored position, in nearby or remote Berber settlements.[12]

The course of peaceful coexistence might have been intermittently interrupted, but the Jew could normally rely on the protection of his patron, employer, or client, and draw some sense of security from the local cultural code which specified rules to safeguard the weak and helpless, such as women and Jews. This position of the Jew, comprising both the inferior status and circumstantial advantages, opened the doors of Berber homes and tribal and sub-tribal territorial borders to the itinerant Jew. 'For us, the craftsmen, there were no borders,' remarked to me one of Amran's former smiths, and thus elucidated the situation he experienced in Morocco.

CONCLUDING NOTE

We started our discussion by presenting a polarity of opinions about the position of Moroccan Jewry. Our case does not fully support either of these viewpoints. It seems as if both Rosen and Stillman described a 'true' but partial reality of the Jewish situation. That perception of reality is not modified by the contradictions of daily existence which some scholars might view as 'non-data,' as, for example, the intervals of economic and social interaction and cooperation between a subordinate ethnic minority and a dominant majority. Accordingly, Rosen and Stillman have drawn clear-cut conclusions; the harmonious perspective versus the conflict perspective in Jewish–Muslim relationships. I have suggested some additional situational and structural factors which affected the position of Jews and their relationships with their neighbors. I emphasized the interpretative element embedded in the Romemites' perception of their experience in Morocco. Their perception and interpretations yield a complex image of Jewish–Muslim interaction evidenced by their paradoxical accounts of harmony and conflict. These presentations are genuine expressions of the existential experience of Atlas Mountains Jews, which cannot be dismissed because of apparent inconsistency. Thus, while most scholars have tried to formulate consistent paradigms, representative of at least, some geographical areas, or certain historical periods, such consistent paradigms may be nonexistent. Also certain rabbinical texts, or other forms of extant records, sometimes arouse disagreement when used as sole basis for interpretation. The verbal communications which I collected about life in Morocco offer a kind of data which is rarely recorded. That type of material, if it survives at all, is with the passage of time absorbed into such forms of discourse as folklore and folk tales.

Notes

The study was supported by the Bernstein Israeli Research Trust, through the Department of Social Anthropology of Manchester University, directed by the late Professor Max Gluckman, and by a grant from the Faculty of Social Sciences at Tel-Aviv University. I am grateful to S. Deshen for his comments and to A. Sommer who helped with the editing.

1. Pseudonyms are given to the village in Israel and to the community in Morocco in order to disguise the identity of the people studied, a standard procedure in anthropological monographs.
2. To avoid identification of the people studied, I used in previous publications the name Etgor instead of Ait Bou Oulli. The district of Ait Bou Oulli comprised several Jewish communities.
3. See my works on kinship, family and religion among Jews in the Atlas Mountains, Shokeid, 1971/1985; Deshen and Shokeid, 1974.
4. Community life in Romema is very much influenced by the conflict and competition between the former traders and the rest of the community (see particularly Shokeid, 1971/1985: 23–8, 101–64; Deshen and Shokeid, 1974: 64–94; Shokeid, 1976).
5. Flamand (1959: 86) also reports that a few families owned land at Ait Bou Oulli.
6. See Gellner, 1972 and Hart, 1972 who describe this system of annual election of tribal chiefs.
7. See also Hart's evidence on the particular relationships between the Berber landlord and his Jewish tenant (1976: 280).

8   See also Flamand who reports on Berbers drinking in the homes of Jews (1959: 99).
9   See my reference to that manner of speech in Romema (1971: 134–5).
10 In rural settlements, Jewish Agency representatives were responsible in many matters related to farming, housing, and financial credit.
11 This comparison is obviously limited by the particular influence of Iranian Shi'ism on the position of Jews (Loeb, ch. 18).
12 The Jews, as other members of pacific groups (of lower or higher status), were exempt from payment of *dhazttat*, the protection fee a traveller paid to go from his own tribe into the territory of another (see Hart, 1976: 303–4).

References

Burke, E. (1976) *Prelude to Protectorate in Morocco* (Chicago: University of Chicago Press).

Chouraqui, A.C. (1968) *Between East and West* (Philadelphia: Jewish Publication Society).

Deshen, S. and Shokeid, M. (1974) *The Predicament of Homecoming: Cultural and Social Life of North African Immigrants in Israel* (Ithaca, NY: Cornell University Press).

Flamand, P. (1959) *Diaspora en Terre d'Islam: Les Communautés Israelites du Sud Marocain* (Casablanca: Presses des Imprimeries Reunies).

Geertz, C. (1973) *The Interpretation of Cultures* (New York: Basic Books).

Gellner, E. (1969) *Saints of the Atlas* (London: Weidenfeld and Nicolson).

Gellner, E. (1972) 'Political and Religious Organization of the Berbers of the Central High Atlas,' in E. Gellner and C. Micaud (eds), *Arabs and Berbers* (Lexington: Heath) 59–66.

Hart, D.M. (1972) 'The Tribe in Modern Morocco,' in E. Gellner and C. Micaud (eds), *Arabs and Berbers* (Lexington: Heath) 25–58.

Hart, D.M. (1976) *The Aith Waryushun of the Moroccan Rif: An Ethnography and History* (Texas: University of Arizona Press).

Loeb, L.D. (1976/reprinted below) 'Dhimmi Status and Jewish Roles in Iranian Society,' *Ethnic Groups* 1: 89–105.

Montagne, R. (1930) *Les Berberes et le makhzen dans le sud du Maroc: Essai sur la transformation politique des Berberes sedentaires* (Paris: Felix Alcan).

Shokeid, M. (1971/1985) *The Dual Heritage: Immigrants from the Atlas Mountains in an Israeli Village*. Manchester: Manchester University Press (augmented edition, Transaction Books).

Shokeid, M. (1976) 'Conviviality Versus Strife: Peacemaking at Parties Among Atlas Mountain Immigrants in Israel,' *Political Anthropology* 1: 101–21.

Slouschz, N. (1927) *Travels in North Africa* (Philadelphia: Jewish Publication Society).

Thomson, J. (1889) *Travels in the Atlas and Southern Morocco* (London: George Philip).

Willner, D. (1969) *Nation Building and Community in Israel* (Princeton: Princeton University Press).

9 Saddiq and Marabout in Morocco
Norman A. Stillman

The chapter by Norman Stillman, Shusterman-Josey Professor of History at the University of Oklahoma, contributes to the study of Middle Eastern Jewry at two different levels. One is that of Moroccan Jewish ethnography where the chapter treats religious leadership, and describes its unique characteristics. In Jewish Morocco marabout-type leadership, and the associated rituals, are late developments, probably not much earlier than the mid-nineteenth century. Later they gained much saliency, and in latter-day Israel attained major dimensions. In precolonial Morocco, although the potential was there, the phenomenon was far less important. This brief but pithy chapter is commensurate with that situation. At another, and implicit, level the chapter addresses a major problem in the comparative study of Jewish societies. As Stephen Sharot argued earlier in his contribution, Jewish cultures are variously informed, sometimes molded, by the surrounding non-Jewish majority. But beyond this general point, on which historians are generally agreed, there are open questions about the nature and details of this influence, which Sharot indicates, but does not explore. In the present study Stillman compares nuances of difference within a particular cultural trait, that is common to Jews and to non-Jews in the same region. This comparison highlights the limits of Jewish acculturation.

'Saddiqim do not die, they keep on living', remarked to me an informant in Sefrou several years ago, when there was still a Jewish community left in that Moroccan town, just south of Fez.[1] The remark is typical, and reflects the profound reverence in which holy men, *saddi'im* in Judaeo-Arabic,[2] are held even after their demise. The same might just as well have been said by a Moroccan Muslim,[3] with the only difference being the word used for 'saint'. The Muslim would have said *wali* ('friend of God') *sālih* ('pure one'), *siyyid* ('lord' – Cl. Ar. *sayyid*), or *mrābit* ('a man bound to God' – Cl. Ar. *murābit*). From the latter is derived the Europeanized form of the word 'marabout'.[4]

Source: Slightly abbreviated version of a paper in I. Ben Ami (ed.) (1982), *The Sephardic and Oriental Jewish Heritage* (Jerusalem: Magnes Press) 1982, 489–500.

The veneration of holy men, both living and dead, is a well-known hallmark of popular religion among Jews and Muslims in Morocco and, indeed, throughout North Africa. The phenomenon has been noted by most observers of the Maghrebi cultural scene for several hundred years – at least as far back as Germain Mouette in the seventeenth century.[5] There is a considerable body of ethnographic and anthropological literature on North African Muslim hagiolatry. Much of this work is descriptive and is devoted to the folklore and cultic practices associated with saints' shrines or with Muslim brotherhoods (*turuq, tariqāt,* or *tawā'if*). There is much less scholarly literature on the Jewish veneration of holy men, although most of the ethnographic work on Moroccan Jews gives it at least a passing mention.[6] In most of the literature dealing with Muslim or Jewish hagiolatry, the approach to the phenomenon is strikingly similar. So too is the analysis when there is any at all. A strong distinction is usually made between official, higher, monotheistic religion and the popular, primitive, hagiolatric religion, which in its most debased form – as viewed by this kind of scholarship – becomes outright anthropolatry.[7]

There is also a great deal of emphasis in the ethnographic literature on atavistic survivals of ancient Berber agrarian religious cults. In the introduction to his *Pèlerinages judéo musulmans du Maroc*, L. Voinot quotes E. Michaux-Bellaire on the importance of taking into account 'non seulement des survivances juives actuelles, mais aussi des survivance païennes ('not only Jewish survivals but also pagan survivals').'[8] Emile Dermenghem, in his excellent survey, *Le culte des saints dans l'Islam maghrébin*, also lays great stress upon the 'continuité du sacré' from pre-Islamic times.[9] This element of continuity is certainly the case *vis-à-vis* many saints' shrines associated with sacred trees, brooks, pools, rocks, and grottos which have been held sacred since earliest times. But such studies, as valuable as they are, do not really get to the main issue of the saints themselves in Moroccan Muslim and Jewish society, and their role, both in their lifetime and after their death. I should add here that there are a few notable exceptions, such as Jacques Berque's *Al-Yousi*, Clifford Geertz' *Islam Observed*, and Ernest Gellner's *Saints of the Atlas*.[10]

Studies of this sort do not exist for Moroccan Jewry, however, and as Issachar Ben-Ami has pointed out in his article on *Sēfer Ma'aseh Nissim*, scholars have still not dealt with the complexity of the phenomenon of hagiolatry among Moroccan Jews.[11] Furthermore, there has not been, to the best of my knowledge, any attempt to compare the Jewish and Muslim phenomena beyond cataloguing the sites of pilgrimage shared in common. Most writers seem to take for granted the essential identity of the two hagiolatries. What I should like to do in this paper is to look briefly from

the point of view of a social historian at the nature of sainthood in
Morocco as understood by Jews and Muslims, and to see to what extent
does the *saddiq* resemble the marabout – and equally important, wherein
do they differ. For we must keep in mind that although Jews and Muslims
shared much in common culturally, nevertheless, they formed two distinct
societies, interacting with one another on a variety of levels, having parallel or tangential developments, but still separate. I should like to pose the
sort of questions that Peter Brown has raised in his fascinating study on
'The Rise and Function of the Holy Man in Late Antiquity'.[12] To para-
phrase Brown, why did the *saddiq* and the marabout come to play such an
important role in Moroccan society? And what light do their activities
throw on the values and functioning of a society that was prepared to
concede to them such importance?

In order to answer these questions, and we can do so only in a most
cursory fashion here, we must turn to several sources in addition to the
ethnographical and historical material. First and foremost are the indigenous Jewish and Muslim hagiographic writings. For the Jews, this literature may be classified under various sub-genres. These include: the *Shivhē
Saddiqim* (Praises of the Saints),[13] *Ma'asē Nissim* (Miraculous Deeds),[14]
and biographical dictionaries, such as R. Joseph Ben Naïm's *Malkhē
Rabbānān*,[15] for which there does not seem to be any generic term, al-
though we may refer to works in this category as *Hayyē Saddiqim*. The
Muslim hagiographic literature is also divided into sub-genres. These in-
clude: the *Manāqib al-Sādāt* (Virtues of the Saints),[16] the *Tabaqāt Ahl al-
Tasawwuf* (Classes of the Sufis), and *Tarājim* (Biographical Dictionaries).
Two well-known Moroccan examples of the latter are 'Abd al-Haqq al-
Bādisi's *al-Maqsad al-Sharif*[17] and Muhammad al-Kittāni's *Salwat al-
Anfās*.[18] In addition to the written hagiographic literature, there are the oral
sources. During the summers of 1971 and 1972, I collected together with
my colleague-wife a considerable quantity of narrative material on saints
from both Jews and Muslims. I hope to publish some of the Judaeo-Arabic
oral texts on this subject in the near future. Recently, Dale Eickelman has
published several Moroccan oral texts dealing with Muslim saints.[19] There
are a number of other oral texts on saints, of both Jewish and Muslim
provenance, that have been published in folklore anthologies and collec-
tions of vernacular readings.[20]

Drawing upon all of these sources, then, we can begin to compare and
contrast the image and the role of saints among Jews and Muslims in
Morocco. At first glance, the respective images of the *saddiq* and the
marabout in both the oral and the written sources is quite similar. Both are
charismatic individuals who possess the powerful spiritual force known in

Moroccan Arabic as *baraka*. The work literally means 'blessing', but defies easy definition.[21] The saintly charisma is also referred to in Judaeo-Arabic as *'ināya* ('divine solicitude') and *zikhut* ('merit', Heb. *zekhūt*). This spiritual force may be used for the aid and benefit of the saint's faithful adherents; but it may also be used to mete out awesome punishments to those who offend him in even the slightest way.[22] The saint's *baraka* is most commonly manifested in acts of blessing, in spiritual guidance, and in intercession with God. This last manifestation is perhaps the most basic and universal function of a saint or holy man in any culture. That is, by his satisfying – in the words of Karl Hase – the 'need to fill the enormous gap between men and God'.[23] Thus, both the *saddiq* and the marabout fulfill the function of making the God of all the world relevant to the believer in a religious society on the individual level.

The saint's *baraka* is also shown from time to time in acts of clairvoyance. The ability to see into the unseen is a faculty that is taken for granted in certain unusual individuals – among them saints. However, it is not considered a miracle or an exclusively saintly power. Both Muslims and Jews recognized that there were gifted members of their own and of the other faith who possessed such powers. I recall that during one of our visits in Sefrou, a Jewish girl we knew went to a Muslim *shewwāfa* (a female seer) to learn whether her impending marriage would be auspicious.[24] In *Malkhē Rabbānān*, R. Khalifa b. Malka of Agadir is reported to have asked a Muslim seer to reveal the future to him. Through his own saintly insight, R. Khalifa knew that what he had been told was true.[25] Both Jews and Muslims generally made a distinction between clairvoyance which came under the category of *shur* (or magic) and genuine divine inspiration. In the Jewish literature, the distinction is quite clear. The Muslim seer in the story of R. Khalifa b. Malka is called a *mekhāshshēf*, that is, a sorcerer who practices one of the abominations of the Canaanite peoples which is strictly forbidden in Deuteronomy 18:10.[26]

The true saint usually exhibits his clairvoyance unsolicited. His knowledge of the unseen (Ar. *'ilm l-ghib*) frequently involves a complex series of events which find their resolution through him.[27] Only rarely, but spectacularly, is the saint's *baraka* demonstrated by outright miracles (Heb. *nissim*; Ar. *karāmāt* or *barāhin*). The more scholarly, orthodox literary sources in both faiths tend to report miracles sparingly. Oral sources and popular devotional works, on the other hand, relate them lavishly and with gusto.

It is with regard to miracles that we come to a primary difference between the saddiq and the marabout. Saddiqim almost never perform miraculous feats during their lifetime. The vast majority of their *nissim* are associated with their tombs: springs of water suddenly gush forth, intruders bent on desecration are struck down or are repulsed by mysterious forces.[28] By contrast, miracles are commonly attributed to living marabouts who not only can suspend the laws of nature, but can fly through the air to faraway places in an instant, spit fire, hold back the sultan and his entire army, or change himself into an animal.[29] This last faculty, which is known in Arabic as *tatawwur*, is a common attribute of Muslim saints. I have not come across any references to saddiqim undergoing a metamorphosis of this sort, although there are stories of saddiqim transforming the wicked into beasts.[30]

In Moroccan Jewish literature, the few miracles associated with saints during their lifetime are frequently not performed by them, but occur, so to speak, around them, as a mark of their blessed presence. For example, it is reported that a marvelous aroma of *etrog* (citron) diffused from the home of R. Hayyim David Serero on the Sabbath eve.[31] Or, there are stories of wild beasts becoming tame in the presence of saddiqim, such as R. Ephraim al-Anqāwa of Tlemcen or R. Elisha b. Ya'ish of Meknes.[32] The narrator of the latter story specifically mitigated the miracle by pointing out that R. Elisha recited a special prayer, whose formula had been forgotten, which was for taming wild animals.[33] In yet another tale, which tells how R. Hayyim Yosef David Azulay, also known as Rav Hida, saves Sefrou from the Mhaws tribe, the saddiq makes himself invisible. However, the narrator did not consider this to be a miracle, but rather a trick, an act of legerdemain.

There are, to be sure, no lack of miracles associated with saddiqim, but they are rarely of the spectacular variety. By far, the most common miracles attributed to them – or rather, to their intercession with God – are the granting of offspring to childless couples and the curing of persons with psychosomatic afflictions. Both of these are standard functions of saints and holy men in traditional societies (and we have only to think of the role of saints in the Roman Catholic and the Eastern Churches) and of minor deities in polytheistic cultures, prior to the advent of modern medicine and psychiatry.

The needs which cause people to turn to the saints are genuine human needs, and they are universal. People will do their utmost to have them fulfilled and will turn to whatever options are open to them. In traditional Moroccan society, the options in such cases were limited outside the realms of folk medicine and popular religion. Within these two areas, however, one might have a multiplicity of options. For example, even though an individual might have a particular patron saint, such as R. Hayyim Cohen or R. Raphael Mūsi el-Bāz, he would have no hesitation in turning to others until his petition was finally granted. The Shaykh al-Yahūd in Settat during the 1930s reported having made pilgrimages with his wife to some thirty saints' tombs before their prayers for a child were answered.[34] As one of my Sefriwi informants observed in another instance of a saint's grace, this was due to his merit and the merit of those who fear God and serve him. The fulfillment of the petition was, however, *di mūlāna* ('from the Lord').

The miraculous element, I believe, is far more subtle and is played down much more in the reality of Moroccan Jewish piety, than one might be led to believe from the descriptions in the ethnographic literature, with its strong emphasis on the exotic and the picturesque. The saddiq is venerated for his piety and learning. Any wonders that occur when he is invoked are only added proofs of his sanctity. However, his being a saddiq is not dependant upon the performance of miracles. Miracles seem to play a greater role in Muslim sainthood. Every Muslim saint is, first and foremost, a *mujāb al-du'ā'*. Yet even here, we find a qualitative distinction is made between the marabout's wonders and those performed by the prophets of old. The prophets performed *mu'jizāt*, truly 'inimitable acts', whereas the saint performs *barāhin*, 'proofs' of his sanctity, or *karāmāt* ('attestations of divine favor').

There is an element of respectful skepticism among the Muslim urban bourgeoisie with regard to the miracles of the saints, just as there is among urban Jewish males with a modicum of religious education. Neither group would go so far as to reject the notion of saints' miracles, since that would involve closing off one of the options I spoke of a moment ago, and that would not be in keeping with Maghrebi practicality. Also, as Kenneth Brown has pointed out in his trenchant study of Salé, there is the important factor of maternal influence on the child's attitude toward saints and their miracles, during the earliest years before the beginning of formal, orthodox education.[35]

The function of the living saddiq is quite different from that of the saddiq who has gone on to *ha'ōlām ha-bā* (to his 'eternal rest.') The living saddiq enjoys great prestige because of his piety and learning. His prestige and his detachment from *l-bi' u-s-sri* (literally, 'buying and selling', but more figuratively, 'daily affairs') make him an excellent mediator in disputes. His learning and his personal integrity make him an obvious advisor and counsellor in time of trouble. Many of the stories told about saddiqim concern the successful mediation of disputes. Frequently, a parent or ancestor was one of the parties involved in the controversy. As in late antiquity, we find that among the primary functions of the holy man are the resolution of tensions, the allaying of anxiety, and the controlling and delimiting of guilt within the community.³⁶ These were, to be sure, among the primary functions of the living Muslim saints in Morocco. However, in their case, there was also considerable overlap with the functions of the dead saint. This is not true of the saddiq, who was rarely a thaumaturge.

Both the saddiq and the marabout offered attractive and desirable alternatives to other forms of authority, such as the central government and its representatives or the institutionalized Jewish communal lay leadership. The government was frequently oppressive and corrupt. In many areas it was ineffectual. And outside the *Bled l-Makhzen* (the land under the direct administration of the sultan), it was almost non-existent. Unlike the government appointed *nāyeb* or *shaykh* and the *tōvē ha-'ir*, the saddiq was not a member of the tiny plutocracy which traditionally dominated the Moroccan Jewish community. If the accounts of European travelers who, admittedly, were not always unbiased observers, are to be believed, the saddiq seems much less likely to have abused his position for material gain than many a marabout.

In addition to these functional differences between the saddiq and the marabout, there were differences in the way in which Jews and Muslims expressed their attitudes toward their respective holy men, and in the way in which they conceived of the very notion of sainthood. The ideology of sainthood was much more highly developed and clearly expressed in Moroccan Islamic culture, which had inherited organized sufism from the Muslim East, but had given it a distinctive stamp of its own. The Muslim saint – in imitation of the Prophet Muhammad – was clearly defined as a *shafi'* (an intercessor) on whose behalf petitions were answered (Ar, *mujāb al-du'ā*). Among sufi saints there was a well defined hierarchy which included the *qutb, ghawth, ikhyār, ibdāl*, and *ibrār*.³⁷ The marabout's theurgic power, his *baraka*, could be passed on mechanistically from master to disciple by the former spitting into the latter's mouth, for example. It could even be imparted without the saint's consent, as when Sidi 'Ali Ben Hamdūsh drank Bū 'Abid Sharqi's vomit.³⁸

Moroccan Judaism possessed neither the refined terminology, nor the notion of hierarchy with regard to its saddiqim. Furthermore, Moroccan Jews perceived sainthood as the culmination of a rational process of piety and learning. This concept was also present in Moroccan Islam, but alongside the other mechanistic notions I have just described. Because of the lack of the mechanistic attitude toward baraka (or *'ināya*) among Jews, Moroccan saddiqim did not need to compete with one another to show who had more charisma, which is a common motif in the stories of Muslim saints.³⁹

Moroccan Jews related to their saintly figures and venerated them in a distinctively Maghrebi way. They did not express a theoretical ideology of sainthood comparable to that of the Moroccan Muslims, nor for that matter, comparable to that of the Hassidic thinkers in Eastern Europe, such as R. Jacob Joseph of Polonoye.[40] But their conception of the saddiq was deeply rooted in the classical Jewish tradition where the saddiq is given the potential for marvelous acts. As the sage Rava says in the Talmud, commenting on *Isaiah* 59:2, 'If saddiqim desired, they could create a world'.[41] That saddiqim could be considered worthy of the sort of veneration shown them by Moroccan Jews is clearly implied by R. Yohannan's remark in the same tractate, 'Saddiqim are to be considered greater than the administering angels'.[42]

References

1. For a brief sketch of the community at that time, see N.A. Stillman, 'The Sefrou Remnant,' in *Jewish Social Studies*, 35, Nos 3-4 (July–October, 1973), 255-63. For an in-depth portrait of Sefrou before the mass exodus of the early 1950s, see R. David Ovadia, *The Community of Sefrou*, 3 vols (Jerusalem, 1974–1975) [Hebrew].
2. On the Hebrew element in Moroccan Judaeo-Arabic, see Wolf Leslau, 'Hebrew Elements in the Judeo-Arabic Dialect of Fez,' *Jewish Quarterly Review* N.S. 36 (1945–1946), 61-78; also N.A. Stillman, 'Some Notes on the Judaeo-Arabic Dialect of Sefrou (Morocco),' in S. Morag, I. Ben-Ami and N.A. Stillman (eds), *Studies in Islam and Judaism, Presented to S.D. Goitein on His Eightieth Birthday*, vol. I (Jerusalem, 1981), 231-51.
3. Edward Alexander Westermarck, *Ritual and Belief in Morocco I* (Repr. New Hyde Park, New York, 1968), 159: 'Properly speaking, a saint never dies; his body is not subject to decay, he is only slumbering in his grave.'
4. See Georges Marçais, 'Ribāt', EI III, 1150-3.
5. *Histoire des conquestes de Mouley Archy etc.* (Paris, 1683), reprinted in H. de Castries (ed.), *Les sources inédites de l'histoire du Maroc: Archives et bibliothèques de France*, Deuxième Série, II (Paris, 1924), 1-201.
6. For example, J. Goulven, *Les mellahs de Rabat-Salé* (Paris, 1927), has a brief descriptive chapter 'Le culte des saints,' 91-8.
7. Thus, for example, Edmond Doutté, *Notes sur l'Islam Maghribin: Les Marabouts* (Paris, 1900) 16-27; or H. de Castries, 'Les sept patrons de Marrakech,' *Hespéris*, 4 (1924), 245-303.
8. Published in Paris, 1948, 1.
9. Published in Paris, 1954, 34-58.
10. Jacques Berque, *Al-Yousi: Problèmes de la culture marocaine au XVIIème siècle* (Paris and the Hague, 1958); Clifford Geertz, *Islam Observed* (New Haven, 1968); and Ernest Gellner, *Saints of the Atlas* (London, 1969).

11 Issachar Ben-Ami, 'Sēfer Ma'aseh Nissim,' in *Yeda' 'Am*, 17, Nos 41–2 (1974), 1. Reprinted in *idem., Le Judaïsme marocain* (Jerusalem, 1975), 199.
12 In *The Journal of Roman Studies*, 41 (1971), 80–101.
13 Concerning this genre, see Issachar Ben-Ami, *Le Judaïsme marocain*, 209–20.
14 See note 11 above; see also Issachar Ben-Ami, 'Ma'aseh Nissim R. Daniel ha-Shōmēr Ashkenazi,' in *Folklore Research Center Studies*, III (1972), 33–59, reprinted in *Le Judaïsme marocain*, 171–207.
15 Jerusalem, 1931.
16 Two Tunisian examples of this genre have been edited with French translation by Hady Roger Idris: *Manāqib d'Abū Ishāq al-Gabanyāni par Abū l-Qāsim al-Labidi et Manāqib de Muhriz b. Halaf par Abu l-Tāhir al Fārisi* (Tunis, 1959).
17 Annotated translation by Georges S. Colin, *Archives Marocaines*, 26 (1926).
18 3 vols, litho (Fez, 1316 AH).
19 Dale F. Eickelman and Bouzekri Draioui, 'Islamic Myths from Western Morocco,' in *Hespéris-Tamuda*, 14 (1973), 195–225; also D.F. Eickelman, 'Form and Composition in Islamic Myths: Four Texts from Western Morocco', *Anthropos*, 72 (1977), 447–64.
20 For example, Dov Noy, *Jewish Folktales from Morocco*, Hebrew edition (Jerusalem, 1964), English edition (Jerusalem, 1965); Louis Brunot and Elie Malka, *Textes judéo-arabes de Fès* (Rabat, 1939); Georges S. Colin, *Chrestomathie marocaine* (Paris, 1951).
21 The anthropologist Westermarck in *Ritual and Belief in Morocco*, I, takes approximately 130 pages to describe the phenomenon.
22 For some telling examples, see Vincent Crapanzano, *The Hamadsha: A Study in Moroccan Ethnopsychiatry* (Berkeley, 1973), 31 and 36; also Dermenghem, *Culte des saints*, 15–17.
23 Cited by Ignaz Goldziher, *Muslim Studies*, II (edited by S.M. Stern and translated by C.R. Barber and S.M. Stern (London, 1971), 259.
24 The *shewwāfa* told her what everyone acquainted with the girl knew – that she and her fiancé were eminently mismatched.
25 Ben Naïm, *Malkhē Rabbānān*, 80a.
26 In an earlier paper, I was somewhat hesitant to 'lay too much emphasis on the term used here to designate the Muslim seer, which may be due to no more than the literary style of R. Ben Naïm the pious editor of the collection'. However, I am now convinced that the term *mekhāshshēf* is used to differentiate clearly between the saddiq and the seer. See Norman A. Stillman, 'Muslims and Jews in Morocco: Perceptions, Images, Stereotypes,' in *Proceedings of the Seminar on Muslim–Jewish Relations in North Africa* (New York, 1975), 24.
27 See, for example, the two stories concerning the clairvoyance of R. Hayyim Pinto of Mogador in Abraham Ben 'Attār, *Sēfer Shenōt Hayyim* (Casablanca, 1958), 12–13.
28 For example, with regard to an attempted desecration of R. Amram b. Diwān's sanctuary, see the legend recounted in J. Goulven, *Les Mellahs de Rabat-Salé* (Paris, 1927), 97. See also *ibid.*, 94–5; and Dov Noy (ed.), *Moroccan Jewish Folktales* (New York, 1966), 39–40.

29 For an example of flying through the air, see Crapanzano, *Hamadsha*, 46; for metamorphosis into animal form, see Dermenghem, *Culte des saints*, 97–101, and Goldziher, *Muslim Studies*, II, 269; for holding back the sultan, see the famous encounter between Mūlāy Ismā'il and Sidi al-Hasan al-Yūsi cited by Geertz, *Islam Observed*, 33–5.
30 Noy, *Moroccan Jewish Folktales*, 131.
31 Ben Naïm, *Malkhē Rabbānān*, 36b (page number is misprinted as 35).
32 For R. Ephraim al-Anqāwa, see Nahum Slouschz, *Travels in North Africa* (Philadelphia, 1927), 324–9; for R. Elisha b. Ya'ish, see note 33 below.
33 Noy, *Moroccan Jewish Folktales*, 131, note.
34 Goulven, *Mellahs de Rabat-Salé*, 94.
35 Kenneth L. Brown, *People of Salé: Tradition and Change in a Moroccan City, 1830–1930* (Manchester, 1976), 106–7.
36 P. Brown, 'The Holy Man in Late Antiquity,' *JRS*, 41 (1971), 97. A similar point is made by Crapanzano with regard to 'Aïsha Qandisha, the powerful female spirit. See Crapanzano, *The Hamadsha*, 227–9.
37 For the literature on this hierarchy, see Goldziher, *Muslim Studies*, II, 265, note 2.; also Dermenghem, *Culte des saints*, 21.
38 Crapanzano, *Hamadsha*, 32.
39 Dermenghem, *Culte des saints*, 16.
40 For his ideology of sainthood, see S.H. Dresner, *The Zaddik: The Doctrine of the Zaddik according to the Writings of Rabbi Yaakov Yosef of Polnoy* (London, 1960).
41 BT, *Sanhedrin*, 65b.
42 BT, *Sanhendrin*, 93a.

Part III
Tunisia and Tripolitania

10 Southern Tunisian Jewry in the Early Twentieth Century
Shlomo Deshen

In this chapter focus shifts to Tunisia. Basing himself on data embedded in rabbinical sources such as religious law tracts, Shlomo Deshen traces the outlines of the structure and institutions of Jewish society in Southern Tunisia in the early twentieth century. The author describes a situation different from that of Moroccan Jewry. Southern Tunisian Jewry has a relatively peaceful history, and the last major anti-Jewish hostility occurred in the twelfth century. The general Berber population, particularly of the island of Jerba, developed in the late nineteenth century a pattern of migrant merchants who operated throughout Tunisia, and retired in their old age to their homes. In this context, the Jews entered local commerce and filled local positions. They did not engage in international commerce or in itinerant trade, roles that Jews commonly filled elsewhere. Jerban Jewry is therefore sedentary and lacking in geographic mobility. As a consequence, the local community is relatively powerful over its individual members, particularly in religious matters, because of the high visibility of individuals. Community organs are highly developed in comparison to other Jewish communities in North Africa.

Southern Tunisia is a region of semi-desert and, prior to the late nineteenth century, the general population engaged mainly in nomadic herding, fishing, and other occupations appropriate to the ecology and proximity of the sea. The Jews, by forming commercial links with groups of semi-nomadic Berbers, fitted into this set-up. Supplying the Berbers with articles of trade and craft, Jews wandered in the footsteps of their customers, and only occasionally returned to their homes (for a study of the local economy see Stone, 1974). At the end of the nineteenth century, with the encouragement

---

Source: A longer Hebrew version appeared as 'An Outline of Social Structure of the Jewish Communities in Jerba and Southern Tunisia From the End of the 19th Century Until the 1950s,' *Zion* 41 (1976): 97–108. Copyright © 1976. Reprinted by permission of the Historical Society of Israel.

of commerce by the French protectorate government, this pattern underwent radical change. In an attempt to strengthen their hold over the peripheral areas of their Tunisian domains, in the east and the south, the French established outposts from where they enforced their administration. Some of these outposts gradually developed into towns which attracted Jews engaged in the service-trades, crafts and petty commerce. On the eve of the massive migration to Israel in the 1950s, the largest Jewish communities were located on the island of Jerba (approximately 6,000 people), and on the mainland, in the nearby town of Gabès (approximately 4,000 people). Another thousand or so Jews were dispersed throughout the other communities, and the total number of Jews in the entire region of Southern Tunisia reached about 15,000. On the island of Jerba the two Jewish communities, Hara Kebira and Hara Sghira, were separate entirely Jewish towns. These were the leading communities in the area and our present knowledge is mainly based on information from there.

The island of Jerba numbered about 60,000 inhabitants at the beginning of the 1950s, a large population relative to the small size of the island, and its limited and underdeveloped economic capacities. The needs of the population had not been sufficiently provided for by the island's economy for at least one hundred years. The Berbers of Jerba overcame the natural and economic limitations of their location by exploiting the commercial opportunities that emerged from the French penetration of the region, and they developed a unique way of life. The male members of the population would spend most of their working lives in other parts of Tunisia where they would engage in trade. They would return home to their wives and families after many months of absence, and then only for short periods of a few weeks. The fact that the Jerba Berbers belonged to a rejected and ascetic Moslem sect, the Ibadie, combined with their particular way of life, ensured their success as merchants. But their neglect of their families caused the Jerba Berbers to be regarded as steeped in bad ways. Towards old age, at the end of twenty or thirty years of work away from home, the traders retired and returned to Jerba permanently. There they invested their savings in their homes and addressed themselves to undemanding tasks, such as the tending of small flocks of sheep, the income from which supplemented their savings. Although relatively large amounts of money flowed into the island, up until the 1950s it was still insufficient to enable the younger generation to explore new means of earning their living, and they were compelled, like their fathers, to start out as migrant traders.

Within this context it was the Jews who, exceptionally and unusually, formed the more settled element. While the Berbers' trading brought them far beyond the coasts of the island, the Jews restricted themselves to commerce and handicrafts, such as wool-carding, associated with the raising of sheep, which was practiced mainly by elderly now sedentary Berbers. The economy of one Jewish community, Hara Sghira, was based almost entirely on the skills associated with wool-processing. Jews also engaged in local trade, in crafts and luxury items, and this economic set-up remained stable and continued to hold within the context of generally peaceful relations between Jews and non-Jews. The economy of the other community, Hara Kebira, was more varied. In addition to the wool trade, the Jews engaged in the processing of precious metals, a skill traditionally associated with Jews in Moslem countries. The Jews were also tailors and shop-owners.

The Jerban Jewish communities were sedentary and lacked geographic mobility. On the whole, the people managed to earn their living at the local market or practiced their trades and crafts in their homes. This lack of mobility, though occasionally found in traditional Jewish communities, was particularly salient in Jerba, and was closely linked to the vitality of the religious and communal institutions of the Jews of Jerba. In many other Jewish communities people were driven to absent themselves from their homes for long periods of time and they were therefore unable to participate in communal activities on a regular basis. But the situation of Jews in Jerba was different. As a result of economic and ecologic circumstances which enabled spatial concentration, social control within the Jerban Jewish community was relatively powerful. On the whole, everyone knew about everyone else's doings. Deviants from the accepted norms were called before the *dayanim* (judges in the religious court), who might exercise their right of excommunication in order to impose obedience. This social control was further strengthened by the large number of *kohanim* (descendants of the ancient priestly caste), a fact which inspired a sense of holiness and exclusiveness in its people. The older of the two communities, Hara Sghira, was originally entirely composed of *kohanim*.

During the last generations, the island of Jerba developed into one of the most important centers of traditional Jewish learning in Northern Africa. This development was new; from medieval evidence it appears that the situation then was very different.[1] Only from the sixteenth century onwards is there occasional evidence indicating the presence of Torah scholars in Jerba, but by the end of the nineteenth century, traditional learning was flourishing. The large number of scholarly works by the sages of Jerba, both printed and hand-written, indicate intensive study. Participation in the study of the Talmud during the evenings was popular. On the Sabbath the sages gave public sermons of various kinds and levels, and also small groups met together to study. There was hardly any male social activity that was completely beyond the context of the synagogues and of traditional learning. The major other opportunity for socializing was provided by the gathering of Jews at the Moslem coffee-houses, and indeed, some complaints pertaining to the phenomenon appear in the sources. But much more saliently, in 1912 a Hebrew press was established in Jerba, which enabled increase in the publication of works written by local sages, and spread their learning to other communities.

During the first decade of this century, the French penetrated Southern Tunisia ever more effectively, and in 1905 the Paris-based philanthropic Alliance Israelite Universelle attempted to establish a modern school for the Jewish community in Jerba. The local rabbinical leaders, however, aware of the secularization potential inherent in modern educational institutions, struggled to prevent the opening of the school. Uniquely in the Mediterranean Jewish orbit, the local community prevailed in the struggle, and the first modern school was opened in Southern Tunisia only fifty years later, when the communities had already begun to disperse. Until that time traditional social institutions remained stable in the south, whereas in the north of the country processes of Westernization had long set in. Traditional life, even in the city of Tunis which, in the past, had been a famous centre in the Jewish world, began to decline. Thus, the gap between the standard of traditional learning of the Jews of the south and of the Jews of other parts of Tunisia gradually increased. Due to the demise of sages in the north, and the lowering of scholarly achievements there, the northern communities were compelled to appoint rabbis and other religious functionaries from Jerba and the south. This greatly strengthened the sense of worthiness and exclusivity among the Jews of Jerba.

In its internal structure the Jewry of Jerba was notable for its homogeneity. There was, albeit, a distinction between merchants and craftsmen, and that was reflected in the taxation system which required representatives of both strata to participate in tax assessments. The distinction does not, however, appear to have given rise to much competitive friction between the strata. In the middle of the nineteenth century, there were rabbis who engaged in trade and in the management of workshops alongside their rabbinical activities, for which latter they received no pay. Debates concerning the discharge of Torah scholars and the pious members of the honorary Burial Society from the burden of community taxes recurred during the nineteenth century. Though the *dayanim* concluded that these dignitaries be granted exemption, the community continued to question this ruling. It cannot be concluded, from the sources, whether the sages to whom these debates referred were scholars whose entire occupation was the study of Torah, or scholars who worked for their living. But the general picture that emerges of the nineteenth century is of a community wherein the stratum of sages was not clearly distinct from that of laymen. Similarly the lack of indications of conflict between merchants and craftsmen suggests that these also were not clearly distinct strata.

The majority of the synagogues in Jerba were private institutions founded by families or groups of migrants, but the local community committees exercised considerable control over the synagogues. Uniquely in Hara Sghira, no Torah scrolls were kept in any of the nine local synagogues. This practice ensured that during days on which the Torah was read, the public would be compelled to gather in one single synagogue, the Ghriba synagogue, which was considered especially holy and venerated, and located at a distance of two kilometers from the town. Underlying this unusual practice was the power of a public capable of overruling the private elements of the various neighborhood synagogues. Comparable arrangements existed in Hara Kebira. On order of the Community Committee, ten out of the 15 synagogues of that community were closed down during the High Holy Days. One aim of this ruling was financial: by the creation of large groups of worshippers, the leaders of the community caused competition for synagogue honors to increase. Honors such as reading from the Torah, or parading the scrolls in synagogue, were most cherished on the High Holy Days. The income from the auctioned honors were on these festivals ordered to be entirely devoted to the general community chest, and not to the benefit of individual synagogues, and the creation of large congregations caused prices to rise. Even those synagogues that were permitted to remain open on the High Holy Days were temporarily forced to resign their financial independence, and give their income to the community chest.

At the head of the Jerban communities stood the Community Committee and the *Beth-Din* (Court of Religious Law). The first body was responsible for the collection of internal taxes, and the majority of its income went towards social welfare, the salaries of the night watchmen, and, at a later period, the salaries of the *dayanim*. The role of the *dayan* was, as is common in Jewish tradition, and in Middle Eastern practice generally, not only that of a judge of the law. The *dayan* also had great moral and religious authority. Not only did he apply the law, but to a considerable extent also formulated rulings and legislation, and moved public opinion. Parallel with this undifferentiated scope of activities of members of the *Beth-Din*, the Community Committee was not only concerned with material and political affairs, but also saw itself responsible for general religious matters. Thus the Committee employed a man to make rounds of the shops on Friday afternoon, in order to ensure that they close their businesses on time well before the beginning of the Sabbath. Most of the income of the communities came from indirect taxation, and had its source in the imposition of a 25 per cent tax on the price of kosher meat sold locally. At the same time the Committee prohibited the import of meat that might cause evasion of payment of this tax. Direct taxes were imposed on the basis of assessments which were determined by committees composed of merchants and craftsmen. The evaluation for this tax was apparently carried out once a year, and the tax itself collected once a month.

During the twentieth century, the Community Committee and the *Beth-Din* underwent formalization. Contrary to the practice during the previous century, the Committee began to pay fixed weekly salaries to the *dayanim*. The change was justified by the notion that a *dayan* compelled to seek his living elsewhere 'risked public humiliation'. This new development was significant in that it increased social distance between *dayanim* and laymen. Parallel to the new financial arrangements, it became customary that only a member of another community and not a local sage, could be nominated a *dayan*. Thus, the *kohanim* of Hara Sghira appointed their *dayan* from among the community of Hara Kebira; while in Hara Kebira, it was customary to appoint a *dayan* from Hara Sghira. Also the Community Committee underwent formalization during this century. In the past, the institution had had no fixed title and was referred to by various terms, but during the twentieth century, the use of the hybrid Hebrew French term *Vaad Hacomité* became permanent. This combination of two equivalent terms appears frequently in the sources, and is practically the only French term used colloquially by immigrants from Jerba in Israel when referring to the institution in the past. Although the Committee acted as an independent body from the *Beth-Din*, and although it in fact appointed the *dayanim*, the Committee remained subordinate to the decisions of the *Beth-Din*. The latter adjudicated cases in which the Committee was involved in litigation with private persons. But the differentiation between the political leadership, the Community Committee, and the religious-legal leadership, was not consistent. Thus, the venerated *dayan* of the 1920s to 1940s, Rabbi Moshe Khalfon HaKohen, was nominated to head the Committee (however he declined the appointment).

Alongside the two principal administrative and legal institutions, there were many voluntary bodies within the community which dealt with various spheres of religion and welfare. The most important of these was the *Vaad Or Torah*, the Committee for the Light of Torah, or more prosaically, the Education Committee. This body extended financial support to needy Torah scholars, to enable them to devote themselves to study. The Education Committee also helped children of the poor in order that they too might study. In addition, the *Vaad Or Torah* provided pupils with books, and placed students in suitable professional positions upon the completion of their studies. By the beginning of this century, also *Or Torah* had reached a significant degree of formalization, as is apparent in the detailed formulation of its rulings. Due to its widespread activities and the considerable financial sources at its disposal, *Or Torah* became an important public focal point. This caused some friction with the Community Committee, but *Or Torah* retained the enthusiastic support of the *dayanim*. *Or Torah* relied on the activities of its individual members, each of whom was responsible for the collection of contributions from his respective synagogue. *Or Torah* reached a considerable degree of internal development, a fact reflected in its employment of a 'truancy officer' responsible for the attendance of the pupils at the various study groups.

Other institutions in Jerba shared a similar structure to *Or Torah*. The *Vaad Bikur Holim* ('Committee for Visiting the Sick') extended financial and medical aid to the sick; it too relied on contributions from the various synagogues. There were also many specific activities and roles that underwent processes of formalization at the beginning of this century. The ritual slaughterers and the circumcisers were required to obtain official qualification, which was granted by experts from among the community who had themselves been authorized by the *dayanim*. The slaughterers were required to have their knives regularly inspected, and this was done by one slaughterer in the presence of two others. Wine imported to Jerba had to be accompanied with proof of its being kosher. Such proof had to be provided by the person who had brought the consignment, but it was not accepted from the owner himself. The latter was not deemed trustworthy in this matter. In addition the person who supplied the proof had to be a Torah scholar. These regulations further illustrate the increasing formalization of communal and religious practices.

By 1920 evidence of the trend toward formalization becomes detailed. The *Beth-Din* ruled that all those engaged in the meat and wine branches must be declared officially to be men of integrity. During the same year a ruling was passed whereby ritual slaughterers had to be paid the same fee, whether or not the slaughtered animal was found to be kosher upon examination. Underlying this ruling was the attempt to ensure that decisions on this matter remained free of considerations other than those imposed by the ritual law. Official qualifications were also demanded of the *menakrim*, ritual pickers of sinews from butchered meat. In 1922 the arrangements for indirect taxation of meat were changed. Until then, the tax assessment had been carried out by the retailer at each individual sale. It was now ruled that the assessment be carried out at the wholesale stage, by an official assessor appointed by the community. Here too, as with the ruling concerning the proof of the kosherness of wine, an element of formality penetrated where, in the past, personal integrity had been held to be sufficient. Similar to this was the development in the organization of the honorary Burial Society. It will be recalled that in the past there had been a call to discharge the members of this society from community taxes. Now in addition to this, formal arrangements were introduced into the work of the society, and it was run on the basis of shifts.

There were similar changes in the sphere of rabbinic duties. In the past, the rabbis appointed by the community were versed in all aspects of ritual and did not specialize in any particular sphere. During the 1940s, however, a rabbi was appointed who specialized in ritual law concerning 'family purity,' which deals with determining the proper times for sexual relations in connection with the menstrual cycle, and the appointment was restricted to this sphere. In the context of the issue of formalization of roles, it is important to note the above-mentioned refusal of Rabbi Moshe Khalfon HaKohen to accept leadership of the Community Committee, and the opposition to the blurring of the distinction between differing roles implied in this rejection. Finally, there were attempts on the part of the *dayanim* over the last decades to resist the multiplication of prayer groups within synagogues, and to ensure that prayer in each synagogue be led by a permanent cantor, at a regular time.

Among the Jewish communities in the region there was a degree of competition, nourished by the activities surrounding the Ghriba synagogue in Hara Sghira. A special committee was responsible for the administration of that synagogue, which was the scene of a great annual pilgrimage, that brought considerable income to the Ghriba. The money was used to support needy elderlies, and also scholars who studied and prayed regularly at the Ghriba synagogue. Though the members of the Ghriba committee were inhabitants of Hara Sghira, they acted independently from their local Community Committee, and commanded the relatively large sums of money, contributed by pilgrims for the financing of the activities of their synagogue. Relations between the general Jewish authorities of Hara Sghira, the *Beth-Din* and the Community Committee, toward the Ghriba Committee, were accordingly ambivalent. While the general community aspired to control the synagogue's income and to put it to its own use, in particular for aid to the local poor, the Ghriba Committee restricted use of the funds for the development of its own institutions, for the support of scholars affiliated with the synagogue, and for the maintenance of the complex of Ghriba buildings. This aroused conflict, but at the same time the Jews of Hara Sghira and its Community Committee held the ancient synagogue in great reverence, and besides, the Ghriba Committee indirectly did bring material benefits to the community.

In spite of the tensions, the people of Hara Sghira and their leaders exerted themselves on behalf of the Ghriba Synagogue. Typically, they were apprehensive that there should be no competition between local synagogues, so that the Ghriba synagogue be paramount among them. However, the repercussions of internal Hara Sghira strains were felt on the level of the relations between Hara Sghira and Hara Kebira. The latter community, which developed at a short distance from the main market town of Jerba, was not autochthonous, as was Hara Sghira. In time, as Hara Kebira became materially established, it attracted more and more Jews from other parts. Among the arrivals was a family of distinguished *kohanim* whose scholarship was famous throughout Southern Tunisia, that claimed descent from Ezra the Scribe (of Biblical renown). In Hara Kebira the members of this family maintained a community framework of their own and did not participate in the general taxation system of Hara Kebira. In doing so they followed the pattern of arrangements that existed in Hara Sghira between the Ghriba Committee and the local Community Committee. The friction surrounding this issue continued in Hara Kebira over a number of generations. Eventually it came to an end when the general public of Hara Kebira took control over the independent body that existed in its midst, and forced its disappearance.

Strain also arose between the two communities, Hara Kebira and Hara Sghira, when members of the Hara Sghira family of *kohanim* eventually came to preside over the *Beth-Din* of Hara Kebira. The new *dayanim* criticized details of the pilgrimage customs held in the neighboring community. Indeed generally, in many communities Torah scholars over the generations used to express disapproval of the folk customs practiced at pilgrimages. But while the rabbis of Hara Sghira were inhibited from expressing such views forcefully (because of the local economic importance of the pilgrimage), the emigrant scholars, resident and prominent in the neighboring community, were now uninhibited and vocal in their criticism.

The social structure of the Jewish communities of Jerba continued to develop along the pattern outlined, until the time of the emigration. Communal institutions became increasingly formalized, and organization based on general rules replaced the former reliance on particular individuals and groups. Traditional learning and scholarship flourished and the Jews of Jerba inherited some of the prestige that was formerly linked to the center of Jewish learning in the city of Tunis. The renown of that community was traditionally expressed in the concept *ha'iyun ha'tunisi* ('Tunisian profundity'). 'Tunisian profundity' is a variant of Talmud-study methodology which was customary both in Tunis and in other communities of Tunisia, and it conceptualized the view that people held of the quality of Jewish scholarship in Tunis. In time, however, traditional Jewish scholarship in Tunis decayed, so that during the twentieth century the Jews of Southern Tunisia became the main heirs and practicers of 'Tunisian profundity.' (for further consideration of the concept see Deshen, 1975, and particularly Boyarin, 1989). The religious status and sensation of self-respect in religious matters of Southern Tunisian Jews soared as a result of this development. While previously Jerba had been a distant backwater, it now outshone the formerly glorious center of Tunis.

Alongside these developments, the Zionist Movement began to make its mark on the Jerban community, at a relatively earlier stage than in many other communities in the Middle East. Already in 1906, a work composed by a sage of Jerba expressed enthusiastic approval of the Zionist movement, and over the years there were more rabbis who lent their vocal and written support to the Zionist cause. In 1919 the *Ateret Zion* movement was established, which, during the 1940s, organized agricultural training and the learning of modern Hebrew. The membership of the movement grew to two hundred by the end of the 1940s. During these years, there were attempts by Zionist activists to encourage clandestine immigration to then Mandatory Palestine. According to all the evidence, it appears that the Zionist element in its midst did not cause conflict in the community. Indeed, one of its most enthusiastic supporters was the forementioned popular Dayan, Rabbi Moshe Khalfon HaKohen. The status of the Zionist Movement within the general structure of the community was similar to that of the other voluntary organizations, such as *Or Torah* and *Bikur Holim*, and Zionism was thus readily accepted within the traditional framework.[2]

To summarize: The Jews of the region enjoyed relatively calm and peaceful living conditions, and were able to remain sedentary and earn a reasonably comfortable living close to home. These conditions brought forth intensive and dynamic communal life. In terms of traditional Jewish society, communities such as Hara Kebira, Gabès and even Hara Sghira were relatively large, very different from the small communities composed of a few extended families that are the majority in certain other Jewish culture areas. Though the family was an important element in social organization in Jewish Southern Tunisia, and especially in the maintenance of links with a particular synagogue over generations, Southern Tunisian communities displayed conventions that went beyond family loyalties. Social organization was relatively dependent on formal written tradition and on abstract rulings, which were given over to the rabbis for interpretation.

All this is closely connected to the particular personality characteristic of Jews from Southern Tunisia. The folk morality of the Jews of the region emphasizes the values of modesty, humility, even bashfulness. According to this, it is fitting for a man to humble himself before others, and especially before rabbis. In the traditional writings of local sages, these values recur, and are recommended as motives for action or for desistance. These factors, together with the calm physical conditions, helped mould quiet and calm personalities.

Notes

1   Detailed reference to the Hebrew rabbinical sources of the statements made here and throughout the paper can be found in the original Hebrew version published in *Zion* (1976).
2   See Udovitch and Valenci (1980, 1984) for a discussion of the nature of tradition in Jerban Jewry, focusing on conditions of the 1970s.

References

Boyarin, D. (1989) *Sephardi Speculation: A Study in Methods of Talmudic Interpretation* (Hebrew) (Jerusalem: Ben-Zvi Institute).
Deshen, S. (1975) 'Ritualization of Literacy: The Works of Tunisian Scholars in Israel,' *American Ethnologist*, 2: 251–9.
Deshen, S. (1976) 'An Outline of the Social Structure of the Jewish Communities in Jerba and Southern Tunisia from the End of the 19th Century Until the 1950s,' *Zion*, 41: 97–108 (Hebrew).
Stone, R. (1974) 'Religious Ethic and the Spirit of Capitalism in Tunisia,' *International Journal of Middle Eastern Studies*, 5: 260–73.
Udovitch, A.L. and L. Valenci (1980) 'Identité et communication à Djerba,' *Annales*, nos 3–4: 764–83.
Udovitch, A.L. and L. Valenci (1984) *The Last Arab Jews: The Communities of Jerba* (New York: Harwood).

11 Communal Organization of the Jews of Tripolitania during the Late Ottoman Period
Harvey E. Goldberg

The Jews of Tripoli trace the formation of their community in modern times to the sixteenth century. Systematic information on communal organization is available from the late eighteenth century onward. In this essay, Harvey Goldberg, Professor of Anthropology at the Hebrew University of Jerusalem, outlines the traditional communal structure, and analyzes changes within the community resulting from the Ottoman reforms over the course of the nineteenth century. Communal organization reflected local traditions as well as influences from Jerba to the west and Eretz Israel to the east. Within the framework of time-honored norms and external changes, individuals and groups sought to shape communal life in accordance with their interests.

The nature of the Ottoman reign in Tripoli, which lasted from 1551 to 1911, varied throughout the period. From 1711 to 1835 the country was ruled by the Qaramanli dynasty which, while retaining nominal allegiance to the Porte, acted independently, making wars and concluding peace at its own initiative. In 1835, Tripoli was recaptured by the Ottomans and placed under direct rule. From the middle of the nineteenth century the reforms within the Empire (*Tanzimat*) began to reshape the administration of the province. These reforms also had far-reaching effects on the Jewish community (Ha-Cohen, 1978; Kahalon, 1972; Simon, 1979; Goldberg, 1990). The present paper will describe organizational aspects of the community during the late Qaramanli period and consider some of the changes in communal life that emerged in response to the nineteenth century reforms.

The Tripoli community attributed the founding of its local religious institutions, in modern times, to Rabbi Shimon Lavi, an important figure

---

Source: This chapter is an abbreviated version of a paper that appeared in *Jewish Political Studies Review* 5: 3–4 (Fall, 1993).

in the kabbalistic tradition.[1] Lavi's origin was among the Spanish Jews exiled to North Africa, and he lived in Fez for a number of years. In the mid-sixteenth century, Lavi left Morocco, heading toward Palestine, where an active community of Spanish exiles had grown. He passed through Tripoli close to the time that the city had been taken by the Turks from the Spanish. Finding a Jewish community which, through lack of contact with other Jewish centers, was both ignorant and lax in observance, Lavi decided to remain in Tripoli and help rehabilitate Jewish life (Goldberg, 1983: 97).

This brief account concerning Rabbi Lavi, reflecting the few facts known, served as a charter myth defining and legitimating the religious life of Tripoli's Jews. The story points to the influence of other Jewish communities of the Maghreb on Tripoli, and it is noteworthy that a parallel tradition concerning Lavi exists among the Jews of Jerba (Udovitch and Valensi, 1984: 16). The story also indicates the centrality of kabbala as an expression of piety, and underlines the orientation toward ultimate redemption in the Land of Israel shared with all Jews. In addition, as will be shown, orientations both west, to Jerba, and east, to Eretz Israel, were sources of influence in the communal life of Tripoli's Jews.

Very little information on the Jewish community is available from the time of Rabbi Lavi until the late eighteenth century. There are echoes of a reaction to Sabbatean propaganda in the seventeenth century, from which Hirschberg (1981: 163ff.) infers that the Jewish community was significant enough in size and organization to respond to the issue. Hazan's study (1989) of the poet Musa Bujnah has shown that one must assume the existence of an active Jewish community at the time. In the mid-eighteenth century, Rabbi Mas'ud Hai Raqah of Izmir, the author of a commentary to Maimonides' *Yad Hazakah*, took up residence in the city, becoming its rabbinic leader as well as the founder of a line of rabbis. It is only from the latter part of that century that there is some continuity of documents providing a consistent picture and glimpse into the organization of the Jewish community (Slouschz, 1908; Hirschberg, 1981; Goldberg, 1987).

From the point of view of the Qaramanli rulers, the Jewish community was headed by an official called the *qaid*. This position enabled the government to place its tax-collecting burden on the shoulders of one man. Much of Jewish communal life revolved around raising funds, both for the external demands of the government and for internal needs (such as provision of charity to the poor, the payment of teachers and ritual functionaries). The ad hoc nature of meeting these needs was striking. As has been discussed for Morocco (Bar-Asher, 1981; Deshen, 1989), the contingencies of collective life were met by an intricate meshing of individual leadership and communal initiatives, in which tradition and rabbinic authority were one set of factors, but wealth and closeness to the authorities were also of central importance. The Tripolitanian Jewish *qaid*, for the time of his appointment, was probably the most preeminent of a set of individuals within the Jewish community who had access to the court. His duties probably were carried out in an irregular manner. Tully (1957: 135), for example, mentions that the *qaid* of the Jews left the town in order to avoid the plague (see below). Occupancy of the position seems to have changed with relative frequency, for it could mean a financial drain on its holder and even bring mortal danger, as well as hold the promise of great benefit.

Most of the available documents (about a dozen) from the late eighteenth and early nineteenth centuries relate to matters of taxation. Some of the taxes served to pay levies imposed by the Muslim authorities, and others were for the purpose of internal communal affairs. In the latter category was a tax of 3 per mil placed upon merchandise imported from abroad or outside the region. Exempt from the tax were several towns to the west of Tripoli which were considered to be part of the province. The first version of this *haskama* (communal ruling) dates from the mid-eighteenth century. It was reconfirmed 18 years later, and again in 1844 (Goldberg, 1987: 172). While the tax clearly was aimed at active merchants only, others affected the Jewish community more widely. One way of raising funds for internal needs was for communal leaders to 'farm out' the right to tax an economic activity central to the Jewish community. This was done both with regard to slaughtering for the purpose of meat and to the production of alcoholic drinks (probably arak). Jews could openly engage in this activity in contradistinction to Muslims. After the Ottoman takeover, the government created a monopoly over the manufacture of arak, and farmed out the right to produce it to a member of the Jewish community (Goldberg, 1987: 174–5).

With regard to the set tax paid to the Muslim authorities, the community would appoint three committees, each consisting of people from a variety of occupations. Every committee would assess the amount to be paid by each family in town, and these assessments would be passed on to the communal leaders. In case of differences between the various assessments, the average of the three assessments would be taken. One source indicates that the following categories of people were exempt from the tax: members of the burial society; *talmidei hakhamim* (sages); beggars; and 'guests' (Goldberg, 1987: 172–3).

The first category may refer to all those who were involved in caring for the dead, including those who sat at the side of a seriously ill person, those who washed the body, and those who were always available, on demand, to bury a corpse. Being available at a moment's notice to engage in these activities meant ignoring one's livelihood. It also should be noted that from 1784–6 Tripoli suffered a severe plague which, according to one report, devastated half the Jewish population. At that time, the government placed an additional tax on Jews for every burial. The same report claims that many Jews sought to avoid this tax by burying the dead inside their homes. This may also explain the large number of people listed as exempt from taxes because of their activities in the burial society (Goldberg, 1987: 174).

Several documents indicate a process of negotiation between individuals and the community leadership over the assessment placed on them.[2] The existence of *haskamot* and unwritten traditions does not imply that individuals always accepted these decrees unquestionably. In fact the periodic reaffirmation of some of the *haskamot* suggests the opposite: that people often sought ways to manipulate the rules to their benefit. This accords with the negotiated aspect of the social structure, emphasized by students of both the Jewish (Deshen, 1989) and non-Jewish (Rosen, 1984) segments of Maghreb society. While some communal rulings concerned straightforward fiscal matters, others carried with them the weight of tradition tied to central social and religious values. Among these were rulings in the realm of inheritance law. One such ruling stipulated that when a woman died childless, her husband would not inherit from her, but her property would return to her father's house. This ordinance was first agreed upon in 1712, reconfirmed in 1783, and was still in force in the mid-nineteenth century (Goldberg, 1987: 176–7).

The degree of control exercised by the Jewish community over its members was partially rooted in the fact that Muslim rule accorded power to the Jewish community in many internal matters. The strength of these arrangements is emphasized by the fact that there were aspects of rabbinic law that had an impact on the affairs of Muslims. The clearest example is found in the laws concerning the leasing of property within the Jewish quarters. While only Jews lived in these quarters, the land on which the houses stood often was owned by Muslims. The principle of *hazakah* gave individual Jews the right to lease property permanently from non-Jews. Other Jews were not allowed to rent that property without paying the holder of the *hazakah*, even if they could outbid the amount of rent being paid the Muslim owner.

In 1835 the Ottoman Empire established direct rule over Libya, and throughout the remainder of the nineteenth century and the beginning of the twentieth took steps to introduce reforms there, parallel to modernizing efforts elsewhere in the Empire (Anderson, 1986). This involved a change in the civil status of the Jews so that they became, in principle, subjects of the empire equal to all other subjects. These changes had an impact on communal organization in a number of spheres, and they emerged over a long period of time, within which several steps are notable.

In the city of Tripoli, changes in the administration of justice were evident a decade after the Ottoman takeover. The *wali* (governor) Mehmed Emin Pasha (1842–7), appointed Rabbi Ya'akov Mimun as head of the Jewish community, and also assigned him a seat in the local court. This was a clear shift from the previous situation in which Jewish communal life was formally separate from that of the Muslims. Mimun's chair in the court was placed to the side of the other magistrates at first.[3] In 1846, as a result of his contribution to the court, a request was sent to Istanbul, to enable Mimun to participate in judicial deliberations on an equal footing with the other justices. An affirmative reply was received in 1847, but by that time Mimun had died. Nevertheless, the precedent of Jewish participation in a system of justice, pertaining to all the citizens, was established.

Under the rule of Mahmud Nedim Pasha (1860–7), the court was reorganized in accordance with the Ottoman Provincial Reform Law, and separate courts – criminal, penal, and commercial – were established. Jewish magistrates were appointed to each, receiving salaries from the government. The pasha no longer sat in the court, as had been the practice during the Qaramanli period, or even during the time of Rabbi Mimun. The separation of executive from judicial power represented a further step in the demarcation of a domain of civil law, common to all citizens of the empire, distinct from the realm of family and personal status law. With regard to the latter, each religious community (*millet*) was governed by its own laws and ordained officials. The new arrangements limited the sphere in which rabbinic rulings could be made with government backing, and formalized the position of religious authority.

The new situation had a complex series of effects on the rabbinic courts and their authority. In general, the rabbinic court was weakened. In the realms of commercial law and internal taxation, it retained jurisdiction only insofar as Jews voluntarily continued to submit to its rule. For example, in early nineteenth century Tripoli, the holder of a *hazakah* right received about twice as much as he paid to the Muslim owner. At the same time, communal ordinances (based on rabbinic precedents) could prevent *hazakah* holders from abusing their privileges (HaCohen, 1978: 222). When the population of the Jewish quarter grew and prices for housing rose, community leaders prevented the amounts paid to the *hazakah* holders from becoming too high. By the third quarter of the century the payment to holders of *hazakah* rights had become a matter of voluntarily accepted custom, which some had begun to ignore (HaCohen, 1978: 222, note 58). A similar process is evident with regard to internal taxation. The tax on the imports of Jewish merchants was reconfirmed in the mid-nineteenth century, but the amount accruing to the community from this tax waned. An attempt to revive communal discipline in the matter in 1912, after the Italian takeover, yielded no results (HaCohen, 1978: 240–1, note 63).

Attempts were also made to reform outdated features of the rabbinic court. Traditionally, there had been a division of intellectual labor in the study of rabbinic sources. The learned of the community were divided into scholars of the Talmud (the theoretical source of rabbinic law) and judges responsible for practical decisions in court.[4] Only the latter would study the literature of the *poskim*, codes which contained concrete judgments (HaCohen, 1978: 257). Within the court there existed the institution of *mursheh* or 'licensee', who in principle could help argue the case of a litigant on the basis of the codes. In fact, however, these licensees never opposed the judges. In the 1880s, a litigant challenged this system by bringing to court a scholar, acting as licensee, capable of challenging the judges. This trend continued, becoming an embarrassment to the court. Mordecai Ha-Cohen (see note 3) suggested that new arrangements should be put into effect, whereby both plaintiff and defendant would be provided with a learned licensee to argue on their behalf, but the practice was not initiated in his day.

Commenting on the overall developments, HaCohen chided the judges of his generation. He criticized their delaying tactics and unwillingness to reach clear and quick decisions, even in cases of personal status which were still explicitly in their jurisdiction. He saw the situation as reflecting the moral fiber of the judges in his day. These men, however, undoubtedly were reacting to the ongoing erosion of their position. They were therefore reluctant to make unequivocal pronouncements, a tactic which further undermined their status and prestige.

An ancient practice, enforced in Tripoli throughout the nineteenth century, provided that payment be made to the judges by the winning litigant. This practice, in fact, was explicitly prohibited in the *Shulhan Arukh*. In the late nineteenth century, pressure grew to change the local practice so that rabbinic judges would receive a salary from community funds. But actual reform in the matter took place only after the Italian conquest (HaCohen, 1978: 255ff.; De Felice, 1985: 37; Khalfon, 1986: 166–8).

At the same time that the government circumscribed the spheres in which rabbinic decisions were binding, its appointment of religious officials also was part of an attempt to maintain power over its Jewish subjects. From that point of view, it reinforced rabbinic authority when it appeared to be in the interest of the rulers of Libya, to support traditionalist claims within the Jewish community, in the face of European cultural currents and political influence. During the days of Rabbi Ya'akov Mimun, we find the pasha upholding a rabbinic ruling applied to a foreign Jew, who was 'freer' in his behavior than generally accepted by local social and religious norms. Later under the Ottoman reforms, tactics took a different turn for governors, who attempted to promote social change and enlist rabbinic support for their program. After having instituted the post of *hakham bashi* (chief rabbi) of the empire (Lewis, 1984: 174–5), the Ottomans appointed, in 1874, a *hakham bashi* of Tripoli, Rabbi Eliahu Bechor Hazzan (Hirschberg, 1981: 176, 181ff.). Rabbi Hazzan was familiar with Jewish communities and general cultural currents in the Mediterranean world. His modernizing orientation was evident in the realm of education, when he sought to introduce the teaching of Italian as part of the standard education of Jewish boys.

This educational effort was very likely linked to an administrative reform instituted by Hazzan. He decreed that the right to tax the slaughtering of kosher meat be farmed out on a yearly basis (HaCohen, 1978: 242). He may have hoped that the income derived therefrom would be used to finance the new school he was planning. This was a major source of income for the support of the Alliance Israélite Universelle school soon to be established in Tunis, where Hazzan had spent some time before his appointment to Tripoli. There were many who were in favor of Hazzan's educational effort, but there also was an opposing conservative element in the community, which claimed that European languages opened the door to the rejection of religion. The school Hazzan planned never materialized.

The split between the conservative reaction of local religious figures, and the official rabbinic position promoted by the Turkish authorities, highlights another characteristic of religious leadership in Tripoli. While during the Qaramanli regime rabbinic leaders were usually local scholars, who were intertwined by family ties with the influential notables, under the Ottomans the trend became clear to appoint rabbinic officials who were somewhat 'outside' and probably 'above' the local religious milieu. This was the case with regard to Hazzan and the chief rabbis appointed after him (Hirschberg, 1981: 183; Simon, 1979). But even a figure like Abraham Hai Adadi, who served as *av beit din* (head of the rabbinic court) in Tripoli in the 1850s, may be considered somewhat of an outsider. Though Adadi was a native of Tripoli, much of his life and the better part of his rabbinic training took place elsewhere (Adadi, 1976: 5–10; Kahalon, 1969).

These appointees, therefore, only represented one level of religious guidance, and there were other, more localized, bases of religious legitimacy.

The Jews of Libya saw themselves as part of the larger Jewish world, but they also had a keen sense of the legitimacy of their own practices and customary forms. They shared a general cultural background with other Maghreb communities, but there were some features which gave Libyan Jewry a distinctive character. The community attributed the founding of its local institutions to Rabbi Shimon Lavi. On the eve of *Yom Kippur*, it was customary for the Jews of Tripoli to recite a memorial prayer listing the names of many of the judges who had been appointed to the *beit din* from the days of Rabbi Lavi to their own day.[5]

The influence of religion in Jewish life was not solely a matter of rabbinic courts. In addition to the authority vested in official levels of leadership represented by rabbis, there also existed local tradition. It consisted of a set of practices viewed as binding and hallowed by years of observance, despite the fact that they may not have been firmly anchored in rabbinic literature. These two 'levels of tradition', as diagnosed by an outside observer, were not conceptually distinct in the eyes of the Jews of Tripoli; they certainly would have resisted any notion that their own praxis diverged from the main norms of Jewish tradition. Rather, the distinction applies to a tendency to keep to familiar ways which had been handed down from one generation to another in communal contexts. This implied that it was not necessary to toe the line with exactitude concerning rules found in rabbinic texts, as these might be pointed to from time to time, even by a scholar of recognized learning and prestige.

From this point of view, calling the local court 'rabbinic' may be misleading. Even though judgments were in principle based on legal rules which evolved in the decisions and writings of rabbis over the generations, those sitting in the courts were experienced and respected members of the community, who were often more versed in local precedent and tradition than in the scholarly tomes of Jewish law codes. HaCohen complained that when the courts handed down decisions, they did not cite the sources upon which their judgment was based. On at least one occasion Rabbi Hazzan was vexed by judgments of the court which flew in the face of accepted rules (HaCohen, 1978: 257), and Adadi, before him, also found himself differing with local practice at times (Kahalon, 1969: 19). HaCohen described a case concerning himself in which he, as a licensee, demonstrated that a decision the judges had taken was at odds with an authoritative written opinion. He was then roundly berated for attempting to intervene in the local judicial process. The judges seemed to act both in terms of their knowledge of binding rules, and a sense of the need for compromise.

While the members of the court would not make an explicit claim to supersede the authority of the texts, they were convinced that their own practice was equally based on learning opinion (HaCohen, 1978: 255–6, 258ff.).

Moreover, the local rabbis' strength, as representatives of a textually-based religious perspective, was attenuated by the fact that, traditionally, they did not have a base autonomous from that of the wealthy notables with ties to the Muslim government (HaCohen, 1978: 148, 266). The attitudes and conduct of this latter class of individuals in various realms, including religion, had an influence on the wider community which rivaled that of formal rabbinic decision.

Yet another aspect of the local nature of religious judicial practices was that, in some matters, there was an overlap between rabbinic law and Muslim jural tradition. The account concerning Rabbi Ya'akov Mimun (above) indicates, that the legal thinking for a decision that Rabbi Mimun took from rabbinic codes was accepted by the court headed by the Ottoman pasha. Mordecai HaCohen himself was familiar with Muslim law, and served as a licensee to individuals who had to appear in the Muslim courts as well as in the Jewish legal forum. It is likely that the well-to-do community elite was familiar with aspects of Muslim law, as commercial activities with Muslims, over the years, including involvement in cases brought to Muslim courts, would have resulted in a common fund of legal-economic understandings. This points to the existence of a kind of 'customary law', not radically different from the norms found in rabbinic (or Muslim) legal tradition, but nevertheless carrying some weight as a significant tradition in its own right (HaCohen, 1978: 149ff., 260, 269).

This sense of local tradition did not make the Jews of Tripoli impervious to external influences. Above, it was suggested that they saw themselves linked to the Jewish world both to the West and to the East. The closest cultural cousins of the Jews of Tripolitania were the communities of Jerba and Southern Tunisia, and there were many contacts between the two groups. In 1832, before the Ottoman takeover, many Tripolitan Jews fled the city during the civil war that was raging among competing members of the Qaramanli family, and sought refuge in Jerba. As a result of this contact, new forms of communal taxation and organization were instituted upon their return to Tripoli, including some of the practices already cited (HaCohen, 1978: 148–9).

Jerba emerged as an active center of rabbinic learning, and in the late nineteenth century a number of rabbis trained there took posts as teachers and religious leaders in the small Jewish communities of the Libyan hinterland (HaCohen, 1978: 148–9; Udovitch and Valensi, 1984: 86ff.;

Slouschz, 1927: 262).[6] These and earlier contacts created an overlapping liturgical culture in which many special features were shared by the Jews of Jerba and those of Tripoli. The Jews of Tripoli were aware of a religious affinity to the Jews of Jerba, and this awareness was shared by the Jerbans as well (Udovitch and Valensi, 1984: 16). Jerba succeeded in resisting the penetration of external influences, and it may be that as the status of Tripolitanian rabbis weakened throughout the nineteenth century, Jerba was more and more perceived as a center of religious inspiration and authority. While a traditionalist orientation existed among the Jews of Tripoli it never became, as in Jerba, a highly self-conscious principle and mark of communal identification. Rather, along with the attachment to their own traditions, Tripolitanian Jewish leaders seemed prepared to incorporate religious notions from a variety of directions, including Jerba but not exclusively from there.

The other major source of rabbinic influence which had an impact on matters of communal organization in Tripoli was Eretz Israel (Goldberg, 1985). As in Jewish communities throughout the world, the arrival of *shlihim* (rabbinic emissaries, sing. *shaliah*) representing religious/charitable institutions in one of the four 'holy cities' was a regular form of contact between the Jews of Tripoli and the Land of Israel. These emissaries would travel to the main urban centers to collect funds, and would also reach small outlying communities. The emissaries worked to regularize the collection and transfer of funds to the institutions in Eretz Israel. This was based on ancient religious values and demanded communal attention. In 1869 an emissary met a refusal to contribute, based on a communal ordinance allowing contributions only once in five years (Ya'ari, 1977: 182). In a document cited by Raccah (1948), a *shaliah* from Jerusalem in the 1870s established a *takkanah* appointing Rabbi Zion Raqah as responsible for all the Eretz Israel funds, and set the percentages due to each community (40 per cent to Jerusalem, and 20 per cent to each of the other three towns, Hebron, Tiberias, and Safed).

Aside from the collection of funds, *shlihim* engaged in activities which contributed to the spiritual life of the community. They might be consulted on matters of ritual practice, or asked to write an authorization for the publication of a book by a local scholar. In one case cited by Ya'ari (1977: 734), a *shaliah*, himself of Tripolitanian origin, suggested to Abraham Adadi that he send a responsum of his to rabbis in Eretz Israel for their reaction. The emissaries were treated with especially great honor in the small communities, where they were a visible manifestation of a link to the spiritual center of Judaism, despite the remoteness of these places from institutions of learning and Torah. Adadi (1865: 62a) mentions a *shaliah* who passed through the region in his day, and acted in the small towns as a judge with regard to civil matters regulated by religious law. Slouschz (1927: 96–103) came across a *shaliah* in his travels in 1906, and described the enthusiasm and honor with which he was received in the small community of Khoms.

At the same time, the arrival of a *shaliah* could be problematic. When two emissaries arrived in Tripoli in the same year, the second was not permitted to collect funds. The community had adopted a *takkanah* that emissaries would be accepted once every several years (Ya'ari, 1977: 182). One *shaliah*, Rabbi Siqli Hakohen, on a visit to the small community of Misurata, describes how his appearance caused people to flee to their homes, instead of his receiving the normal enthusiastic welcome (Ben-Zvi, 1964).

From the last decade of the eighteenth century, we begin to get a fuller picture of the internal structure of the community, and this includes the activity of *shlihim*. Rabbi A. Khalfon, one of the communal leaders at that time, entered into his ledger a record of the arrival of *shlihim* (Raccah, 1948), and the arrival of no less than seven emissaries during that decade is noted. The visits of emissaries continued throughout the nineteenth century. To survey this activity we have summarized from Ya'ari's work (1977) the material which relates to Tripoli. During the years 1800 to 1909 at least 27 *shlihim* were sent from Eretz Israel to Tripoli. This, on the average, represents one visit every four years, but the visits were not spread out evenly in time. Concentration of visits appears in two separate decades, the 1850s (six emissaries) and the 1870s (seven emissaries). It is only possible to speculate what may be associated with this concentration. In the 1850s, the Ottomans completed their pacification of the whole of Tripolitania, and in the 1870s they appointed the first chief rabbi. Both of these are developments which would seem to encourage more active institutional life within the Jewish community.

Several emissaries from Eretz Israel eventually became spiritual leaders of the community. This was the case of Rabbi M. Raqah in the middle of the eighteenth century, and of Rabbi A.H. Adadi (who in fact was born in Tripoli) in the nineteenth century (Adadi, 1976/1849). The first rabbi to fill the newly created Ottoman office of *hakham bashi*, Eliahu Bechor Hazzan, assumed the post in 1874, at the end of a mission as a *shaliah* in North Africa (HaCohen, 1978: 147, 168).

The prestige attached to religious leaders from Eretz Israel did not mean that the community automatically fell in line with their expectations. We have already mentioned the differences between R. Hazzan and local leaders over the opening of a new school which planned to teach Italian. In 1875, various rabbinic leaders of the Tripoli community wrote to the chief rabbi in Eretz Israel seeking to enlist his aid in their opposition to the school. Hazzan in turn presented his own views, and called upon many rabbinic leaders throughout the Mediterranean, all of whom sent messages supporting his stand.[7] Like other elements in the tradition, the religious aura of Eretz Israel could be situationally mobilized to strengthen one's position.

During the course of the nineteenth century, Jewish communal life in Tripoli underwent significant change. In addition to the formal reorganization discussed, there were internal and external developments which provided new challenges. The Jewish population of Tripoli grew, from about one thousand families in 1853 to well over 10,000 people at the time of the Italian conquest. It appears that the number of voluntary charitable organizations began to grow during this period. One noticeable development was a women's organization which collected funds for caring for the sick, and which also seems to have approached the Rothschild family for assistance in its activities (HaCohen, 1978: 242). These activities represented the initiatives of many individuals, not the coordinated steps of a central communal organization.

During the same period of time, the Jews of Tripolitania, as Jews elsewhere in North Africa, were becoming ever more deeply affected by developments in European society and within European Jewry. Not only were they linked to various sources of rabbinic and religious tradition, but they became more and more exposed to competing European models. The efforts of Rabbi Hazzan to start a new school took place in a context, in which competing new frameworks for education were being suggested from a number of directions.[8] This was a further centrifugal force within the Jewish population. The Jews remained formally a *millet* and still paid taxes to the Ottoman government as a unit. But otherwise they were pulled in a variety of directions. The Jews showed the capability of joint action, more in their ability to oppose reforms which seemed harmful to them (Goldberg, 1990), than in formulating and institutionalizing new directions. Only under the Italians would there be an attempt, from above, to restructure the community in an extensive fashion (De Felice, 1985).

Notes

1 Lavi was also the author of a hymn in honor of Bar Yohai, a central figure in the kabbalistic tradition. This hymn has become widespread in the liturgy of Sephardi groups and of the Eastern European Hasidim.
2 A well-connected Jew might use his ties to weaken the hold of the Jewish

community on him, and one document may even indicate that a wealthy Jew fought the communal assessment of taxes, by intimating that he had the option of converting to Islam (Goldberg, 1987: 182, note 14). While such a step was indubitably rare, it underlines the nature of the dynamic social field in which Jewish life played itself out.

3   The story of Rabbi Ya'akov Mimun in the court, and much of the subsequent material on the rabbinic court, are taken from the principal source of Jewish history in Libya during the nineteenth century, the book of Rabbi Mordecai HaCohen (1978: see p. 151 for the incident concerning Mimun). HaCohen (b. 1856) was himself a licensee in the rabbinic court. Some of the materials on the changes in the nineteenth century have been analyzed in greater detail by Goldberg and Segrè (1989).

4   The first category may be exemplified by Rabbi Ya'akov Raqah (b. 1800), a scholar who published a number of books (Raqah, 1987), but who never accepted an official position (Zuaretz et al., 1960: 73–4).

5   A similar custom, naming different rabbis, exists among the Jews of Jerba. On the influence of Jerban Jewry on the Jews of Tripoli, see below.

6   In the communities of the hinterland, religious leadership entailed leading prayers, teaching boys in synagogue, slaughtering animals in accordance with the laws of *kashrut*, and conducting marriages. Matters of a more complex legal nature, including divorces, had to be brought to the court in Tripoli. Individuals who carried out these basic religious tasks generally were addressed as *rebbi*, but were not considered full rabbis unless they had much more extensive training.

7   Hazzan's responsum is found in his *Ta'alumot Lev, Yoreh De'ah, Siman Dalet* (Hazzan, 1879: 14a–16b), and the *haskamot* are on 17a–18a of that work.

8   Attempts to innovate in the realm of education are discussed by Goldberg and Segrè (1990).

References

Adadi, A.H. (1865) 'Quntres makom she-nahagu,' in *Vayikra Avraham* (Leghorn: Ben-Amozegh).
Adadi, A.H. (1976/1849) *Ha-Shomer Emet*, edited by F. Zuaretz and F. Tayyar (Tel Aviv: Va'ad Kehillot Luv Be-Yisrael).
Anderson, L. (1986) *The State and Social Transformation in Tunisia and Libya, 1830–1980* (Princeton: Princeton University Press).
Bar-Asher, S. (1981) 'The Jewish Community in Morocco in the 18th Century: Studies in the History of the Social Status and Self-Government of the Jews of Fes, Meknes and Sefrou,' PhD dissertation, Hebrew University of Jerusalem (in Hebrew; English summary).
Ben-Zvi, Y. (1964) 'The Travels of a *Shaliah* from Safed by Rabbi Ya'akov Sikli Kohen,' *Otzar Yehudei Sefarad* 7: 77–86 (Hebrew).
De Felice, R. (1985) *Jews in an Arab Land: Libya, 1835–1970*, Trans. by J. Roumani (Austin: University of Texas Press).
Deshen, S. (1989) *The Mellah Society: Jewish Community Life in Sherifian Morocco* (Chicago: University of Chicago Press).

Goldberg, H. (1972) *Cave Dwellers and Citrus Growers: A Jewish Community in Libya and Israel* (Cambridge: Cambridge University Press).
Goldberg, H. (1983) 'Language and Culture of the Jews of Tripolitania: A Preliminary View,' *Mediterranean Language Review*, 1: 85–102.
Goldberg, H. (1985) 'Between Tripolitania and Eretz Israel in the Nineteenth Century,' *Pe'amim* 24: 87–92 (Hebrew).
Goldberg, H. (1987) 'Ottoman Tripoli,' in Y. Dan (ed.), *Culture and History: Ino Sciacky Memorial Volume* (Hebrew) (Jerusalem: Misgav Yerushalayim) 171–84.
Goldberg, H. (1990) *Jewish Life in Muslim Libya: Rivals and Relatives* (Chicago: University of Chicago Press).
Goldberg, H. and C. Segrè (1989) 'Holding on to Both Ends: Religious Continuity and Changes in the Libyan Jewish Community, 1860–1949,' *The Maghreb Review*, 14: 161–86.
Goldberg, H. and C. Segrè (1990) 'Mixtures of Diverse Substances: Education and the Hebrew Language among the Jews of Libya, 1875–1951,' in S. Fishbane and J. Lightstone (eds), *Essays in the Social Scientific Study of Judaism and Jewish Society* (Montreal: Concordia University Press) 151–201.
HaCohen, M. (1978) *Higgid Mordecai: Histoire de la Libye et de ses Juifs* (in Hebrew) (ed.) and annotated by H. Goldberg (Jerusalem: Ben-Zvi Institute).
Hazan, E. (ed.) (1989) *The Piyyutim of Rabbi Musa Bujnah of Tripoli* (in Hebrew) (Jerusalem: Ben-Zvi Institute).
Hazzan, E.B. (1879) *Ta'alumot Lev*, Part I (Leghorn: Ben-Amozegh).
Hirschberg, H.Z. (1981) *A History of the Jews in North Africa, vol. 2 From the Ottoman Conquest to the Present Time* (Leiden: Brill).
Kahalon, Y. (1969) 'Rabbi A.H. Adadi: The Man and the Community of Tripoli in the Nineteenth Century,' MA thesis. Bar Ilan University (Hebrew).
Kahalon, Y. (1972) 'La lutte pour l'image spirituelle de la communauté de Libye au XIXe siècle,' in H.Z. Hirschberg (ed.), *Zakhor le-Abraham: Mélanges Abraham Elmaleh* (Jerusalem: Comité la communauté marocaine) (in Hebrew: French summary) 79–122.
Khalfon, H. (1986) *Lanu u-Levanenu* (Hebrew) (Netanya: Published by the author).
Lewis, B. (1984) *The Jews of Islam* (Princeton: Princeton University Press).
Raccah, G. (1948) 'Shlihei Eretz-Yisrael be-Tripolitania' (in Hebrew), *Yerushalayim*, 1: 109–13.
Raqah, Y. (1987) *Shulhan Lehem Ha-Panim: Hilkhot Shabbat* (Edited) by L. Nahum (Jerusalem: Machon Hai Hai).
Rosen, L. (1984) *Bargaining for Reality: The Construction of Social Relations in a Muslim Community* (Chicago: University of Chicago Press).
Simon, R. (1979) 'The Jews of Libya and their Gentile Environment in the Late Ottoman Period,' *Pe'amim*, 3: 5–36 (Hebrew).
Slouschz, N. (1908) 'La Tripolitaine sous la domination des Karamanlis,' *Revue du Monde Musulman*, 6: 58–84, 211–32, 433–53.
Slouschz, N. (1927) *The Jews of North Africa* (Philadelphia: Jewish Publication Society).
Tully, R. (1957) *Letters Written During a Ten Years' Residence at the Court of Tripoli*, Introduction and notes by S. Dearden (London: Arthur Baker).
Udovitch, A.L. and Valensi, L. (1984) *The Last Arab Jews: The Communities of Jerba, Tunisia* (Chur: Harwood).

Ya'ari, A. (1977) *Sheluhei Eretz Yisrael* (Hebrew) (Jerusalem: Rav Kook Institute).
Zuaretz, F., A. Guweta, Z. Shaqed, G. Arbib, and F. Tayar (eds) (1960) *Sefer Yahadut Luv* (Tel Aviv: Va'ad Kehillot Luv be-Yisrael).

Part IV
Syria and Iraq

12 Syrian Jews and their Non-Jewish Neighbors in Late Ottoman Times
Walter P. Zenner

As the chapters by Mark Cohen and Allan Meyers show, relations between Muslims and non-Muslims are governed both by the dictates of Muslim law and by a variety of local circumstances. Relations change under different regimes, as we find in Iran (Loeb, ch. 18). The situation in Syria in the late Ottoman period presents a still different situation. It is a context in which the large indigenous Christian minority and powerful Europeans play important roles. Economic rivalry and jockeying for power and prestige remain important forces in this environment, alongside the insecure Muslim majority's efforts to remain dominant.

Among folk-stories recorded about the rabbis of Aleppo are three, which exemplify aspects of relations between Jews and their Gentile neighbors

The First Story

When the body of a rather ordinary man was exhumed thirty years after his death, the gravediggers found that it had not decayed at all. The diggers went to the distinguished Rabbi Raphael Solomon Laniado (died 1794), and told him of the miracle. At night, the man appeared to the rabbi and told him his story. He had been a weaver, and a maker of loops and hooks. Every day he set aside some money which he put into a clay vessel, to be used only for a special purpose. One day a new governor was appointed. The Gentiles petitioned him, and the governor issued a decree that forbade the Jews to engage in embroidery. Two hundred families were thus deprived of their livelihood. People came to the embroiderer and asked him to help. The humble embroiderer decided to go the governor. He waited until the Sabbath had concluded, and went to the governor's house, taking the money in the clay vessel with him. The man asked if the governor wanted to deprive his subjects of their livelihood, and he gave the governor the money which he had saved. The governor annulled the decree. Now the rabbi understood (Laniado, 1980: 196).

The Second Story

A Muslim Arab had a contract with the government to supply the army with provisions. When he requested payment by the Pasha, the latter refused several times. Days passed. Then an Arab friend suggested to him to go to the *hakham* of the Jews, Rabbi Hayyim Mordecai Labaton (died 1869), for a solution. The Arab went to the rabbi and showed his account book, including his expenses. The rabbi saw that his request was in order. He then wrote a letter to Abraham Kamondo, treasurer of the Ottoman government in Istanbul, and told the provisioner to go with that letter to the capital. The Arab did so, and delivered the letter to Kamondo. Thereupon the latter paid him what was his due. The Arab praised the rabbi in particular, and Jews in general (Laniado, 1980: 191).

The Third Story

One day before Passover a Christian boy by the name of Musan disappeared in Aleppo. The Christian priests started a rumor that the Jews had kidnapped the boy, and used his blood to make *matza*. The Pasha invited Rabbi Hayyim Mordecai Labaton, and told him that if the boy was not found, he would expel the Jews from the city. The rabbi assembled the Jews to pray to avert the evil decree. He then went to the place where the boy had been kidnapped, and overheard two boys whispering, that Musan had been taken to the church. When the rabbi heard this he went to the pasha's house, requesting that he and the governor should go to the church without prior notification. The governor agreed. When they arrived at the church they were greeted by the priests. Suddenly the governor saw Musan walking about the church courtyard, and he ordered the priests jailed. In memory of the miracle, that day, the 14th of Sivan, became a day of rejoicing (Laniado, 1980: 195).

The stories show that Syrian Jews saw the setting in which they lived as full of uncertainties that stemmed from their neighbors, the market, and the government, as from the natural habitat. Therefore, the study of Syrian Jewry in the late Ottoman empire entails examination of a complex environment: the imperial administration, the European-driven world economy and relations between Muslims, Christians, and Jews. Competition and cooperation between Jews and Gentiles in various arenas of life will be considered here.

THE CHARACTER OF JEWISH–GENTILE RELATIONS

Unlike North Africa, where Jews were the only native non-Muslim group, Jews in Syria had Christian as well as Muslim co-residents. They all lived distinct lives while sharing a common habitat. Each group had its own set of loyalties, norms, and courts of law, and each used its own norms and symbols for judging others. While the dress of all was adapted to the climate, the costumes of each group were distinctive. At the same time they were all economically interdependent.

In Syria, the various groups shared Arabic as their everyday language, as well as many values and customs. All lived under one monarch, although many Muslims and non-Muslims did not recognize the Ottoman sultan as fully legitimate. The readiness with which non-Muslims sought the protection of foreign consuls was a sign of this. No group permitted unrestrained marriage. The Muslim law that allows Muslim men to marry Christian and Jewish women is only apparently permissive, and is, in fact, an assertion of Muslim male dominance. The forms of prayer of the three religions are quite different from each other. Muslims are forbidden to drink alcoholic beverages, permitted to Jews and Christians. Jews and Muslims have similar, but not identical, dietary laws. While all groups have periods of abstinence, the time and manner that they were observed was not the same. No one would mistake Ramadan, Lent, or the Jewish Days of Awe for one another.

Each religious tradition had its own indicators of identity and idiom, transmitted by its own network of communications. The Greek Orthodox and Catholic (Uniate) churches used Greek, the Armenians Armenian, the Muslim *ulemā* (religiously learned) used classical Arabic, and Jews used Hebrew. An Armenian (Uniate) Catholic would be connected to the Mekhtiarist monastery in Venice, while the Armenian Apostolic priests might correspond with a bishop in Echmiadzin. The Sunni *qādī* (judge) had contacts with Cairo, Istanbul and Mecca. The rabbi had his books printed in Leghorn (Livorno), and received Jewish pilgrims from Poland on their way to Jerusalem and Safed.

Modernizing styles moved along similar religio-ethnic lines. A Maronite might receive a western education in the French clericalist atmosphere of St Joseph University in Beirut, while an Armenian would go to an Armenian nationalist school, and a Jew would receive the European tradition in a French laicist form in the Alliance Israélite Universelle school. The corporate structure in which these religious communities lived side by side has been labeled the *millet* system, the term for either a religious or an ethnic community. Since the nineteenth century it has been applied to formally recognized religious communities, who were granted the right to administer the personal law of their adherents. While communal pluralism existed prior to the nineteenth century, no single formal administrative structure governed the various non-Muslim communities, nor were the hierarchies of the different groups parallel to each other. As a result of nineteenth century reforms, the Ottomans demanded to confirm communal heads. Ottoman bureaucrats, however, allowed local religious authorities a great deal of freedom in dealing with the everyday affairs of their communities.

Despite separatism, the various groups had some familiarity with each other's religious law. Such knowledge is found in the inter-religious jokes of Lebanese, Syrians, and Palestinians. The following is an example by a Damascus Jew:

> Once a Shi'ite, of whom there were few in Damascus, came to a rabbi and asked, 'How can it be, that when the Messiah comes, we will be the donkeys of the Jews, since Jews are many and Shi'ites are few in number?' The rabbi replied, using a chant used for reading the Qur'an, that the Shi'ites would be such big asses that they could carry all the Jews.

Part of the shared interfaith ideology is found in the rhetoric of fatalism (interspersing Arabic phrases like *inshallah*, 'if God wills', in one's speech), beliefs in the evil eye and the use of talismans against it. People of all groups crossed religious boundaries to be cured, although this might be a commercial, rather than religious, transaction. The story about the Arab who went to Labaton suggests that a holy man of another religion might be honored for his own personal qualities. In that story, the rabbi did not perform a supernatural miracle. This could also occur on a communal level during emergencies like droughts, as in the tale of a Lebanese Jew:

> [There was a drought]. All the Mohammedan (sic!) and Christian religious leaders prayed for rain and it didn't come. They came to the rabbi and said he should pray and blow the *shofar* (ram's horn). He declared a fast and took the children from the Talmud Torah (Jewish school) to the cemetery, and before they finished [their prayers], the rains came. Then, after the rabbi's death, they went to his grave. He is powerful. He was the teacher of my oldest brother.

The graves of saints and shrines of each group were revered by the others, although sometimes in seemingly perverse ways. Jews tell stories about Muslims attempting to bury bodies of rabbis in their own cemeteries. On the other hand, when synagogues in Aleppo were destroyed in 1947, a local *sheikh* protected the Jewish shrine of Ezra the Scribe.

Visiting in the homes of members of different groups was infrequent. It was probably more common in Aleppo where Jews and Muslims shared courtyards than in Damascus. When Jewish peddlers traveled in rural areas, they often had to spend the night in Gentile homes, and there were Gentile guests at Jewish weddings, especially of the elite. In the eighteenth century, Turkish ladies came to view the *sukkōt* (booths) during the feast of Sukkot (Russell, 1794 II: 56–88). At the end of Passover Muslims might bring Jewish acquaintances bread and cheese. Beginning with the nineteenth century, when European schools, including those of missionaries and the Alliance, were attended by people of various religions, interfaith friendships formed. Equally, in the period from 1840 to 1877, the homes of wealthy Jews were attractions for European Christians, and were visited regularly by them (Harel, 1992: 44). In the Mandatory period Jewish men would meet Gentile acquaintances in cafes, but rarely invited them home.

THE OCCUPATIONS OF SYRIAN JEWS

From 1800 until World War I Jews played specialized roles. They were not only craftsmen or local traders, but were also involved in international commerce. In Aleppo and Damascus there were both craftsmen and traders, though in Aleppo there were more traders among the Jews than in Damascus. The first story, about the embroiderer, which is set in the eighteenth century suggests, however, that certain occupations, that later were not Jewish niches, were practiced by Aleppine Jews in the eighteenth century. At that time craft specialization was narrowly defined, and organized into guilds, each with its own headman and rules. In Aleppo in the mid-1700s, there were 157 such guilds. The guilds however, were not generally organized along religious lines, but included members of different religions (Marcus, 1989: 158–9; there were some exceptions).

In Damascus, eighteenth-century records of Muslim courts indicate the following as occupations of Jews: moneychangers, physicians, makers and/or sellers of soap and wax, various textile-related trades (e.g. dyers and printers), food-related crafts (including butchers, bakers, millers, and wine sellers) perfume sellers, carpenters, goldsmiths and barbers. Several of the men in these records are identified as 'master craftsmen' (Al-Qattan, 1992). Several of the crafts were also practiced by non-Jews. The records show that also money lending was multi-directional. Jews and Muslims, as well as Christians, engaged in it. In northern Syria, by the late nineteenth century, we hear of Jewish goldsmiths, tinsmiths (especially in rural areas), and people who prepare food, such as slaughterers, butchers, and cheesemakers. After World War I, when there was some hostility between Armenian refugees from Anatolia and Jews in Aleppo, Armenians tended to become silversmiths, as opposed to Jews who were goldsmiths. Such division of labor mitigated the sharpness between the groups.

At the beginning of the twentieth century, most Jews in Damascus were engaged in the engraving of copper and wood, as weavers, shoemakers, carpenters and smiths. The former occupations specialized in manufacture for the tourist trade. There were also some bankers and moneychangers, small merchants, and a handful of government employees (Franco and Gottheil, 1903). Due probably to the economically depressed times, some women were professional singers, a stigmatized occupation. While some crafts and industries included Muslims and non-Muslims, in others particular tasks were ethnically or religiously marked. Muslim, Christian, and Jewish shoemakers in Damascus each made different varieties of shoes (Gibb and Bowen, 1950 I: 294). In one Damascus factory Jews engaged in metal engraving, Christians processed mother-of-pearl, and Armenians did the woodwork (Goitein, 1955: 117).

With guild monopolies and narrow definitions of crafts, the first story indicating religious discrimination, remains plausible. Members of ethnic groups might exclude others from their craft. The guild of pastry-makers in 1770 explicitly excluded Jews and Christians, on account of the demand to maintain Muslim purity. Conversely, Muslims were not allowed to sell alcoholic beverages for religious reasons (Marcus, 1989: 264–5). The case of the pastry-makers suggests that the kind of discrimination described in the story about the embroiderers was based on a history of ethnic economic conflict. In Aleppo there were many inter-religious partnerships, sometimes between a merchant and a craftsman, or even a herder. One supplied the capital and the other was the producer of goods. Some partnerships were between Muslims and Christians, and others between Jews and Muslims (Marcus, 1989: 183).

Provision of credit was an important part of the commercial economy. The partnerships mentioned above were often *de facto* loan arrangements. Peddlers and itinerant craftsmen would provide goods and services to peasants in one season, to be repaid with agricultural produce at harvest time, thus in effect extending loans. Urbanites would lend peasants money for taxes. Professional moneychangers (*sarrāfs*) in Damascus particularly, were mostly Jews, and often acted like bankers. They took deposits, made transfers and lent money, even to state officers. For a few wealthy Jews in mid-nineteenth century Damascus, lending money at high interest rates to peasants was major income (Harel, 1992: 55–6, 368–74; Marcus, 1989: 184). Moneylending entailed competition with lenders of other religions, conflict with the borrowers, and altogether provoked much hostility (Zenner,

1991). But when the Ottoman empire defaulted on loans in 1875, most of the money-lenders who had invested heavily in Ottoman bonds were ruined, and their influence diminished (Harel, 1992: 57-8; Braver, 1945/6).

Syria had long been situated across trade routes between Africa, Europe, and Asia. At the end of the eighteenth century Syria conveyed raw materials and finished goods, particularly silk and cotton to Europe. Much of the international trade was carried on through European monopolies, such as the English Levant Company. This company viewed Jews and Armenians as potential competitors, and tried to shut them out. They rarely hired them as interpreters or agents. But by the end of the eighteenth century Italian Jews, particularly merchants from Livorno, settled in Aleppo and formed a separate grouping among the Jews of that city (Marcus, 1989: 46-7; Masters, 1988: 88-90). The nineteenth century brought drastic economic changes, as effects of European industrialization came to be felt. The new industrialization and new commercial trade coincided with commercial treaties made between the Ottoman Empire and Europe. This caused European goods to flood the markets of the empire, and Christian and Jewish traders prospered more than Muslims (Zenner, 1987; Maoz, 1968: 182). One Muslim reaction was to impede Christians from practicing certain crafts. Thus in Damascus in 1842, the local council forbade Christians from producing certain kinds of silk products (Maoz, 1968: 193-4).

The industrial revolution caused a reversal in the flow of trade, as did the commercial treaties, and later the Suez Canal opening. Syrian craftsmen of all backgrounds faced unemployment as their goods were displaced by cheap imports. Aleppine merchants who had relied on the caravan trade were driven to adapt to the new conditions. Aleppines of all religions, including Muslim shipping merchants, opened offices in Manchester, England, with the object of selling British textiles in the Levant. In Aleppo, local merchants would then give these *manafaktura* goods on consignment to shopkeepers and peddlers, to sell in the city and the countryside. Thus Jewish merchants and peddlers helped change the relationship between Syria and the world economy.

SYRIAN JEWS AND THE OTTOMAN STATE

Until the reforms of the nineteenth century, persons with the legal status of slave held high positions in the administration. The officials were ethnically diverse – Turks, Slavs, and Albanians – and many did not even speak Arabic. The population was thus generally subject to an administration of strangers. Though the local governor was sometimes independent of the Istanbul government, he was often seen as exploitative and arbitrary. For Muslims this was mitigated by the courts which administered Islamic law, and that had judges who were often of local origin. Gerber (1994) points out that this administration of justice gave the Ottoman regime a fairly rational bureaucratic character, quite different from the way many scholars imagined it.

For non-Muslims the situation was different. Jews and Christians in the Ottoman empire were *dhimmi*, protected communities, that had to abide by regulations imposed by Muslim authorities, which marked their submission and inferiority. Before the nineteenth century reforms these rules prohibited rebuilding houses of worship, ordered the wearing special garb, and generally required maintaining a low profile. Certain regulations governing the *dhimmis* were actually enforced (Marcus, 1989: 41), but in certain cases the testimony of Jews and Christians was accepted in Islamic courts, despite Islamic law's impulse to discriminate against non-Muslims (Al-Qattan, 1992).

Dhimmis were often oppressively taxed. For instance, in the eighteenth century, the Aleppo Jewish community was led to consider selling sacred synagogue ornaments to pay taxes. Taxation was viewed as vexatious, sometimes as theft by the government, *gazlanuta demalkhuta*, rather than legitimate imposts, *dina demalkhuta*. Changes in tax laws, such as lifting tax exemptions of religious scholars placed new burdens on that class. When Jews and Christians were put on a single tax roll in Aintab, Christians protested because they felt that this increased their tax burden unduly (Harel, 1992: 180–93). In the nineteenth century the ancient discriminatory *jizya* tax, which *dhimmis* had long paid Muslim governments, was transformed into a tax for escaping military conscription, but in practice taxation differences continued to exist. After the Young Turk regime took over in 1908, Jews and Christians became subject to actual conscription which they, like their Muslim counterparts, resented. Escape from military service was one of the forces behind emigration from the Ottoman empire at that time.

In the wake of the nineteenth century *tanzimat* reforms, some of the discriminatory symbols were abrogated (Maoz, 1968: 188–99; Harel, 1992: 139–56). The *tanzimat* reforms also entailed the establishment of bodies of local notables, and also tribunals, that included Jews and Christians. The establishment of a government-appointed chief rabbi (*hakham bashi*), to represent the Jews as a counterpart to Christian bishops in newly-established local councils, was part of this effort. To a large extent, the chief rabbis served to mediate between the Jewish community and the Ottoman authorities. They were politicians more than spiritual leaders or legal authorities for Jews, though some were rabbinic scholars (Zenner, 1982: 166–7; Harel, 1992: 64–76). Local Muslims, however, particularly in the 1850s, blocked the participation of Jews and Christians in the local councils. Only through Ottoman pressure, and the appointment of officials committed to reforms, was *dhimmi* participation enforced. Generally Christians worked to enforce the reforms, while Jews tended to act in a manner which did not offend Muslims, and did not fight assertively against discrimination (Harel, 1992: 203–8, 241–52; Maoz, 1968: 202–9).

The reforms aimed at removing discrimination of *dhimmis* were due to pressure from European powers on the Ottoman government, and were resented by Muslims. They saw them as threats to their status and religion. The reactions included non-compliance, and violence against non-Muslims, especially Christians. Violence was particularly marked against Christians in Aleppo in 1850, and in Damascus and Lebanon in 1860, in ways typical of groups who feel that their entitlements are threatened (Horowitz, 1985; Maoz, 1968: 200–5).

The changes in participation in councils and tribunals were accompanied by changes in the administrative structure. This requires a recapitulation of earlier eighteenth century conditions. Before the *tanzimat* reforms, Jews and Christians often contracted with the government to perform certain services. Such contracting often resulted in rivalry between members of *dhimmi* groups, such as over tax-farming rights from foreign merchants (Masters, 1988: 137–43). In Aleppo a consortium of Jewish families held the contract for customs collection in the eighteenth century. Retired members of this group received a portion of the commission, besides those actively involved. But the consortium was accused of embezzlement and displaced, when a Christian, who had been a dragoman of the Venetian consul, received the contract in their stead. Eventually one of the Jewish families recovered the contract, and it remained in their hands well into the nineteenth century (Zenner, 1987; Masters, 1988; Harel, 1992: 165). The rivalry with Christians had bearing on the blood libels referred to above, in the third story.

In the late eighteenth and early nineteenth centuries, Jews and Christians, employed as bankers (*sarrâf*), for governors, became tax-farmers. They provided surety for governors, who had to pay the equivalent of expected revenues for their positions. The tax burden was particularly harsh on peasants. Those living on government land paid according to the Muslim lunar calendar, which rarely coincided with the agricultural cycle. Therefore they had to borrow money to meet their obligations, and the bankers were blamed for the hardships. While the Muslims perceived the *dhimmi* bankers as representatives of Jews and Christians, most of the ordinary *dhimmi* did not benefit much from the bankers' activities, since the latter identified with the governor's interests, to protect their investments.

The rivalry with Christians for banking and tax-farming positions was quite intense. In Egypt, Syrian Catholics replaced Jews as customs collectors in 1763. In Aleppo, over the centuries, customs collectors alternated between the three religions. The rivalry between the Jewish Farhi family and the Greek-Catholic Bahris was a factor in tensions between the communities, that led to the infamous 'Damascus Affair' in 1840, the accusation that Jews had murdered a Catholic priest, and imprisonment of the Jewish leadership of Damascus.

The third story above, about the disappearance of a child, is an example of numerous such incidents that occurred during that period. As the story shows, both groups concerned sought to enlist Muslim authorities and European powers against each other. While economic rivalry provided an impetus, the blood libels must also be seen in terms of the Christian view of the Jew as 'Christ-killer'. Catholic, Orthodox, and Armenian Christians supported such accusations, but Protestant missionaries, some of whom were converts from Judaism, did not, and for a time the latter were seen by Jews in a favorable light because they defended them against libel (Harel, 1992: 273–82). This might be an explanation for a certain receptivity of Near Eastern Jews for missionary schooling in the nineteenth century.

One of the most prominent of the Jewish bankers in the eighteenth century was Hayyim Farhi who served three pashas of Acre, until he was executed in 1819. His brothers served in this capacity in Damascus, but after 1820 rivalry with Christians increased and they were displaced. Another Farhi brother later recovered the position, but the post of *sarrâf* was abolished and Jewish financiers lost much of their power (Harel, 1992: 164–9). The kind of mixed private and public positions, which the positions of *sarrâf* and customs collector represented, was replaced by a more modern style of bureaucracy. Christians and Jews were admitted to this new 'civil service', but the informal power which the *dhimmi* notables had previously held was no more (Krikorian, 1977; Franco and Gottheil, 1903). Dignitaries of the kind of the Farhis disappeared from the scene after the mid-nineteenth century. The power of independent worthies declined, as the nascent modern bureaucracy made its first assertive gestures and appointments.

CONSULS

Consular protection accompanied European commercial penetration of the Ottoman Empire. In the early period of European relations with the Ottoman Empire, such protection secured trade, but it was subject to abuse, since the Europeans and their local protégés were immune from local law. Thus in Aleppo in the eighteenth century, the *signores francos*, the European Jews (many from Livorno) successfully fought to be free of taxation by the local Jewish community.

In 1788, Rafael Picciotto, one of the *signores francos*, became Austrian consul in Aleppo, and in 1806 he was knighted. From then the family provided consuls for most Western powers until the 1880s. As Austrian consul, the protection of one of the Picciottos extended to the Catholics of Aleppo, and others were consuls in Damascus (Cohen, 1971). The Picciottos were generally unpaid, and continued to run their own enterprises while serving as consuls. Through the middle of the nineteenth century they were seen as protectors of Jewish interests in Aleppo. For instance, they helped obtain governmental permission to rebuild the shrine of Ezra in Tedif al-Yahud, a major Jewish pilgrimage site in northern Syria. During the Damascus Affair, a member of the Picciotto family was instrumental in gaining Austrian assistance for the Jews who had been imprisoned. The Picciottos, however, also used their power to protect their own class interests. When the Alliance Israélite Universelle wanted to set up a school to serve both the affluent and the poor, the Picciottos and other wealthy Jews objected.

By the 1870s the conflicts of interest between the roles of the Picciottos as consuls, protectors of Jews, and private entrepreneurs entangled them, and made them less useful to both the powers and to their fellow-Jews. Increasingly they were seen as corrupt, especially by the British and French consuls, who were fully paid agents of the two great powers in the region. The Picciottos' personal conflicts with non-Jews made the Jewish community as a whole a target for Muslim and Christian hostility. In addition, the Picciottos' opposition to the opening of the Alliance school went against the interests of the majority of their fellow Jews. But though it lost its consular positions, the family has survived and continues to be important in the Syrian-Jewish diaspora to this day (see Harel, 1992, for detailed accounts of these notables).

From 1840 on, wealthy Jews in particular gained the protection of the British and later the French. With British assistance, the Jews of Damascus fended off continued accusations of ritual murder and charges of complicity in the Muslim massacres of Christians in 1860 (Baron, 1933, 1940;

Harel, 1992: 365–6). Up to the 1870s Syrian Jews viewed the British, and Protestants generally, as friendly to Jews, while the French, the traditional protectors of Catholics, as inimical. But in the 1870s relations between Syrian Jewry and the French consuls became warmer, and more Syrian Jews received protection from the French. As the power of the Jewish Picciotto consuls dwindled, larger numbers of Syrian Jews received foreign protection. Importantly, the dependence of Jews on foreign protection further alienated them from their Muslim neighbors, and paved the way for the later worsening in the relations between Syrian Jews and Muslims.

CONCLUSION

The relationships of Jews and Muslims must be seen as augmented by the relations of both with European and local Christians. The three stories cited at the beginning, one set in the eighteenth century and the others in the nineteenth, give us a flavor of the times in which Jews and members of other religions competed with each other, but could also collaborate. The second story also shows that while the Jewish self-image did not depend on the favorable views of others, Jews still valued the approbation of non-Jews. While the Muslims continued to be the dominant religious group in the Ottoman empire, they felt that they were weak *vis-à-vis* Christian Europe. This defensiveness was reflected in the behavior of the Ottoman government and of the masses, resulting both in the *tanzimat* reforms and in Muslim reactions against it, including pogroms. The protection which Christians and Jews sought from European consuls, and their mutual rivalry, also reflect the growing power of the European states. Despite all of this conflict, the various religious groups in Syria remained inter-dependent and continued to live together during the nineteenth century, as often at peace as in conflict.

Note

The list of references for this chapter figures with that for ch. 13.

13 Jews in Late Ottoman Syria: Community, Family and Religion
Walter P. Zenner

During the nineteenth and twentieth centuries, Syrian society moved from a period when the authoritative basis of traditional Islam, Judaism and Christianity were not questioned, into one in which all of these competed with new ideologies which came from Western Europe. Zenner provides a reconstruction of internally oriented institutions (communal structure, religious and educational institutions, and the family and household). Also the impact of European cultural models in Syrian Jewry is discussed. The changes which occurred in Syrian Jewry in this period paralleled developments in Iraq, Tunisia, and elsewhere.

In the previous chapter, relations between Muslims, Christians and Jews in the late Ottoman period showed the impact of the increasing European influence on Syria. The internal institutions of Syrian Jewry during this period also began to show this transformation, but most of these areas of activity also continued to exhibit patterns of life derived from the Middle Eastern Jewish tradition. Traditional educational institutions, however, faced severe competition from European-style institutions.

JEWISH COMMUNAL ORGANIZATION

Jewish communities in the larger Syrian cities were not directly dependent upon other Jewish communities. Despite the imperially confirmed *hakham bashi*, each Jewish community was not bound to a hierarchy. Because they often had only one rabbi, Jews in small towns within the northern province of Aleppo, such as Killiz, Marash or Urfa, were forced to bring cases before rabbinical courts (of three rabbis) in the larger cities. They could however choose, as did the Jews of Diyarbekir, whether to send the case to Aleppo, or to other major communities such as Baghdad and Istanbul.

Source: A revision of 'The Inner Life of the Jews in Late Ottoman Syria' (Hebrew) *Peamim* 3: 45–58 (1979). © Copyright Ben Zvi Institute 1979. Reprinted by permission.

The factor integrating all Jews was the common acceptance of one body of tradition as authoritative. Like traditional Jews everywhere (outside of sects such as the Karaites), Syrian and Turkish Jews considered the Hebrew Bible and Talmud as sacred. The common body of law or lore, to which rabbis in Aleppo, Izmir, and Warsaw referred, made it possible for them to communicate. All wrote in Hebrew and were concerned with similar problems. Many of the responsa and other works of Syrian rabbis were published in Livorno, Italy, while other works were published in Izmir, Istanbul, Aleppo, and Jerusalem. The shared identification and the common tradition made it possible for Spanish, Italian and even East European Jews to be assimilated into the Syrian Jewish communities.

In Aleppo, rabbinic authority was strong until World War I. An English visitor writes of the great authority of the *hakham* (*kakhan*):

> In general the Jews were more sober than [native] Christians. Many were secured from intemperance by poverty, besides which their attendance twice a day at the synagogue, on all festivals, and their living so much under the eye of their Kakhans render it more difficult to conceal debauchery, than it would be under a more numerous people. (Russell, 1794: 61)

The *hakham* was distinguished by the size and color of his turban and by the long-wide sleeves of his outer garments. He was, according to Russell, more respected by his community than the Christian bishop was by his flock. His civil jurisdiction was restricted and parties could appear before the *mahkama*, the governmental Muslim court (Al-Qattan, 1992). But this privilege of appeal was exercised warily, since it might result in having to pay bribes (Russell, 1794: 64). The cases which came before the rabbinic court were of many types – Jewish rituals, marriages, divorces, inheritance, business contracts, loans, torts, building regulations (especially with regard to placement of windows opposite a neighbor's house). The penalties available to the rabbinic court in enforcing its decisions were excommunication, fines and corporal punishment. These, especially the latter, were used by individual teachers and rabbis. The story is told of a father who was drunk, and protested to the *hakham* because his son's schoolteacher had bastinadoed the boy. The *hakham* had the father given the same punishment. There is a story that a *hakham* once had some young men beaten for violating the Sabbath, and such practices continued into recent times. A woman teacher at the Alliance School in Aleppo in the 1920s reported that a father brought his adolescent son, with hands bound, to be whipped for disobeying the father. The teacher refused.

Quasi-magical powers attributed to rabbis added to their standing, and this is reflected in legends (Zenner, 1965b). I was once told that a rabbi had been ordered by the rabbinic court to curse a sinner and thereupon the man died; the rabbi refused to use his holy powers in such a manner thereafter. Rabbis prayed at the bedside of the sick and wrote amulets against the evil eye. After the death of a saintly rabbi, people would pray at his grave. This reinforced the powers of rabbis, and made a rabbinic excommunication particularly forceful.

The rabbis were divided into those who were members of the rabbinic court, led by the head of the Court (*av bet din*), teachers at various levels, and private scholars. Teachers at the primary school level (*kuttab*) had a relatively low status. A 'private scholar' is an individual who is known for his erudition, but does not hold office as teacher or judge. He may work as a *shohet* (slaughterer), or as a businessman. Businessmen might take scholars on as partners, sons-in-law, or as tutors for their children. A merchant might endow a small *yeshivah*, where scholars would assemble and study the Talmud.

Selection of judges of the court, the various heads of the community, including the chief rabbi (who was confirmed imperially) and assessment of taxes, were the functions of what was later known as 'the committee'. This body was made up of both 'notables' and the rabbinical judges of the court. In Aleppo, the notables were a self-perpetuating body, since there were no elections to the committee. Wealth and family position played an important role in appointment to these posts and, over the years, similar names of incumbents recur. In controversies that revolved around an individual with powerful connections, such as a pasha's banker, a consul, or a *hakham bashi*, the power of the state might be invoked against the leaders of the community (Nehmad, 1941). In the small community of Saida (Sidon, Lebanon), discord arose over the appointment of two judges to the rabbinic court. There were only two suitable candidates in the city, but to prevent the appointment of a candidate whom they disliked, one faction was willing to see an unqualified candidate appointed by lot. Thereupon the other faction appealed to rabbis in Damascus for help.

The income of communal organizations was raised from several sources: the sale of kosher meat, taxes assessed by the committee, voluntary contributions pledged in the synagogue at the Torah readings and on other occasions, and fines. After the World War I period a large part of the community's finances came from remittances sent by Syrian Jews who had emigrated. On minor festivals, such as the 15th of Ab (in July–August) or Lag B'omer (May), there were celebrations in the evening at which songs were sung and contributions made. These contributions were not only on behalf of the synagogue, but also for charitable societies, such as the Burial Society, the Food for the Poor Society, Clothing, Dowries (for needy girls), Study, and the Visiting the Sick Society. By use of the endowment (Arabic *waqf*, Hebrew *heqdesh*) an individual could dedicate property for a sacred purpose or a religious institution. A man could provide that the rental from a building he owned would be used hereafter on behalf of a school.

During the nineteenth century, communal discipline weakened, but rabbinic authority was still generally recognized (Harel, 1992: 72–5). Shortly before World War I the rabbis proclaimed a warning to the community concerning violation of the Sabbath and excommunicated violators. But at that time, only a few violated the Sabbath. After the War communal discipline weakened further.[1]

SCHOOLS

Traditionally boys were sent to school at the age of three or four, but many did not complete the full curriculum of studies. Those whose parents were poor often left school early and could barely read. In small communities schooling was irregular, since teachers did not stay there for extended periods of time. The curriculum of the *kuttab* started with the Hebrew alphabet, followed by vocalization of the Hebrew letters (since they represent consonants only), then the benedictions and prayers, the weekly portion of the Torah read in the synagogue, and other parts of the Bible. *Leviticus* was the first book of the Pentateuch that was taught, followed by *Genesis* and the remainder of the Torah. Scripture was accompanied by *sharh*, a traditional translation into literary Arabic. The teacher, or his assistant, would collect the boys from their homes in the morning to remain in school all day. There were also study sessions on the Sabbath. Discipline was maintained by corporal punishment, including the bastinado, and students sat on the ground before the teacher.

Arithmetic was the only secular subject taught. In recent generations, the traditional school added Arabic, French, and similar subjects to the curriculum. This was partly due to competition from other schools which had been opened. Traditionally, teaching of Scripture was followed by *'Ein Ya'aqov*, a collection of the non-legal sections of the Talmud. At about age ten or eleven, the student began the study of Talmud, first with Rashi's commentary and then proceeding with the more advanced commentaries of the Tosafot. By this point, most boys quit school, while a minority continued into the *midrash* (or *yeshiva*), the advanced rabbinic school.

In their adolescence, students were expected to learn independently, without the help of a teacher or rabbi. Two differences between Aleppene (Heb. *halebim*) and Ashkenazi Jews are that while the latter studied only the Pentateuch in school and not the rest of the Scripture and they stressed Talmudic casuistry, the Aleppenes studied the Bible more extensively and the Talmud more straightforwardly. According to one informant, a characteristic of Halebi learning was *'iyun halebi*, Halebi deliberation or concentration, which meant that thorough learning of the text received more weight than casuistic distinctions. One Aleppene rabbi believed that Sephardic superiority in learning lay in their more thorough knowledge of texts. But an Ashkenazi criticized Syrians for 'reading the Talmud like a story', rather than studying it through argumentation.[2] Until the 1870s there were several schools that taught Talmud in both Aleppo and Damascus. The rabbis of Aleppo, however, maintained a high level of Talmudic study into the twentieth century, while most of the yeshivot in Damascus closed when their supporters fell on hard times (Harel, 1992: 85–6).

THE FAMILY AND HOUSEHOLD

The family and household was the basic unit of social organization, as well as the initial base of socialization. Until the twentieth century, the home in Aleppo or Damascus, for peoples of all religions, was in a courtyard. Often several families shared a courtyard, and lodgings were overcrowded. European travelers repeatedly commented on the impoverished condition of Jewish quarters. One reason for their poor appearance was the Middle Eastern pattern, of an impoverished public façade which contrasted with a private display of luxury. Isabel Burton (1879: 102ff., 129) described such a traditional Jewish home with its 'mean' doorway and narrow winding staircase – leading into a luxurious home. Even when the motivation was not to conceal one's wealth from tax-collectors or itinerant beggars, the traditional Middle Easterner desires the privacy of his home and the veiling of his women. A number of legal responsa deal with the problem of who should bear the cost when a property-owner or tenant intrudes on the privacy of a neighbor, by installing a new window or opening a shop opposite a courtyard entrance. Such privacy was protected both by Talmudic and Islamic law (Abu-Lughod, 1987).

There is a report of the 1830s (Bowring, 1840: 49–50) that the lot of the ordinary Syrian compared favorably with that of working class people in England (then at the height of the Industrial Revolution). Bread was readily available and mutton was consumed several times a week, sometimes with rice or bulgar pilaf. Clothing was mainly of cotton, and lodging, despite the congestion, consisted usually of a separate set of rooms per family. Wages were low, but so were costs. Epidemics, however, were frequent, and by the turn of the century conditions had deteriorated. Many Syrians of all religions faced extreme poverty, and sought better conditions abroad.

The attitude of children towards their parents in the traditional household was one of respect. It was customary for a son to kiss his father's hand when greeting him. On the Sabbath, the father blessed his children and grandchildren, placing his hand on their heads. An informant said that children did not drink coffee or crack pistachios until they were mature. A father in Syria could punish even an adult son bodily, and older brothers also had authority over their younger siblings. The birth of a son was a time for rejoicing, while feelings at the birth of a daughter were mixed. Before the opening of the schools of the Alliance Israélite Universelle, and the mission school in Damascus, girls did not go to school. Girls from poorer families worked as domestics in wealthy Jewish homes, sometimes beginning at the age of eleven or twelve (Russell, 1794: 84). The movement of young girls was carefully controlled. Many boys began to work in their adolescent years. Some continued their studies, but most became apprentices either in commerce or with craftsmen. Unless they emigrated, they were expected to live in their parents' home and their income belonged to the family.

The role of the family in determining an individual's occupation was significant. Certain positions in the community had a quasi-hereditary nature. Business concerns were often partnerships organized along familial lines. Posts such as financier to the governor and those of the customhouse were often passed on in the family. A trade, such as that of goldsmith, was generally learned from one's father or uncle. But the positive role of the family in this realm could only apply when a skill could be learned or a position passed on. The many unskilled workers in Aleppo and Damascus could not always rely on their kin. As court cases concerning inheritance show, Syrian Jewish families could be arenas for competition, as well as refuge from a hostile world.

Marriages were generally arranged by the parents, although a young man might indicate to his mother his interest in marrying a particular girl. Some parents betrothed very young children, while others waited until a few months before the marriage. Most people were married before they reached the age of 18 or 20. By the 1920s however, according to informants, men frequently married in their late 20s when they were already established in business. In Aleppo, there was an exchange of gifts between the family of the groom and the family of the bride, as well as between the bride and the groom, and there was a society to provide dowries to poor and orphaned girls. But these women were often wed without substantial dowries. The emphasis of the exchange was on a dowry which the father of the bride gave his son-in-law. In contrast, in southeastern Turkey, the hinterland of Aleppo, the property exchange at marriage emphasized bride-price.

Marriage contracts could contain clauses which dealt with a number of situations, that might arise in marital life. These included the desire of a man to marry a second wife without the consent of his first wife, his desire to move to another city, and the distribution of property exchanged at the time of the marriage, in case of death of the wife or of divorce. There were standard formulas for different contingencies, some of which leaned in favor of the wife, while others favored the husband. There were also ordinances decreeing that weddings should be performed in the presence of a quorum of ten men, to prevent elopements and other untoward marriages (Zenner, 1980).

Once married, the couple would generally live with the husband's parents. They might share a kitchen, and have a separate room in the courtyard. There were cases where the couple was so young that the husband's parents had to help them, but one woman related that it was her parents who helped them. Another woman related that her parents were only thirteen years old when they were married. The husband's parents had to entertain the bride because the boy could not yet consummate the marriage. This type of arrangement of 'two women in one kitchen' often resulted in conflict. On holidays, generally a man's sons and daughters-in-law would eat at his table. There were also situations in which couples lived with the wife's parents or in a separate apartment or house. In any case, the couple usually lived in the same city with one set of parents or both and mutual visiting was frequent. Proximity facilitated close relationships between the parents and their married children. A woman could frequently obtain support from her own family if she had trouble with her husband's, assuming she had not shamed her own kin.

During the eighteenth century, according to an English physician who recorded his impressions of Aleppo life, Jewish women were veiled in the presence of strangers and did not eat at the same table with the men, except on Sabbath and holidays.

> From the common circle of several families living in the same house and inter-marriage among near kindred, it happens that Jews live more familiarly with women than Turks or Christians, and women are more

negligent in veiling before persons of their own nation. (Russell, 1794 II: 63)

The European Jewish ladies in Aleppo would stroll in public unveiled, scandalizing the rabbis. In the nineteenth century, one *hakham* wrote harshly about the laxity of Jewish women in their dress, and their negligence in covering their faces. He also complained about the new trend toward men and women's eating together at wedding feasts (Antebi, 1960/1: 118–21). By World War I, European styles of dress for both men and women were becoming popular in Aleppo, but had not yet completely replaced traditional dress (Segall, 1910).

According to Russell, women domestics remained in service until they were with child. Jews, more than Christians, used wet nurses. They seldom continued to suckle after the next pregnancy, he writes. Otherwise the child was kept at the breast from eighteen to twenty months. Jews were more prolific than Christians or Turks. He claimed that intrigues among Jewish domestic servants were more common than among Christians, but that Jews were no less chaste, only more often exposed to temptation. Matters were handled discretely so as to prevent a scandal or the exaction of a fine. An unmarried girl with child might be sent to another town, or be provided with a husband. Poverty made it difficult for the poor to marry. Venereal disease, however, was rare (Russell, 1794 II: 84). A sage warned the wealthy about the dangers of having male domestics in the house, and saw dangers in leaving a maid and a bachelor servant alone in the house, exposing them to temptation (Antebi, 1960/1: 32–33).

Information on extra-marital affairs is difficult to obtain. One person reported about a married couple who had a widow as neighbor. The husband became ill, and it was determined that the widow was performing love-magic to attract him. Divorce could only be initiated by the husband and was in any case considered shameful. In the discussion of married life in Aleppo and Damascus, features such as divorce and inheritance are emphasized, while normal interaction is neglected. Our reconstruction is based primarily on court cases and memories rather than on observation, although some inferences are made on the basis of oral testimonies (also see Zenner, 1980).

But a wife could precipitate divorce. Such is the case of the *moredet*, a woman who rebels against her husband. She may flee her husband's home, and return to that of her father. If she does this, she is liable to lose the rights guaranteed her in the marriage contract. She can provoke her husband's anger, in which case, he may threaten to leave her an *agunah*[3] 'till her hair whiten', that is, without the possibility of remarriage. Even if the *moredet* is granted a divorce after forfeiting her rights, she may still try to claim the return of gifts made to the couple from her side of the family. In other cases of divorce too, the provisions of the marriage contract are at issue in the court cases, not so much the rights or wrongs of actually granting a divorce.

The internal stresses and strains to which families were subject also emerge in inheritance cases. According to Jewish law, sons are the first in line to inherit, followed by daughters if there are no sons, then brothers of the deceased (Num. 27; Shulhan Arukh, Hoshen Mishpat, 276: 1). Men could ensure that members of their family not in line to inherit would receive gifts such as providing for a daughter's dowry. These legal provisions for widows and orphans often became issues on which litigations were based. For instance, a man's half-brothers and his full sister might battle for property, which he had inherited from his and his sister's maternal grandmother. Such cases were produced by a combination of circumstances stemming from death and other conditions, as well as human acquisitiveness. They serve to illustrate the imagery of 'peril and refuge', which Gulick (1976: 39) sees as a theme running through Middle Eastern institutions, including the family. Kinsmen are both an individual's 'first line of defense' and his 'last resort'. While they may be relied upon, this high expectation often cannot be met, and 'overdependence breeds disappointment, which in the absence of alternatives perpetuates overdependence.' The bitter quarrels of kinsmen, as well as the factiousness of close-knit communities, can thus be explained.

RELIGIOUS AND LEISURE ACTIVITIES

Syrian Jewry in the nineteenth century lacked the compartmentalization of the sacred from the profane, and the magical from the religious, which characterized Western Europe in that period. As I have noted elsewhere, great rabbis were considered figures who helped bring rain and otherwise direct supernatural aid to their people (Zenner, 1965a). The interweaving of the religious with the secular occurred in many aspects of life. All areas of existence could be adjudicated by a religious court, or would be subjected to comment and censure by a preacher. Aleppo, however, was not a sacred society in the sense that some nostalgic religious families in Jerusalem today remember it, 'a community of saints and scholars'.[4]

The use of leisure-time can be used to illustrate the connection of what to us are separate realms. As one rabbi wrote, the most extreme attitude was that every moment not needed for subsistence was to be spent in some form of sacred activity, whether prayer, learning, or devotional song. Hymns to God, even if written to the music of Arabic or Turkish love songs,[5] were praiseworthy, though the moralists deplored the songs on which they were based (Antebi, 1960/1: 10). Some young men sought physical prowess, but there was little time for this, and doing it on the Sabbath was a violation. Again, Antebi wrote:

> It is necessary to erase that which Jewish bachelors, lads empty of Torah and *misvot* (holy obligations) [do]. For they also go out on the Sabbath without license, to walk in the gardens, to swim in the water, and to hurl stones to each other, and to violate the Sabbath in public. (1960/1: 96).

Legend has it that several decades later Rabbi Saul Dwek, in the late nineteenth century, eliminated this custom, first by punishing these young men, and then forming them into teams for the purpose of singing competitively and vigorously in synagogue. The rabbi also arranged that the singers be paid small sums of money. Thus natural urges were harnessed to worship. But such conversion of public singing and dancing by women, considered profoundly immoral, was more difficult. One rabbi denounced what he considered to be an innovation, when women danced before the bride at a wedding with male musicians playing (Antebi, 1960/1: 119). In the early twentieth century a rabbi upbraided people going to cabarets to watch performances by women singers (Dwek, 1913/14: 17b; Adler, 1905). Gambling, particularly backgammon, dice and playing cards, was a common form of recreation. As elsewhere, it led to abuse, including theft, and sometimes it was a cause for divorce (Antebi, 1960/1: 10). In the early twentieth century, women of means spent time at card parties.

Sacred and mundane leisure activities came together during Sabbaths and holidays, and then clashes would occur. Antebi (1960/1: 10, 96) condemned Sabbath walks which people took in gardens around Aleppo. He feared both technical violation of the Sabbath and the development of morally dubious relationships. Instead, he counseled the men to sit at home and study sacred lore. Travel and performing a sacred duty were combined in pilgrimages. Jerusalem, Safed and Tiberias were in reach of many Syrian Jews during the Ottoman period. Aleppo Jews also went to Tedif al-Yahud, the reputed grave of the biblical Ezra. The favored time for visiting that shrine was the period between the Fast of the 9th of Av (July–August) and the High Holydays (September–October). While a separate realm of leisure was not recognized in the modern sense, there were professional entertainers, including musicians, dancing girls, clowns, singers and storytellers. People would also come together to listen to a good teller of tales, especially on Saturday nights.

CREEPING WESTERNIZATION

With the incorporation of most of the world into a single political and economic system and with the improvement of communications, the nineteenth and twentieth centuries have been marked by a tendency to cultural homogenization. The introduction of Western educational institutions was part of this development. The Protestant 'London Society for Promoting Christianity amongst the Jews' maintained a mission in Damascus during most of the nineteenth century and into the Mandatory period. Jews had ambivalent attitudes towards the Protestant missionaries for, unlike other Christians, they defended the Jews against blood libels. But attempts to convert Jews met with resolute opposition. For a time, the rabbis strongly opposed the activities of the Protestant mission, but by World War I a *modus vivendi* was reached: Jewish children obtained a modern English education with Christian overtones, and a rabbi came to the school to provide Jewish instruction (Gidney, 1897: 107–35; 1908: 101–8; Cohen, 1973: 137; Harel, 1992: 273–82; informants).

The Alliance Israélite Universelle founded a boys' school in Aleppo in 1869, followed by the establishment of schools for both boys and girls in Damascus and Beirut, and a girls' school in Aleppo in 1889 (Harel, 1992). Both Christian and Jewish schools often helped prepare Syrian Jews for foreign trade and emigration, since they taught French and English, as well as Hebrew and Arabic. In 1900 more than half of the students did not pay tuition and were supported by foreign philanthropy (Adler, 1905; Cohen, 1973: 137–40; Harel, 1992: 381–2). The Aleppo notables and rabbis went through a number of periods of either support or opposition to the Alliance schools. In the 1860s, some notables opposed the Alliance policy of integrating poor and well-to-do students in the same school, while rabbis supported the Alliance. Later, as the Alliance became more secularistic and the rabbis were influenced by ultra-orthodox Ashkenazim in Jerusalem, they became hostile to the Alliance (Harel, 1992: 87–100). In the 1960s, in orthodox circles in Jerusalem, stories were still told about the religious practices of the first Alliance principal who came to Aleppo, pretending to be an observant Jew. A rumor was circulated that he put on phylacteries, but when the phylacteries were examined, some of the scrolls in the phylacteries were found to be missing. The rabbis also opposed the founding of Masonic and B'nai Brith lodges in Aleppo.

In the areas of fashion, taste, and morals, Westernization was gradual and still very incomplete by the end of the Ottoman period. Syrian Jews had European models, such as the Italian Jewish merchants who settled there in the eighteenth century. The laxity of which moralists complained with regard to veiling and sexual segregation may have been influenced by these wealthy foreigners. Western dress became more common during the late nineteenth and early twentieth centuries. Syrian Jews also came into contact with Western Christian tourists, whom some entertained in their homes, as well as with European Jews (Segall, 1910: 99–104; Harel, 1992: 44). In the twentieth century there is a shift in the remonstrances of the preachers. Whereas Antebi in the early nineteenth century complained of women dancing at weddings in the presence of men, Dwek a century later, condemns the cabarets. It was only in the 1920s and 1930s, however, that mass media, such as films and radio, were introduced into the Levant and that speeded the process of homogenization.[6]

Berger (1976: 186) has defined 'modernization' as 'a shift from giveness to choice on the level of meaning'. What had previously been unquestioned as a 'fact of life' now became an individual option. By the end of the Ottoman period, this process was well underway in the cities of Syria. The Jews continued to adhere to much of their traditional Jewish and Middle Eastern patterns, but they had been profoundly affected by European culture.

Notes

1   By that time, many of the rabbis had emigrated, as had many of the wealthiest member of society. In the Mandatory period (1920–1940) synagogue attendance on the Sabbath was still generally observed. On other issues, however, such as that of women going to cafés outside the home, the rabbis had more difficulty (Ne'eman, 1927). During the 1920s there was serious quarrelling between the rabbis and the younger men on this kind of issue. A Jerusalem informant, who visited Aleppo, was shocked when she saw belly-dancing at a party, and card playing as a major leisure-time activity.
2   How 'iyun halebi actually differs from Ashkenazic forms of studying Talmud requires examination. There is also an 'iyun tunisi in Tunisia – see ch. 10 above.
3   An *agunah* is a woman whose husband is missing without proof of death, or who has deserted her without a divorce, thus not releasing her from the status of being a married woman.
4   This view already existed in the early nineteenth century, when Antebi wrote about a former generation, which rose early at night to study and to pray, and which used each spare moment for sacred learning (1960/1: 3–5).
5   On such songs using Arabic melody-types but in Hebrew, known as *baqashot*, see Zenner (1980) and Katz (1970). The problem of Jewish toughs who played games on the Sabbath appeared in Tripoli (Libya), as well as in Aleppo (Goldberg, 1990: 31–3).
6   But it should be noted that the new media also helped sustain and develop a modern form of Arabic music.

References

Abu-Lughod, Janet L. (1987) 'The Islamic City: Historic Myth, Islamic Essence, and Contemporary Relevance,' *International Journal of Middle Eastern Studies*, 19: 155–76.

Al-Qattan, Najwa (1992) 'The Damascene Jewish Community in the Latter Decades of the Eighteenth Century: Aspects of Socio-Economic Life based on the Registers of the *Sharia* Courts,' in Thomas Philipp (ed.), *The Syrian Land in the 18th and 19th Century*, Berliner Islamstudien, vol. 5 (Stuttgart: Franz Steiner).

Adler, E.N. (1905) *Jews in Many Lands* (Philadelphia).

Antebi, A. (1960/61) *Hokhmah u'musar* (Jerusalem).

Baron, S.W. (1933) 'The Jews and the Syrian Massacres of 1860,' *Proceedings of the American Academy for Jewish Research*, 4: 3–31.

Baron, S.W. (1940) 'Great Britain and Damascus Jewry in 1860–61,' *Jewish Social Studies*, 2: 179–208.

Berger, Peter L. (1976) *Pyramids of Sacrifice* (New York: Doubleday).

Bowring, John (1840) 'Report on the Commercial State of Syria,' *Parliamentary Papers*, 21, Reports of Commissioners, London.

Burton, Isabel (1879) *The Inner Life of Syria, Palestine and the Holy Land* (London).

Braver, A.J. (1945/6) 'The Jews of Damascus After the Blood Libel of 1840,' *Zion*, 10: 83–108 (Hebrew with English abstract).

Cohen, H.J. (1971) 'Picciotto,' *Encyclopedia Judaica*, 13: 498.

Cohen, H.J. (1973) *The Jews of the Middle East, 1860–1972* (Jerusalem: Israel Universities Press).

Dwek, J.S. (1913/14) *Derekh emunah* (Aleppo).

Franco, M. and Gottheil, R. (1903) 'Damascus,' *Jewish Encyclopedia*, 4: 415–21.

Gerber, Haim (1994) *State, Society and Law in Islam: Ottoman Law in Comparative Perspective* (Albany, NY: State University of New York Press).

Gibb, H.A.R. and Bowen, H. (1950–7) *Islamic Society and the West*, 2 vols (Oxford: Oxford University Press).

Gidney, W.T. (1897) *Sites and Scenes: Descriptions of Oriental Missions* (London).

Gidney, W.T. (1908) *A History of the London Society for Promoting Christianity amongst the Jews, 1808–1908* (London).

Goitein, S.D. (1955) *Jews and Arabs* (New York: Schocken).

Goldberg, Harvey E. (1990) *Jewish Life in Muslim Libya: Rivals and Relatives* (Chicago: University of Chicago Press).

Gulick, John (1976) *The Middle East: An Anthropological Perspective* (Pacific Palisades: Goodyear).

Harel, Yaron (1992) 'Changes in Syrian Jewry, 1840–1880' (in Hebrew). Unpublished PhD dissertation, Bar-Ilan University.

Horowitz, Donald (1985) *Ethnic Groups in Conflict* (Berkeley: University of California Press).

Karpat, Kemal (1978) 'Ottoman Population Records and Census of 1881/2–1893,' *International Journal of Middle Eastern Studies*, 9: 237–74.

Katz, Ruth (1970) 'Mannerism and Culture Change,' *Current Anthropology*, 11: 465–75.

Krikorian, M.F. (1977) *Armenians in the Service of the Ottoman Empire, 1860–1908* (London: Routledge and Kegan Paul).

Laniado, David (1980) *Li'qedoshim asher ba'ares* (Jerusalem).

Maoz, Moshe (1968) *Ottoman Reform in Syria and Palestine* (London: Oxford University Press).

Marcus, Abraham (1989) *The Middle East on the Eve of Modernity: Aleppo in the Eighteenth Century* (New York: Columbia University Press).

Masters, Bruce (1988) *The Origins of Western Economic Domination in the Middle East: Mercantilism and the Islamic Economy in Aleppo, 1600–1750* (New York: New York University Press).

Nehmad, M. (1941): 'Lament on the Quake,' *Ha Olam*, 3 April (Hebrew).

Nehmad, M. (1943) 'The Family of Ha'dayan,' *Ha'mishor*, February 26, 1933 (Ben-Zvi Archives, Hebrew).

Neeman, P. (1927) 'Jewish Communities: Beirut (12 Av), Sidon (3 Av), Damascus (10 Elul), Aleppo (24 Elul)'. Articles in *Ha'aretz* daily (Hebrew, Tel-Aviv).

Philipp, Thomas (1984) 'The Farhi Family and the Changing Position of the Jews in Syria, 1750–1860,' *Middle Eastern Studies*, 20: 37–52.

Russell, Alexander (1794) *The Natural History of Aleppo*, 2 vols, 2nd edn (London).

Segall, J. (1910) *Travels Through Northern Syria* (London: Society for Promoting Christianity Amongst the Jews).

Zenner, Walter P. (1965a) 'Syrian Jewish Identification in Israel,' PhD Thesis in Anthropology, Columbia University (Ann Arbor: University Microfilm Order No. 66–8536).

Zenner, Walter P. (1965b) 'Saints and Piecemeal Supernaturalism among the Jerusalem Sephardim,' *Anthropological Quarterly*, 38: 201–17.

Zenner, Walter P. (1980) 'Censorship and Syncretism: Some Anthropological Approaches to the Study of Middle Eastern Jews,' in F. Talmage (ed.), *Studies in Jewish Folklore* (Cambridge, Mass.: Association for Jewish Studies) 377–94.

Zenner, Walter P. (1982) 'The Jews in Late Ottoman Syria,' in S. Deshen and W.P. Zenner (eds), *Jewish Societies in the Middle East*, Washington DC: University Press of America, 155–210.

Zenner, Walter P. (1987) 'Middleman Minorities in the Syrian Mosaic: Tradition, Conflict and Image Management,' *Sociological Perspectives*, 30: 400–21.

Zenner, Walter P. (1991) *Minorities in the Middle* (Albany, NY: State University of New York Press).

14 Baghdad Jewry in Late Ottoman Times: The Emergence of Social Classes and of Secularization
Shlomo Deshen

Mesopotamian Jewry is most intriguing. For over a millennium it was a major center of Jewry in terms of both size and cultural vigor. During much of that period Mesopotamian Jewry was in fact the predominant center of the Jewish people, and an abundance of historical sources sheds light on the social structure of the community, until the High Middle Ages. Then, quite abruptly, the community virtually disappears from the historical record, not to reemerge until the eighteenth century. Historians explain this as a result of the havoc that the Mongolian invasion wrought in the thirteenth century. In the nineteenth century the community suddenly undergoes enormous demographic and economic expansion, and blooms as a religio-cultural center. Cultural creativity continues (until again, the sudden demise of the community in 1950), and becomes diversified as a result of a rather unique form of modernization and secularization. Baghdad Jewry produced inter alia *literary artists, who depicted both conditions in their land of origin and reflections based on their experience as a result of emigration. But study of this major Jewish society struggles far behind that of other communities, including some that are far less weighty. The present contribution is an attempt to plumb some of the available sources, while raising issues comparable to those that sociologically-oriented historians have raised on other Jewish societies.*

In late Ottoman times and until the end of the British Mandate in 1932, the community in Baghdad was one of the glories of modern Jewry. Among

---

Source: Abbreviated version of a paper in *Association of Jewish Studies Review*, 19 (1994): 19–44.

contemporary Middle Eastern communities, Baghdad Jewry was unrivaled in size and institutions. But despite its prominence, and that of its descendants in Israel today, Baghdad Jewry has been studied very little. Our understanding of Jewish societies in obscure regions such as Yemen and Tripolitania is more advanced. This paper offers the outlines of a sociological portrait to fill that gap. The thesis of the present study is that late Ottoman Baghdad Jewry was characterized by increasing complexity. The population grew dramatically and became socially heterogeneous; new strata emerged and new organizations were founded. The main sources for the study are the legal responsa of local sages.

In the nineteenth century the Ottomans reasserted their sway over their Mesopotamian province, improving its security. Baghdad began to play a role in the British India trade, and the Jewish community greatly increased. In 1794 the number of Jews there is reported to have been about 2,500, or 3.3 per cent of the population of the city (about 75,000).[1] By 1893 the Jews are reported to have increased to about 50,000, no less than 35 per cent of a population of about 145,000. The Jewish community thus would seem to have increased twentyfold, while the city as a whole barely doubled its population. The number of Baghdad synagogues increased ten-fold, from three to about 30. Moreover, synagogues were generally overcrowded. The causes of the increase in the second half of the nineteenth century are migration from Persia, where Jews were particularly oppressed, and from Kurdistan and Syria.

The reassertion of Ottoman rule in the nineteenth century coincided with the *Tanzimat* reforms, which tightened the hold of the central government over the provinces. The effect on the Jewish community was to encroach on the prerogatives of old-established families, and to favor newly-installed government-backed functionaries and institutions. The innovations coincided with a great expansion of commerce, resulting from British policies in India. Baghdad, and in particular its Jewish sector, became a commercial hub. The opening of the Suez Canal caused ancient inland routes of commerce to stagnate, and international commerce to move southward to the port of Basra.

The outcome of all this was a general expansion. In addition to population increase, new institutions and social classes grew. Baghdad Jewry became increasingly polarized economically, as the number of wealthy financiers on the one hand, and of the poor on the other, increased. Uniquely in Jewish social history we hear of mass political mobilization. In 1883, 1,700 people signed a petition protesting taxation; in 1884, some 400 signed a petition protesting the appointment of an unpopular sage to the office of *hakham bashi* (chief sage). On another occasion a protagonist in a dispute found it necessary to explain why he had not circulated a mass petition to advance his cause. People beyond the limited circle of hereditary notables became politically active.

In the 1820s Baghdad Jews began to establish colonies of merchants and industrial entrepreneurs in India and throughout the Far East, and by the end of the century they were also in England. The Jewish presence in Baghdad trading was so salient that Saturdays were slack days. A European visitor in 1880 reports characteristically, 'On Sabbath days all the stores close, and a holy repose (*dumiat qodesh*) prevails in the city'. But we also hear of people who could not make a living, and of people who were forced to search for food among the refuse.

Mesopotamian Jewry had a venerable tradition of having been governed by scions of the royal Davidic family of ancient Judea that went back at least as far as the beginning of the common era. The *nasi'* (president, pl. *nesi'im*) of the community was a member of that circle, who owed his position to his acting as a financier for the local Muslim governor. The *nasi'* was responsible for collecting taxes and sundry extortions from the Jews, and provided the governor with loans and securities. Sometimes the *nasi'* advanced the community's payments out of his own resources. The community had little say about the appointment of the *nasi'*. This was a personal transaction between the Muslim potentate and a wealthy financier. The *nasi'* maintained his position by having recourse to the potentate's authority. In contrast to other Jewish societies, eighteenth-century Baghdad Jewry lacked an independent group of sages who, in comparable Jewish communities of Northern Europe and Morocco for instance, constituted a resourceful and powerful stratum. Appointments to judicial and religious positions in those communities lay partly in the hands of the sages themselves and partly in the hands of lay leaders. Sometimes the sages had more say (as in pre-colonial Morocco), and sometimes (as in European Jewry) the lay community had more say, with gradations in between in other Jewish societies. But in eighteenth-century Baghdad we hear of a single-handed appointment, solely by the *nasi'*. Moreover, after appointment the *nasi'* interfered in court procedures, which elsewhere were governed exclusively by rabbinical discretion.

Towards the middle of the nineteenth century the relative standing changes: the number of sages increased and they are found operating in academies (*yeshiva* or *midrash*, pl. *midrashim*), making legal decisions over matters that are brought to the attention of senior sages, and which are then reviewed by them. And the *nasi'* is no more heard of in the sources. Rabbis Yosef Hayim and 'Abdulla Somekh, the major nineteenth century sages of Baghdad, often remark that they allow junior sages and disciples, referred to as 'the sages of the academy' to deliberate over matters that were brought before them as senior sages. The importance of this new stratum of sages is also evident in cases of public disputes: they take sides for or against particular appointments to the office of *hakham bashi*, and on matters of income and taxation.

Baghdad Jews had numerous terms to designate differences of social status. These terms are consistent with the class situation, the emergence of a new stratum of religious scholars and the decline of the old political elite. Care in religious practice was expressed in a variety of honorific terms, *medaqdeqim* ('punctilious'), *zehirim* ('careful'), *'anshei ma'aseh* ('men of [good] deeds'). The awareness of the category of sages and painstaking people also produced awareness of the opposite category, of persons who are 'boors', *'am ha-'ares*. Similarly, we hear of customs of 'the common people', *hamon ha-'am* in a derogatory context. People of lower class are referred to stereotypically: butchers are 'complete evildoers', and 'most bakers are boors'. A particular custom that a sage disapproves of is categorized in terms of a putative low-class origin. It is termed a custom that the synagogue-sextons 'have fabricated', (*badu*). When sages were called upon for advice about ritual practices, they imposed strict practice upon boors, because 'it is proper to be stringent (*le-hahmir*) with [them].' This is phrased as a virtual principle of rabbinical pastoral teaching in the community. Comparable Moroccan and Tunisian material has no trace of such expressions.

This overt and cognitive categorization of people in terms of wealth, and further, the linkage of the difference, as a matter of course, with socio-religious practice, is remarkable. We find it at certain times and places in traditional Jewish and other societies, for instance in sixteenth and seventeenth century central European Jewry. But by no means is it universal. An 1874 Baghdad journal report is illuminating. Writing for a European publication, a member of the community described a local philanthropist who had given grants to 150 men, to study Torah:

> There are many completely uncultured people here who are ignorant of Bible and Mishna, [lack] good manners, and are a disgrace to the Jewish people. For eight months now this man has prevailed upon [one hundred and fifty of] them to improve themselves, teaching them the Torah of the Living G-d, so that they should be considered like all our wealthy brethren (*nehshavim ke-khol 'aheinu ha-'ashirim*) ... They have come ... to keep the precepts like all Israel ... rising early to prayers and staying late in the evening in synagogue, and study diligently ... We hope that in the future there will be no more boors in Baghdad ...

Evidently, the writer has a conception of material affluence as being normally and naturally tied to excellence in religiosity, and conversely – poverty in his view dovetails religious laxity. Seen in terms of class theory these conceptions, linking material differences with symbols of differentiation of other spheres of life (such as religion), are a fundamental element of social class formation.

A sage, discussing the possibility of a person using the *talit* and *tefillin* (prayer shawl and phylacteries) of another person without permission, remarks, 'In our times most people are particular that others should not put on their *talit* and *tefillin* [which they left in synagogue]'. In many Jewish communities people are not particular about others using the ritual objects that are normally left in synagogue after daily services, provided they are properly returned to their place. But in Baghdad men were fussy about this. The impression we gain is that decorum, formality, and distance between people were marked.

Differences in status were entrenched. In a discussion on synagogue etiquette Rabbi Yosef Hayim calls on people to restrain their expressions of obeisance to superiors while in synagogue. He requests that one act according to *halakha*, which requires worshipers to offer gestures of respect only to one's parents, the learned, and the aged. The sage rules:

> When a rich notable (*gevir*) who is neither aged nor learned enters synagogue, one should not rise in his honor, because such a gesture would imply a lack of honor to Heaven. Such is the case even concerning a rich notable whom one would honor outside synagogue. However, if the case happens to be of a famous rich notable of the community leaders (*mi-yehidey ha-qahal*), and he is insistent about this, then it is permissible to rise in his honor, so as to avert strife.

The sage does not conceive that people might err by being disrespectful. He worries that they might expand improperly the categories of people entitled to overt gestures of respect, and that he considered unseemly in a house of worship. This kind of concern can arise only among people who are highly conscious of status, and who strongly adhere to symbolic gestures that differentiate individuals.

Status consciousness also had its effects on marriage arrangements. Families were more or less respectable, and the term 'of good family' is often used. Public opinion, honor and shame were important. A case came before the sages in which a married woman was suspected of adultery. Halakhic law requires divorce when such a suspicion is confirmed. In the case at hand the sage ruled that suspicions were unfounded and cleared the woman's name, but the husband nonetheless insisted on divorce, on the grounds that it would be shameful for him to remain married to a woman who had even been suspected of such a thing. In another case the father of a young man, engaged to be married, belatedly discovered that the father of the bride made his living as a school teacher. The man wanted to break his son's engagement on the grounds that this made the match 'shameful for him'. A sage has a discussion about 'loss of face': he concludes that this is most grievous when a person is among people of 'his own kind'.

Brides universally like to appear in finery, but the rationale that the Baghdad sources suggest for this, as a matter of course, are revealing. It is 'to advertize the distinction of the bride's family'. The status element is emphasized. Some girls rejected offers of marriage, and threatened suicide if the father persisted with a particular match. In one case the father of a bride gave the girl's age as eight years less than it actually was. The groom was apparently of modest background and the bride was of a notable family whose menfolk were scholars. Presumably, because of the bride's advanced age, her family were resigned to a less than optimal groom, but they still had to resort to deception. Such deception could arise only where the families, and certainly the young people concerned, did not know each other, a condition that must have been common in the growing and heterogeneous community of Baghdad. Families new to the city would have little familiarity with the parents or with the child concerned.

The contrast with the Moroccan Jewish family is striking. In the much more extensive material we have for traditional Morocco there is hardly any indication of friction over matchmaking. I suggest that this is probably because the Moroccan communities were more homogeneous in both origin and class, and numerically much smaller. Matches were therefore between people who were likely to be familiar and comfortable with each other in advance.

Formalization and institution-building devolved primarily on sages. In the mid-nineteenth century the Ottomans, as part of the *Tanzimat* reforms, created the office of *hakham bashi* (chief sage), by which they sought to tighten their hold over their subjects and weaken the old aristocracy, the lay *nesi'im*. The *hakham bashi*, appointed jointly by the authorities and notables of the community, replaced the *nasi'* and came to fill both religious and administrative functions. This appointment was often a source of dissent, and incumbents changed frequently. Some of the sages who held the post of *hakham bashi* had little standing in the community, but the mere fact that the role was earmarked for sages was of significance. It added to the power of sages, and detracted from that of lay notables, who were represented side by side with the sages in the committee for secular affairs (*va'ad ha-gashmi*) and the committee for religious affairs (*va'ad ha-ruhani*); the head of the joint committee was the *hakham bashi*.

Whereas the old regime of the *nesi'im* was historically rooted in the community, that of the *hakham bashi* was largely an alien bureaucratic appointment of a particular sage, which was often controversial. The new regime, therefore, in contrast to the old one, was not fully legitimate in the eyes of people of the community. Consequently sages who were members of notable and wealthy families often avoided being appointed to the legally-dubious position of *hakham bashi*. By avoiding this role those sages gained superior, albeit unofficial, standing within the community. This is true in particular of the leading sages of the period, Rabbis 'Abdulla Somekh and Yosef Hayim, and other sages, members of the latter's family. After the *Tanzimat* reforms – the disappearance of the *nasi'* and the creation of the novel *hakham bashi* position – the remaining traditional role, of the sage who was independent of the general authorities, became enhanced in the eyes of people. In particular, those sages who combined aristocratic lineage and independent wealth with superior personal qualities, were respected.

In contrast to the *nasi'* of old, the *hakham bashi* was not usually a member of a wealthy notable family, and thus did not command his own resources. He maintained his office out of a tax on kosher meat and out of endowments. Sometimes he was supported by wealthy laymen who belonged to his clique. This kind of community head was new for Baghdad. The cost of the office of the *hakham bashi* was paid by the imposition of a new tax by the Ottoman authorities, that the *hakham bashi* collected. Petitions circulated among the affluent who had to shoulder this burden; and employees, junior sages, and professionals in religious affairs (such as teachers and *shohatim*) demonstrated and even went on strike. They fought to retain their age-old privilege of immunity from community taxation. But in view of the weight of the new tax, and probably also because of the newly-increased number of sages who requested immunity, the affluent were called upon to shoulder what they regarded as an unreasonable burden. This aroused their ire and led to unprecedented social tension.

The ensuing configuration of social arrangements entailed increasing stratification by social class. The nineteenth century sources indicate vague recognition of this reality on the part of contemporaries. Thus, the forementioned 1874 journal reporter did not conceptualize the reality he described with explicit class terms. But by the beginning of the twentieth century class formation was evident to all. A British consular report of 1910 written by a local Jewish employee, repeatedly mentions 'class' divisions within the community, and 'class' identities of individuals. A sermon delivered around the same time describes class differentiation vividly. Speaking about the community's old religious school, Rabbi Shim'on Agassi, one of the senior sages, expressed his anguish at innovations:

> There are now some [people] in our community who have raised an uproar about the Midrash Talmud Torah that caters to nearly 2,500 boys, learning Scripture and a little Rabbinics. Most [of the boys] come from poor homes ... [Those people] say that the Midrash consumes a vast sum [out] of the community treasury ... and the returns are not worth the expense, because most of those who leave that house ... become porters and disposers of refuse on donkeys, cleaners of latrines, and similarly despised and degrading occupations, that do not bring honor to our people (*lelo kavod la'uma*) and [that] also are useless to the individuals themselves (*rehoqim mi-to'elet 'asmam*) ... for these degraded occupations do not enable a livelihood ... All that in contrast to the graduates of the Alliance schools ... who know how to write, and [know] foreign languages, and make a good living, some as clerks of the merchants, and [others] have themselves become big businessmen ... Therefore, [those people say], 'It is better for us to hand over the management of the Midrash to the Alliance!'

The sage concludes with a forceful response to that suggestion:

> Those people should know that even if, Heaven forbid, there remain in our community (*qehal 'adateinu*) only the porters, disposers of garbage and cleaners of latrines – through whom they despise us (*mevazim 'otanu bahem*) – we will nevertheless manage to continue and supply all the needs of this school!

This reaction and the whole tenor of the speech reveal antagonism between the classes of well-to-do merchants and others, fueled by the tendency of divisions of wealth to nurture religio-cultural differences.

Several social classes figure in this preacher's sermons: dwelling on the sins that, in his view, led to a drought in 1914, he called on his audience to mend their ways:

> If the sages do not do anything [about this] can you remain passive ...!? The Torah that the sages study protects them. [Therefore] though eventually they also will suffer from rising prices, they will not suffer as much as you ... I myself am a merchant like you. I understand your troubles. Also the wealthy do not feel all the troubles that visit us, as everyone knows ... Only you suffer from the drought ... the high costs, and from the authorities who constantly make demands ... why therefore do you remain lax ...? Why don't you help yourselves? How long will you go on dreaming, relying on the sages!?

The preacher clearly distinguishes between three classes – ordinary merchants, wealthy merchants, and sages – characterized both by material and by religio-cultural features, and he is poignantly aware of the tension between them. At the turn of the century Baghdad Jews were becoming increasingly cognizant of social classes.

Secularization was another major process, of which contemporaries were becoming aware. Beginning in the 1870s, Baghdad reporters for Jewish periodicals published in Germany, Poland and India note instances of disregard for orthodox Jewish practice, such as patronizing of coffeehouses and music-making on the Sabbath and, after the turn of the century, writing in commercial ledgers on the Sabbath. But these desecrations do not figure as major concerns to the rabbis. Comparing the responsa of eighteenth- and nineteenth-century sages, one sees little difference in concerns for religiosity and orthodox practice. The nineteenth-century Baghdad sages seem to be secure, just like their predecessor, that theirs was a stable world.

The 1910 consular report states rather sweepingly that 'in contradistinction to past days the clergy enjoy no influence over their co-religionists'. An illuminating sermon of 1913 adds to this. The preacher, complaining about the new ways (particularly women's dress and relaxed segregation of the sexes), called on his audience not to rely on the sages to correct matters. The latter have no influence any more, he laments. Therefore, the preacher advised, lay people should correct matters. In the past, he explained, the sages were allied with 'the rich', and the latter used to execute the directions of the sages. The two strata governed the community jointly. But now wealthy men do not devote themselves much to public affairs, but concentrate on commerce, 'and since the rich are not effective, neither are the sages effective', he concluded.

The preacher sees traditional self-rule falling apart, but he does not rail at villains. He is notably mild. The wealthy are not described as radical, or even innovative, certainly not as heretics. He sees them just as very busy men who choose not to devote themselves to Jewish public affairs. Those whom the preacher berates are presented as part of a society that he conceives as unified, and from which he detaches neither himself nor his audience. It is possible that the people whom the preacher berated were actually in his audience. The religio-social disintegration that is reflected in the sermon is not far-reaching.

In late Ottoman times secularization was slow in coming to Baghdad and reaction to it mild. Abandonment of religious practices in Baghdad was not coupled with a supporting secular ideology and did not turn into an actual movement of secularization, in contrast to European Jewry where, beginning in the eighteenth century, secular ideologies and movements did develop. The Baghdadi sources reflect an unawareness of changing times. Baghdadi sages evaluated the transgressors of religious norms as people who succumbed to old-time, all-too-familiar, human failings, not as innovators; hence the mildness of their castigations. Secular schooling, in the guise of the Alliance Israelite system, was conceived in terms of the traditional world view, objectionable when it clashed with religion, but not threatening in a fundamental way, the forebodings of a transformed godless world. We come to an important conclusion: late Ottoman Baghdad Jewry, while it did undergo change, was not radically recasting itself. People conceived their community as one in which the pious were losing control; with such mutations they were familiar from their folk-culture, the Bible and rabbinic texts, and they took them in their stride. Cultural change was seen as neither innovative nor threatening.

Another conclusion concerns the social stratification of the community. The data are replete with indications that people conceived themselves as belonging to particular classes. Symbols of status dovetailed with occupations and material standing. At the same time we hear little of kin ties, the major element of social organization in premodern societies. In contrast to the numerous indications of class differentiation in late Ottoman Baghdad, evidence that kinship was potent in public life is scarce. Also the relative silence of the sources on another point is remarkable: Commonly in Jewish societies, certainly since the late Middle Ages, social life revolved around migrant groups or quasi-ethnic groups, leading to the formation of synagogue congregations of people of particular common origin. One would have expected these to appear in Baghdad, since the community included many migrants from other places, such as Persia and Kurdistan. But in all the sources and secondary materials I have reviewed, there is no trace of such a development. So how did people in this vast community conceive themselves, and how did they organize themselves? The foregoing cluster of data clearly indicates the direction of class formation.

Note

1 Full citation of sources may be found in the expanded versions of the paper, in *Association of Jewish Studies Review*, and particularly in the French version in *Annales*.

15 The Religious World of Jewish Women in Kurdistan
Susan Starr Sered

Despite a promising early beginning, with the work of Erich Brauer in the 1930s, followed by Dina Feitelson in the 1950s, Donna Shai and Yona Sabar in the 1970s, the study of Kurdish Jewry has not developed much over the years. Those scholars attempted to reconstruct conditions in Kurdistan on the base of fieldwork among immigrants in Israel, and they contended with the difficulties of 'doing ethnography at a distance'. But they lacked an advantage that other scholars had, who worked in a similar way in the field of North African Jewry. The latter benefited from a tradition of major anthropological scholarship, the work of Westermarck, Gellner, Geertz and numerous other leading anthropologists. That led to a rich corpus of theory, and hence the interest in the work of both Judaists and Islamists of North Africa. Work in the Kurdish field had little theoretical focus. The importance of the work of Susan Sered, Associate Professor of Anthropology at Bar-Ilan University, is that it breaks away from the old model of work in the Kurdish field, and operates with a theoretical model. It is part of the wave of feminist anthropology, which evinces a fresh sensitivity to the activities of women and explores their particularities. This probing leads the present study, devoted to religiosity, to the discovery of a shade of piety that, Sered argues, constitutes a female speciality. The women were concerned in particular with practices that would be auspicious for the home and its members. They were little concerned with matters beyond the circle of intimacy. Sered brings evidence that Kurdish Jewish women even conceptualized the great Jewish national themes in terms of personally relevant matters. The author suggests that these traits constitute a 'nurturing characteristic' of Kurdish Jewish women's religiosity. The theoretical thrust of the paper leads the author at the end to raise questions in the general field of religion.

Much of the religious world of women in traditional Jewish communities has remained concealed, both from historians and from ethnographers. The reasons behind this concealment are worthy of discussion for the insight they provide into the content and structure of women's religious lives. The invisibility of traditional Jewish women's religiosity is not merely a function of disinterest on the part of historians and ethnographers, but an inherent feature of women's religious conduct. Embedded within the profane, centered upon individuals, domesticated, sexually segregated, and non-written, the religiosity of traditional Jewish women was bound to escape the notice of Western scholars.[1] In this chapter I focus upon Jewish women in Kurdistan, but many of my observations would hold true for other Jewish communities, and indeed for other groups of women around the world as well (cf. Loeb, 1992).

The foremost ethnographer of Kurdish Jewish culture, Erich Brauer, meticulously documented the secular and religious activities of women. At the beginning of a chapter devoted to women's lives Brauer wrote:

> While the Yemenite Jewish woman (who is in general more gentle and sensitive than the Kurdish woman) expressed her Judaism in certain [identifiable] ways, it is difficult to see in what the Judaism of the Kurdish Jewish woman is expressed except in outward observances of religious law. (Brauer, 1947: 248)

In the present chapter I seek both to document the rich religious life of Kurdish Jewish women, and to explain how Brauer could have so grossly misinterpreted the data which he himself had so carefully collected.[2] In addition, I shall draw certain parallels between the religious mode of Kurdish women and Jewish women of other communities.

My own experience with Kurdish Jewish women was in 1985-6 when I carried out fieldwork among a group of elderly women in Jerusalem (see Sered, 1992). Although the goal of the fieldwork was to understand their current religious world, in the course of my work I learned a great deal about their religious practices in Kurdistan. In writing this chapter I have supplemented what I heard from my informants with the ethnographic writings of Erich Brauer, Yona Sabar, and Donna Shai. Like myself, all of these anthropologists have reconstructed Kurdish Jewish life through the recollections of immigrants living in Israel. My own work, like Brauer's, was with women who had come from Kurdistan in the first decades of the century; some of the other anthropologists studied the Kurdish Jews who came to Israel during the 1950s. To the best of our knowledge, there are no more Jews living in Kurdistan. Everything that we can say about the traditional religious life of Kurdish Jewish women is twice filtered: once through the memories of our informants, and again through our own Western anthropological worldview. While it is difficult to unravel all of the myriad biases which this double filtering entails, I believe that the two most critical issues (at least for the purposes of this paper) are the tendency of Kurdish Jews in Israel to shape their narratives of Kurdish life to make it look more in keeping with 'normative' Israeli Judaism, and assumptions on the part of Western anthropologists that our conceptions of 'religion' and 'gender' have cross-cultural applicability.

THE FAMILY

In Kurdistan women's religious world was inseparable from their domestic lives; indeed, it is impossible to understand their religious practices without placing them within the context of women's family relationships. The central emotional link for Kurdish Jewish women was their children. This link was a tenuous one – infant mortality rates were high and many rituals were aimed at averting child death. While we have no systematic demographic data concerning infant mortality in Kurdistan, many of my informants related stories such as, 'My neighbor who gave birth to ten children, all of whom died'. Another one of my informants described her own family history, 'I had four children who died in the Old Country, and four who lived in Israel'. The emotional bond between mothers and children, coupled with the very real fear of child death, set the stage for a large portion of the religious beliefs and practices of Kurdish Jewish women. Much of the religious life of the women had to do with warding off the evil eye and evil spirits, which were believed to endanger children and pregnant women.

Fertility and infertility were seen as women's responsibilities. Again, we lack demographic data, but from the number of rituals aimed at enhancing fertility we can assume a high rate of fertility problems. If this indeed was the case, the reasons for low levels of fertility most probably had to do both with poor nutrition (exacerbated by the fact that women typically ate after men), and with the custom of marrying girls at so young an age that many young women would not attain reproductive maturity until they had been married for several years. In the struggle to stay alive and keep one's children alive, women were dependent upon the support of other women. Whether a woman received enough food to eat often hinged upon her good relations with her mother-in-law. Since women rarely went out of the house (except for bringing water from the river or well and washing clothes at the river), and social contact with men was rare, women relied upon the women of their extended families for social contact and support. Neighbors and kinswomen taught young brides about pregnancy, they served as midwives at birth, and they cared for the new mother during the post-partum rest period.

Relationships with husbands tended to be problematic. According to Brauer, when a girl menstruated for the first time she would be told that from now on 'the bread of her father's house is forbidden her' (Brauer, 1947: 90). In other words, she soon must marry and leave her natal family. My informants reported only positive memories of their parents' houses; thus we can assume that being told that she must leave was an unhappy event for most girls. Marriages were arranged, and in many instances young girls were married to men who already had children from a previous marriage, in which the wife had died (often in childbirth). My informants spoke with resentment about their marriages, and were disinterested in describing wedding rituals. Girls were often married at age fourteen, and the marriage could be consummated before the young women had reached physical maturity. The young married woman would be likely to give birth to her first child before completing her own body growth, and ensuing mortality rates were high.

From the work of Donna Shai (1982: 279) we know that women's wedding songs spoke about the reluctance of brides to leave their natal families.

> You will cry enough, sleep more tonight.
> Tomorrow you are going.
> Say good-bye to your sister-in-law
> And your three brothers.
> As much as you cry, it won't help you,
> You are going.
> Why are you running to the mountains?
> The bridegroom's parents are taking you.
> Don't hide yourself, it won't help you
> To hide yourself in the mountains.
> Come and go, it is best for you.
> Why are you standing against the wall crying?
> Go with the parents of the groom.
> That will be best for you!
> They take her and go.

In Brauer's book there are close to thirty-five pages on wedding rituals. But I find it difficult to understand how Brauer managed to so closely document wedding rituals, as my own informants were utterly disinterested in discussing their weddings. For this reason, I have chosen not to repeat Brauer's descriptions, but refer the interested reader to the appropriate chapter in his book (Brauer, 1947: 90–125). The songs collected by Shai seem to reflect better the recollections of my informants of their weddings.

The position of the wife in the patriarchal extended family in Kurdistan was uncomfortable. A young wife was often the last to receive food. Men could divorce their wives rather easily, whereas women could not divorce their husbands. If a woman was adamant about ending the marriage, her two options were to return home to her parents and never remarry, or to convert to Islam and cut herself off from her family forever. In the event of divorce, children remained with the father, a situation which my informants described with a great deal of anger. Brauer's informants described how Kurdish Jewish men would beat their wives at slight provocation and even in public. 'In this way the husband would try to show his dominance to others' (1947: 152).

Brauer documents wedding rituals which reflect the tension between men and women, and the inherent insecurity of a woman's position. For example, at the marriage ceremony, as the 'Seven Blessings' were read, the groom placed his right foot on the bride's left foot to symbolize his dominance over her. Yet according to Brauer, it sometimes happened that the bride would refuse to cooperate (Brauer, 1947: 110). Again, the first time that the bride and groom were alone together the groom would ask the bride for a glass of water, and when she gave it to him he would let the glass fall onto the floor. The meaning of this ritual was that he would rule her. 'Smart parents would warn their daughters ahead of time about this custom, and so she would not put the glass into his hand, but would place it in front of him [so that he would take it himself]' (Brauer, 1947: 118).

Conflict between men and women is an underlying theme in Kurdish culture, and this is expressed in many of the women's rituals. For example, Brauer describes how on the third day of the intermediate days of Passover young women would go out into the hills and dance. They would carry in their hands branches of a certain kind of tree, and when one group met another they would beat each other with branches. Also 'if they would meet a young man, they would surround him and beat him with the branches' (Brauer, 1947: 244). Similarly on Purim, groups of girls would meet and sit on a porch to eat. The boys would climb onto the roof and begin taunting the girls, and the girls would return their taunts. The whole affair would turn into a shouting match (Brauer, 1947: 291). It is against this background of inter-gender conflict and intra-gender cooperation that we can begin to unravel the religious world of Kurdish Jewish women.

SEXUAL SEGREGATION

One reason that historians and ethnographers have tended not to see women's religious lives is so prosaic that it hardly needs mentioning – Kurdish Jewish religious life was sexually segregated. Male ethnographers simply would not have had access to many women's rituals. Similarly, historians who study texts which were written by men would be limited by the fact, that the men who wrote the texts were not able to see what women were doing. My informants recalled spending most of their work and leisure time with other girls and women. According to Brauer, boys and girls were separated from the age of ten. Laws of menstrual purity were strictly observed. A menstruating woman could not hand her husband anything, nor would a father take anything from the hand of his menstruating daughter. Given the extended family household organization, it is likely that other women would have been able to replace menstruants in tasks which involved contact with men.

The synagogues had no women's section, and the only women who would go to synagogue were very old women who would sit outside in the yard or in the synagogue wearing veils (Brauer, 1947: 215). The exclusion of women from the synagogue was fairly common among Eastern Jews. In Yemen women were explicitly barred from the synagogue, and it was considered a sin for a woman to learn to read, or to enter a synagogue (Katzir, 1976: 38). In Kurdistan at every stage in the life-cycle men's and women's ceremonies differed. To take one example, after a death only men would go to the cemetery on the day of burial. Women would visit the grave the next day and spray rose water over it. The women continued doing this for three or seven days. When the female family members of the deceased visited the grave they were accompanied by many other women, who brought clothes of their own dead family members to place on the grave. The women would cry over the grave. When the women returned from the cemetery they washed their hands in the river. Men who saw them turned away so as not to meet them (Brauer, 1947: 168–9).

The life-cycle events which received the most ritual attention from women were pregnancy and birth. Here is how Brauer describes the events subsequent to a young woman announcing her first pregnancy: She would go to her parents' house. Her mother and female relatives would bring cloth and sew clothes for the baby. The special job of sewing the diapers was assigned to an old woman who had already delivered many healthy boys and girls of her own. They would invite singers, a drummer and other musicians, and the women would sing and dance. The pregnant woman would be given advice about how to take care of herself. In the evening a festive meal would be served at her husband's house (Brauer, 1947: 126). Birth was attended by midwives, who were typically older women. They would stay at the home of the new mother for eight days after the birth. According to Brauer, Jewish midwives were also popular among non-Jews, and folk stories even tell about demons who would ask for Jewish midwives to assist at their births (Brauer, 1947: 129). For an extended period (typically forty days) after birth, the new mother was confined to her room, and during this time women would come to visit her (Brauer, 1947: 132-5). It seems that men would not enter the room of the post-partum woman.

Holy days were celebrated separately. For example, on Shabbat morning while the men were at synagogue, the women would do the necessary housework, and then dress in their Shabbat clothing and go out to visit brides, new mothers, and mourners. The young women would meet to dance, or sit on rooftops and sing (Brauer, 1947: 217-25). On the first day of Shavuot men would go to visit family and holy graves, while women would go on the second day (Brauer, 1947: 246). On the women's day there was a great deal of celebration. Women would dance and sing, approach the grave, kiss it, and make requests. They would bless each other, and pledge to charity money that they had saved all year for this purpose. The most popular tomb was that of the prophet Nahum.

The greatest elaboration of girls' rituals occurred during the weeks preceding Purim. The first Shabbat of the month of Adar was known as 'Girls' Shabbat'. On the preceding Friday girls would organize into groups, each with a leader, and go around the village and ask for wood to build a fire. They would sing traditional songs, act in a rowdy manner, and symbolically steal firewood from people who refused to give them wood. They then sold part of the wood, and used the rest to heat the oven in which they made special cakes, and to build fires to heat their bath water. The bathing was communal and festive. On Shabbat the girls would continue to celebrate with singing and dancing. They would pour sweet-smelling rose water on their heads, and go to the fields outside of town and play games. On the evening of Purim the girls would again bathe in water heated with the wood they had collected. Girls and mothers would meet at one house, make *henna* (a red dye used for ritual purposes), and paint all of the girls. The mothers would wash their daughters and sing to them, and throw roses and nuts at them (Brauer, 1947: 279ff.).

The degree of sexual segregation varied in traditional Jewish communities. In Shiraz, Iran, for example, women not only attended synagogue, but had the right to interrupt the service in order to request that the men remove the Torah from the ark, and carry it over to the women to see and kiss (Loeb, 1992: 3). In contrast, Yemenite Jewish men and women were so thoroughly segregated that each group developed its own musical traditions: men and women sang different songs, in different languages, and in different musical styles (Katz, 1971). At home Yemenite men and women sat separately. During menstruation and for the week following, the separation between men and women was particularly strict. And while young girls sometimes played with their fathers, after puberty there was little contact between fathers and daughters (Gilad, 1982: 59–61). Among the Habbani, a small Jewish community in south-east Yemen, men were itinerant silversmiths who spent most of the year away from home. Women, left alone with children and old men, shared a ritual and daily life of their own with other women:

> [In] the absence of menfolk, and totally illiterate, Habbani women evolved elaborate ... rituals ... Hannuka was celebrated as a woman's holiday with song, dance and games. Shabbat and holidays were sanctified by special dress, grooming and ornament ... (Loeb, 1992: 7)

Loeb particularly notes the wedding rituals performed by women: the elaborate ceremonial braiding of the bride's hair after rubbing in numerous spices, the 'Bride's Shabbat' on which large numbers of women spent the day feasting and singing with the bride, and the *hinne* – a full-day ceremony at which the bride's hands and feet were decorated with henna dye (Loeb, 1992: 8).

In many Jewish cultures sexual segregation in religious life meant that the spatial loci of men's and women's rituals were different. While men congregated in the synagogue, women congregated at holy tombs and at home. Among Iranian Jews, for example, the shrine of Serah bat Asher was briefly visited by men during the forty days preceding Yom Kippur, whereas women would come daily and stay for hours (Loeb, 1992: 4). Yemenite informants in Jerusalem have told me of a shrine in Yemen, where women would camp out for days, often until they received a sign that their petition had been accepted by the saint (see also Mernissi (1977) on Muslim women at shrines in Morocco).

THE SACRED IN THE PROFANE

Even in Jewish communities in which women were active visitors at shrines, the home remained the most important location for women's religious activities. This spatial circumstance leads to the second reason that women's religion is missed by ethnographers and historians: it does not fit neatly into academic notions of 'sacred' as opposed to 'profane'. I am not surprised that it was particularly in relation to women's initiation rituals that anthropologist Bruce Lincoln observed:

> Ritual makes it possible for people to derive profound emotional and intellectual satisfaction from otherwise pedestrian affairs, because it points to something cosmic, transcendent, or sacred concealed within the tedium of mundane existence. (1981: 107)

Much of women's religion is indistinguishable from everyday life – cleaning, needlework, tending the ill, and visiting neighbors are all potentially religious activities. The clearest example of this pattern is cooking – a holy activity which is so totally embedded within the everyday world, as to cast doubts upon the usefulness of holy and profane as meaningful analytic categories.

Cooking is a multi-faceted religious activity. On the most obvious level, by observing Jewish dietary laws a woman who cooks even the simplest meal is engaged in holy work. On a deeper level, an important religious act for women in Kurdistan was that of giving food to itinerant beggars. A woman who sought religious expression often found it in the simple form of passing over part of her family's meal to a hungry person who was passing through her village. Going deeper still, food preparation is what places the stamp of culture on the most essential bit of the natural world – that bit of the natural world which is actually ingested by human beings. In Kurdistan, as in other societies, women rarely served their families a plain bowl of boiled rice or a piece of meat which was thrust onto the fire. Women's sauces and seasonings transformed their basic ingredients into edible expressions of tradition. This process was most apparent at holiday seasons, but it was also part of daily food preparation. To a large extent, what made a Kurdish Jew into a Jew was the food preparation carried out by the women. In Kurdistan, according to my informants, relations with non-Jews were good, but 'we wouldn't eat their food. It's not kosher'. Food, in other words, is what set the social limits between Jews and non-Jews; eating kosher food was one of the key markers of Jewishness.

Women used foodstuffs in many of their rituals, even when the ritual itself had no evident connection to food. For example, when a new house was built the housewife (senior woman) would throw a handful of wheat and break a dish. In earlier days the women would spill water and wave a piece of cloth while calling out 'Get out, go away evil spirits, come in spirits of life [good spirits], you should have boys and girls, grooms and brides.' Afterwards, 'the men would sit around and learn holy texts [*mishnayot*] for several hours' (Brauer, 1947: 62).³ The contrast between the men and the women is instructive. The male ritual act involved books; the female ritual act involved food. The male ritual object was set apart from daily events and objects. The female ritual objects were wheat, flour, and cloth – pedestrian substances. Not surprisingly, the male ritual act is much easier for Western scholars to identify as sacred.

On numerous occasions I asked my informants how they celebrated a particular holiday in Kurdistan. The answers almost always had to do with food preparation. 'For Rosh HaShana, flat breads, *kube* [dumplings], stuffed chicken, stuffed grape leaves. Much work.' For Kurdish women food was the essence of holidays. Holidays whose historical or theological meanings may not have been very clear were distinguished by the special foods which they prepared. Engagement and wedding festivities also included a great deal of cooking on the part of the women. The morning after the engagement was publicized, women from the bride's and groom's families gathered at the groom's house to prepare rice, cook and sing. They would put a mixture of cooked rice and peas in a large pot covered with a silk kerchief. The groom's mother would add clothing and gifts for the bride, and young men would then carry the bundle to the bride's house. Along the way neighbors would throw sweets and nuts onto the pot. An old woman would stand on the roof of the bride's house, and when the procession arrived, she would throw wheat at the revelers while telling the evil eye to go away (Brauer, 1947: 93–5). When one reads Brauer's detailed description of the lengthy engagement and wedding festivities, one gets the impression that the bride's and groom's female relatives spent the entire wedding year cooking!

Many of the food customs surrounding marriage were symbolic of fertility or, to be more precise, were aimed at ensuring fertility. For example, as the bride entered her husband's house for the first time, relatives would throw wheat at her, splash her with water, and bombard her with raisins, nuts, and candies. All these foodstuffs are potent fertility symbols (Brauer, 1947: 110–15). Food from the bride's plate at the wedding meal was considered a charm, and much desired by people with problems. Given that those standing near the bride in this sexually-segregated society were probably women, we can guess that the food from her plate was most commonly used as a fertility charm or to ward off disaster from young children. At the wedding feast, the bride herself turned into a symbol of fertility.

Cooking was not the only aspect of women's lives which lent itself to sacred interpretation. When I asked my informants how they celebrated Rosh HaShana (the New Year) in the Old Country, many of the answers had to do with cleaning. 'We cleaned our houses before Rosh HaShana. In Kurdistan we would whitewash the walls and scrub the floors and tables with stones.' The important point that emerges is that cleaning was not just preparation for the ritual observance of the New Year; rather, cleaning was the actual ritual observance of the New Year. Women's sewing also tended to blur the lines between the sacred and the profane. In order to prepare the bride's trousseau, seamstresses would work at the bride's house for a month before the wedding. When the first piece of cloth was cut, the women would trill with excitement and exclaim, 'Blessed, blessed be the clothes, and they should be dirtied by sons and daughters, by grooms and brides' (Brauer, 1947: 98). In a similar vein, the scraps of clothing left over from sewing the shroud of a holy man were much desired by mothers, as amulets for their children (Brauer, 1947: 160).

Women used domestic substances to cure their families of a variety of illnesses. My informants told how they would spread coffee or egg yolk on the forehead for headaches, cigarette ash or coffee to stop bleeding, and fried onions or dates for pain. This sort of healing had two dimensions, both of which were recognized by women. On the one hand, the substances themselves had certain curative properties. On the other hand, none of these substances were efficacious unless one believed in them. In the words of one of my informants:

> I remember an Arab woman who couldn't get pregnant. He [a Jewish man] scribbled something on paper and folded it and gave it to her. She got pregnant, because she believed. Belief is the biggest thing . . . Arabs [Kurds] had eye problems and asked Jews for powder to cure it. Where would we get powder from? Jews would go outside and pick up dust [ashes] and make it into a fine powder and give it to them. In the morning their eyes would be better, because they believed. Also the Jews would use this.

Not only does women's religiosity tend to blend into the everyday world of profane activity, it also tends not to fit neatly into the prevalent academic model of religion as liminality – as something apart from everyday reality, as outside of the ordinary, as 'betwixt and between.' This non-adherence to a supposedly universal pattern has been observed by scholars who have studied women's religiosity in a number of different cultural contexts. For example, in her work on medieval Christian holy men and women Caroline Bynum maintains that the pattern of women's lives shows fewer ruptures. In critique of anthropologists Victor Turner's and Arnold van Gennep's model of religious experience as liminal, Bynum writes:

> Women's images and symbols – which, according to Turner's model, should reflect either inversion . . . or elevation . . . do not quite do either. They rather continue or enhance in image (for example, bride, sick person) what the woman's ordinary experience is. (1984: 108)

The argument that I am making here is not an essentialist one: I do not believe that women and men have inherently different religious proclivities. Rather, I suggest, in Kurdish society, like in many other societies, social reality constrains women more than men, and prevents women from engaging in the violent ruptures and conversions that men describe and experience. Women – and especially mothers – cannot get up and walk away from regular life in the way that men can. Because women tended to be limited in their freedom to break away from daily life in order to engage in rituals, many of the ritual observances of Kurdish Jewish women had to do with abstaining from certain kinds of work, and specifically from the kinds of work whose omission would not immediately affect men. Both Brauer and my informants related that during the weeks preceding the 9th of Av (the day of mourning for the destruction of the Temple in Jerusalem and subsequent exile), on Rosh Hodesh (the festival of the new moon), and during the intermediate days of the Passover holiday women would not sew or do laundry, although they would cook and clean the house. The simple act of delaying laundry from one day to the next was an important religious expression for Kurdish Jewish women.

Kurdish women's religion, embedded within and continuous with everyday life, tended to center upon relationships with specific, known, and loved individuals. A great deal of the religious effort of Kurdish women was directed towards safeguarding their families. Frequently symbols and rituals taken from 'great tradition' Judaism were modified by the women, and applied to the particular real-life situations for which the woman felt responsible. I call this the 'domestication of religion' – a process in which people who profess their allegiance to a wider religious tradition, personalize the rituals, institutions, symbols, and theology of that wider system, in order to safeguard the well-being of particular individuals (Sered, 1988). For instance, my informants explain that when they light the Shabbat candles (symbolizing the onset of Shabbat) they ask God to preserve the health of their children. The women go beyond the obligatory two Shabbat candles, and light one candle for each of their children; lighting the candles alerts God to the needs of these particular human beings. In this way the women transform a 'great tradition' ritual, which ostensibly has nothing whatsoever to do with family health, into an intensely personal, domestic ritual.[4]

A wonderful example of the domestication of religion can be found in the Kurdish women's rituals of the holiday of Tu bi'Shvat – the traditional and very minor Jewish holiday on which trees are reckoned as one year older, the 'New Year for the Trees.' On Tu bi'Shvat women performed a number of fertility rituals, in many of which the theme was that the fate of women is connected to that of trees. If it rained or snowed the women declared that the trees had dipped in the *mikveh*, ritual bath, and so could become pregnant now. This would be interpreted as a good omen for their own fertility. They would also plant sweets around the trees to increase their own fertility and that of the trees. Barren women would hug fruit trees at night to encourage the fertility of the tree to pass on to them (Brauer, 1947: 275).

Another example of the domestication of religion concerns the traditional dirge recited by Kurdish women on the eve of the 9th of Av. On this day which commemorates the destruction of the Temple in Jerusalem, Kurdish women told stories in which history was personified into the experiences of a young man and two young women (Sabar, 1976). In these stories one of the women escaped rape by seven infidel men by drowning herself in a *mikveh*. The women who listened to this would themselves have the practice of immersing in a ritual bath after menstrual periods and after childbirth, so the imagery was very real to them. All the more so because their *mikveh* was the local river, which at certain times of year would be freezing cold, or flowing in torrents. The story of the other woman recounted that she was killed by her father-in-law, as a sacrifice imposed by divine edict, in order to end a drought. For women who were sent at a young age, often against their will, to live with their husband's families, the imagery here must have been compelling.

IS WHAT THEY DO REALLY JEWISH? IS WHAT THEY DO REALLY RELIGION?

In the preceding sections I have shown how the very structure and focus of women's religion tends to make it invisible to Western scholars. Much of what women do men are not allowed to see; other of their activities are accessible to men, but highly embedded within profane life. In this final section I suggest another reason for the invisibility of Kurdish women's religiosity: it does not 'look' Jewish to Western scholars or even to Western Jews.

Let me begin by noting that writers on Kurdish Jews, and – more specifically – about Kurdish Jewish women, commonly remark on how so many of their customs are 'borrowed' from the local non-Jewish population (see Squires, 1975: 16, for a review of the literature). It does seem to have been the case that the religious activities of Kurdish Jewish women often overlapped with those of non-Jews. For example, as Dina Feitelson notes, Jews and Muslims consulted the same wise men, and visited the same holy graves (Feitelson, 1959). And one need only glance through the wonderful collection of Kurdish-Jewish amulets collected by the Israel Museum to see that many of their ritual objects – and especially the ritual objects used by women – have no overt 'Jewish' content. The fact that Kurdish Jewish women were illiterate meant that their rituals and ritual objects tended not to use written texts. Given the central role of written texts in Jewish [male] religious culture, this in and of itself would tend to make Kurdish Jewish women's religion invisible.[5]

Not only are Kurdish Jewish women's ritual objects uncomfortably 'non-Jewish', but they also look uncomfortably 'non-religious'. In fact, they look a great deal like what Westerners call 'magic' or 'superstition'. Everyone who has written about the religion of Kurdish Jews has noted their extensive use of amulets (e.g. Fischel, 1949: 558–9). Women tended to wear more amulets than men, because of the enhanced danger that they confronted during pregnancy and childbirth. Women also sewed a variety of amulets onto their children's clothing. All women wore a silver amulet from girlhood on, and children's and women's clothes were embroidered with blue beads and triangles and circles, which were believed to keep evil away. Many of the amulets had to do with protecting a pregnant woman from miscarriage or death. Examples of such amulets included a special lock, a snakeskin, multi-colored threads, and various written passages in which the names of angels were prominent. One interesting amulet was made of copper (a material which in and of itself was believed to have protective properties). The pregnant woman would ask for money from seven sexually immature girls and from seven sexually apathetic post-partum women. She would give this money to a Jewish jeweller, who would fashion for her copper plates, which a Jewish holy man would then inscribe with the names of certain demons (Brauer, 1947: 127). The woman then wore these plates during pregnancy. Other techniques for avoiding miscarriage included hanging a shoe from a nail over the pregnant woman's door, and bringing her to her parents' house.[6]

Almost all of the rituals performed by Kurdish Jewish women, and especially the rituals they performed on behalf of their children, are considered to be magic or superstition by Western scholarship. This is especially noticeable when we look at rituals having to do with death, and especially with the death of children. Death rituals performed by men –

the funeral service and synagogue prayer – are construed as obedience to divine law, and as participation in the life of the community. Kurdish Jewish women leave candles, food, or pieces of cloth at graves, acts which tend to strike Western scholars as magical and superstitious practices. This distinction is also made to some extent by Kurdish men and women, but is emphasized far more by Western scholars.[7] A pervasive problem in much of the academic study of religion is the tendency to treat the formal, communal synagogue prayer as more noble, important or primary than leaving cloth on tombs. I believe that it is necessary to reject this sort of treatment for being ethnocentrism and androcentrism at their worst. There is no reason to assume that the experience of the holy is any more genuine or estimable to a man who makes use of written liturgical formulae, than to a woman sewing amulets to protect her family.

In his otherwise excellent book, Brauer repeatedly uses the word 'magic' to describe women's religious practices, and almost all ethnographers who have written about Kurdish women follow this usage. It seems to me that there are two dimensions in the religious rituals of these women which entice scholars to disparage them as 'magical'. In the widely accepted Durkheimian model, the essence of religion is its social character whereas the essence of magic is its private character (Durkheim, 1954: 58ff.). Given that in Kurdistan – as in most cultures – women are associated with the private domain and men with the public (Rosaldo, 1974), we come to the inevitable conclusion that women's spiritual expressions are by definition 'magic' – which is, by definition, inferior to both science and religion (cf. Frazer, 1911–1915). I am convinced that it is indeed the case that religious practices which attract women are typically (although not always) characterized by a preference for expressing ultimate concerns in the language of personal relationship. But Western religious studies has constructed conceptual categories in which the specific is less valued than the abstract, and in which women's practices – associated with private or personal rather than with public concerns – are automatically substandard or invisible. From an anthropological perspective, defining the abstract or the public as 'better' than the specific or personal is simply a culture-bound value judgment.

The second reason that Western scholars are lulled into calling Kurdish women's religion 'magic' has to do with the notion (made famous by Frazer) that religious acts are characterized by an attitude of uncertainty and supplication, whereas in magical acts the practitioner believes that his or her performance has an automatic effect upon the desired outcome. According to this line of reasoning, the use of amulets, for instance, appears to indicate an expectation that simply sewing a particular shape is sufficient to keep away the evil spirits, especially when (as in the case of Kurdish women) the fabrication of amulets is not accompanied by a prayer. I suggest that we would be incredibly naïve to think that women who lost four, five or more children in infancy would believe that an amulet has automatic powers. My informants were very clear in explaining that one has to believe in order for the ritual or amulet to be efficacious. My guess is that Western scholars have misread Kurdish women's ignorance of formal Jewish prayers as constituting a deficiency in spiritual sophistication.

The very elements which make the religious world of Kurdish Jewish women invisible to Western scholars – its sexual segregation, its domesticity, its embeddedness in everyday life, its interpersonal focus, and its lack of orientation toward holy texts – are also what gave that world its richness and its internal cohesiveness. Situated in a society in which men could not be depended upon not to harm one, in which children all too often died, and in which other women were one's only allies in the struggle for existence, Kurdish Jewish women developed a religious world which safeguarded and sacralized those relationships which gave life meaning.

Notes

1. From the outset, I wish to emphasize that many of the points I raise about women are also true of the male non-elite. The issues that I raise in this paper are as linked to power as they are to gender.
2. I do not mean to imply that Brauer was not a good ethnographer. He carefully collected customs that no one else at the time was paying attention to, and unlike many of his contemporaries he did document women's lives. The very fact that we can learn about women's religious practices from reading his book is proof of his – for his day – extraordinary sensitivity to gender issues.
3. The recollection of men sitting around and studying holy texts is very probably an Israeli gloss on Kurdish life; few Jewish men in Kurdistan were literate.
4. I have no proof that in Kurdistan the process was identical, but Jewish women in Kurdistan did light Shabbat candles, and given the interpersonal orientation of their religious world, I would guess that what my informants describe as doing today is similar to what their mothers did in Kurdistan.
5. One could argue that if these activities seem non-Jewish, then perhaps they really are non-Jewish. My own work with Kurdish women in Jerusalem absolutely negates this stance. My informants constantly used the expression 'it is written in the Torah' to describe their rituals and beliefs – even when

the particular ritual or belief in question had absolutely no textual basis in the Torah (something the women themselves could not know because they were illiterate). The point is that the women perceived these beliefs and rituals to be ancient and sacred Jewish beliefs and rituals. From an anthropological perspective it is sufficient proof of the 'Jewishness' of practices that Jews consider them to be Jewish.

6   This last technique had the added advantage of removing the woman from what was likely to be an uncomfortable situation, at her in-law's house, and returning her to the warmth of her natal family. Aside from any ritual considerations, one can see how the move from low status daughter-in-law to loved daughter might have beneficial effects upon the pregnant woman's mental and physical health.

7   The men's formal liturgy is studied by Judaica scholars; women's tomb rituals are studied by folklorists.

References

Brauer, E. (1947) *Jews of Kurdistan* (Jerusalem: HaMaarav Press).
Bynum, Caroline Walker (1984) 'Women's Stories, Women's Symbols: A Critique of Victor Turner's Theory of Liminality,' in Frank Reynolds and Robert Moore (eds), *Anthropology and the Study of Religion* (Chicago: Center for the Study of Religion) 105-25.
Durkheim, Emile (1954) *The Elementary Forms of the Religious Life* (New York: Free Press) (originally published by George Allen and Unwin, 1915).
Feitelson, Dina (1959) 'Aspects of the Social Life of Kurdish Jews,' *Jewish Journal of Sociology*, 1: 201-16.
Fischel, Walter (1949) 'Jews of Kurdistan,' *Commentary*, 8: 554-9.
Frazer, J.G. (1911-15) *The Golden Bough: A Study in Magic and Religion* (London: Macmillan).
Gilad, Lisa (1982) 'Yemeni Jewish Women,' PhD dissertation, Cambridge University.
Jews of Kurdistan: Lifestyle, Tradition, and Art, Israel Museum Publication 216, Jerusalem, Summer-Winter 1981-2.
Katz, Nina Dubler (1971) 'Culturally Determined Dichotomy in the Musical Practice of the Yemenite Jews.' Paper given at the American Anthropological Association Annual Meeting, November.
Katzir, Yael (1976) *The Effects of Resettlement on the Status and Role of Yemini Women: The Case of Ramat Oranim, Israel*, PhD dissertation, University of California, Berkeley.
Lincoln, Bruce (1981) *Emerging from the Chrysalis: Studies in Rituals of Women's Initiation* (Cambridge, Mass.: Harvard University Press).
Loeb, Laurence D. (1992) 'Religious Imperatives and Women's Behavior in Two Middle Eastern Jewish Communities.' Paper given at the American Anthropological Association Annual Meeting, December.
Mernissi, Fatima (1977) 'Women, Saints, and Sanctuaries,' *Signs*, 3: 101-12.
Rosaldo, Michelle Z. (ed.) (1974) *Woman, Culture and Society* (Stanford: Stanford University Press).

Sabar, Yona (1976) 'Lel-Huza: Story and History in a Cycle of Lamentation for the Ninth of Ab in the Jewish Neo-Aramaic Dialect of Zakho,' *Journal of Semitic Studies*, 21: 138–62.

Sered, Susan Starr (1988) 'The Domestication of Religion: The Spiritual Guardianship of Elderly Jewish Women,' *Man*, 23: 506–21.

Sered, Susan Starr (1992) *Women as Ritual Experts: The Religious Lives of Elderly Jewish Women in Jerusalem* (New York: Oxford University Press).

Shai, Donna (1982) 'Family, Conflict, and Cooperation in Folksongs of Kurdish Jews,' in Shlomo Deshen and Walter Zenner (eds), *Jewish Societies in the Middle East* (Lanham Md.: University Press of America) 273–84.

Squires, Pamela (1975) *Dance and Dance Movements of Iraqi Kurdish Jews in Israel*, MA thesis, University of California, Los Angeles.

Part V
Yemen

16 The Social Structure of Jewish Education in Yemen
Shlomo D. Goitein

> *More than any other Middle Eastern community, Yemenite Jewry has captured the imagination of scholars and observers. One reason for this is the combination of traits that Yemenites have exhibited until recently: passionate attachment to the Jewish literary tradition and the background of an exotic country, untouched by Westernization. In this pioneer treatment, the late S.D. Goitein of the Institute of Advanced Studies at Princeton, discusses one aspect of this combination. The chapter is an abbreviated version of a longer article, published in the early 1950s, on the basis of Goitein's fieldwork among Yemenite immigrants freshly arrived in Israel. The author's theoretical orientation is informed by a background in Talmudic scholarship. In the fuller version of this paper Goitein explored the question as to the extent to which Yemenite Jewry exemplified socio-cultural traits, that figure in classical rabbinic sources of late antiquity. Implicitly, that romantic concern colors also the present selection. Also, the reader should bear in mind that when the author purports to depict contemporary Israeli conditions those pertain to the early 1950s. Nevertheless the paper retains its vitality to date.*

In order to assess correctly the educational activities of the Yemenites we should take into account two demographic factors: firstly, the small size of the population, and secondly its distribution over an immense area. In Israel today there are perhaps 80,000 Yemenite Jews. During the past two generations the number of Yemenites in their own country did not exceed 100,000. The 48,000 Yemenite immigrants who entered Israel since the inception of the Jewish State – not all of whom could be asked to furnish particulars about themselves – had lived scattered over more than 1,000 different settlements in Yemen prior to their migration. This means that the size of Jewish communities in Yemen was extremely small. If we add

---

Source: Abbreviation of 'Jewish Education in Yemen as an Archetype of Traditional Jewish Education,' in C. Frankenstein (ed.), *Between Past and Present*, 109–46. By permission of the Szold Foundation, Jerusalem. © Copyright 1953.

to this the fact that communities in the actual sense of the term did not exist in Yemen, but that Jewish life centered round the synagogue, it becomes clear how limited the organizing power of Yemenite Jewry was.

The dispersion of the Jewish population over the whole of Yemen was somewhat weakened in its effects by another characteristic feature of their lives, their constant migrations within that territory. This led to the intermixing of Jews resident in different zones and, together with the predominance of the Jewish community of the capital Sana'a (which has been on the decline only during the last few decades), to a certain degree of unity. Nevertheless, the fact that the Jews of Yemen were split into divisions and subdivisions, differing greatly among themselves, should make us wary of generalizations. About 80 per cent of the Yemenite Jewish population lived in villages or townlets, whereas all investigations into their mode of life refer solely to urban areas. During the past year I have given my attention mainly to the rural population, but the scope of my research is very limited and this publication can only be considered as preliminary. As regards the details given below they stand open to correction and supplementation.

THE NEGATIVE ATTITUDE OF THE YEMENITES TO CHILDHOOD

Many educationalists are inclined to regard their conceptions of the child's place in society as axiomatic, and to believe that they were held to be valid throughout all ages and among all nations. Nothing is further from the truth. Our evaluation of childhood, and our views on the rights of the child and his natural independence, have only evolved during the last few generations. If we want to appreciate and understand the methods of education in force among a people of different culture – such as the Yemenite Jews – then we must put aside all our modern prejudices and ask ourselves, what theory of education prevailed in that civilization and was consciously or unconsciously applied in the upbringing of children in its various stages.

Throughout the civilization of the Middle East during the Middle Ages the view prevailed that the state of childhood had no intrinsic value and no rights of its own. It was merely the state of a person who was not yet complete, a phase through which one should pass as quickly as possible. In the colloquial language of the inhabitants of Yemen, a child was called 'jahil', meaning not only 'ignorant' but also 'one who does not want to know', for 'the impulses of man are evil from childhood'. It is this spirit which pervaded and determined every phase of Jewish education in Yemen. No one doubted that the evil spirit must be driven out of the child's mind by the use of the rod and the strap; that its strength must be sapped by the study of the Torah, and that the evil spirits must be conquered, although, it must be noted, extreme cruelty on the part of the teacher was not tolerated in Yemen and could lead to the teacher's dismissal.

Even the child's loving, devoted and gentle mother did not refrain from using the stick on her little son to prevent him from committing evil deeds, such as quarrelling with his playmates, although, as he grew up, she was frequently moved to save him from the greater severity of his father. When she brought her child to the teacher for the first time, she would say to the latter: 'I have brought you flesh, return bones to me', which meant, 'don't spare him'. She did this out of the conviction that only the discipline of the Torah, and the chastisement of his teacher, could make a man of her little boy. It was the aim of parents and children alike that the boy should become a man, and that he should leave the state of ignorance as soon as possible. The good child was the one who behaved like an adult, who sat quietly without moving, 'like a cup of arrack' that is, a cup which stands firm and without motion, although the wine bubbles and foams. The manner of dressing was an expression of the same attitude. Nowadays when even adults wear shorts and open-necked shirts, go bareheaded and in sandals, and generally adopt a mode of dress which a generation ago was permissible only to street urchins – the little Yemenite boys and girls in their long clothes seem like dolls masquerading as adults. So we often have to admit the aim of likening the child to the adult has been achieved with considerable success. Even in Israel today – where the influence of environment pulls in the opposite direction – we can still see small boys, sitting next to their elders in the synagogues, silent for hours on end.

NO BAR-MITZVAH CEREMONY

The negative attitude of the Yemenites towards the state of childhood, as a state in its own right, is also reflected in the fact that, as far as our information goes, there is no ceremony by which the boy enters adult society, such as the Bar-Mitzvah ceremony of the Sephardi or the Ashkenazi Jews. Such an 'initiation' ceremony is given great prominence by many nations. Yet it is completely lacking among Yemenite Jewry, just as it was non-existent in Israel during the Talmudic era, although it is true that the age of 13 is sometimes mentioned in Talmudic literature as the age when the youth must begin to observe the commandments. The expression 'Praise be to the Lord who has freed me of the punishment which might be meted out to this child', usually uttered by the father on the day of his son's Bar-Mitzvah, is also of Talmudic origin, but a Bar-Mitzvah ceremony for every boy was evolved only much later. The lack of a precise Hebrew term for the ceremony, as well as the marked difference between the Ashkenazi and the Sephardi customs, are significant. The Yemenites, moreover, have no fixed age for putting on of phylacteries, or for reading from the Torah. Some Yemenite boys start putting on phylacteries at the age of ten or even eight and others wait until they are 13 or 14. One finds village boys aged 15 who have not yet started putting on phylacteries. The reading from the Torah in the presence of the congregation is not restricted to the age group which is obliged to keep the commandments, for with the Yemenites, according to the Mishnah (Megila 4.6 and 4.5), 'the little ones may read in the Torah and may translate from it', and they may also read from the Prophets. On the Sabbath young boys are given the honor of being called to the Torah in the sixth place. thus neither the putting-on of phylacteries nor the first calling to the Torah is celebrated by a meal or any other form of festivity.

THE SYNAGOGUE AS THE PRINCIPAL CENTER OF EDUCATION IN YEMEN

It can be said that in the main the education of Jewish boys in Yemen was carried out within the synagogue, by the synagogue and for the synagogue. From a very early age the child spent many hours at synagogue, especially on the Sabbath and holidays. He rises before daybreak – and often several hours before it – and sits in the synagogue with his father, from the beginning of the service until the very end. Anyone visiting a Yemenite synagogue in Israel will be impressed by the deafening 'Amen' coming from the mouths of the smallest children. How natural then that in a country with a high infant mortality rate, the father should be anxious to ensure a place for his son in the world to come as early as possible. On weekdays, it is true, schoolboys prayed in the place where they studied, but since they studied for a few years only, especially in villages, we find that the synagogue was the only communal center for the education of adolescents. There were many children who received their entire education in the synagogue. To this category belonged orphans, children of poor parents, children who had run or been driven away from home, and thus had not studied with a teacher for over a year or longer. It seems that the brighter and more alert among them profited from their participation in the studies of their elders, more than from the instruction of their teachers.

Moreover, all the details of the syllabus of the Yemenite school were arranged so as to ensure the child's participation in the life of the synagogue as early as possible. The syllabus and the school had one aim, namely to teach the child prayers, the reading from the Torah, the appropriate passages from the Prophets and their translation and the Oral Law, so as to enable the boys to follow the discourses which were a regular feature in Yemenite synagogues. They learned nothing which lacked direct bearing on the life of the synagogue. The fact that the school was of secondary importance as compared with the synagogue can also be inferred from the fact that it had no name of its own. In those parts of Yemen where the synagogue was called *kenees*, the school was likewise called *kenees*, and in those districts where the synagogue was called *ma'alama*, meaning 'house of study', the school was called by the same name.

In its educational influence, too, the Yemenite school could not compete with the synagogue. Neither the school room, nor the teacher, nor the system of instruction was of a type likely to instill feelings of love and respect in the children. The synagogue, however, though often housed in a small and most primitive building, inspired deep feelings. Anyone who has ever joined Yemenites in villages in their prayers, must have become aware that, in some measure, the conduct of the people transformed the most primitive place into a sanctuary. The old men and other adults usually sat along the walls, on hassocks or fur-skins. At their feet or in the center of the synagogue the boys were grouped, the supervision of whom was the duty not only of their fathers, but also of all the adult members of the congregation. The fact that the child spent hours amidst a congregation, whose members were studying and praying, implanted in him a firm feeling of belonging to the community of Jews as a whole, which his community, no matter how small it might be, represented to him.

The joint recital or, more correctly, the joint shouting of prayers, was a form particularly suitable for children because of their natural bent towards activity; and it strengthened still more the boy's feeling that he was a member of a strong and closely-knit community. When the 'Shmoneh Esreh' prayer was recited, a complete silence reigned in the synagogue. The recital of this prayer, repeated three times daily, made a deep impression even on the small boy, and aroused in him the feeling of God's omnipresence and of the reality of spiritual existence. What is perhaps even more important is that the regular and constant study in the synagogue awakened in the boy the desire to emulate the adults, and he was given constant opportunity for doing so.

THE SUBORDINATE POSITION OF THE SCHOOL AS COMPARED TO THE HOME

The Yemenite school was subordinate not only to the synagogue as a channel of education, but also to the parental home. As in all other spheres of life, the Yemenite Jew obeyed the law literally, that it is the father's duty to instruct his son in the Torah, a duty of which he cannot absolve himself by paying a fee for his son's instruction. The teacher in Yemen was only a 'Makrei Dardekei', that is, one who teaches small boys to read aloud. Thus he was also called derisively in the Yemenite colloquial tongue, 'Megarri'. But the teacher was not an educator, whose task it was to teach the child the significance of the text to be memorized. This quality of the teaching role applied not only to the initial stages of study (prayers, the Bible and the Aramaic translation), but also to advanced subjects, such as the Mishnah. Also, as far as these texts were studied at all, the children were taught to read them aloud with the correct intonation, but the teacher did not consider it his task to elucidate their contents. Very seldom a teacher could be found who 'explained' as well as 'read'. This was in conformity with the view prevailing in Oriental schools, that memorizing, or at least reading aloud, should precede explanation and understanding. There was a widespread belief to the effect that explanation before reading was harmful to the child's mind.

The Yemenite school generally resembled the Eastern European *heder* insofar as the system prevailing in it was to teach by memorization. The system of education differed however, in that the Yemenite Jew gave pride of place to the parental home in the instruction of the child. The child acquired his real understanding of things, as far as he attained it at all, from his father and not from his teacher. The father considered this an ancient tradition and a holy duty. He did not content himself with explaining difficult points to the child when the latter repeated to him the text he had learned at school. Even after the boy had left school he continued to benefit from his father's instruction, and it was from his father that he acquired higher and more profound knowledge, such as the laws of ritual slaughter. The latter can be considered a sort of 'secondary school education' for the Yemenites, and they were also studied under special teachers. This practice applied to sons of ordinary artisans, as well as to sons of educated men.

A man from Saada told me that after he had left school at the age of 13, he sat for two years in his father's workshop and learned the Scriptures. While the father carried on with his work, the son read to him from the sources, and received the necessary explanations. A man from Goran told me that at school the children used to read various religious texts without any explanation. In the evening, the boys of the family, that is my informant, his brothers and a cousin, used to sit together with his father, his uncle, his grandfather and his grandfather's brother. The adults would carry on with their work while the children were examined in what they had learnt at school, and together read the book 'Reshit Hokhma', a mystical commentary on the Pentateuch, and received adequate explanations whenever the text was not clear to them.

A system which entrusts to the family the imparting of learning and education can only succeed where education is restricted to the knowledge and understanding of a certain number of holy books, which every adult and every pater familias can know. Children of the poor who were wholly preoccupied with the task of making a living, or children of uneducated parents and especially orphans, grew up without any education at all, unless they had the initiative and the luck to find a teacher among the men who regularly attended synagogue. On the other hand, the system was based on a noble conception of the relationship between the generations: the father who begot a son had the duty of introducing him to the lofty sphere of intellectual life. Here lies the source for the honor accorded to the father, which is carried to great lengths in a good Yemenite Jewish family.

THE MATURING INFLUENCE OF ADULT SOCIETY

The synagogue and the parental home thus determined the life of the Yemenite child much more than did the school. The boy was drawn into the life of adult society from the day he began to think and, perhaps, we might say, even a little sooner. We must remember that life in a Yemenite home was crowded. Apart from the parents a considerable number of other adults – grandfathers, uncles, grown-up brothers – frequently already married – all lived together. Moreover, Yemenite Jews in general are a very sociable people, and festive gatherings as well as mourning ceremonies are numerous and long drawn out. The children join the adults in the prescribed meals, such as wedding celebrations lasting a whole week or celebrations of circumcision, or meals arranged for the consolation of mourners. The Yemenite child has been trained not to raise his voice in the company of his seniors. It is amazing to see the restraint of which these small children are capable for hours on end. The time is not wasted: the child is all eyes and ears. He absorbs the adults' conversation, and quickly learns to understand hints and allusions. It can be said that while modern education now tends to prolong the age of childhood artificially, the Yemenites shortened it to a minimum, which to us appears unnatural. An Arabic proverb which has also gained currency among Yemenite Jews says: 'When your son grows up make him your brother.' Yemenite Jews, however, do not wait until the child grows up, but accustom him at an early age to consider himself responsible for his actions.

THE GRANDMOTHER AS THE MISTRESS OF THE HOUSE

The paternal grandmother plays an important part in the childhood memories of Yemenite Jews. The young couple generally lived in the house of the bridegroom's father, and when the Yemenite woman gave birth to her first children the care and upbringing devolved to a large extent upon the mistress of the house, i.e. the grandmother. A Yemenite proverb says: 'The mother has the joy and the grandmother the mess' (since it was the grandmother who washed the child and laundered his linen). The grandmother often took her grandson or granddaughter to one of the many festivities which were so characteristic a feature of Yemenite life, and tried on such occasions, not always successfully, to teach good manners. It seems that the grandmother was accorded this status not only for these practical reasons, but also because she occupied the position of the mistress of the house, i.e. the position accorded in all ancient Eastern households to the husband's mother. The author of the 'Travels of Habshush' describes such a grandmother. Round her neck she wears an iron chain to which all the keys of the house are attached, and whatever is done in the house is decided by her, even though her son may have two or three wives. The part played by the grandmother in the child's upbringing often gave rise to quarrels between her and the young wife. Nevertheless, it seems that the supervision of the upbringing of small children by a mature woman with her greater experience of life could be counted as a blessing, and years later she was remembered with affection.

THE ROLE OF THE YEMENITE WOMAN IN THE EDUCATION AND UPBRINGING OF CHILDREN

In the urban as well as the rural areas, the Yemenite Jewish woman was illiterate. A famous proverb says: 'He who reads aloud to his mother will never make a mistake.' Moreover, no woman knew the prayers, a fact which is certainly surprising in the Yemenites, for they pay meticulous attention to the letter of the Law and are so exact in its observation, and it is specifically laid down in the Mishnah and by Maimonides that women are obliged to pray. On the other hand, there were in Yemen, again in accordance with Jewish law, women acting as slaughterers of animals. The position of Jewish women in Yemen was determined by an excessive emphasis on laws dealing with uncleanliness and purity (which was also the reason for the exemplary cleanliness of Yemenites in urban areas, stressed by all those who have visited the country). For fear that women might attend services during the periods of menstruation, women were excluded from all communal prayers. Thus women did not recite the Hebrew prayers, not even the grace after meals, since there was no point in teaching it to someone who did not know the principal prayers. Women were incapable of giving their children religious education, the only type of education recognized in Yemen. Also the secular education of Yemenite women was extremely limited. The Yemenite Jewish woman knew innumerable proverbs; her songs were very beautiful and distinguished by great emotional power and splendid imagery. But the subject matter was restricted to only a few themes.

Considering her scanty education, the influence of the Yemenite woman on her children was far greater than would be expected. It is not correct to say that her educational tasks ended with the child's admission to school, and that she was only in charge of his physical well-being and care, teaching him, for instance, habits of personal cleanliness. As a Yemenite boy has put it in an essay: 'At noon the children go home in order to eat and talk to their mothers.' The father's duty, like that of the teacher, was to be strict, for he taught the child, but the mother could talk to her son like one human being to another. From her he could receive what an adult can give to a young person. We also have to consider the older sister, who took her brothers to school and often sat with them for hours looking after them. It would be worthwhile investigating the mother's influence on her sons, in adolescence and even after their marriage. The bitter complaints of the aging mother – which we meet in proverbs and songs – that her son has betrayed her, and delivered himself body and soul to his young wife, is indicative of what was considered the normal state of affairs in these matters.

If a man was successful in his life, it was said that 'his mother has prayed for him', or 'happy is she that bore him.' On the blessing of his mother, rather than on the discipline imposed on him by his father, depended a man's fortune in life. The central point of a Yemenite wedding was the solemn moment, when the door leading from the room of the women to the hall of the men was opened, and the bridegroom walked up to his mother and kissed her knee, asking her forgiveness for all his sins in word or deed against her. For the son belonged first and foremost to the one who 'suffered and toiled for him and who watched over him during the night.' In critical moments he turned first to her – 'all the boy's comings and goings center round his mother'. And when a man was cursed in Yemen, the evil-wisher prayed that he should be in distress, without his mother's knowing about it. The allocation of educational tasks in the Yemenite home can be easily discerned from the expression of the parents' faces. The father's face was, as a rule, stern and set, whereas the mother's smile testified to her cheerfulness and practical wisdom.

THE EDUCATION AND UPBRINGING OF GIRLS

From her earliest childhood the mother taught her daughter to recite the short prayers, to which she herself was accustomed. On various occasions during the year, for instance before the grinding of flour for the unleavened bread of Passover, the women recited short prayers. They were generally in the habit of addressing themselves to the Lord of Creation, or, as a little girl put it: 'Mother tells God whatever she likes', in contrast, of course, to the father who could only say what was written in the book. However, the fact that religious education in Yemen was based exclusively on classical sources which were mainly Hebrew, set up a barrier between the girls and religious teaching. Substitutes in colloquial Arabic did not occupy an important place. Nearly all instructors who have taught Yemenite immigrant girls confirmed the fact that these girls had very little knowledge of biblical stories. A clear proof that the latter were not very familiar to Yemenite women is the surprising fact that biblical names of women were hardly to be found among them.

Only the regulations for women concerning impurity and a few of the Passover laws, as well as the stories about Hannah and her seven sons, and similar material, were specially edited in a language they understood. It is therefore all the more surprising to note the profound Jewishness, the mental alertness and the strong character of these little girls, who have now come to us in their thousands. This applies in particular to those who were born and bred in places where there was a Jewish community of some size. The upbringing of girls in Yemen proves that the home atmosphere was of paramount importance as an educational factor, and that educational activities occupy a secondary position only. The home atmosphere provided the child with a living example of a strong faith in absolute values, and of their realization in daily life.

Girls also did not attend synagogue on the Sabbath. At most they sat in the courtyard of the synagogue in the afternoon, all dressed up, not in order to listen to the 'learning' or recital of prayers, but to chat and to listen to the talk of grown-up women. They could not take part in the religious discourses at the family table, but the Sabbath was a day of rest for them. While for the boy it was a day of study with the adults, to the girl it afforded an opportunity for friendly social contacts. Yet the girls too observed the Sabbath strictly. The Yemenite woman was brought up to be a Jewess even though she did not enjoy systematic instruction in the tenets of Judaism.

It is, however, not quite correct to present the Yemenite girl as lacking all 'formal' education. I gathered from my conversations with girls from all parts of Yemen that Yemenite women had a special system for the gradual introduction of girls to the fields of domestic work, to matters concerning conduct and to vocational training. Training for needlework meant for the girl what admission to school meant for the boy. A small town girl told me: 'When I began to learn embroidery I ceased to play.' Up to the age of five she used to play in the street – games such as 'five stones.' When this girl began to learn embroidery she remained at home. A similar story was told by a girl from Sana'a when she recounted the course of her vocational training. At first one made a Khirkah, a simple kerchief, worn over the skull-cap of the Arab woman, and then the Tarjulah, simple embroidery on the trousers of Moslem girls. At the age of eight the girl was capable of making two Tarjulahs weekly. She would bring her work to the Jewish merchant at the market, who sold it to Moslems. For her work she received one-quarter of a rial per Tarjulah, or half a rial per week – while for her brother's studies a sum of one-eighth rial was paid every week. At the age of nine the girl thus managed to take her place in the life of the community, just as did her brother if he showed promise in his studies, in which case he could put on phylacteries already at that age.

I have heard of isolated instances of fathers who had no sons giving instruction to their daughters, and of the daughters having become learned. There is the case of Sham'ah, the daughter of the poet Shalom Shabazi, and of Miriam, the daughter of Benayah the scribe, who wrote a scroll of the Pentateuch while still nursing a child.

THE TRANSITION FROM THE HOME TO THE MORI

The word *mori* is derived from 'mar', the Aramaic equivalent of 'Master,' whereas 'rav' is an Assyrian word which has been incorporated into

Hebrew. The teacher or spiritual guide was called 'Master,' for the relationship between him and his pupil was like that between a master and his servant. The Talmud prescribes that a pupil should do for his teacher all the work that a servant is supposed to do for his master, except for the 'untying of his boots' (Ketubboth 96.1), and this precept was valid in Yemenite Jewish schools too, although there were not many opportunities for its application. The word 'mori', 'my master', thus had the formal meaning of 'Rabbi' or 'Monsieur'.

Since the teacher's task was merely that of making children memorize texts for use at the synagogue and at home, it required little expert knowledge. Also, since the state of childhood had no value of its own, a man dealing with children was not be accorded an important position. As a rule, only those who had either no talent for, or success in, other more remunerative types of work, turned to the teaching profession. It is particularly surprising that in scores and perhaps hundreds of places in Yemen boys, some of them very young ones, aged nine or ten, served as teachers. More than once the villagers presented a young lad to me, mentioning with pride that since he was an orphan, they had provided for him by making him an infant-teacher. It was not difficult for a clever Yemenite boy, who had run away from home, to find refuge as an infant-teacher in one of the small towns or, since such boys were fond of wandering, in several small towns in succession. Boys whom we would still consider children wrote down for me in minute detail the outlines of the syllabus, according to which they taught, and the conditions of work at every place in which they had been employed.

This phenomenon can perhaps best be explained by the fact that in Yemenite schools, where as a rule several age-groups of children learned together, young boys were given opportunities to serve as infant-teacher, and the step from infant-teacher to real teacher was not very big. At the other end of the scale there were very old men who, on reaching the retiring age, had taken up teaching. Young lads and very old scholars were often employed together as teachers Neither was suitable, but it would seem that a very old teacher was preferable to one who was an immature boy. There were, however, also professional teachers in Yemen who learned their calling from their fathers, as was the rule in all trades in Yemen, and who continued studying and teaching all their lives. Such teachers were usually to be found in the cities, and if they lived in villages they also served as rabbis, performing marriages and granting divorces, and might also serve as the head of the synagogue or as the local slaughterer. Sometimes these teachers were strangers in the locality and its foremost intellectuals. Usually there were one or two additional teachers and the children passed from one to the other.

There was no certification for teaching, and anyone so desiring could practice. In the towns this was a question of free competition. In the villages the local inhabitants usually agreed on the appointment of a particular teacher, and the latter did not often stay long in one place. Whereas no one could be a ritual slaughterer, let alone a minister of religion without an authorization – and as a rule this letter of authorization had to be renewed by a recognized rabbi at set times – I have never yet seen a teacher's letter of authorization, and it need hardly be mentioned that there was no teachers' training college. It is most significant that even in Sana'a, where in recent years there were some twenty teachers, and in other towns where there were between three and six, it occurred to no one that they might join together and found a school comprising several classes. There were marked differences in the standards of instruction between the various teachers, but there was no system of promotion. Some boys 'read' with several teachers, others received instruction from the same teacher over the years. It was not before the beginning of this century that, as a result of outside influence, a school was organized in Sana'a, but even that experiment was short-lived.

Until about a generation ago schoolrooms commonly served also as hostels for poor wayfarers. Only after it was noticed that children became infected with diseases by wayfarers, were special *midrash* (literally 'school') institutions, founded in some places to shelter strangers. The link between the school and the duty of hospitality existed to the last in all parts of Yemen. When a poor man came to a place where there was a Jewish congregation he would turn to the school as a matter of course, for there he would always find someone, whereas an individual householder might be busy with his work. The teacher would send one or more pupils home to fetch food for the wayfarer, and thus children learned to dispense charity from their earliest youth.

However, not everywhere could a schoolroom be found next to the synagogue. When a man wanted to practice charity he sometimes threw open the door of one of his basement rooms for the use of a teacher. Only a minority of schoolrooms belonged to this category, and they were more frequent in towns than in villages. Since teaching in Yemen was a private or, more correctly, a semi-private occupation, there were also teachers who rented rooms for themselves, and others who taught in their own houses, or even adapted their houses to the requirements of teaching. The furniture and equipment of the schoolroom was very simple. The children sat on mats or on fur skins on the floor, and used bricks or small wooden props brought from their homes for their books. For the mats or fur skins every member of the synagogue paid a certain sum. The teacher had a special raised seat, and woe to the child who dared to sit on it, even in jest.

As a rule, the books belonged to the boy's parents. Love for books was one of the outstanding characteristics of Yemenite Jews, even of those living in villages. They clung to the ancient custom of teaching the child to read sideways and upside-down, apart from reading in the normal way, even in such places where there was no shortage of books. In order to avoid the wear and tear on books, the children used a small stick with which they pointed to the passage being read without touching the book itself. Essential parts of the teacher's equipment were a whip and a stick. The maintenance of teachers fell decidedly into the category of charity. The underlying idea was that the work of the teacher is not actually the type of work by which a man should earn a living. In addition to tuition fee, the boys after their lunch brought a 'mitzvah' ('deed of piety'), in the form of a loaf of bread for the teacher's household, which he would consume or sell. Some teachers never collected the fees due to them, and when the parent did not send the money, the teacher would not claim it. If the parents could not find the means, the teacher would usually not bar the child from attending school. Yet the system worked, and generally even the poorest parents did not evade payment. But not all teachers conformed to the norm, and there were children who, after the death of their father or upon economic ruin, could not continue to study.

We must distinguish between two different types of teachers. On the one hand there was the teacher who had come down in life, whose main work consisted of teaching and who supplemented his meager income by pursuing some other occupation of a despised type, such as spinning. On the other, there was the respected craftsman, such as a silversmith who (especially in small towns) taught as a sideline, in addition to his main work. The latter usually gathered only a small number of pupils around himself, from among members of his own family. It would seem that the best-qualified professional teachers were to be found in the larger cities, although there were also many miserable 'moris'. In the small townlets the general status of the teacher was higher.

THE YOUTH AGE GROUP

Just as the entry into school took place only after prolonged preparation, so also the leaving of school was not an abrupt process. The boy continued his studies, apart from the discourses in the synagogues, in which he had participated from the time he had joined the advanced class in his school. He learned from his father, either while receiving instruction in a trade or at another time. Furthermore, it was widely accepted that a boy did not work full time upon leaving school. After breakfast he would return to one of the synagogues for two or three hours of study. This arrangement did not place a great burden upon the father, for the son usually took up his father's trade and worked in his house.

Childhood was considered only as a preliminary stage subordinate to adulthood, and the child lived within the adult society from the day he started his conscious life. But it seems to me that the age group of adolescents was more united and marked off from other age groups. It had a distinct character within Yemenite society. In Sana'a there was an ancient custom, preserved up till the time of the exodus from Yemen, according to which the bachelors of the community sometimes assembled on Friday night, shortly after midnight, in 'the Alsheikh synagogue'. The older men would vacate the synagogue that night, and the young men would chant special hymns, customary 'Tikkunim' and psalms. They also prayed for a good and beautiful wife. Occasionally the young men held special gatherings outside the precincts of the synagogue, such as a special party on the seventh day of Hanukkah. The organization of youth into groups of their own within the framework of the Jewish community thus did exist in rudimentary fashion.

17 The Authority of the Community of San'ā in Yemenite Jewry
Yosef Tobi

Jewish communities throughout the world face the problem of how to maintain unity and adherence to a common code of practice, within a context of dispersion. In this essay, Yosef Tobi, Associate Professor of Comparative Literature and History at Haifa University, shows how this was tackled in Yemen during the past two hundred years. Unlike most of the contributors to this volume, Tobi's work shows how historians utilize documents to reconstruct social and political relationships. He infers ways in which the ancestry, personality and scholarly reputation of rabbinic leaders led to social acceptance, against a background of other forces which shaped the communities.

The community of Jews of San'ā, the capital of Yemen, has for long been regarded as the spiritual center for that country's Jews, and its religious courts and rabbis were regarded as supreme by all the Jewish communities of Yemen.[1] In the first part of this chapter, we review general data of the last two hundred years concerning details of the authority of the San'ā community, and in the second part, we present historical documents that exemplify the topic.

In the middle of the seventeenth century an important event took place that caused great changes in Yemenite Jewry – the temporary expulsion of the San'ā community in 1679 to the littoral desert. Thereafter Jews were subjected to intensified degradation, and engaged, more than previously, in Messianic activities (Ratzabi, 1972), and Yemenite Jewry lost many of its ancient traditions. On the other hand, ties with the world-at-large expanded. Scholar-travellers, such as Christian Niebuhr, and emissaries from Eretz-Israel came in considerable numbers. Trade movement, from both the Persian Gulf and the Red Sea, increased. There were also the missionary activities of Joseph Wolf and Aharon Stern in the nineteenth century and, more importantly, in the second half of the century the conquest of Yemen

---

Source: Slight abbreviation of a chapter in S. Deshen and W.P. Zenner (eds), *Jewish Societies in the Middle East*, Washington, DC: University Press of America, 1982, 235–50.

by the Turks. As a result of all these developments, information about the Jews of Yemen increased, and we now possess a considerable number of historical sources (see Tobi, 1976a).

Until the tenth century the correspondence of the head of Mesopotanian Jewry, 'The Gaon of Babylonia', reflects the supremacy of the San'ā community. In the three centuries that follow, we find that the *negidim* (heads of community) of Aden, and the Aden community generally, wielded authority and power, that were recognized by all the communities of Yemen (Goitein, 1967). The standing of the city of San'ā was diminished during the eleventh to thirteenth centuries, partly because in the middle of the twelfth century, the royal court moved to the town of Jiblah in the south, and also Jews moved there (Goitein, 1953: 48). Thus during the period from the eleventh to the thirteenth centuries leadership of Yemenite Jewry passed from San'ā to another community, that of Aden. Much international trade proceeded at that time from India via Aden to Egypt and Europe, and Jews played a significant role in it. In the fourteenth-century San'ā once more regained its previous eminence, but the position of the Jewish community there was not undisputed. The rabbis of the Sa'dah community, in the north of the country, did not accept the decision of the rabbis of San'ā in an issue concerning allegorical interpretations of the Torah. But after excommunication was pronounced by the San'ā sages the rivals consented to submit the matter to sages from Eretz-Israel, and to accept their judgment (Qāfih, 1951). Thereafter, it appears that the authority of the San'ā community remained unchallenged.

In the middle of the eighteenth century, we hear of the activities of two distinguished personalities in San'ā, the results of whose work were felt right up until the emigration in our times. Rabbi Shalom ben Aharon Ha-Kohen (known also as 'Irāqī) and Rabbi Yihyā ben Yosef Sālih, who officiated in the parallel functions of head of the community (sheikh) and head of the rabbinical court (bet-din). Rabbi Shalom 'Irāqī was of a family that came to Yemen from Egypt in the sixteenth century, and which was prominent in the public life of Yemenite Jewry over several generations. In the eighteenth century the 'Irāqī family produced community leaders and royal counsellors and ministers, and during the lifetime of Rabbi Shalom ben Aharon the 'Irāqī family attained its greatest renown. The standing of the family was practically uncontested, both at the court and among the Jews, and Rabbi Shalom's renown reached even the Jews of Eretz-Israel. Upon his father's death, Rabbi Shalom inherited his position as royal adviser, and served two monarchs (imams) over a period of thirty years (1731–61).[2] There can be no doubt that the eminence of Rabbi Shalom in the royal court strengthened his status as leader of Jewry. This we may learn, for example, from his order to arrest in 'royal custody' anyone transgressing the minor ritual prohibition of cutting one's hair during the 'Omer period in late spring. As most Yemenite Jews did not have this custom, this was an innovation, but it accorded with the practice of most Jewish communities in other countries (Sālih, 1964 II: 57–66).

Rabbi Shalom was active on behalf of the members of his community, both in the royal court as well as within the community itself (teaching Torah, aiding the needy, building synagogues and ritual baths), and became known by the honorific title 'Sayyednā al-Shaikh Sālim' (our Master the Head Shalom), as well as by that of 'al-'Ustā' (the master craftsman), apparently bestowed by the Imam. Rabbi Shalom expanded his charitable activities to include other communities, such as Dhamār, 'Ibb and Mochā. The attitude of the Jews of his own community towards Rabbi Shalom was, however, ambivalent, and some of his actions aroused opposition. He attempted to introduce to Yemen the form of prayer of Eretz-Israel. This action was apparently aimed at increasing his stature in the community (for it may be assumed that his family which originally came from Egypt, did not worship according to the Yemenite rite but according to that of Eretz-Israel), and that caused controversy. Ultimately, Rabbi Shalom failed on this issue. San'ā legend reports another controversy in which he was involved, the destruction of the genealogical records of the Jewish families of San'ā, because of a refusal to give a local bride to Rabbi Shalom's son in marriage, on the claim that the latter's family which stemmed from Egypt lacked distinguished ancestry (Sappir, 1866: 100–2).

It would seem at all events that Rabbi Shalom 'Irāqī was the outstanding secular leader of Yemeni Jewry of recent centuries. No such figure emerged under Turkish rule, in the nineteenth century, when communal institutions were more formally organized by the authorities (Tobi, 1976c: 104–17). Rabbi Shalom's activities undoubtedly enhanced the standing of the San'ā community, and particularly the status of the Bet-Din of San'ā. That body was headed during the second half of the eighteenth century by Rabbi Yihyā Sālih. Rabbi Yihyā was elected to the Bet-Din of San'ā in 1758 when still a young man, and from then until his death in 1805 he was the religious leader of San'ā Jewry, and of the Jews of Yemen as a whole. Rabbi Yihyā was the outstanding religious figure of recent centuries in Yemen, and was regarded as ultimate authority. His treatises were so highly considered that everything that followed was based on his work. The *Tiklāl* (prayer-book) that he drafted, together with his exegesis, is the accepted text used by the Yemenite Jews, and all subsequent prayer-books are derived from it. And so too, the particular way of reading of the Pentateuch in Yemen was henceforth based on Rabbi Yihyā's treatise

Heleq ha-Diqduq. That determined the accepted custom to which the Yemenite Jews adhere to this day. The same is true in the area of *halakha* (religious law), for his work of responsa, entitled *Pe'ulat Saddiq*, together with three other works, on laws of slaughtering and ritual purity, are considered to be the ultimate of religious judgment among Yemenite Jews. Rabbi Yihyā's status was acknowledged throughout the country, and in his work we discover that he was approached for decisions by many communities. Even the sages of the distant communities of Aden to the south and Habban to the east base themselves to a great extent on Rabbi Yihyā's treatises. He also had renown outside Yemen, and maintained ties of correspondence with communities in Egypt, India and the Balkans (Ratzabi, 1967: 248–77; Greidi, 1938: 134–7).[3]

Concerning the nature of the authority that was exercised by the San'ā community over other communities, the evidence indicates that until the end of the nineteenth century this was of a moral nature only. The authority of San'ā depended upon the personalities of the individuals involved.[4] Only with the conquest of Yemen by the Turks in 1872 was the head of community appointed and officially recognized by the ruling powers. Thus we find that Rabbi Shelomo Qārah was appointed that same year as *Hakham Bāshī*, the title conferred by the Ottomans on the representative of the Jewish community in their Yemenite domains (Tobi, 1976b: 104–17; 239–45). From the 1870s on there is increasing information concerning intervention by the authorities, first by the Turks and later by the local Yemenites, in the appointing of leaders of the community (Nahshon, 1972).

We do not possess the document of appointment of Rabbi Shelomo Qārah, but deducing from 'the Royal Decree' given to the first *Hakham Bāshī* in Jerusalem, Rabbi Abraham Hayyīm Gagen (Luntz, 1894: 203–8), it would appear that his powers were extensive, and that he was supported by the authorities. We find support for the assumption, that the leadership of the Yemenite community was organized in Turkish times according to the manner prevalent in other parts of the Empire, in the form of the signatures of the leaders of the community in those days. The seal of office of Sālem ben Yihyā Jamāl, who officiated as *Hakham Bāshī* in the years 1897–9, reads in translation, 'The Chief Rabbi of San'ā and environs and the [Jewish] community of the Yemen.' The seal of the sages of the learned academy of San'ā reads, 'The scholars of the academy of the holy community of San'ā (May the Lord find it well), the spiritual committee' (Ratzabi, 1970). From these formula it appears that the Turkish authorities appointed, as they did elsewhere in the Empire, two committees, one for religious matters and one for material affairs, and that the authority of the *Hakham Bāshī* encompassed all Jews of the country.

During the twentieth century, however, it seems that the head of the San'ā community was not entrusted with officially recognized authority over all Jews of Yemen. This may be learnt from at least two documents. One of these, from the year 1905, when the monarch Imam Yahyā succeeded in forcing the Turks out of San'ā for a brief period, is a 'Religious Regulations for the Jew' given to the Jews by the Imam (Hibshush, 1937: 220–3). This document abrogated the rights granted to the Jews by the Ottomans, and regulated the relations of the government with the Jews on the traditional basis that the Jews were *dhimmi*, strangers under protection. Remarkably, the document refers to the Jews of San'ā only, and nothing is said of other communities. Another document, from the year 1932, appointing Rabbi Yihyā ben Shalom Abyad as Head of the community, and also issued on behalf of Imam Yahyā, similarly indicates that Rabbi Yihyā ben Shalom is appointed over the Jews of San'ā, and nothing is said of other communities (Qorah, 1954: 76–7). The Imam thus abolished the function of *Hakham Bāshī* of Yemen as a whole, perhaps because he did not desire an official who might act on behalf of the whole of Yemenite Jewry. As a result of this policy, the head of the San'ā community dealt with the collection of the poll-tax of his community only, and not with that of other communities. The Imam appointed the heads of individual communities throughout the country, and these were responsible for collecting the local poll-tax (Tobi, 1976b: 65–111).

This formal change did not, however, cause a radical change in the actual position of the San'ā community. Thus Rabbi Yihyā Yishak Halevi, who was *Hakham Bāshī* under the Turks, and who continued to serve as Head of the Bet-Din in the time of Imam Yahyā, was active among the communities outside San'ā. He appointed an emissary on behalf of the Bet-Din of San'ā, who visited various communities in order to ascertain that ritual slaughterers and the officials at marriages did their work properly, and were qualified to do so (Qorah, 1954: 45). Rabbi Yihyā Yishak Halevi also certified, on behalf of a Moslem ruler in a provincial town, a permit to slaughter, which had previously been given to a Jew of that town (Goitein, 1953: 52, also Tobi, 1976b: 111–15).

In the second part of the chapter we now examine a series of new documents that throw light on the nature of the relations between the community of San'ā and other communities. The original sources figure in Tobi (1976a: 191–209).

I   Memorandum of the Bet Din of San'ā to the community of 'Arjāz concerning the safeguarding of morality, 1809 (?) (Adler Geniza, Ms. 2561, Ben Zvi Institute, photograph file 417)

The document is a rather stern appeal to the members of the 'Arjāz community, concerning the slackening of morality and religion, and the need to abide by orders of the courts of the Moslems. The document refers in particular to the apparel of women, and complains about the lack of modesty when women leave the Jewish quarter and enter Moslem neighborhoods. The authors of the memorandum dwell at length on the importance of modesty, and of the dangers implicit in the lack of this virtue:

> And one more observation concerning women when there is no difference between those of Israel and the heathen, for not only do they add to their sinfulness by adorning themselves with all kinds of ornaments and parade among the nations without any trepidation and the Gentiles mock at us, but they also behave in a lewd manner.

Moslems used to set their eyes upon Jewish women, therefore the rabbis of San'ā ordained that women be prohibited from wearing jewelry, except on the Sabbaths and holy days, and then only in the seclusion of the Jewish quarters. Men too were prohibited from wearing white garments except on Sabbaths, in order not to attract the attention of Moslems. The writers of the document threaten all who do not heed them with excommunication, and bestow upon the leaders of the 'Arjāz community power to excommunicate (by refraining from providing ritual services, such as ritual slaughtering and circumcision).

The document is torn at the margins so we do not know the names of the signatories or of their community. But it may be assumed that the signatories were members of the San'ā Bet-Din, for we cannot conceive of such forceful language being that of any other figures. If our hypothesis is correct, and the rabbis of San'ā were the authors of the memorandum, then we may learn from here that the San'ā Bet-Din considered itself duty-bound to ensure the preservation of social and moral standards among all Jews, even though this authority was not granted to it by the general authorities. This emerges more clearly from the documents that follow.

II A letter of rebuke from Rabbi David ben Abraham Sālih to the community of Dāle' concerning the sale of wine to Moslems (before 1839) (Ben Zvi Institute, Ms. 1118, pp. 111b–112a)

Rabbi David Sālih, grandson of Rabbi Yihyā Sālih, was a judge in San'ā Bet-Din during the years 1827–1839, headed at the time by the Rabbi Yosef Qārah. Rabbi David rebukes members of the Dāle' community for having sold wine to Moslems. In the nineteenth century Dāle' was outside the region ruled over by the Imams; it came under the jurisdiction of independent sultanates. In spite of this, the rabbis of Dāle' saw fit to inform Rabbi David that some Jews in the community were selling wine to Moslems, which was prohibited both by general Islamic law and by the regulations of the local Jewish community. Rabbi David's letter of rebuke was apparently penned in response to a request of the local rabbi. So, although Dāle' did not belong politically to Yemen, its Jews regarded themselves as subject to the rabbis of San'ā. But it is unclear why Rabbi David wrote this letter of rebuke, and not the greatest of the rabbis of San'ā and the permanent head of its Ben-Din at the time, Rabbi Yosef Qārah. Possibly the rabbis of Dāle' addressed themselves to Rabbi David as the grandson of the revered Rabbi Yihyā Sālih.

The structure and style of the letter are of interest. The first part deals with the state of Jews in the diaspora and their relationship with God, and the need for repentance in order to hasten divine redemption. The letter was written in the month of Ellul, and constitutes an exhortation connected with the upcoming High Holy Days. Rabbi David goes on to speak of the Tabernacles festival which follows the High Holy Days, and on which one is enjoined to make merry with wine and song. In this connection he reminds the community of Dāle' of the prohibition from selling wine to Moslems. Only after that lengthy introduction does the author come to the point. Moreover, he repeats that he does not aim to rebuke people, but only to remind them that dire consequences are likely to follow transgression, both from the Almighty (the postponement of divine redemption), and more concretely from the Moslem rulers. The letter is written in a moderate style, probably because a mildly-worded reprimand was considered more likely to be effective. But also perhaps because Rabbi David lacked the authority that his ancestor, Rabbi Yihyā Sālih, had possessed. In any event the document expresses the moral authority of the rabbis of San'ā over other communities.

III A letter of rebuke from the San'ā Bet-Din to the members of the Jabal 'Amr community concerning moral decline (1853) (Ms. of Mr. Y. Dahūh, Tel Aviv)

This letter too demonstrates the intervention of the rabbis of San'ā in the lives of people of other communities. Here is the background of events: In the latter months of 1852 tribal fighting took place north of San'ā, and as a result the inhabitants of Jabal 'Amr[5] were apparently driven to leave their homes. After the disturbances abated, people began to return to their hometown, but their institutions, and religious and moral life had apparently deteriorated. Also, personal relations among people were disturbed, to the extent that they used to address themselves to the Moslem town-governor over trivial issues, instead of settling disputes within the Jewish community, as normatively required. As the letter puts it, 'One sin brings a more grievous one in its wake. Since every person who quarrels with his fellow even over a trivial matter comes before the governor of the town. So through this quarrelling they transgress our Holy Law.' Jews opposed at all times having recourse to common law courts, but this community was disordered and its institutions were not effective.

When rumors about this state of affairs reached the San'ā Bet-Din they addressed themselves to the heads of the Jabal 'Amr community, the brothers Rabbi Sālim and Rabbi 'Awād, sons of Yosef Yishak, warning them that, as leaders of the community, they were duty-bound to strive for the restoration of orderly communal life. The brothers replied to the San'ā Bet-Din that, due to their suffering and their preoccupation with their own families, they had no choice but to neglect their duties, and 'their words are words of truth, and the time is one of pressing need.' Rabbi David ben Sālim Dahūh, sent to the San'ā Bet-Din by the elders of Jabal 'Amr, explained to the sages that the elders were not neglecting their duties, and were doing all in their power to restore order. In spite of this the rabbis of San'ā appointed Rabbi David on behalf of the San'ā Bet-Din to be head of the Jabal 'Amr community, and to run local affairs assisted by the brothers, Rabbi Sālim and Rabbi 'Awād Yishak.

The punishment with which the Bet-Din threatened anyone who disobeyed Rabbi David was moral and not material, since they did not have authority to impose the latter. The signatories are the members of the San'ā Bet-Din – the Head Rabbi Sulīmān ben Yosef Qārah (d. 1889), his brother Rabbi Yihyā (d. 1887), Rabbi Yihyā ben Shalom Ha-Kohen (d. 1867), Rabbi Yihyā ben Ya'aqov Sālih (d. 1859), and Rabbi Yosef ben David Manzilī (d. 1899). Again we learn that the authority of the San'ā community was essentially a moral one, conditional upon the consent of the Jews of other communities. In the days of a forceful and respected Head of Court such as Rabbi Sulīmān Qārah, the San'ā Bet-Din could manifestly intervene in the life of another community, and even appoint on its behalf and as it saw fit, a supervisor over local affairs.

IV *The verdict of the emissaries of the Bet Din of San'ā with regard to a dispute between the members of the community of Hufāsh and the local rabbi, 1885 (Sassoon, Ms. 973, pp. 99–100, Ben-Zvi Institute, photograph file 296)*

Rabbi Yihyā ben Hayyim al-Shaikh and Rabbi Hayyim ben Rabbi Sālim Habshūsh were sent on behalf of the San'ā Bet Din to other communities of the Yemen, in order to inspect affairs in these communities. On their arrival in the town of Hufāsh, which lies some three days walking distance to the west of San'ā, they found themselves confronted with a dispute 'over authority in the synagogue and ritual slaughtering, and all sections of the community assembled before us for judgment, including their leaders and dignitaries, and we heard all their testimony with regard to their quarrel with their rabbi, Sa'īd Suwailim.' The emissaries decided in favor of the community, and the rabbi agreed to abide by the judgment. As emerges from the document, the affair later came to the knowledge of Shaikh Yihyā Mūsā, the secular head of the community. He was apprised of the judgment and added his signature beside that of the above-mentioned emissaries. Evidently in this case, the San'ā Bet Din took the initiative in supervising this community; that is, it did not take action only when requested. Furthermore, the authority of the Bet-Din of that particular time was notable. The Head of the Bet-Din was Rabbi Shelomo *Qārah*, considered as the *Rosh Galuta* (Head of the Diaspora), and his Court was known as the *Bet-Din Ha-Gadol* (Supreme Court).

The wording at the beginning of the document is as follows:

> ... [W]e the undersigned being sent on a divine mission by the Rosh Galuta of the Bet Din of San'ā (may the Lord find it well), in order to inspect the affairs of the Jews outside the city of San'ā, in such matters as the slaughterers and inspectors and religious laws and disputes, and whatever greatly requires the powers invested in us by the Supreme Bet Din of San'ā.

The activity of the Bet-Din of San'ā has to be viewed against the background of the comparative quiet that prevailed in the 1880s under Turkish rule, and stems from the fact that the Bet-Din had official recognition of the authorities. Another notable point is that the emissaries of the Bet-Din associate their ruling with the local shaikh. In small communities there were not always ranking rabbis, and the shaikh frequently had a standing superior to that of the local rabbi.

V *The appeal of Yosef ben Shukr of Mahwīt to the Bet Din in Jerusalem against the judgment of the rabbis of San'ā, 1890 (Elyashar, 1891: 60a–63a)*

This responsum by the nineteenth-century Chief Rabbi of Jerusalem, Rabbi Ya'aqov Sha'ul Elyashar, reveals an episode in the relations between the San'ā community and other communities. Yosef ben Shukr Busānī, from the town of Mahwīt, northwest of San'ā, addressed himself to the Bet Din of San'ā, requesting the annulment of a divorce granted to his wife, on the grounds that, as he claimed, he had been compelled to give it against his free will. The husband claimed that, because he was afflicted with boils, his wife had left him. Consequently a dispute errupted between him and the wife's relatives in the town and, therefore, the case was transferred away to the bet din of another town. That bet din decreed that the husband grant his wife a divorce and also pay a fine. The husband refused, and thereupon the shaikh of the Jewish community intervened. He ordered that if the husband disobeyed now, he would have to pay a fine to the Muslim authorities. The shaikh also threatened to imprison the husband. In his plea the husband writes:

> At the time they caused me to become depressed by telling me that if I disobeyed ... I would suffer torture at the hands of the authorities, and would be compelled to divorce.

After having gone from town to town unsuccessfully to find support for his cause, the husband turned to the rabbis of San'ā. The Bet Din of San'ā addressed itself to the local bet din that had reached the first verdict, received a full report, and gathered new testimony. Thereupon the rabbis of San'ā, basing themselves on the code of Maimonides, ruled that the divorce was valid. But the husband continued to appeal to the rabbis of other communities, and eventually obtained opinions against the judgment of the San'ā rabbis, that the divorce was invalid. Those rabbis argued that the decision ought to have been made according to the code of Rabbi Yosef Karo, and not that of Maimonides, because judgment in Yemenite communities outside San'ā customarily followed that code.[6] Eventually the husband presented the case to the rabbis of Jerusalem, and they again ruled against him, that the judgment of the San'ā rabbis was correct, and that the divorce was valid.

We learn from the case of tension between the rabbis of San'ā and those of other communities, which hinged on adherence to different schools of *halakha*. The ruling of the rabbis of San'ā is stamped with a sense of superiority, but that was neither absolute nor final, since the authority of the rabbis of Jerusalem was superior. With the entry of Yemen into the Ottoman orbit we find the Yemenite rabbis of various communities addressing themselves to Jerusalem, without having recourse to the San'ā Bet Din (Tobi, 1973: 286–91). We also learn of the considerable power of the local shaikh, who could imprison and impose fines. The shaikh was evidently supported by the Moslem authorities, for the fines he threatened to impose were earmarked for them. The authority of San'ā thus had clear limits.

Notes

1. See Goitein (1953, especially 50–3); Nahshon (1972: 45–9) devotes a chapter to the power and influence of the San'ā community. See also Tobi (1981: 12–18, 204–11). On the Jewish community of San'ā in general see Qāfih (1968) and Goitein (1953: 48).
2. Towards the end of his life Rabbi Shalom fell from royal favor. He was imprisoned and heavily fined, and the Imam decreed the locking of all synagogues in San'ā.
3. Many poems, mostly still in manuscript, were written in eulogy of Rabbi Shalom, see Tobi (1974: 268–9).
4. The correspondence between the Jewish courts of Aden, and San'ā in the years 1812–1834, concerning the issue of the San'ā court's authority over that of Aden, demonstrates this point. See Nahum (1981: 75–107).
5. This town lies to the northwest of San'ā. For a note about its Jewish community see Dahūh (1964: 7). I am grateful to Mr Dahūh for having made available the document discussed here.
6. Maimonides (twelfth century) was accepted by the Jews of Yemen as supreme rabbinic authority. He was contested from the seventeenth century on by Rabbi Yosef Karo's Code of religious law. The dispute between these two rabbinical schools continued to the last days of the Jews in Yemen, in our times.

References

Dahūh, Y. (1964) 'Ha-yehudim lo hit'arvu ba-goyim,' *Da'at* (Tel Aviv) 8.
Elyashar, Y.S. (1891) *Ma'ase Ish* (Jerusalem).
Goitein, S.D. (1953) *'Al ha-hayyim ha-tzibburiyyim shel ha-yehudim be-eretz-teman*, in Jubilee Volume for M. Kaplan, Hebrew Section. (New York) 43–61.
Goitein, S.D. (1967) 'Negide eretz teman,' in *Bo'i Teman*, Yehuda Ratzabi (ed.), Tel Aviv, 1964: 15–25.
Greidi, S. (1938) 'Kavvim le-toldot yehude teman ba-me'ah ha-yod-het (1700–1800),' in Shimon Greidi and Israel Yesha'yahu (eds), *Me-teman Le-tzion* (Tel Aviv) 106–38.
Hibshush, S. (1937) 'Eshkelot Merorot Va-Halikhot Sheva,' in Shlomo D. Goitein (ed.), *Kovetz 'Al Yad* 2: 197–230.
Luntz, A.M. (1894) *Yerushalayim* IV.
Nahshon, Y. (1972) *Demutah shel Ha-Hanhagah Ha-yehudit Be-Teman*, unpublished MA thesis, Bar Ilan University, Ramat Gan.
Nahum, Y.L. (1981) *Mi-Yetzirot Sifrutiot Mi-Teman*, Yosef Tobi (ed.), Holon.
Qāfih, Y. (1951) 'Ketav haganah mi-teman 'al ha-shitta ha-alegorit be-ferush ha-mikra,' *Kovetz 'Al Yad* 5: 39–63.
Qāfih, Y. (1968) 'Kehillat San'ā shebe-teman,' *Mahanayim* 119: 36–45.
Qorah, A. (1954) *Sa'arat Teman*, Shimon Greidi (ed.), Jerusalem.
Ratzabi, Y. (1967) 'Mahritz u-veto,' in *Bo'i Teman*, Yehuda Ratzabi (ed.), (Tel Aviv, 1964) 248–77.
Ratzabi, Y. (1970) 'Kehillat San'ā bi-shnot 5659–5673 (1899–1913),' *Sinai* 67: 202–18.

Ratzabi, Y. (1972) 'Gerush mawza' le-or mekorot hadashim,' *Zion* 37: 197–215.
Sālih, Y. (1946–64) *Pe'ullat Tzaddik*, Tel Aviv, 2 vols.
Sappir, Y. (1866) *Even Sappir*, vol. 1, Lyck.
Tobi, Y. (1973) 'Yediot 'al yehude teman mi-tokh she'elot u-tshuvot,' *Shevet Va-Am* 7: 272–91.
Tobi, Y. (1974) 'Peniyyat pekide kushta el ribbi shalom iraqi nesi yehude teman bi-shnat 5502 (1742),' *Shalem* 1: 257–69.
Tobi, Y. (1976a) *Yehude Teman Ba-Me'ah Ha-Yod-Tet* (Tel Aviv).
Tobi, Y. (1976b) 'Ha-kehilla ha-yehudit be-teman,' in Yosef Tobi (ed.), *Moreshet Yehude Teman* (Jerusalem): 65–117.
Tobi, Y. (1981) 'Ha-Merkazim ha-Yehudiyyim be-Asya,' in Yosef Tobi, Ya'aqov Barna'i, Shalom Bar-Asher and Shemu'el Ettinger (eds), *Toldot Ha-Yehudim Be-Artzot Ha-Islam*, Jerusalem, 3–70, 197–244.

Part VI
Iran

18 Dhimmi Status and Jewish Roles in Iranian Society[1]
Laurence D. Loeb

The relationship of Muslim and dhimmi *is a Middle Eastern example of a traditional system for regulating the interaction of dominant and subordinate populations in a complex society. When the relationship between these populations shifts to open hostility on the part of the dominant population, the subordinate one may be required to make far-reaching adjustments in its life style. Laurence Loeb, Associate Professor of Anthropology at the University of Utah, explores the nature of these adjustments in the particular setting of Persian Jewry. The author conducted fieldwork in Shiraz in the late 1960s. Conditions at that time do not reflect traditional times, which terminated with the onset of Pahlevi rule in the 1920s, and the creation of modern Iran. But in a provincial city like Shiraz the pace of change was slow, and the present material may to an extent reflect traditional conditions. Be that as it may, Loeb's work is of particular value, because it is uniquely based on fieldwork in situ, in contrast to most of our contributions that do not have this advantage. The author demonstrates that Iranian Jews survived in a social climate of oppression, by adopting a posture of low social visibility, and rendering important economic and social services. The social invisibility that Jews adopted is noteworthy in this account. The oppressive 'law of apostasy,' which entitled apostates to Islam the inheritance of all family property, must have had an important ramification, namely, a trend toward disavowal of extended kin ties, and maintenance of secrecy about details of family relationships. Loeb's material thus raises important questions about the nature of the Jewish extended family system. A full version of Loeb's work is his* Outcaste, *London 1977.*

Using the community of Shiraz, located in the southern Iranian province of Fars, as our principal focus, we shall consider the relationship of Jew and Muslim in traditional Persian society. Utilizing informant-reporting

---

Source: Abbreviation of a paper in *Ethnic Groups*, 1 (1976): 89–105.

and participant-observation techniques, to supplement available historical sources, we shall demonstrate that the survival strategy adopted by Iranian Jews was not dictated by the 'protection' afforded by second-class citizenship, but by their status as a ritually impure outcaste group. Given the ideological commitment to remain Jews in the face of open hostility, on the part of the Muslim population, and the possession of the means of reinforcing ethnic identity through the Jewish 'Great Tradition', Iranian Jewry developed appropriate defense mechanisms. The tactics employed by the Jewish minority in confronting Persian society were typically passive, and oriented towards maintaining a low social visibility. And Persian society permitted the survival of Iranian Jewry for purely pragmatic reasons – the proper articulation and functioning of Persian society.

HISTORICAL BACKGROUND

Together with Christians and Zoroastrians, Jews were considered *dhimmi*, or 'protected minority'. *Dhimmis* were not to be forced to convert to Islam, but in return for this favor, they were expected to shoulder a considerable portion of the tax burden. Originally the granting of *dhimmi* status does not appear to have had immediate, major consequences for Iranian Jewry. Urban Jews continued their interests in trade, banking and handcrafts, while rural Jews were sedentary horticulturalists or pastoral nomads. At the end of the thirteenth century, Jews became influential in Persian politics. A Jew, Sa'ad ad-Daula, became chief vizier of the Mongol ruler Hulagu, and Jewish governors were appointed over Baghdad, Mosul and Shiraz. The eventual downfall of such notables, and subsequent pogroms, signaled the end of Jewish political power in Iran. Thereafter links between Persian Jewry and the outside world were severed, and the fortunes of Iranian Jewry declined.

While the creation of *dhimmi* status appears to have been a mere *modus vivendi*, it soon became apparent that certain Islamic restrictions, which interfered with the smooth functioning of normal commerce, could be circumvented by non-Muslims. Thus, *dhimmis* were not only a lucrative source of tax revenue, but a willing and able supplier of credit services for the entire population – a task forbidden to Muslim merchants. Nevertheless, the rights and obligations of *dhimmis* were, at best, those of a second-class citizen, whose exploitation and harassment were chartered as early as the eighth century in the 'Covenant of Omar' (Baron, 1957: 129–30). It was not until the sixteenth century, however, as a result of a Muslim religious revitalization, i.e. the adoption of the *Shi'a* form of Islam as the national religion, that Persian Jewry was actually reduced to the status of 'persecuted minority', an outcaste group.

Bernard Lewis (1960), among others, has concluded that the origin of Shi'ism among the seventh century peasants of Iran could be explained, as a rebellion of rural serfs against their urban landlords – native Persian *mawali* against the alien Arab master. The religious schism engendered by this movement was felt soon after in Mesopotamia, Egypt and Yemen. In Iran itself, although the official religion remained orthodox *Sunni* Islam, many peasants unwilling or unable to divest themselves completely of their Zoroastrian beliefs and customs, clung to sectarian Shi'ism in a continuing protest against the authorities. Eventually, in 1502, Shah Isma'il proclaimed Imami Shi'ism the state religion; it has remained so ever since.

Commencing with the reign of Abbas I (1587–1629), Jews suffered forced conversion, mass expulsion and murder. The Jew was required to identify himself as a *dhimmi* by various external signs, e.g. by wearing a colored patch or 'badge of shame' on his cloak, a multicolored hat and non-matching shoes (Bacher, 1906: 237). Under a code called the *jam abbasi*, Jews were further restricted as to mobility under various circumstances, public behavior, house and synagogue construction, property rights, legal rights and vocation (Mizrahi, 1966: 36). Revived and renewed after a lapse of several hundred years, the old 'Covenant of Omar' was meticulously refined as it was applied to Iranian Jews. During the nineteenth century, under the Qajars, the constraints and prohibitions became ludicrous. Branded a ritual polluter by the Shi'ite clergy,[2] Jews were forbidden to walk in the rain lest the water washing the Jew come in contact with a Muslim. Nor could Jews sell ritually slaughtered animals to a Muslim, touch merchandise to be purchased from a Muslim, speak loudly in public, or permit their women to appear in public with their faces veiled (Benjamin, 1859: 258–60; *BU*, 1892: 49–50). According to Shirazi informants, these and other practices continued, until outlawed by Reza Shah in 1926. However, in the northwestern part of the country, informants claim that some restrictions are still enforced. My wife and I witnessed prohibitions on Jewish use of water facilities, ostensibly shared with co-owners in Burujerd, on touching market food in Hamadan and Burujerd, and on using the public baths in Yazd.

Jews used to be publicly ridiculed in a variety of ways. Part of the head might have been shaved (*BU*, 1910: 20), or part of the beard removed in public (*BU*, 1892: 50). 'Side locks' were clipped (*BU*, 1902: 110), clothes torn to shreds (*BU*, 1903: 110), and hats cut into triangles like an ass's bonnet (*BU*, 1905: 95). Perhaps the greatest public humiliation was described by Wills in the following terms:

> At every public festival – even at the royal salaam, before the King's face – the Jews are collected, and a number of them are flung into the *hauz* or tank, that the King and mob may be amused by seeing them crawl out half-drowned and covered with mud. The same kindly ceremony is witnessed whenever a provincial governor holds a high festival: there are fireworks and Jews. (1887: 231)

Making sport of the Jew was known as *jud baazi* ('Jew-game'), and that same term was applied to describe the most abject person pitifully begging for his life. Persians coined the expression *jud kosht* ('Jew-murder'), for the most exquisitely painful forms of death imaginable.

JEWISH ECONOMIC ROLES

In response to these circumstances Iranian Jews were driven to develop an appropriate adaptive strategy. One critical area requiring substantial re-adjustment was subsistence. Segregated for hundreds of years Jews were relegated to ghetto living, and proscribed from owning property external to it. The rise of Shi'ite Islam, and resulting seizures of Jewish landholdings, gave impetus to a decline in Jewish participation in horticulture. By the end of the seventeenth century, Jews were limited to tenant farming. Because of the accusation of ritually polluting food Jews touched, they may well have been entirely excluded from food-crop production. In Fars, Jews were probably restricted to silk and opium farming, as these were the prime non-nutritive crops. But silk farming disappeared in the early nineteenth century, and because opium growers were obliged to pay as much as eight-ninths of their crop to their landlord (Lambton, 1969: 318), Jews were not attracted to opium farming.

As Jews were excluded from most guilds, they were prevented from engaging in crafts such as mosaic-making, ceramics, carpentry and painting. In Fars, Jews were not even employed as cobblers, tailors or bakers. Among the crafts, Jews were to be found only in gold- and silversmithing, and in these cases they established their own guilds. Hirschberg (1968: 140) explains:

> Islamic law regards the wage received for work in precious metals as usurious profit, and lays down that no more may be charged for gold and silver articles than the metal value, that is to say, without remuneration for the work and without compensation for the wastage.

For this reason, gold- and silversmithing were in the hands of non-Muslims throughout the Middle East. Jewish manufacturing roles were limited to spinning, warp-winding, masonry, liquor and drug production. Most Jews were gradually forced into service roles as itinerant peddlers, money-lenders, musicians, dancers, actors, healers, fortune tellers, amulet makers, cloth merchants, carters, tinkers, shopkeepers, haberdashers and cesspool cleaners. Jewish women engaged in peddling, midwifery, bone-mending and prostitution.

The most degrading of professions was that of entertainer, whose manner of soliciting employment, i.e. by performing outside the walls of a house until invited in or constrained to leave, was condemned as akin to begging. The debauchery traditionally associated with musicians, actors and especially dancers (who were usually prepubescent boys), was notorious. Rumors circulated within the Jewish community that ran the gamut of impropriety, from their eating non-kosher food to their participation in sexual orgies. Jewish entertainers were exploited by the Muslim population, at least in part, because such activity was expressly forbidden to them by their clergy. Liquor manufacture and sale, like music-making, was expressly forbidden to Shi'ite Muslims, and was therefore an ideal occupation for a limited number of Jews. The traditional importance of liquor-making and entertaining may be measured by the large number (15 per cent) of Shirazi Jews thus employed in 1903 (*BU*, 1903: 108). Hundreds of Shirazi Jews were engaged in the clandestine liquor trade, or employed as entertainers, as late as 1950. In present-day Shiraz, entertaining and liquor selling are still identified as Jewish vocations by the Muslim population.

At the turn of the century, at least 40 per cent of employed Shirazi Jews were itinerant peddlers. Peddling was not disreputable, only erratic, often unprofitable and dangerous. Peddlers would visit far-off villages and nomad camps, remaining away for weeks at a time, frequently to be robbed and sometimes murdered. Despite these hazards and competition from Gypsies, Muslims and other *dhimmis*, peddling attracted large numbers of Jews. Because Iranian Jewry had an excellent system of credit, Jews could venture into peddling with a minimal capital outlay. And Jewish peddlers can still be found trading in many of the far-flung villages of western and southern Iran. Some Jews were beggars, or engaged in menial labor, while others served the community as teachers, ritual slaughterers, prayer readers, synagogue caretakers and washers of the dead. Those Jewish women who serviced the Muslim population as prostitutes, usually did so to support their children, in a family whose male head had deserted, was a drug addict or an inept provider.

The Jewish commercial role of moneylending was particularly important, because Islamic law forbade the faithful to engage in this activity.

Any Jew with surplus capital could be a part-time moneylender, and many made it a full-time vocation. For their part, Muslims liked to borrow from Jews knowing that they could not be legally compelled to repay. No collateral could be demanded by the Jewish moneylender, and the only threat he held over the borrower was the withholding of future credit – a boycott which could be enforced throughout the country, when necessary. Moreover, the Jews, dispersed throughout the country, formed a vast credit network. The traditional process of raising capital remained essentially unchanged in modern Shiraz in the 1960s. The moneylender leases a piece of his property for a lump sum of money, payable in advance. He, the lessor, receives usufruct rights to this 'key' money for the lease period, while the lessee has usufruct rights to the property. At lease termination, the principal is returned to the lessee, while the property and improvements to it revert to the owner. In recent years, Jews have leased out large tracts of land in the center of fast-growing urban areas, and have become wealthy from property improvements and from the interest obtained from lending the 'key' money.

Those Jewish occupations that were not entirely intra-community oriented, shared, to a great extent, the following traits: (i) they were necessary to Persian commerce, but were not basic subsistence skills; (ii) they produced marginal income; (iii) they were despised by Shi'ite Islam or were suspect in the eyes of the ruling elite, hence (iv) they were occupations normally avoided by the populace.

The occupations of peddler, entertainer, liquor-seller, moneylender and prostitute, imply considerable face-to-face interaction with diverse elements of the population. People engaged in these activities are therefore in a position to exchange information with a wide variety of social groups, and thus may be said to perform the task of communicator or disseminator of ideas. According to Sjoberg (1960: 135–7), it is because of this extra-occupational role, that such vocations were viewed with suspicion by the elite in feudal autocratic preindustrial societies. The elite concerned with maintaining the status quo, considered the diffusion of potentially disruptive radical ideas a threat to the authority structure, and desired to insulate society from all such corrupting heresies. Since the above-mentioned vocations were deemed necessary for economic reasons, it was advantageous to the authorities to have them filled by people who were not taken seriously by the populace. Outcaste groups, ridiculed and segregated, served this function well; thoughts communicated by them would be ignored or dismissed as valueless by the masses.

In Iran, the marginal, menial, low-paying and disreputable service occupations were linked with *dhimmis*. The Shi'ite clergy and the elite constantly reiterated that such employment was unworthy of consideration by the lowliest of the Muslim faithful; even begging was to be preferred. Thus potential Muslim competition for these service roles was effectively eliminated. Simultaneously, the *dhimmis* were socially ostracized and physically segregated from the populace by religious sanction of the clergy, who accused them of ritual pollution.

Not only were the Jews traditionally the largest, most widely dispersed and probably the most despised minority in Iran (cf. Malcom, 1905: 108), but as we have seen, they were also firmly entrenched in these service roles.[3] The Jew's potential value to Persian society as newsbearer, social and political commentator and mediator or disseminator of ideas, was restricted, because in essence, he had little meaningful social access to the masses. As a segregated, ridiculed social outcaste, the ideas and views he expressed met with minimal acceptance. Therefore, whether or not it was so intended, the Iranian Jew functioned as a safety valve for social and political heresy. Radical ideas proposed by one sector of society, and thence mediated and diffused by Jews, rarely evoked a response from the rest of the populace. The Jew, rather than communicating ideas, thus in effect acted to insulate the various segments of the population from one another. This implicit service to the elite, coupled with direct economic benefits to Persian commerce, made the Jew invaluable to Iranian society.

SOCIAL DEFENSE

As the protective features of *dhimmi* status gradually disappeared, Iranian Jews found it necessary to defend themselves as individuals, kinsmen and members of a community. We shall demonstrate that in all three aspects of Shirazi social life, the main strategy of defense was one of social invisibility – a pattern discernable in role differentiation, i.e. the avoidance of vocational confrontation, or competition between *dhimmi* and Muslim, previously alluded to in the economic sphere.

As in most societies, the primary unit of social structure among Iranian Jews was based on kin relationships. The main kin-based group and unit of familial stability was the tri-generational patrilineal, patrilocal extended family, known as the *khanevadeh*. The *khanevadeh* provided for the subsistence of its membership, the education of the young, and the formation of marital alliances. Since inheritance of property was, with rare exceptions, wholly patrilineal, i.e. from father to sons, property tended to remain within the *khanevadeh*, until the residence became so overcrowded that it became necessary for the unit to fission. Despite the apparent benefits of the *khanevadeh*, a unit common to many Iranian populations, it was a structure maladapted to at least one important fact of Iranian Jewish life – the 'law of apostasy.'

This law, promulgated in the seventeenth century, provided that any *dhimmi* convert to Islam would legally inherit the entire estate of all relatives within seven generations (Carmelite Chronicles, 1939: 366), and it was enforced until the early part of this century. In 1903, a representative of Alliance Israélite Universelle reported that there was not a single family in Shiraz without a *jadid al-islam* ('new Muslim') waiting for his inheritance (*BU*, 1903: 107). In Shiraz, far from the capital, local authority was all but autonomous, and the 'law of apostasy' rigorously applied. In an obvious effort to avoid its consequences, some Jews distributed their property before death. Jewish girls were married off at age six or seven, to ensure the receipt of a proper dowry, from fathers who could not assure this after death. In a region where bridewealth is the rule, the Jewish pattern of dowry is conspicuous. Its origin notwithstanding, the dowry pattern is uniquely well-suited to the exigencies arising from the 'law of apostasy', by ensuring the conservation of wealth within the community.

From the testimony of informants, it appears that the 'law of apostasy' was only applied patrilineally. This might explain some apparent anomalies in the Shirazi Jewish kinship system. When asked why they could rarely name their grandparents, or identify forebears of their patriline more than two generations removed, people responded that their ancestors would have been remembered if they had accomplished anything noteworthy. In no case could an informant name a consanguine more than six degrees, or three generations, distant. Named patrilineal kin four degrees or more removed from ego were invariably younger than ego, and the latter were usually unable to reciprocate the identification. The importance of this convenient 'loss' of genealogical memory in the dissipation of the effects of the 'law of apostasy' should be noted; it probably effectively limited its application to no more than three generations.

The low visibility of the patriline was further enhanced by the emergence of a non-corporate bilateral kindred, the *famil*, as the major extended kin group. Included within this group are consanguines, five or six degrees distant from ego, and affines four to five degrees distant from ego. No distinction is made between patrikin and matrikin with regard to rights and obligations, which are largely limited to life crises rituals. More distantly related kin are called *qom* ('tribe'), but when pressed to reveal the precise relationship between themselves and *qom*, Shirazi Jews are rarely able to do so. They sheepishly admit that they all are probably related anyhow.

The social 'invisibility' necessitated by the 'law of apostasy' was complemented by political 'invisibility' vis-à-vis the outside world. The head of the Shirazi community was once known as *nasi*, the Hebrew term for 'headman', and is now referred to by its Persian equivalent, *re'is*. Traditionally this was not a position sought after, nor was it a position of substantial power. Although the *nasi* was a man of prestige within the community, he was either chosen or approved by the government. To the authorities he symbolized the Jewish community, and was thus the prime recipient of official abuse and punishment. Ostensibly, the *nasi* led the community with the aid of a committee of elders, known as the *'ene ha'eda* ('eyes of the community'). The latter, however, were not infrequently at odds with the *nasi*, sometimes provoking external intervention with tragic results (Loeb, 1970: 34).

The main concerns of the *nasi* and *'ene ha'eda* lay in the field of relations between the Jewish community and the dominant population. Major internal disputes were brought before them only when they threatened to erupt beyond the ghetto confines. Membership in the *'ene ha'eda* was generally limited to the wealthy and prominent, although others piously volunteered their services. Membership visibly demonstrated prestige within the community, yet this status was not widely coveted. The *'ene ha'eda* represented the community in public, and many of the members were imprisoned, wounded or murdered while petitioning the authorities on behalf of the community, or while trying to dissuade Muslim mobs from invading the ghetto (Melamed, 1951: 366). Being highly conspicuous, these men were constantly endangered, and consequently they tried to avoid making decisions which might have met with objection from Persian society. Avoidance of decision-making has become a common behavioral pattern among Shirazi Jews, and it still paralyzes the apparatus of community management.

That the Jewish community managed to thrive despite the vacillations of this pusillanimous body was largely due to an invisible political structure, elsewhere dubbed 'the council of the pious' (Loeb, 1970). At its head was the *dayan* (judge), who was the religious counterpart of the secular *nasi*, and in the view of many Shirazis, more important than the latter. Less concerned about exposure, the *dayan* was not averse to making decisions affecting the future of the community. The *dayan* more or less presided over the 'council of the pious,' whose membership included *darshanim* (preachers), *hazanim* (synagogue overseers), *gabayim* (collectors and disbursers of community funds), *shlihe sibbur* (prayer leaders), *mohalim* (circumcisors), *shohatim* (ritual slaughterers) and pious concerned laymen.

The 'council of the pious' collected funds from charity and taxes on meat and wine, appropriating sums for schooling, relief and communal projects. Decisions regarding day-to-day problems within the community were in its hands, and its influence was considerable. Decisions of the council were arrived at by consensus, and while dissenters sometimes ignored them, rulings in the all-pervasive sphere of religious life were usually adhered to by everyone. Membership in the council was informal and participation extensive, thereby contributing to the overall low visibility of this political body. The prestige of the councillors, involving neither wealth nor government sponsorship, did not attract outside interest or jealousy. Since its area of interest rarely impinged directly upon Persian society, the 'council of the pious' was a more effective political structure than the *'ene ha'eda*. Although in recent times there has been a decline in its political influence, and a sapping of its economic base due to external forces, the 'council of the pious' continues to exert a powerful moral influence upon the Jews of Shiraz.

Until recently, personal security was non-existent for Iranian Jews. Men were harassed, beaten, incarcerated and murdered. Women faced the additional hazards of kidnap and rape. Typically, passivity, humble demeanor and servility marked Jewish public behavior, whose goal was to avoid Muslim hostility. Yet, even the home was not inviolate. Shirazi Muslims, for example, felt no compunctions about walking into any Jewish home, and taking anything that pleased them. Jews learned to hide their wealth in walls or under floors, living a threadbare existence, no matter what their actual economic condition was. The *mahalleh* (quarter) in which Jews were constrained to reside, served to restrict contact between Jew and Muslim. Architectural features, such as: (a) long, high, unbroken walls around each house; (b) low, narrow, twisting entrances; (c) long, narrow, dead-end alleys with five-foot high overhangs and (d) connecting roofs, functioned to protect Jews from marauders.

Although Shirazi Jews have gradually been leaving the *mahalleh* since 1945, until a few years ago no one dared to build a plush house or purchase modish furnishings. The pattern of affecting poverty, necessitated by the fear of theft as well as by a desire to hide wealth from potential *jadid al-islam* heirs, fostered a reluctance among the wealthy to donate to charity. The wealthy claim they cannot afford to contribute, citing their own evident lack of material possessions. As a result, Shirazi charity has traditionally meant the redistribution of the resources of the poor among themselves. Personal insecurity has, furthermore, encouraged an ethos in which labor is not considered a virtue, because its fruits are likely to be stolen. It has also engendered an encompassing intense fear for personal, familial, communal and ethnic survival, incessantly expressed and displayed by young and old.

Excluded from meaningful interaction with the rest of Persian society, Jews have compensated for this deprivation by means of a formal system of intracommunal honor exchanges. Daily public social contact among Jews involves intricate maneuvering, aimed at improving one's prestige and thus intracommunity ranking. The rank order is determined by kinship, education, occupation, piety, religious knowledge and, most of all, affluence. It is in this context alone that conspicuous displays of wealth are made in the synagogue (and are therefore not manifest to outsiders), as expressions of piety and prestige. But even here, people are reluctant to give evidence of their true worth, so that the bidding for auctioned ritual honors is no reliable guide to the absolute or even relative wealth of the bidders.

CONCLUSIONS

While Persian society has long been stratified, it is not immediately apparent why the presence of an outcaste ethnic group such as the Jews is tolerated. Furthermore, in a complex preindustrial society marked by sharp social distinctions, including landlord/peasant, nomad/sedentary, urban/rural and elite/proletarian, one wonders what possible need there could have been to add a believer/*dhimmi* category.

Islam extended to Jews the status of *dhimmi*, 'protected minority'. Although this 'protection' was provided an ideological rationale, its function was the economic and social exploitation of a subordinate population. Under the auspices of Shi'ite Islam, extremist clergy classified the Jew as a ritually impure outcaste, to be strictly segregated from the faithful. As a consequence, the Persian elite found the Jews valuable agents in their efforts to control the populace. With Jews acting in roles normally requiring extensive social contact and subsequent dissemination of ideas, the Persian masses were at least partially insulated from prevalent social heresies. At the same time, the Jew was able to fulfill important economic and social roles that were morally or religiously prohibited to Shi'ite Muslims. The Jew became so expert at these roles that some of them are still completely identified with him. The critical nature of these roles for the normal functioning of Persian life is attested to by the continued survival of the overwhelming majority of Jewish communities, despite the opposition of the powerful Shi'ite clergy.[4]

The institution of identifying dress, specialized vocational roles highly differentiated from those of the Muslim population, restricted legal rights and constrained public behavior, marked the Jew as a highly visible target for ridicule and humiliation – in short, a potential scapegoat. Thus, the major strategic problem for Persian Jewry was the maintenance of a low, if not invisible, public profile. Despite their conspicuousness, Jews by and large succeeded in this endeavor by avoiding public physical, economic and social confrontation with the Muslim population. This adaptation required important adjustments in the personal, familial and communal life of the Jew, as well as the development of appropriate defense mechanisms.

Whether the analysis presented here might serve as a model for *dhimmi*/Muslim relations throughout Iran, and to what extent it holds true elsewhere in the Muslim world, is not at all clear. There is some evidence that Armenians, Nestorians, Gypsies and, to a lesser extent, Zoroastrians have traditionally played a role paralleling, overlapping and conflicting with that of the Jew. As yet, too little research has been done to draw any conclusions from it. On the other hand, material on Jewish communities elsewhere in the Muslim world suggests that while the middleman/broker role was widely associated with the Jew, there was considerable variation with respect to other aspects of Jewish/Muslim relations, requiring further investigation and clarification.

The concept of 'outcaste group' would probably apply to all the *dhimmis*, though differentially, and outside of Iran it may be applicable to other non-Muslim populations. In Yemen, however, it would be more appropriate to speak of *dhimmis* as a low-caste, since Yemen possesses a true caste system. The evidence presented here suggests that the relationship of dominant and subordinate populations in complex society could benefit from a closer examination of traditional long-term contact systems, such as the *dhimmi*/Muslim link. Diaspora populations in general and the Jews, in particular, are especially useful in this context.

Notes

1   An earlier version of this paper was presented at a symposium entitled: 'The Ethnology of Traditional Jewish Communities,' at the Seventieth Annual Meeting of the American Anthropological Association, New York, 1971. I wish to express my appreciation to my wife, Nomi, who collaborated in fieldwork and to Prof. Eric Wolf for his helpful comments. The field research in Iran (1967–1968), upon which this study is based, was facilitated by grants from the Cantors Assembly of America, The Memorial

2 Shi'ite preoccupation with ritual pollution, and its emphasis on unbelievers as a major source of contamination, is of probable Zoroastrian origin (cf. Loeb, 1970).
3 In some of the highly specialized *dhimmi* professions, Jews faced intense competition from other *dhimmis*. In Shiraz, for example, Jewish-Armenian competition, especially in wine manufacture and music-making lasted hundreds of years, continuing into the late nineteenth century. In this case the Jews triumphed and the vanquished Armenian community all but disappeared. In Isfahan, however, the Armenians gained the upper hand. In Yazd, the outcome of competition with the Zoroastrians could not be properly evaluated.
4 The Shi'a clergy made numerous attempts to end the Jewish presence in Iran. Community-wide forced conversion to Islam was a common occurrence in Iran, beginning with the reign of Shah Abbas I. Although there is considerable evidence (Loeb, 1970) demonstrating that occasionally the conversion was complete and irrevocable, most of the time, pragmatic commercial considerations led to acquiescence to 'backsliding', or outright repeal of the conversion decree. The last major conversions took place in Shiraz (circa 1830) and in Mashhad (1839). The former community gradually returned to Judaism, whereas the latter is famous for having remained outwardly *jadid al-islam*, while maintaining a meticulously observant Jewish tradition within the home. Jews openly returned to Judaism in Mashhad after World War II. Lacking any *dhimmis*, Mashhad allowed these *jadid al-islam* to continue their traditional vocations, despite the contradictions inherent in such a policy.

References

Bacher, W. (1906) 'Les Juifs en Pèrse au XVII et au XVIII siècle d'après les chroniques de Babai Loutf et de Babai B. Farhad,' *Revue des Études Juives*, 52: 237.

Baron, S.W. (1957) *A Social and Religious History of the Jews*, Revised edition, vol. 3 (New York: Columbia University Press).

Benjamin, I.J. (1859) *Eight Years in Asia and Africa – from 1846 to 1854* (Hanover).

(BU) Bulletin Mensuel de l'Alliance Israélite Universelle, various issues.

Carmelite Chronicles (1939) *A Chronicle of Carmelites in Persia and the Papal Mission of the XVIIth and XVIIIth Centuries* (London: Eyre & Spottiswoode).

Hirschberg, H.Z. (1969) 'The Oriental Jewish Communities,' in A.J. Arberry, *Religion in the Middle East*, vol. 1, 119–225 (Cambridge University Press).

Lambton, A.K.S. (1969) *Landlord and Peasant in Iran*, 2nd edition (London: Oxford University Press).

Lewis, B. (1960) *The Arabs in History* (New York: Harper & Row).

Loeb, L.D. (1970) *The Jews of Southwest Iran: A Study of Cultural Persistence*. Columbia University. PhD dissertation.

Malcom, N. (1905) *Five Years in a Persian Town* (New York: E.P. Dutton).

Melamed, E. (1951) 'Hayyhudim Befaras Lifne Shishim Shana,' *Sinai* (Hebrew) 29: 359–70.
Mizrahi, H. (1966) *Toldot Yehude Paras Umshorrehem* (Hebrew) (Jerusalem: Rubin Mas).
Sjoberg, G. (1960) *The Preindustrial City* (New York: Free Press).
Wills, C.J. (1887) *Persia As It Is*, 2nd edition (London: Sampson, Low, Marsten and Rivington).

19 Prestige and Piety in the Iranian Synagogue[1]
Laurence D. Loeb

There are significant differences in the social organization of traditional synagogues. The Moroccan synagogue, for instance, is essentially a private institution that revolves around an aristocratic sage. The Yemenite synagogue, at the other extreme, strives to be egalitarian and tolerates few social distinctions in its religious functions. Congregants there fill religious roles according to rotation. Between these polar extremes there is a variety of social systems in the synagogues of various Jewish societies. In the Iranian variant described here, congregants have formal religious roles, but together with the formalism there is scope for individuals to assert themselves. Such assertion would not be tolerated among egalitarian Yemenite Jews, whereas among Moroccans it would not usually be possible due to the dominance of the sage. In the Iranian situation we see the synagogue as an arena, that permits dynamic and overt assertations of status, in which people can gain and also lose prestige. These dynamics have so far been described only by Loeb for the Iranian synagogue. Activities of this kind exist with differences of nuance, also in other Jewish societies, and await further study. The chapter is additionally notable for providing a rare description of a form of traditional Jewish etiquette and social skill.

Despite frequent assertion by sociologists and social historians that the synagogue is the central institution in traditional Jewish society, there is a remarkable dearth of competent description or analysis of synagogue behavior. Most of the available material is limited to discussions of the synagogue's physical structure and the ideal mechanics of its organization and operation, but little is said about social dynamics (Deshen, 1972, 1974; Heilman, 1975, 1976). This article focuses on certain procedures of the synagogues of Shiraz, observed during 1967 and 1968.[2] Much of the accompanying analysis is somewhat applicable to behavioral patterns observed in other, oriental as well as some occidental, synagogues. The

---

Source: Slightly abbreviated version of a paper in *Anthropological Quarterly*, 51 (1978): 155–61. © Copyright 1978: Catholic University of America Press. Reprinted by permission of Catholic University of America Press.

procedures described also supplement the literature currently available on the formal mechanisms of Middle Eastern face-to-face interaction, and presents a perspective on their function, which differs somewhat from those proposed by Bourdieu (1966) and Abou-Zeid (1966), among others.

THE SETTING

The Jews of Shiraz have been harassed and intimidated more than most Iranian Jews, and their lives less secure than in many other places where Jews have lived. One result of frequent persecution has been the inhibition of free social development, marked for example, by the lack of visible political structures (Loeb, previous ch., 1977). Jews treated political power with ambivalence, fearing involvement with the authorities.

The only social institution in which the entire Jewish community participates is the *knisa*, synagogue,[3] of which there are a considerable number in the city. Here, largely concealed from the outside world, men can vie for a measure of influence in procedural decision making. The decision making process culminates in a consensus only after the issues have been disputed, and factions formed to support the contending personalities. The weight of communal opinion depends primarily on the relative religious and secular prestige of the protagonists. The main 'bone of contention' in Shirazi Jewish social life is prestige, which the elite (top ranked) have and wish to deny to others. Everyone else wants a greater share.

Although Shirazi Jewish society is clearly not egalitarian, neither can it be sharply demarcated into bounded classes nor strata. Rather a ranking system is operative, whose composite scale is the product of several prestige scales. Prestige (influence) is measured by indices of kin, affluence, occupation, religious knowledge, piety and education. Like Stirling (1965: 233), I am unable to derive the precise rank of all Shirazis since: (i) it is difficult to evaluate the relative weight given the various indices in each particular case, and (ii) prestige fluctuates through accrual or loss of honor. In the past, social mobility among Shirazi Jews was very limited. Kinship, perhaps the most important single factor in rank, is not subject to major alteration. Great wealth always guaranteed acceptance into the elite, but wealth was unavailable to most potential social climbers. Bettering one's occupation might enhance one's prestige, but this alone did not guarantee acceptance into the elite. Today, some can circumvent the tedious struggle to achieve higher rank by use of a shortcut, such as by becoming college-trained professionals (doctors or engineers), or by becoming high-level government employees. But for most potential social climbers, only traditional means are available.

Two traditional mechanisms which simultaneously serve to (i) reinforce rank differences, and (ii) allow social mobility are *ta'arof* (the Persian code of formal behavior) and the auctioning of *kvodot* (ritual honors Hebrew). Each of these is a procedure dealing with transactions involving honor, and will be considered presently.

HONOR

In Iran, as throughout the Middle East and circum-Mediterranean, honor is the critical factor in social relations (cf. Peristiany, 1966). Jews considered devoid of honor were publicly insulted, and forced to suffer various indignities by the population at large. Nevertheless, within Jewish community life, honor, with its traditional Persian ramifications, became an essential complex in the Jewish value system. Despite the Shirazi Jew's preoccupation with physical survival – perhaps because real wealth and security were unattainable goals – honor became as much sought after as wealth.

Honor is associated with relative prestige, which may be exchanged in face-to-face situations. It is also a valuation, composed of two factors: (i) an individual's self-estimation (pride), that is his claim to rank; (ii) society's acknowledgment of this claim (deference, respect), confirming his right to rank. Honor can be acquired, added to, saved, exchanged and even spent (for example, in exchange for loans, political power, and so on). The whole system of honor exchange could be fruitfully analyzed in economic terms. The loss of honor (shame) among Shirazi Jews, no matter how slight, is a very serious matter. The offended withdraws, becomes sullen and often sulks by himself. He avoids the offender at all costs. If amends are not made, the offended individual may attempt to enlist support, and has been known to spread rumors about the offender. Defense of one's honor is almost always verbal. When, infrequently, outright anger ensues, it is always contained before it reaches the point of violent. In this presentation, the concern is with personal honor, which, in most situations among Shirazi Jews, outweighs other kinds (e.g. family honor).

TA'AROF

Ta'arof refers to the Persian system of polite formal behavior, verbal and non-verbal, by which means honor exchanges are transacted in face-to-face situations. Descriptions of ta'arof are found in Chardin (1923: 188), Waring (1807: 101–3), Bishop (1891, 1: 196–7) and Wills (1887: 28–32), among others. It used to be most strictly observed by the elite to reinforce rank differentiation, and it was considered the model of proper behavior, much imitated by the rest of the population. Among contemporary Jews of Shiraz, the elite affects Western manners, and less frequently initiates ta'arof exchanges. In its pristine form, ta'arof is best preserved among society's more conservative elements, the aged, religious and poor. But altogether Shirazis maintain ta'arof to a degree rarely observed elsewhere in Iran.

The fundamental meaning of ta'arof ('offer') gives a clue to its most important process. The offer may, for example, be in the street, when acquaintances meet, *befarmayid!* ... 'please' (come along, be my guest, and so on), by which the speaker implies that the other should accompany him to his house. Such offers are never accepted, nor are they meant to be. A variety of offers are made in situations of hospitality.[4] The guest is offered a seat of honor, *bala*, 'up front', away from the entrance. He may then be offered the water pipe, tea, nuts, raisins, fruit (the order varies), and perhaps a meal. At the meal, the guest is offered the choice portions of food to the point of satiation and beyond, for the host may finally resort to placing the food in the protesting guest's mouth. The guest, on the other hand, no matter how hungry he is and no matter how little food he is given, must leave food on the plate to demonstrate that the host has been overly generous. Should a chance remark slip from the guest's mouth, that some item belonging to the host pleases him, the latter will press the guest to accept it as a gift, for the host will declare, *manzel-e-man, khod-e-tun!* – 'my house is your own!'

The target of the offer is expected to politely refuse. Repeated offers are declined, and great power of persuasion may be necessary to force their acceptance. If more than one guest is present, the initial target of the offers must attempt to defer the honor of acceptance to the others. Eventually, each person present will accept the offer in rank order, from highest to lowest. Should someone accept out of turn, everyone else who considers himself to have been slighted, will adamantly refuse to accept at all.

TA'AROF IN KNISA

Ta'arof is the foundation of the traditional code of synagogue behavior. With regard to seating, the most prestigious sit nearest the western wall (in which the Tora scrolls are kept), away from the entrance, and visitors are asked to sit *bala*, honorifically up front. The ta'arof mechanism is of central importance, particularly in one of the synagogue's critical procedures, the selection of the *sheliah zibbur* (prayer leader). Each knisa has one chief sheliah zibbur and several regular substitutes, and at some time or other, nearly every male, literate in Hebrew, acts in this role. The chief sheliah zibbur, who ranks high on indices of piety and learning, is considered among the knisa's elite, although usually not being wealthy, he ranks considerably lower in the community's overall ranking. The opportunity to perform as sheliah zibbur is eagerly sought after, since it identifies one as pious and learned, qualities highly respected in Shiraz.

If the chief sheliah zibbur is present, he usually begins by offering the honor of leading worship to someone else, with the words: *aghaye* so-and-so, *bekhavod*, 'Mr. so-and-so, be honored' (using the Hebrew terms for 'honor'). Mr. so-and-so declines the offer and offers it back, or, less often, defers to someone else. The chief sheliah zibbur may now offer the honor to someone else, to several others, perhaps returning to his original choice, or he may persist immediately with his first choice.[5] The *kavod* (honor) is frequently first offered to the substitute *shlihey zibbur*. Next it is offered to others in order of general rank, with somewhat more weight given to knowledge of Judaica and piety than in secular ta'arof situations. One need not wait to be offered a kavod, but may take the initiative in offering it to others at any time, providing one is literate.

Such ta'arof is a game, albeit a serious one. Its object is for the individual to accrue as much honor as possible. One scores by (1) accepting the offer after much protestation, (2) deferring the honor upward to the individual who accepts it, (3) magnanimously bestowing it on someone lower in rank, (4) pressing it on a near equal. All participants in these exchanges gain honor, though in different measure depending on their rank, posture during the exchange, and other variables. Non-participants suffer relative loss however slight.[6] Other things being equal, it is best to accept the honor offered, after appropriate refusal. One should not, however, accept an honor offered by someone very much higher in rank, should he make the mistake of offering it. He would appear to be mocking the recipient, and this is frowned upon, both parties sharing a consequent loss of honor. The proper strategy is to defer the honor elsewhere, preferably upward, to avoid embarrassment. One may accept an honor offered from below, since such is one's due.

The ta'arof exchange for selecting a sheliah zibbur usually lasts two or three minutes, and only 8 to 10 men, out of a much larger congregation, participate in the selection. Congregants can inject themselves into the transaction at any point and do so. After the first exchanges, the participants usually sense who is eventually going to accept the kavod. The signs are subtle: the recipient's attempts at deferring are quieter and less convincing than those of the others; instead of gesturing with the offer and looking toward the potential recipient he will studiously look at the floor. Even if initial offers are not directed at the eventual recipient, he will initiate his own offers. In terms of total number, the eventual recipient tends to make more frequent offers than anyone else. In this way, he covertly proclaims that he wants the kavod while overtly demonstrating his modesty, apparently only accepting the honor because everyone is deferring to him.

One who has *yerze'it*, the annual memorial day for a deceased relative, or is in mourning, may feel that he has a priority claim to this honor on a given day, without regard to rank. He may seize the honor without even perfunctory deferral, usually without loss of honor. Honor-gaining strategies also depend on mood. One may simply not want to act as sheliah zibbur, and will instead accept a lesser honor by deferring. One of high rank may defer to one of lower rank, who is more pious or learned or has a better voice. The elite need not participate at all, without penalty, since as Julian Pitt-Rivers (1966: 37) put it, 'Just as capital assures credit, so the possession of honor guarantees against dishonor'. Sometimes however, one of low rank may cut through the ta'arof and seize the honor of leading the worship. Such mavericks lose more honor than they gain, since this is in violation of the rules. The ultimate loss of honor faces those who frequently resort to such tactics. They may be stopped by the *hazzan*, the overseer, of the knisa and asked to desist.

THE PURCHASE OF KVODOT

The second mechanism to be considered is the purchase of synagogue honors. *Kvodot* (sing. *kavod*, lit. honor) are certain ritual acts and objects which are auctioned off in knisa. These include the opening of the ark and removal of the Tora, various *aliyot* (being called to 'go up' to the reading of the Tora), 'ownership' of various parts of the knisa for specified periods (e.g. the eternal light), the right to lead certain short prayers, and (rarely) to act as general sheliah zibbur. The various kvodot are of unequal merit. Thus among the aliyot the last, *maftir*, is the most important, followed by *mashlim* (next to last), *shelishi* (3rd), *samukh* (3rd from end), the 4th and 5th. Some are restricted, such as the first one which belongs to the *kohanim*, 'priests', and rarely will a non-priest purchase it, since he cannot make use of it himself. The absolute value of the kvodot varies with the occasion. On the Day of Atonement, they are worth most, on Sabbaths and Festivals less, and during the week, least. During weekday worship the cost of bidding is well within the reach of the poor, therefore the mechanism of *kvodot* tends to be less exclusive than that of ta'arof. Also, in order to purchase and use a kavod, one need not be literate in Hebrew.

The purchaser of a kavod demonstrates his wealth, and that is the only traditional example of conspicuous consumption among Shirazi Jews. In the past, Jews were not permitted to own real property, and expensive household items such as carpets were kept to a minimum, for fear that they would be seized by Muslims. Only within the confines of the knisa, through auctioning of kvodot, could one demonstrate relative wealth. The elite, who need not support their claim to honor, but fear to express lack of piety (as would be assumed if they totally abstained), try to purchase kvodot at low prices. The rest of the congregation competes to keep the bidding up, thus justifying claims to position on this important wealth prestige scale.

The purchaser of kvodot demonstrates reverence for the knisa and Tora – important markers of piety – since the high bidder's money goes for synagogue maintenance and improvement. During mourning especially, when the merit of these purchases accrues also to the deceased (at the same time protecting the purchaser from *neshamot* ('spirits') one buys many kvodot, thus testifying to one's respect for the dead.

THE SOCIAL CLIMBER IN KNISA

Since the knisa is Shiraz's only public Jewish forum, the social climber exhibits a marked interest in synagogue problems. The social climber must verify his claim to higher rank by demonstrating increased wealth. To solidify this claim, he must prove his piety and by participating in synagogue ta'arof, constantly improving his image and increasing his prestige. The social climber becomes a vigorous advocate of synagogue improvement, and if his attendance had been erratic in the past it now becomes more regular. The social climber tries to be friendly with those who sit bala, and at weekday services, he gradually moves *balatar* (further from the entrance), often at the insistence of his new friends who ta'arof him to do so. He may eventually establish himself up front. Also eventually, he may leave the ghetto knisa of his family, and join a more prestigious one out on the main streets.

The social climber endeavors to call attention to himself for socially correct reasons. Thus he may enter knisa a few minutes late, puts on his *tallit* (prayer shawl), and *tefillin* (phylacteries), while loudly reciting the appropriate blessings. Worship is then momentarily suspended as everyone replies, 'Amen!' After receiving an *'aliya'* to the Tora, he like everyone else, waves the fringe of his zizit over the congregation and wishes them, *kulkhem tihyu berukhim*, 'may you all be blessed'. Afterwards, he goes to the elders of the congregation, touches the fringe to their heads and kisses it, personally giving them his blessing. The social climber participates frequently in the auction of kvodot. His bids are conspicuous, and mostly directed to attain the more meritorious honors. He must have the audacity to challenge the elite of the very wealthy in the bidding. By outbidding the latter, or forcing them to bid much higher than they normally would, he gains great honor. Another honor-gaining strategy is to outbid someone and then, after some ta'arof, bestow the honor on the opponent. By thus purchasing the honor, for someone who cannot afford to bid for it, the social climber gives evidence of benevolence. These last two strategies pay the added dividend of obligating the target of such generosity to reciprocate in some way.

Through participation in public ta'arof exchanges with the elite, the social climber clinches his claim to higher rank, showing that he is considered a quasi-equal by them.[7] A common vehicle for this exchange is the selection of the sheliah zibbur, as previously described. At first, no offers are made to the social climber. He must himself take the initiative by offering honor to others. But his moves must be subtle, to avoid appearing brazen. If he can establish himself as a respected sheliah zibbur, so much the better; he should act the role on at least one occasion. His aim is not so much being sheliah zibbur, as it is to regularly participate in the selection process, thereby benefiting from the continual (though lesser) honor of deferral. On occasion, by acting as sheliah zibbur, the social climber can convince the congregation of his learning and piety, as he demonstrates his acceptance among the elite through direct ta'arof exchanges. The underlying assumption of the social climber is, that by constantly adding small increments of honor, he can enhance his prestige and subsequently his rank. One might summarize: accumulated honor leads to increased prestige (influence), and that leads to higher rank.

CONCLUSION

The manipulation of the appearance of piety by the social climber serves to validate the primacy of piety within the hierarchy of Shirazi Jewish values, while maintaining the importance of rank distinctions within Jewish society. Since some indices of prestige are not within the province of personal control (e.g. family, wealth), individuals seeking to maintain or better their position within the community are often compelled to resort to the manipulation of prestige, through pious behavior. This should not be misconstrued to suggest that all public manifestation of piety is insincere, nor on the contrary that acts of synagogue piety alone suffice to raise one to high rank. Rather, synagogue practice sets the parameters by which Shirazi Jewish men may be judged. For most of the men social status is subject to upward and downward fluctuation, and the synagogue, being the most important public forum, is the nexus of community consent or dissent over their relative self-estimation.

Notes

1   An earlier draft of this paper was presented at the annual meeting of the American Anthropological Association, 1969. Fieldwork was conducted from August 1967 to November 1968. Financial support was provided by the Memorial Foundation for Jewish Culture, the Cantors' Assembly of America, and the State of New York.
2   During a brief return visit to Shiraz in October 1977, I observed that the formal behavior described here had diminished somewhat, as the older generation dies out and younger people assume responsibility. But the relative ranking of my main informants seems to have changed little. The data herein derives from participant observation and interviews of informants during the research period. At the time, Fredrik Barth's 'Models of social organization' (1966) was not available to me, and I did not attempt 'transactional-analysis' in the field. I have been nevertheless highly stimulated by Barth and his critics, especially Paine (1974), in analyzing the procedures presented here.
3   All of the foreign terms used in the article are utilized by Shirazi Jews. With the exception of Hebrew terms centering on ritual and the synagogue, the words are of Persian origin (see Loeb, 1977: 301–6).
4   Among Shirazi Jews, the guest house or guest room is not institutionalized. Guests are invited to come for particular purposes or on specific occasions.
5   These are weekday procedures. On Sabbaths and festivals, the chief sheliah zibbur is expected to lead worship, and the offers are then made only *per forma*, since no one would accept on those occasions.
6   Because illiterate congregants cannot participate in these knisa exchanges, the prestige gap between them and literate congregants would be ever-widening, were there no countering mechanisms in operation.
7   The parallels between this behavior and potlatching are duly noted. Even the purposed social ends attainable by both procedures are similar.

References

Abou-Zeid, Ahmed (1966) 'Honor and Shame Among the Bedouins of Egypt,' in J.C. Peristiany (ed.), *Honor and Shame* (Chicago: University of Chicago Press).

Barth, Fredrik (1966) 'Models of social organization,' Occasional Paper No. 23 (London: Royal Anthropological Institute).
Bishop, Isabella (1891) *Journeys in Persia and Kurdistan* (London: John Murray).
Bourdieu, Pierre (1966) 'The Sentiment of Honour in Kabyle Society,' in J.C. Peristiany (ed.), *Honor and Shame* (Chicago: University of Chicago Press).
Chardin, Sir John (1923) *Sir John Chardin's Travels in Persia* (London: Argonaut Press).
Deshen, Shlomo (1972) 'Ethnicity and Citizenship in the Ritual of an Israeli Synagogue,' *Southwestern Journal of Anthoropology*, 28: 69–82.
Deshen, Shlomo (1974) 'The Varieties of Abandonment of Religious Symbols, and Ethnicity and Citizenship in the Ritual of a Synagogue of Tunisian Immigrants,' in S. Deshen and M. Shokeid (eds), *The Predicament of Homecoming* (Ithaca: Cornell University Press).
Heilman, Samuel C. (1975) 'The Gift of Alms: Face-to-Face Almsgiving Among Orthodox Jews,' *Urban Life and Culture*, 3: 371–95.
Heilman, Samuel C. (1976) *Synagogue Life: A Study of Symbolic Interaction* (Chicago: University of Chicago Press).
Loeb, Laurence D. (1977) *Outcaste: Jewish Life in Southern Iran* (New York: Gordon and Breach).
Paine, Robert (1974) 'Second Thoughts about Barth's models,' Occasional Paper No. 32 (London: Royal Anthropological Institute).
Peristiany, John C. (ed.) (1966) *Honor and Shame* (Chicago: University of Chicago Press).
Pitt-Rivers, Julian (1966) 'Honour and Social Status,' in J.C. Peristiany (ed.), *Honor and Shame* (Chicago: University of Chicago Press).
Stirling, Paul (1965) *Turkish Village* (London: Weidenfeld & Nicolson).
Waring, E.S. (1807) *A Tour to Sheeraz* (London: T. Cadell and W. Davies).
Wills, C.J. (1883) *In the Land of the Lion and Sun, or Modern Persia* (London: Macmillan).

Recommended Readings

For further study of traditional Middle Eastern Jewish communities we recommend the readings of this list. We have selected works along the lines that guided us overall in the compilation of the volume. Hence the recommended readings are primarily of a socio-historic nature. But we have also included some additional works, either because of their importance as landmarks in the early study of our field, or because, despite various reservations, they constitute the only works available on particular, little studied, communities or topics. For those reasons too, we have included a few books in Hebrew and in French.

I General Introductions to the Middle East

Bates, Daniel and Rassam, Amal (1983) *Peoples and Cultures of the Middle East* (Englewood Cliffs, NJ: Prentice-Hall).
Davis, John (1977) *People of the Mediterranean: An Essay in Comparative Social Anthropology* (London: Routledge & Kegan Paul).
Eickelman, Dale F. (1989) *The Middle East: An Anthropological Approach*, 2nd edn (Englewood Cliffs: Prentice-Hall).
Gulick, John (1976/1983) *The Middle East: An Anthropological Perspective* (Pacific Palisades: Goodyear; reprinted Washington DC: University Press of America).
(These works provide overviews of the Middle East as a whole, both over time and space.)

II General Works on Middle Eastern Jews

The Jewish Encyclopedia (1903–7) (New York: Funk & Wagnalls).
Encyclopaedia Judaica (1971) (Jerusalem: Keter).
(These reference works are uneven in quality. The old *Jewish Encyclopedia* contains descriptions of communities as they were in 1900. One can learn much by looking up Middle Eastern countries, cities, and individuals. Much of the material is unavailable in other English language sources.)
Attal, Robert (1993) *Les Juifs d'Afrique du Nord, bibliographie: édition refondue et élargie* (Jerusalem: Ben-Zvi Institute).
(An immensely erudite, multi-language work, comprising no less than 10,062 items.)
Ben-Zvi, Yitzhak (1957) *The Exiled and the Redeemed* (Philadelphia: Jewish Publication Society).
(The late Israeli President Ben-Zvi took an active interest in the study of Jews in Middle Eastern countries, and the institute named in his honor has been a center for their study. This book reveals his own outlook on these communities.)
Braude, Benjamin and Lewis, Bernard (eds) (1982) *Christians and Jews in the Ottoman Empire* (New York: Holmes & Meier).
Cohen, Hayim J. (1973) *The Jews of the Middle East, 1860–1972* (Jerusalem: Israel Universities Press).
(An historical account, concentrating on the Near East and Iran.)

Cohen, Hayim J. and Yehuda, Zvi (1976) *Asian and African Jews in the Middle East, 1860–1971: Annotated Bibliography* (Jerusalem: Ben-Zvi Institute).

Cohen, Mark R. (1994) *Under Crescent and Cross: The Jews in the Middle Ages* (Princeton, NJ: Princeton University Press).

Dobrinsky, Herbert C. (1986) *A Treasury of Sephardic Law and Customs* (New York: Yeshiva University Press).

(A compendium of the ritual practices of Syrian, Moroccan and Spanish/Portuguese Jews, mainly in North America.)

Gerber, Jane S. (1992) *The Jews of Spain: A History of the Sephardic Experience* (New York: Free Press).

(Four chapters of this general book attempt to trace the history of the Spanish exiles in their places of settlement, particularly North Africa.)

Goitein, Shlomo D. (1955) *Jews and Arabs* (New York: Schocken).

Goitein, Shlomo D. (1969–92) *A Mediterranean Society: The Jewish Communities of the Arab World as Portrayed in the Documents of the Cairo Geniza*, 6 vols (Berkeley: University of California Press).

(While these works of Goitein concentrate on the early and middle Islamic periods, they reflect his general overview of Jews in the Middle East. *A Mediterranean Society* has become the key work in the study of medieval Jews under Islam and is invaluable. It is particularly pertinent in relation to Egypt and Tunisia.)

Levy, Avigdor (1992) *The Sephardim in the Ottoman Empire* (Princeton, NJ: Darwin Press).

Lewis, Bernard (1984) *The Jews of Islam* (Princeton, NJ: Princeton University Press).

(An overview by one of the senior world experts, focusing on the Near East.)

Noy, Dov (ed.) (1963) *Folktales of Israel* (Chicago: University of Chicago Press).

(A sample of Jewish tales, including many from the Middle East.)

Patai, Raphael (1971) *The Tents of Jacob* (Englewood Cliffs, NJ: Prentice-Hall).

Patai, Raphael (1986) *The Seed of Abraham: Jews and Arabs in Contact and Conflict* (Salt Lake City: University of Utah Press).

(These are works by a pioneer in Jewish ethnography, of a general survey nature, and the conclusions should often be seen as hypotheses for further research.)

Rodrigue, Aron (1993) *Images of Sephardi and Eastern Jewries in Transition: The Teachers of the Alliance Israélite Universelle, 1860–1939* (Seattle: University of Washington Press).

(A study of communities in transition, based on the correspondence of the French-oriented teachers and their Paris head office.)

Stahl, Abraham (1993) *Family and Child-Rearing in Oriental Jewry: Sources, References, Comparisons* (in Hebrew) (Jerusalem: Akademon).

(A valuable wide-ranging compilation of primary sources gleaned largely from remote rabbinic texts.)

Stillman, Norman (1979) *The Jews of Arab Lands* (Philadelphia: Jewish Publication Society).

Stillman, Norman (1991) *The Jews of Arab Lands in Modern Times* (Philadelphia: Jewish Publication Society).

(These two volumes, on medieval and modern times respectively, feature comprehensive overviews, followed by selections of hundreds of original documents. The volumes balance the unequal geographic stress on the Near East of other books, by also offering much material from other parts of the Middle East and North Africa. They are particularly useful on Jewish–Muslim relations, using accounts by European observers.)

Tobi, Yosef, Bar-Asher, Shalom and Bernai, Ya'akov (1981) *The Jews of the Middle East* (three volumes, in Hebrew) (Jerusalem: Shazar Center).
(A comprehensive history textbook, similar in structure to the Stillman volumes, with the various chapters authored by experts on particular communities.)

Zimmels, H.J. (1958) *Ashkenazim and Sephardim* (London: Oxford University Press).
(A general introduction to the relations between Jewish communities emphasizing ritual differences. While emphasizing European communities, it provides a good background to the manner in which Jewish law deals with clashes of local custom. The historical process described by Zimmels can complement Dobrinsky's compendium.)

III Morocco

See the references to works by Geertz, Rosen and Stillman noted at the end of chapter 5.

Ben-Ami, Issachar (1990) *Cultes des saints et pèlerinages judeo-musulmans au Maroc* (Paris: Maisonneuve & Larose).

Brown, Kenneth L. (1976) *The People of Salé: Tradition and Change in a Moroccan City, 1830–1930* (Manchester: Manchester University Press).
(While concentrating on the Muslims, the volume gives a good picture of the context in which Jews existed in urban Morocco.)

Chouraqui, André N. (1973) *Between East and West: A History of the Jews in North Africa* (Philadelphia: Jewish Publication Society).
(A popular history of North African Jewry as a whole, seen from the perspective of a French-educated writer.)

Deshen, Shlomo (1989) *The Mellah Society: Jewish Community Life in Sherifian Morocco* (Chicago: University of Chicago Press).
(A portrait of the community based on an anthropological analysis of rabbinical legal materials.)

Flamand, Pierre (1959) *Diaspora en terre d'Islam: Les communautes Israelite du Sud-Marocain* (Casablanca: Presse d'Imprimeres Réunies).
(An account of Jewish life in the Berber hinterland during the French colonial period.)

Hirschberg, Hayim Z. (1974) *A History of the Jews in North Africa* (Leiden: Brill).
(A synthesis of North African Jewish history.)

Gerber, Jane (1980) *Jewish Society in Fez, 1465–1700* (Leiden: Brill).

Goldberg, Harvey (1978) 'The Mimouna and the Minority Status of Moroccan Jews,' *Ethnology* 17: 75–87.
(An anthropological analysis of the major folk festival of Moroccan Jewry, focusing on the role of the festival in relations between Jews and Muslims.)

Goldberg, Harvey (1990) 'The Zohar in Southern Morocco: A Study in the Ethnography of Texts,' *History of Religions* 29: 233–58.

Laskier, M.M. (1983) *The Alliance Israélite Universelle and the Jewish Communities of Morocco, 1862–1962* (Albany, NY: State University of New York Press).

Laskier, M.M. (1994). *North African Jewry in the Twentieth Century: The Jews of Morocco, Tunisia and Algeria* (New York: New York University Press).

Schroeter, Daniel (1988) *Merchants of Essaouira: Urban Society and Imperialism in Southwestern Morocco, 1844–1886* (Cambridge: Cambridge University Press).
(A study of a former major city, similar to the aforementioned book by Brown.)

Shokeid, Moshe (1971) *The Dual Heritage* (Manchester: Manchester University Press) (augmented edition, Transaction Books, 1985).
(Follows immigrants from the Atlas Mountains to their adjustment in Israel.)

Shokeid, Moshe (1979) 'The Decline of Personal Endowment of Atlas Mountains Religious Leaders,' *Anthropological Quarterly* 52: 186–97.
(Similar to the above work, but focuses on rabbis and illuminates their situation in the past.)

Stillman, Norman (1988) *The Language and Culture of the Jews of Sefrou, Morocco: An Ethnolinguistic Study* (Manchester: Manchester University Press).

IV Algeria, Tunisia, and Tripolitania

The general overviews of North Africa, such as Chouraqui and Hirschberg, are also pertinent for these regions.

Bahloul, Joëlle (1992) *La maison de mémoire: ethnologie d'une demeure judéo-arabe en Algérie (1937–1961)* (Paris: Métailié).
(A modern ethnographic reconstruction of life in a small community, which may possibly also reflect on conditions in much earlier times.)

Briggs, L.C. and Guede, N.L. (1964) *No More For Ever: A Saharan Jewish Town*, Peabody Museum Papers 55:1 (Cambridge, Mass.: Harvard University Press).
(A study of a southern Algerian community on the eve of its emigration in 1962.)

De Felice, R. (1985) *Jews in an Arab Land: Libya, 1835–1970* (Austin: University of Texas Press).

Friedman, Elizabeth (1988) *Colonialism and After: An Algerian Jewish Community* (South Hadley, Mass.: Bergin & Garvey).

Goldberg, Harvey E. (1974) 'Tripolitanian Jewish Communities: Cultural Boundaries and Hypothesis Testing,' *American Ethnologist* 1: 619–34.

Goldberg, Harvey E. (1981) *The Book of Mordecai* (Philadelphia: Institute for the Study of Human Issues).
(An important and unique chronique by an early twentieth century Tripolitanian sage, edited and published from manuscript.)

Goldberg, Harvey E. (1990) *Jewish Life in Muslim Libya: Rivals and Relatives* (Chicago: University of Chicago Press).
(A synthesis of documentary and oral history research based to a considerable extent on the account of the previous item.)

Goldberg, Harvey E. (1994) 'Jerba and Tripoli: A Comparative Analysis of Two Jewish Communities in the Maghreb,' *Journal of Mediterranean Studies* 4: 278–99.
(A rare attempt at systematic comparison between particular communities.)

Memmi, Albert (1961) *Pillar of Salt* (New York: Orion Press).
(Memmi's novel gives a picture of Jewish life in Tunisia during the 1930s and 1940s, when Jews stood between assimilation to the French way and a nascent Arab nationalism.)

Simon, Rachel (1992) *Change within Tradition among Jewish Women in Libya* (Seattle: University of Washington Press).
Udovitch, Abraham L. and Valensi, Lucette (1984) *The Last Arab Jews: The Communities of Jerba, Tunisia* (New York: Harwood).
(An account based primarily on numerous short visits by two historians, which reflects in particular the religious atmosphere of Djerba, and probably also that of many other traditional communities.)

V Egypt, Syria and Iraq (Baghdad)

Baron, Salo W. (1940) 'Great Britain and Damascus Jewry, 1860–61,' *Jewish Social Studies* 2: 179–208.
(The status of Jews in Damascus at the time of the Lebanese massacres of 1860 is delineated here in local and international terms.)
Ben-Yaakob, Abraham (1979/1965) *The Jews of Iraq from 1038 to 1960* (in Hebrew) (Jerusalem: Kiryat-Sepher).
Ben-Yaakob, Abraham (1980) *The Jews of Iraq in Modern Times* (in Hebrew) (Jerusalem: Kiryat-Sepher).
(The two major historical studies of Baghdad region Jewry, replete with documentary sources, but presented somewhat unsystematically.)
Deshen, Shlomo (1994) 'Baghdad Jewry in Late-Ottoman Times: The Emergence of Social Classes and of Secularization,' *Association for Jewish Studies Review* 19: 19–44.
(An expanded version of the chapter that is included in this volume.)
Krämer, Gudrun (1989) *The Jews of Modern Egypt, 1914–1952* (London: Tauris).
Landau, Jacob (1969) *Jews in 19th Century Egypt* (New York: New York University Press).
(A community undergoing incorporation into the modern world, including European immigration.)
Livingston, John W. (1971) 'Ali Bey al-Kabir and the Jews,' *Middle Eastern Studies* 7: 221–28.
(The rivalry of Jews and Greeks in Egypt for government jobs during the late eighteenth century.)
Philipp, Thomas (1984) 'The Farhi Family and the Changing Position of the Jews in Syria, 1750–1860,' *Middle Eastern Studies* 20: 37–52.
(An account of the rise, decline, and later history of a notable Damascus family.)
Rejwan, Nissim (1985) *The Jews of Iraq: 3000 Years of History and Culture* (London: Weidenfeld & Nicholson).
(A useful though very general overview.)
Sassoon, David Solomon (1949) *A History of the Jews in Baghdad* (Letchworth: Hertz).
(An unsystematic community history by a member of a distinguished Baghdad family.)
Shamir, Shimon (ed.) (1987) *The Jews of Egypt: A Mediterranean Society in Modern Times* (Boulder, Colo.: Westview).
Shamosh, Amnon (1979) *Michel Ezra Safra & Sons* (Hebrew) (Tel-Aviv: Massada).
Shamosh, Amnon (1979) *My Sister, the Bride* (Tel Aviv: Massada).
Sutton, Joseph A.D. (1988) *Aleppo Chronicles* (New York: Thayer-Jacoby).
(Shamosh and Sutton are Aleppo emigrés. The former is a distinguished Israeli

writer living on a kibbutz, the latter a retired New York businessman. These works contain portraits of how Jews remember the Aleppo community, and also memories of various places to which they migrated.)

Zenner, Walter P. (1965) 'Saints and Piecemeal Supernaturalism among the Jerusalem Sephardim,' *Anthropological Quarterly* 38: 201–17.

Zenner, Walter P. 'Censorship and Syncretism: Some Anthropological Approaches to the Study of Middle Eastern Jewry,' in F. Talmage (ed.), *Studies in Jewish Folklore* (Cambridge, Mass.: Association for Jewish Studies) 377–94.

Zenner, Walter P. (1982) 'Jews in Late Ottoman Syria: External Relations,' in S. Deshen and W.P. Zenner (eds), *Jewish Societies in the Middle East* (Washington DC: University Press of America) 155–86.

Zenner, Walter P. (1987) 'Middleman Minorities in the Syrian Mosaic: Trade, Conflict, and Image Management,' *Sociological Perspectives* 30: 400–21.

(These items cover areas which are not dealt with in as much detail in Zenner's contributions to the present volume, such as saints and magic, the critique of responsa, singing *baqashot*, etc.)

Zohar, Zvi (1986) 'Halakhic Responses of Syrian and Egyptian Rabbis to Social and Technological Change,' *Studies in Contemporary Jewry* 2: 18–51.

Zohar, Zvi (1993) *Tradition and Change: Halakhic Responses of Middle Eastern Rabbis to Legal and Technological Changes (Egypt and Syria, 1880–1920)* (Hebrew) (Jerusalem: Ben-Zvi Institute).

(A sophisticated socio-historical study with an emphasis on talmudic and legal issues. Enlarges on the previous item.)

VI Yemen

Ahroni, Reuben (1986) *Yemenite Jewry: Origins, Culture, and Literature* (Bloomington: Indiana University Press).

Ahroni, Reuben (1994) *The Jews of the British Crown Colony of Aden: History, Culture and Ethnic Relations* (Leiden: Brill).

Eraqi Klorman, Bat-Zion (1993) *The Jews of Yemen in the Nineteenth Century: A Portrait of a Messianic Community* (Leiden: Brill).

Goitein, Shlomo D. (1955) 'Portrait of a Yemenite Weavers' Village,' *Jewish Social Studies* 16: 3–26.

Goitein, Shlomo D. (1980) 'Research Among Yemenites,' in F. Talmage (ed.), *Studies in Jewish Folklore* (Cambridge, Mass.: Association for Jewish Studies) 121–36.

Goitein, Shlomo D. (1983) *The Yemenites: History, Communal Organization, Spiritual Life* (Hebrew) (Jerusalem: Ben-Zvi Institute).

(The late Goitein was, and probably still is, the major figure in Yemenite ethnography. The 1955 paper is one of his major studies, while the 1980 paper contains general reflections. The Hebrew book contains the most important of Goitein's Yemenite research.)

Loeb, Laurence D. (1980) 'Jewish Life in Habban: A Tentative Reconstruction,' in *Studies in Jewish Folklore* 201–18.

(An anthropologist describes life on a remote South Yemeni oasis, on the basis of interviews with immigrants in Israel.)

Nini, Yehuda (1991) *The Jews of the Yemen, 1800–1914* (London: Harwood).

Tobi, Yosef (1976) *The Jews of Yemen in the 19th Century* (in Hebrew) (Tel-Aviv: Afikim).
(Nini and Tobi are leading historians of Yemenite Jewry and work with documents. Most of Tobi's work remains untranslated.)

VII Kurdistan

Ben-Yaakob, Abraham (1961) *Kurdish Jewish Communities* (in Hebrew) (Jerusalem: Ben Zvi Institute).
Brauer, Erich (1993) *The Jews of Kurdistan* (Detroit: Wayne State University Press).
(Brauer was the pioneer of Kurdish-Jewish ethnography, who worked with immigrants in Israel in the 1930s. Raphael Patai has recently published this newly edited English translation.)
Feitelson, Dina (1959) 'Aspects of the Social Life of Kurdish Jews', *Jewish Journal of Sociology* 1: 201–16.
(An anthropological reconstruction based on interviews of immigrants in Israel.)
Fischel, Walter J. (1944) 'The Jews of Kurdistan 100 Years Ago,' *Jewish Social Studies* 6: 196–226.
Magnarella, Paul J. (1969) 'A Note on Aspects of Social Life among the Jewish Kurds of Sanandaj, Iran,' *Jewish Journal of Sociology* 11: 51–8.
(A somewhat preliminary reconstruction by an anthropologist, then a graduate student, on the little-studied Iranian Kurdish Jews.)
Sabar, Yona (1978) 'Multilingual Proverbs in the Neo-Aramaic Speech of the Jews of Zakho, Iraqi, Kurdistan,' *International Journal of Middle Eastern Studies* 9: 215–35.
(Provides documentation for Kurdistani multi-culturalism.)
Shai, Donna (1980) 'Changes in the Oral Tradition Among the Jews of Kurdistan,' *Contemporary Jewry* 5: 2–10.
Shai, Donna (1982) 'Family Conflict and Cooperation in Folksongs of Kurdish Jews,' in S. Deshen and W.P. Zenner (eds), *Jewish Societies in the Middle East* (Washington, DC: University Press of America).

VIII Iran

Fischel, Walter J. (1950) 'The Jews of Persia: 1795–1940,' *Jewish Social Studies* 12: 119–60.
Fischel, Walter J. (1953) 'Isfahan: The Story of a Jewish Community in Persia,' in *Joshua Starr Memorial Volume. Jewish Social Studies Publication* V: 111–28.
Fischel, Walter J. (1960) 'Israel in Iran: A Survey of Judeo-Persian Literature,' in L. Finkelstein (ed.), *The Jews: Their History, Culture and Religion* (Philadelphia: Jewish Publication Society) 1149–90.
(Fischel was the pioneer in the study of Iranian Jewish history and literature.)
Goldstein, Judith L. (1980) 'The Jewish Miracle-Worker in a Muslim Context,' in F. Talmage (ed.), *Studies in Jewish Folklore* (Cambridge, Mass.: Association for Jewish Studies) 137–52.
(An Iranian Jewish tale is examined in order to understand Jewish–Muslim relations.)

Loeb, Laurence D. (1977) *Outcaste: Jewish Life in Southern Iran* (London: Gordon and Breach).
(A comprehensive ethnography of the Jews of Shiraz during the 1960s, based on fieldwork in Shiraz.)
Soroudi, Sorour (1981) 'Jews in Islamic Iran,' *Jerusalem Quarterly* 21: 99–114.
(Although focused on contemporary issues, the paper also illuminates conditions of the past.)
Soroudi, Sorour (1994) 'The Concept of Jewish Impurity and its Reflection in Persian and Judeo-Persian Tradition,' in S. Shaked and A. Netzer (eds), *Irano-Judaica* 3 (Jerusalem: Ben-Zvi Institute) 142–70.

IX Turkey and the Balkans

Several of the works that we note in this section stress the post-Ottoman periods, when Jews began to live under the new Balkan nation-states, while they are scant on the period that is the focus of concern in our volume. Some of the authors also tend to view the late-Ottoman period merely as one of decline. From the particular comparative perspective of this volume, the Ottoman and Balkan heartland of Sephardic Jewry, despite its importance, has been studied less than some other communities.

Angel, Marc D. (1978) *The Jews of Rhodes* (New York: Sepher-Hermon Press).
(A history with some ethnographic materials.)
Argenti, Philip (1970) *The Religious Minorities of Chios: Jews and Roman Catholics* (Cambridge: Cambridge University Press).
(Part of a longer history of the island of Chios.)
Attal, Robert (1984) *Les Juifs de Grèce de l'expulsion d'Espagne à nos jours: Bibliographie* (Jerusalem: Ben-Zvi Institute).
(A multi-language bibliography.)
Benardete, Mair Jose (1952) *Hispanic Culture and the Character of the Sephardic Jews* (New York: Hispanic Institute in the United States).
(An essay of the relationship of Ladino-speaking Sephardim with their Spanish heritage.)
Benbassa, Esther (1993) *Une diaspora sepharade en transition: Istanbul xix–xx siècles* (Paris: Cerf).
Benbassa, Esther and Rodrigue, Aron (1993) *Juifs des balkans: espaces Judéo-ibériques xiv–xx siècles* (Paris: La Découverte).
Dalven, Rae (1990) *The Jews of Ioannina* (Philadelphia: Cadmus Press).
Freidenreich, Harriet P. (1979) *The Jews of Yugoslavia: A Quest for Community* (Philadelphia: Jewish Publication Society).
Glazer, Mark (1979) 'The Dowry as Capital Accumulation among the Sephardic Jews of Istanbul,' *International Journal of Middle Eastern Studies* 10: 373–80; also in *Jewish Societies in the Middle East*, 299–310.
Haskell, Guy H. (1994) *From Sofia to Jaffa: The Jews of Bulgaria and Israel* (Detroit: Wayne State University Press).
Levi, Avner (1992) 'Social Cleavage, Class War and Leadership in the Sephardi Community: The Case of Izmir, 1847,' in A. Rodrigue (ed.), *Ottoman and Turkish Jewry: Community and Leadership* (Bloomington: Indiana University Press, Turkish Series) 183–202.

(A treatment of an important topic, but mainly on the basis of a single source.)
Rodrigue, Aron (1990) *French Jews, Turkish Jews: The Alliance Israelite Universelle and the Politics of Jewish Schooling, 1860–1925* (Bloomington: Indiana University Press).
Shaw, Stanford (1991) *The Jews of the Ottoman Empire and the Turkish Republic* (New York: New York University Press).
Weiker, Walter (1992) *Ottomans, Turks and the Jewish Polity* (Washington, DC: University Press of America).

Index

Abbas I, Shah 249
Abikhezir, Rabbi A. 74, 80
Abraham ibn Daud 61
Abraham ibn Ezra 61
Abrahamic monotheism 60
Abyad, Rabbi Y. ben Shalom 236
acculturation 35–49
  environmental culture and social structure 40–6, 183
  see also modernization; westernization
Adadi, A H. 150–1, 151, 153–4, 154
Aden 233
administration/civil service 42–3, 167–8, 169, 170
adolescents 230–1
adult society 223–4
adultery 180, 191–2
Africa, North 44, 66–7
Agassi, Rabbi S. 194
agriculture 13, 250
Aith Waryaghar 90
'Alawî dynasty 86
Aleppo 164, 165, 171, 173, 181, 184
  Alliance schools 183
  communal organization 174, 175
  customs collection 169, 170
  economic activities 165, 166, 167
  family and household 177, 178–9, 180
  folk-stories 161–2
  Talmudic study 177
Algeria 66
Alliance Israélite Universelle 21, 67, 150, 196
  school in Jerba 136
  Syria 171, 178, 183
Almohades 44, 61–2
amulets 210, 211–12
Anqāwa, E. al- 125
Antebi, A. 182, 184
Anti-Atlas 89

anti-clericalism 67–8
anti-Jewish doctrine 59
Antonius, G. 51
'apostasy, law of' 254
appearance 39
  see also dress
'Aqnin, J. ben Joseph ibn 61
Arabian Peninsula 60
Arabic 36, 75, 80
Arabs 114–15
  and Berbers 84–5, 95–6, 99, 117
  Palestine 51, 52
  pluralism 44
arak 146
'Arjāz community 236–7
Armenians 166, 167, 258, 259
Ashkenazi Jews 3, 30, 39–40, 177
  see also shtetl society
Ashkenazic rabbis 71
Ashour, Said Abdel Fattah 51
Ateret Zion movement 142
Atlas Mountain Jews 109–20
  circumstances of Jewish life 112–15
  intermediary role 115–18
auctioning of *kvodot* 137, 266–7, 268
Augustine, St 59
authority 31
  rabbis 174, 176, 184
  saddiq and marabout 126–7
autonomy, community 101–8
Azulay, Hayyim Yosef David (Rav Hida) 125

'badge of shame' 249
Bādisi, Abd al-Haqq al- 123
Baghdad 78, 173, 187–96
  Jewish school 70–1
  Jewish social classes and secularization 187–96
  synagogue lighting 72–3
Bahris 170

280

Balkan Jewry 7-8
Bar-Mitzvah ceremony 219-20
baraka (charisma) 123-4, 127
Basra 188
Bat Ye'ar 51, 55
beggars 205
Beirut 183
belief 207, 211-12
Ben-Ami, I. 122
Ben-Shim'on, Rabbi M.H. 74, 75
Ben-Shim'on, Rabbi R.A. 71, 79
Bene Israel 38-9, 43-4
Berber 'kingdoms' 89-90
Berbers
  and Arabs 84-5, 95-6, 99, 117
  Atlas Mountain Jews 109-20
  Jerban Jews and 133-43
Berque, J. 122
Beth-Din (Bet-Din) (Court of Religious Law)
  Jerba 137, 138, 139, 140, 141
  San'ā 234, 236-7, 238-41
Bible 36, 60-1
birth 203
Black Jews 38
blacks 116
blood libels 52, 170
B'nai Brith lodges 183
books 230
boors 190
Braithwaite, Captain J. 91-2
Brauer, E. 198, 200-3 *passim*, 207, 211, 212
'Bride's Shabbat' 204
Britain 171-2
Brown, K. 126
Brown, P. 123
Buddhism 38
Bukhara 18-19
bureaucracy *see* administration/civil service
burial society 136, 140, 146-7
Burton, I. 177
BusānI, Yosef ben Shukr 240-1
Bynum, C. 207-8

Cairene Jews 78
caste system 38, 39, 43, 48
casuistry 10-11

Central High Atlas 94
change
  Sephardic rabbis 9, 68-77
  tradition and modernity 26-7, 34
charisma *(baraka)* 123-4, 127
charity 229, 230
chastisement 219
chief rabbis *(hakham bashi)* 150, 168-9, 192-3, 235, 236
childhood, negative attitude to 218-19
children
  education in Yemen 217-31
  Kurdistan 199, 201
  Syria 178
China 37, 37-8, 41, 42-3, 47, 48
Chouraqui, A.C. 109
Christianity/Christians 10, 44, 48, 105
  comparison with Judaism 40, 45-6, 163
  dhimmi status 14-15, 16, 168
  Jews under in Middle Ages compared with Jews under Islam 50-63
  Syria 167, 169, 170, 171
  see also Europe
church: and state 10, 55-6
  see also Christianity; Roman Catholicism
cities 14, 87-8
civil service/administration 42-3, 167-8, 169, 170
clairvoyance 124
classes, social *see* status
cleaning 207
Cochin Jews 38
commercial guilds 53
'Committee for Visiting the Sick' *(Vaad Bikur Holim)* 139
communal organization 17-19, 45
  Syria 173-6
  Tripolitania 144-58
communal protection 85, 87-90, 93-5, 98-9, 100
  see also dhimmi status; patronage
Community Committee 137-8, 139, 140

282   Index

community leaders 18
  Baghdad 189
  Iran 255
  Morocco 101–2
  San'ā 235–6
  Tripolitania 145–6
Confucianism 38, 42, 43
Constantine, Emperor 59
consuls 171–2
conversion to Islam 104–5, 114, 259
  martyrdom and 61
cooking 205–6
corporate organization 58
'council of the pious' 255–6
courts
  millet 73–4
  Morocco 103–4
  rabbinic 17, 148–9, 151–2, 173–4, 175
  Tripolitania 148–9, 151–2
'Covenant of Omar' 248, 249
craftsmen 112–13, 136–7, 165–6, 250–1
credit *see* moneylending
Crusades 57, 59
culture areas 7–9
curriculum 70–1, 176
'customary law' 152
customs collection contract 169

Dadès Valley 89–90
Dahūh, Rabbi D. ben Sālim 239
Dālé community 237–8
Damascus 165–7, 169, 171, 177, 183
'Damascus Affair' 170, 171
Daula, Sa'ad ad- 248
Davidic (royal) family 189
dayanim (judges in religious courts)
  see judges
death rituals 202, 210–11
decentralization of power 32–3
defense, social 253–7
demographic distribution 40–1, 86, 93, 217–18
Dermenghem, E. 122
despotism 94
Devil 52
dhazttat/zattâta (protection fee) 91, 120

dhimmi status (protected minority) 14–16, 109
  Iran *see* Iran
  Jews under medieval Islam and Christianity 55–8
  Morocco 85, 87–90, 93–4
  Syria 168–9
discrimination 44–5, 57–8
  see also humiliation; restrictions
disputes
  saddiqim and 126–7
  San'ā Bet-Din 238–41
disseminators of ideas 252–3
dissident regions (*bilâd al-sîba*) 88–90, 93, 117
diversification 54
Divine Image 75–6
divorce 180–1, 191–2, 201, 241
domestic service 178, 180
domestication of religion 204–9
dowry 178–9, 254
dress 39, 115, 180, 184, 219
Druzes 15, 16
Durkheim, E. 211
Dwek, Rabbi S. 182, 184
dyadic relationships 84–5, 90–1, 93–5, 99–101, 101
  see also patronage; protection

economic activities/roles 12–14
  Atlas Mountain Jews 112–13
  Christianity, Judaism and Islam 53–5
  Iranian Jews 250–3, 259
  Jerban Jews 134–5
  Morocco 86, 99–100
  Syrian Jews 165–7, 178
  tradition and modernity 33
  Tripolitanian Jews 146
education
  Jewish in Yemen 9, 217–31; adolescents 230–1; girls 226–7; grandmother 224; lack of initiation ceremony 219–20; maturing influence of adult society 223–4; negative attitude to childhood 218–19; school's subordinate position 221, 222–3; synagogue as centre of

education – *continued*
 education 220–1; teachers 219, 222, 227–30; women's role 219, 224–7
 modernization and 20–1, 66–7
 secular studies 70–1, 176
 tradition and modernity 27–8, 28–9, 29–31
 see also schools
Education Committee (*Vaad or Torah*) 138–9
egalitarianism 94
Egypt 7, 13, 44, 80, 170, 249
 millet courts 73–4
 modernization 66–7
Eickelman, D. 123
elders, visiting of 106
electrical lighting 71–2
Elon, M. 65–6
Elyashar, Rabbi Y.S. 240–1
emancipation 72–3
embroiderer, story of 161
embroidery 227
emissaries, Eretz-Israel 153–4, 232, 233
'ene ha'eda ('eyes of the community') 255
engagement festivities 206
English Levant Company 167
enjoyment 31–2
entertainers 251, 252
environmental culture 40–6
Eretz-Israel 153–5, 232, 233, 234
Europe 95
 coalescence of orthodoxy 65–6
 educational organizations 20–1, 66–7, 183
 influence on Syrian Jews 183–4
 Jewish acculturation in Christian Europe 10–11, 39–40, 41, 46, 48
 Jews in compared with Jews under Islam in Middle Ages 50–63
 and Ottoman Empire 167, 171
 values central to modernity 75–6
 see also Christianity/Christians
explanation of texts 222–3
extra-marital affairs 180, 191–2

Ezra the Scribe 141
 shrine 15, 164, 171, 182

family 19–20
 Kurdistan 199–201
 Morocco 106, 108
 Syrian Jews 177–81
 tradition and modernity 29, 31
'family purity' 140
Farhis 170
farming 13, 250
Feitelson, D. 210
fertility 199, 206, 209
15th of Ab 175
finance 17, 175–6
 see also taxation
Flamand, P. 110
folk-stories 161–2, 209
food 199, 205–6
Foucauld, C. de 94
France 66, 172
 and Southern Tunisia 134, 136
Frazer, J.G. 211
friendship 100–1, 112, 113–14, 165

Gabès 134
Gagen, Rabbi A.H. 235
gambling 182
'Gaon of Babylonia, The' 233
Gaon of Vilna 31
gas-lighting 72–3
Geertz, C. 111, 122
gender roles 19–20
 see also women
genealogical records, destruction of 234
generational turnover 26
gentiles: employment on Sabbath 72–3, 79
Gerber, H. 168
gestures of respect 191
Ghali, Ibrahim Amin 51
gharâma see jizîya
Ghriba synagogue 137, 140–1
girls 226–7
'Girls' Shabbat' 203
Goitein, S. 5, 13, 26
Goldberg, H. 101, 110, 146–7

Gora ('White Bene Israel') 39
grandmother 224
graves *see* shrines
guilds 53, 165, 166, 250
Gypsies 258

Habbani 9, 204
HaCohen, Rabbi M. 148–9, 150, 151–2, 152, 156
hagiographic literature 123
hakham bashi (chief rabbis) 150, 168–9, 192–3, 235, 236
Hakim, Khalif al- 44
HaKohen, Rabbi M.K. 138, 140, 142
HaKohen, Rabbi S. ben Aharon (Rabbi Shalom 'Irāqī) 233–4, 242
Hakohen, Rabbi Siqli 154
halakha see religous law
HaLevi, Rabbi H.D. 69–70, 76, 78
HaLevi, Rabbi Y.Y. 236
Hamdūsh, Sidi 'Ali Ben 127
Hara Kebira 134, 135, 137, 138, 141
Hara Sghira 134, 135, 137, 138, 140, 141
Harris, W. 89–90
Hart, D. 90, 117–18
Hasidei Ashkenaz ('pious men of Germany') 39
haskama (communal rulings) 146, 147
Hayyim (Hayim), Rabbi J. (Y.) 70–1, 78, 189–90, 191, 193
hazakah rights 147, 148–9
Hazan, E. 145
Hazan, Rabbi I.M. 71, 79
Hazzan (Hazan), Rabbi E.B. 68, 78, 150, 154–5, 155
healing 207
Hebrew 36
Hebrew Bible 174
High Atlas Mountains 94
High Holy Days 137
Hinduism 38, 39, 43–4
hinne 204
Hirschberg, H.Z. 145, 250

holidays (holy days) 71, 79, 137, 203, 206
holy men: Morocco 117, 121–30
see also shrines
home
Kurdistan 204–9
Yemenite Jewish education 222–3, 226
see also family
honor 257, 263
auctioning of *kvodot* 266–7
social climbers 268
ta'arof (honor exchanges) 263–6
hospitality 264
household 177–81
see also family; home
houses, new 205–6
Hufāsh community 239–40
humiliation 55, 116, 249–50

Ibadie 134
Iberian peninsula 40
imperial cities 87–8
India 188
Jewish communities 37, 38–9, 41, 43–4, 47, 48
industrial revolution 167
infant-teachers 228
informing 104–5
ingurramen see marabouts
inheritance 178, 254
law 108, 147, 181
'initiation' ceremony 219–20
interethnic relations 14–17
interfaith friendships 165
interfaith partnerships 166
interfaith utopia, myth of 50, 51
intermediary role 115–18
international networks 18–19, 163
international relations 76
international trade 167, 233
invisibility 253–7
Iran 203–4, 247–70
dhimmi status 15, 116, 247–50; Jewish economic roles 250–3, 259; social defense 253–7 synagogue behaviours 12, 261–70
Iraq 7, 15
Irāqī family 233

Islam 10, 35
  conversion to *see* conversion to Islam
  Jewish view of 105
  Jews under in Middle Ages compared with Jews under Christianity 50–63
  Judaism and 35–6, 37
  pluralism and monopolism 44, 45
'Islamic reform' movement 78
Isma'il, Shah 249
Israel 33–4, 34, 111, 198, 199, 219
  Eretz-Israel 153–5, 232, 233, 234
  expectations of migrants surpassed 115
  mass migration to 4, 34, 110–11, 115
Istanbul 14, 173
Italy 8, 18, 46, 167
itinerant craftsmen/peddlers *see* traders

Jabal 'Amr community 238–9
Jamāl, Sālem ben Yihyā 235
Jerba 14, 133–43, 145, 152–3
Jerusalem 71, 182, 240–1
'Jewish badge' 55
Jewish quarter (*hara/mellah/millâh/mahalleh*)
  Iran 256
  Morocco 87, 98, 99; social contours of autonomy 101–8
'Jewishness' of Kurdistan women's rituals 209–12
Jewish retainers 15–16
Jewish Scripture 60–1
  see also Talmud; Torah
Jiblah 233
jizîya/jizya (communal tribute) 88, 168
  see also tax; tributes
jud baazi ('Jew-game') 250
judges
  Jerba 135, 136, 137, 138, 140
  Shiraz 255
  Syria 168, 175
  Tripolitania 148, 149, 151–2
justification, religious 26

Kaifeng Jews 37–8, 42–3
Kala ('Black' Bene Israel) 39
Kamondo, A. 162
Karo, Rabbi Y. 241, 242
Katz, J. 65
Katzburg, N. 65
Katzin, Rabbi R. 78
'key' money 252
Khaduri, Chief Rabbi 78
Khalfon, Rabbi A. 154
khanevadeh (patrilocal extended family) 253–4
Khirkah 227
kinship 106, 253–4
  see also family
Kittāni, Muhammad al- 123
knisa see synagogues
kohanim (descendants of priestly caste) 135
Kook, Rabbi I.H. 75
Kurdistan 8, 13
  religiosity of Jewish women 197–214; domestication of religion 204–9; family 199–201; Jewishness of religious practices 209–12; sexual segregation 202–4
kvodot, purchase of 266–7, 268

Labaton, Rabbi H.M. 162
'lachrymose conception' 50, 52, 61
Ladino (Judezmo) 7–8
Lag B'omer 175
landlords 113–14
Laniado, Rabbi R.S. 161
Lavi, Rabbi S. 144–5, 151, 155
law
  Egyptian and *millet* courts 73–4
  inheritance 108, 147, 181
  legal interpretation 10–11
  religious *see* religious law
  Tripolitanian Jews 147–9
  see also courts; judges
'law of apostasy' 254
leaders, community *see* community leaders
Lebanon 169
legal codes 56–7, 58

legal rights 75-6
Leghorn (Livorno) 8, 18, 174
leisure activities 181-2
Lempriere, W. 87, 88
Lewis, B. 52, 62, 249
lighting 71-2, 72-3, 79
liminality 207-8
Lincoln, B. 205
lineage 40
liquor-sellers 251, 252
literacy 9-12
Livorno (Leghorn) 8, 18, 174
local sheikhs 112, 113, 241
local traditions 28, 151-2
Loeb, L.D. 204
London Society for Promoting Christianity amongst the Jews 183

magic 11, 36-7, 40, 174-5, 210-12
mahalleh see Jewish quarter
Maimonides, M. 50, 61, 62, 68, 69, 241, 242
makhzan/makhzen (central government) 88-9, 93, 93-4, 98-9
male superiority 19
Malka, Khalifa B. 124
Mannheim, K. 26
marabouts 117, 121-30
Marrakech (Marrakesh) 87, 107
marriage 19-20
  Baghdad Jews 191-2
  contracts 179
  Kurdistan 200-1, 206
  Syrian Jews 178-9
  see also wedding festivities; wedding rituals
martyrdom 61
Mashdad 259
Masonic lodges 183
massacres 59, 60, 171
meat 139-40
Mecca 54
mediation 126-7
Medina, Jews of 60
Meknes, Jews of 101
mellah see Jewish quarter

menstruation 200, 202
merchants see traders
Mesas, Rabbi J. 71-2, 79
Mesopotamia 188, 249
Michaux-Bellaire, E. 122
Middle Ages 50-63
Middle Atlas 89
Middle East 10-11, 177
  Jewish acculturation 35-7, 41, 44-5, 47, 48
  Sephardic-Oriental Jews 66-7
  see also under individual countries
midwives 203
migrant groups 196
migration
  to Baghdad 188
  mass migration to Israel 4, 34, 110-11, 115
  to Yemen 217, 218
military service 168
millâh see Jewish quarter
millet system 148, 163-4
  courts 73-4
Mimun, Rabbi Y. 148, 152
Mimuna Jewish folk festival 101
miracles 124-6, 174-5
Miriam 227
missionaries, Protestant 170, 183
modernity
  Sephardic rabbis' responses 9, 64-80
  tradition and 6, 25-34
modernization 20-1
Mohammed, Prophet 44, 54, 60
moneylending
  Iranian Jews 248, 251-2
  Jews under Christianity compared with Jews under Islam 53-4, 54-5
  Syrian Jews 166-7, 169-70
monopolism 44, 47, 48
monotheism 61
  Abrahamic 60
moral decline 238-9
moral sanctions 92
morality, safeguarding 236-7
moredet (woman who rebels against husband) 180-1
mori (teachers) 219, 222, 227-30

Morocco 7, 13, 18, 192
  Atlas Mountain Jews 109–20;
    intermediary role 115–18
  community life in 19th century
    98–108; social contours of
    mellah autonomy 101–8;
    structure of Muslim-Jewish
    relations 98–101
  patronage and protection 83–97;
    dhimma and status of Jews
    87–91; sanctions 91–3
  saddiqim and marabouts 121–30
mother 219, 224–6
  see also women
Muhammad, Prophet 44, 54, 60
Mūsā, Shaikh Yiḥyā 240
mystical rationalism 69
mysticism 11
  saddiqim and marabouts 121–30
  see also magic

nagid (community representative)
  101–2
Nahum 203
Naïm, Joseph Ben 123
nasi (community leader) 189, 255
'neo-lachrymose conception' 51–2,
  62
Nestorians 258
networks 18–19, 41, 163
new houses 205–6
New Year 206–7
Niebuhr, C. 232
9th of Av 208, 209
non-Jewish society, solidarity with
  72–3
North Africa 44, 66–7
Northern Tier 8, 9
notables 175, 183

occupations *see* economic activities
'Omar, Covenant of' 248, 249
oral reports 5
orthodoxy 65–6
Ottoman Empire 7–8, 44, 62
  Baghdad Jewry 187–96
  modernization 66, 67
  Syrian Jews *see* Syria
  trade with Europe 167, 171
  Tripolitanian Jews 144–58
  Yemen 232–3, 235, 236, 241
ownership of synagogues 102, 107,
  137

Pact of 'Umar 52, 55, 56, 57, 58
Palestine 18, 51, 52, 66, 75
  see also Eretz-Israel
Papacy 46
  see also Roman Catholicism
parents
  children's attitudes to 178
  girl's reluctance to leave 200
  living with after marriage 179
partnerships, interfaith 166
Pasha, Mahmud Nedim 148
Pasha, Mehmed Emin 148
Passover 201
pastry-makers' guild 166
patronage 13, 15
  Morocco 83–97, 99–101, 103–4,
    108; Atlas Mountains 112,
    113–14, 118; *dhimma* and status
    of Jews 87–91; sanctions
    91–3
  see also protection
peddlers *see* traders
persecution 46, 59–60, 61–2, 91–2
Persia 8, 188
  see also Iran
personal relationships 211–12
Peters, J. 51–2
phylacteries, putting on 220
Picciotto consuls 171, 172
piety *see* religious practice
pilgimage to saints' tombs 11, 36,
  182
Pitt-Rivers, J. 266
plague 147
pluralism 42–6, 48, 57
political invisibility 255–6
political mobilization 188–9
political rights 75–6
political system
  internal community organization
    17–19; *see also* communal
    organization
  role of state and interethnic
    relations 14–17

pollution, ritual 249, 253, 259
Poppers, Rabbi J. 72–3
'popular' religion 11, 36–7
  see also magic; superstition
potlatching 269
power, decentralization of 32–3
prayer leader (*sheliah zibbur*)
  264–6, 268, 269
prayers, education and 221, 226
pregnancy 202–3, 210
prestige 261–70
  honor 263
  purchase of *kvodot* 266–7
  social climbers 267–8
  ta'arof 263–6
privacy 177
private scholars 175
private synagogues 102, 107, 137
professions *see* economic activities
property exchange 178–9
  see also dowry
property leasing 147
prostitutes 251, 252
protection
  communal 85, 87–90, 93–5, 98–9, 100
  consular 171–2
  dyadic relationships 84–5, 90–1, 93–5, 99–101, 101
  Morocco 83–97, 99–101, 118; sanctions 91–3
  tribal 89–90, 91, 99–100
  see also dhimmi status; patronage
Protestant missionaries 170, 183
Provincial Reform Law 148
Purim 201, 203

qaid (community leader) 145–6
Qaramanli dynasty 144, 152
Qārah, Rabbi S. 235, 240
Qāsim, Qāsim 'Abduh 51
qualifications, official 139

rabbinic courts 17, 148–9, 151–2, 173–4, 175
rabbinic officials 149–51
  see also chief rabbis
rabbis 11
  and Alliance schools 183

  Ashkenazic 71
  authority 174, 176, 184
  Baghdad 189–90, 192–3, 194–5
  economic activities 136
  and 'family purity' 140
  folk-stories 161–2
  magical powers 174–5
  Morocco 102, 106
  private synagogues 107
  and secularization 195
  Sephardic and modernity 9, 64–80
  see also chief rabbis; marabouts; *saddiqim*
ranking system 262
  see also prestige
Raqah, Rabbi M.H. 145, 154
Raqah, Rabbi Zion 153
rationality, common 73–5
religion 9–12
  domestication 204–9
  justification in terms of 26
  nature of and acculturation 41–6, 47–8
  see also under names of individual religions
religious law 39–40, 65–6
  gestures of respect 191
  interfaith knowledge of 164
  Sephardic rabbis and dynamic nature 68–77
  Tripolitania 147–9, 151–2
  see also courts; judges
religious officials 149–51
  see also chief rabbis
religious practice
  care in 190–1
  Iranian synagogues 12, 261–70
  Morocco 106
  Syrian Jews 181–2
  women in Kurdistan *see* Kurdistan
'Religious Regulations for the Jew' 236
residence
  pattern 19–20
  segregation 45, 47–8; *see also* Jewish quarter
respect, gestures of 191

restrictions 45, 55, 87, 249
retainers, Jewish 15-16
Rhee, S.N. 43
Rhineland, Jews of 59
ridicule 249
  see also humiliation
Rîf, Moroccan 90, 93
rights 75-6
  hazakah rights 147, 148-9
Ritter, Rabbi Dr B.L. 75, 80
ritual objects 191
ritual pollution 249, 253, 259
ritual sanctions 92
rituals see religious practice
robbery 100, 114
Roman Catholicism 46, 56, 57
Roman Empire 59
Rosen, L. 84, 84-5, 109-10, 116-17, 118
Rosh HaShana (New Year) 206-7

Sabbath 12, 182, 195, 203, 227
  candles and women 208, 212
saddiqim 121-30
Safed 182
safety/security 91, 99, 110, 114-15, 118, 256-7
sages see rabbis
Saida 175
saints (holy men) 117, 121-30, 174-5
  shrines see shrines
Sālih, Rabbi D. ben Abraham 237-8
Sālih, Rabbi Y. ben Yosef 233, 234-5, 238
Sammet, M. 70, 77
San'ā (Sana'a) 218, 229, 231
  authority of San'ā community 232-43; San'ā Bet-Din 234, 236-7, 238-41
sanctions 91-3
scholar-official class 42-3
scholars 40, 135-6, 149
  private 175
schools
  Baghdad 196
  Jerba 136
  secular subjects 70-1

Syria 171, 176-7, 183
tradition and modernity 30-1
Tripolitania 150, 154-5, 155
Yemen: subordinate position 221, 222-3; wayfarers' hostels 229
  see also Alliance Israélite Universelle; education
science 71-2
secular rulers 55-6
secular subjects 70-1, 176
secularization 10, 195-6
security/safety 91, 99, 110, 114-15, 118, 256-7
Sefrou 84-5, 106
segregation 55
  residential 45, 47-8; see also Jewish quarter
  sexual 19, 37, 202-4
senses, stimulation of 12
Sephardic Jews 40
  rabbinic responses to modernity 9, 64-80
  tradition 107-8
Septimus, B. 62
Serah bat Asher 204
Serero, R. Hayyim David 125
service roles 251-3, 259
services, withdrawal of 92
seudat mitzva (festive meal) 31
sewing 207, 227
sexual segregation 19, 37, 202-4
'Shabbes Goy' 72-3, 79
Shai, D. 200-1
Sham'ah (daughter of Shalom Shabazi) 227
Sharqi, Bū 'Abid 127
Shavuot 203
sheikhs, local 112, 113, 241
sheliah zibbur (prayer leader) see prayer leader
Shi'ism 251, 259
  Iran 248-9, 250, 252-3, 257
  Yemen 45
Shiraz see Iran
shlihim see emissaries
shrines 122, 164, 204
  pilgrimages to 11, 36, 182
shtetl society 3
Shulhan Arukh 27, 149

sîba (dissident regions) 88-90, 93, 117
slaughterers 139
Slouschz, N. 154
social change *see* change
social classes *see* status
social climbers 267-8, 269
social defense 253-7
social gatherings 31-2
social invisibility 253-4
social sanctions 92
social status *see* status
social structure
  acculturation and 40-6
  Christianity and Islam 57-8
  Iran 253-7
  Jewish education in Yemen 217-31
  mellah autonomy in Morocco 101-8
  protection and 94
Sofer, Rabbi M. 77
solidarity
  Indian 43-4
  with non-Jewish society and state 72-3
Somekh, Rabbi A. 72-3, 79, 189-90, 193
songs 182
sovereignty, right to 76
Spain 44, 46, 62
specialization 14, 165
Srinivas, M.N. 43
state
  and church 10, 55-6
  Ottoman 167-70
  role of 14-17
  solidarity with non-Jewish 72-3
status
  Atlas Mountain Jews 109-10, 116, 117, 118
  dhimmi see dhimmi status
  and economic activity 12-13; *see also* economic activities
  Jews in precolonial Morocco 86-7, 87-91
  social classes and synagogue behaviour 12, 187-96
Stern, A. 232

Stillman, N. 52, 62, 84, 85, 86-7, 94, 109-10, 118
stranger role 13-14
submissive state 46
Suez Canal 188
sufi saints 127
sultans: and protection 87, 88-9, 98-9, 100
Sunnis 16
supernatural sanctions 92
superstition 210-12
  see also magic; 'popular' religion
support, social 199-200
Sûs 89
Suwailum, Rabbi Sa'id 240
synagogues 12, 55
  Baghdad 188
  gas-lighting 72-3
  Iran 12, 261-70; purchase of *kvodot* 266-7; social climbers 267-8; *ta'arof* 264-6
  private 102, 107, 137
  women in Kurdistan 202
  Yemen 227; centres of education 220-1
syncretism 42-6, 47
Syria 7, 66, 161-86
  character of Jewish-Gentile relations 163-5
  communal organization 173-6
  consuls 171-2
  family and household 177-81
  folk-stories 161-2
  Jews' occupations 165-7, 178
  Ottoman state 167-70
  religious and leisure activities 181-2
  schools 171, 176-7, 183
  westernization 183-4

ta'arof (honor exchanges) 263-6
  synagogue behaviour 264-6
Tafilalt 100
Tarjulah 227
Talmud 61, 174, 176, 177
Talmudic scholars 40, 149
Tanzimat reforms 168-9, 188, 193
Taoism 38

tax
  Baghdad 189, 193
  internal: Jerba 136, 138, 139–40;
    Morocco 88, 103–4;
    Tripolitania 146, 149
  Iran 248
  to sultan in Morocco 87, 88
  Syria 168; collection 169–70
  Tripolitania 146–7
  see also tributes
teachers 219, 222, 227–30
technology 71–2
Tedif-al-Yahud 15, 171, 182
Temple 71–2
texts, explanation of 222–3
Tiberias 182
tolerance, limited 46
tombs see shrines
Torah 176
  eternality of 68
  reading from 220
  'Torah prohibits the New' slogan
    65–6
Torah scholars 136
trade, international 167, 233
traders 13–14
  under Christianity and Islam 53, 54
  class divisions in Baghdad
    194–5
  Iran 251, 252
  Jerba 134, 136–7
  Morocco 112, 114; protection fees
    99–100, 113
  Syria 165
tradition 107–8
  literacy, religion and 9–12
  local tradition 28, 151–2
  and modernity 6, 25–34
  Syria 174
travellers 99–100, 113, 120
  see also traders
trees 209
tribal protection 89–90, 91, 99–100
tributes: for protection 87, 88,
    89–90, 90, 91, 120
  see also tax
Tripolitania 144–58
Tu bi'Shvat 209

Tunisia 18, 133–43, 152
'Tunisian profundity' 141–2
Turkish Jewry 7–8
Turner, V. 207

Udovitch, A.L. 56
ulamā 56
'Umar, Pact of 52, 55, 56, 57, 58
Urfa 9
Urmia 9
usury 53–4, 54–5
  see also moneylending
Uzziel, Rabbi Ben-Zion M.H. 68–9, 75–6

Vaad Bikur Holim (Committee for
  Visiting the Sick) 139
Vaad Or Torah (Education
  Committee) 138–9
values 75–6
Van Gennep, A. 207
violence 57, 100, 169
  see also massacres
visiting
  elders 106
  interfaith 165
vocational training 227
  see also education
Voinot, L. 122
Volozhin 71

wayfarers 229
wealth 40
  concealment except in synagogue
    256–7, 267
  social classes in Baghdad 194–5
Weber, M. 42
wedding festivities 31, 206
wedding rituals 200–1, 204, 225–6
  see also marriage
westernization 183–4
wet nurses 180
White Jewish caste 38
Willner, D. 110
Wills, C.J. 249–50
wine
  koshemess 139
  sales to Muslims 237–8

wise men: interfaith respect 15
  see also marabouts; rabbis;
  saddiqim
withdrawal of services 92
'witness', doctrine of 59
Wolf, T. 232
women
  degradation of Jewish women by
    Muslims 20
  illiteracy 12, 40
  religiosity of Jewish women in
    Kurdistan see Kurdistan
  sexual segregation 19, 37,
    202-4
  Syria 182
  Yemen 198, 202, 204, 237; role
    in education 219, 224-7
women's suffrage 75-6

Ya'ari, A. 153
Yahūd, Shaykh al- 126
Yahyā, Iman 236
Ya'ish, R. Elisha B. 125
Yazîd, Molay al- 92

Yemen 8-9, 16, 18, 249, 258
  authority of San'ā community
    232-43
  distinctiveness of Jewish
    communities 37
  Jewish education see education
  oppression of Jews 45
  women 198, 202, 204, 237; role
    in education 219, 224-7
  Zohar and Shulhan Arukh 27
yerze'it (annual memorial day)
  266
Yiddish 39
yirat horaah (reluctance to make
  rulings) 66
Yishak, Rabbi 'Awād 239
Yishak, Rabbi Sālim 239
youth age group 230-1

zattâta/dhazttat (protection fee) 91,
  120
Zionist Movement 142
Zohar 11-12, 27
Zoroastrians 57, 249, 258

www.ingramcontent.com/pod-product-compliance
Lightning Source LLC
Chambersburg PA
CBHW022038290426
44109CB00014B/905